The

Dr. Tony Baron
Azusa Pacific University

Becoming more human

Exploring the interface of spirituality, discipleship

and therapeutic faith community

Becoming more human

Exploring the interface of spirituality, discipleship

and therapeutic faith community

Peter R. Holmes

PATERNOSTER

First published 2005 by Paternoster Press
Paternoster is an imprint of Authentic Media
9 Holdom Avenue, Bletchley, Milton Keynes, Bucks, MK1 1QR, U.K.
and 129 Mobilization Drive, Waynesboro, GA 30830-4575, USA

www.authenticmedia.co.uk/paternoster
Authentic Media is a division of Send The Light Ltd.,
a company limited by guarantee (registered charity no. 270162)

11 10 09 08 07 06 05   7 6 5 4 3 2 1

British Library Cataloguing in Publication Data
A catalogue record for this book is available from the British Library.

ISBN 1-84227-388-4

Photography with thanks to Ian Giles
www.iangilesphotos.co.uk

Printed and bound by J. H. Haynes & Co. Ltd., Sparkford
Cover design by fourninezero design

*To Mary, my wife,
who has honoured me,
by continually giving me back my calling*

Contents

Appendices
To view the appendices for this book, please visit:
www.authenticmedia.co.uk/paternoster/Becoming More Human

PREFACE

This book is a journey for both of us, for me over the last 40 years and you as you read. But before you even begin a short explanation is needed. Back in the 1970s and 1980s I found myself facing a range of mental and emotional illnesses in those who came to me for help. I never pretended to be able to help them, but suggested I knew someone who could, the Lord Jesus Christ. I told them I believed He wanted to lead them out of the maze of their trauma, compulsions and addictions. So with a growing range of skills and experience learned over many years I taught them to seek the voice of the Lord, talking to them about themselves and their plight. As He did, I helped them apply what He was saying, step after step. This book summarises some of the key points I and others are discovering on this interesting journey.

But that is not the end of the matter, it has just the beginning. What we had learned found its way into the congregation of Christ Church Deal after it was formed in 1998. The knowledge continued to expand, continually changing as members adapted the principles that Mary (my wife), Susan Williams (my colleague and former client) and I had taught them. We had started with a ministry for those at the 'hard end' of mental illness. But this began to change into a series of positive life-changing Biblical principles that anyone could use to help them become more whole. What was forming organically was an innovative type of discipleship journey. It incorporated ways of both deepening relationship with Christ, and easing the plight of anyone needing to positively change, or to let go of their toxic past. Most of us want to know Christ more intimately, and what we have been learning positively contributes to this desire.

Looking back, what the Lord has done has been remarkable. This book, along with others now being published, illustrates just how remarkable. As I have reflected over the years on the difficult ways the Lord has led us, I see few other options for Him introducing to me the possibility of us being able to live 'as though our past no longer clings to us'. He had to teach me from a hard place, against much scepticism and prejudice both in me and the wider faith community. But with my clients and friends as my teachers, and the faithfulness of all those who have sought me out, transformation and its wholeness has increasingly become the norm.

As you read this book I would not want to give the impression I have found a cure for mental illness, though we have been able to help some. Neither would I want to give the impression the journey is only for those who are ill in this way. This would have been my mindset maybe 15-20 years ago, but it is not now the case. Instead, what the Lord has led us into, and what I introduce in this book, is an intellectual, theoretical framework both theologically, therapeutically and sociologically, that now under-girds the discipleship model that several thousand people are already living (Williams and Holmes 2004, Holmes and Williams 2005) across the continents.

Much work has still to be done, as I believe we are only scratching the surface of what the Lord wants to lead us into. However, what my own life's work has so far taught me is of a God of grace able to meet people in their darkest moments, and their most complex of needs, leading them by His word into a place where they can know Christ and become more Christ-like, as they become more fully human.

MY THANKS...

Someone wise once told me that it takes fifty years for a young oak tree to form its first acorns. So even though it may now be rather blasé to speak of a book being written over many years, in my case this is genuinely true. Many of the concepts, words and ideas in this book I have been wrestling with for decades, helped by numerous people.

In paying tribute to these, I must first honour Mr and Mrs Cooper, London City Missioners at Norman Road Mission, South Wimbledon, who have sadly now passed on, but in the early 1960s led me into the Kingdom and into Christ. But forty years later, in writing up my PhD, (on which this book is based), I am now indebted to many more people. Revd Dr Kenneth Wilson, formerly of Westminster College, Oxford and Queens Foundation, Birmingham, was my PhD supervisor, and has been a key ally in this enterprise. Without his gentle spirit, sharp intellect, and continual encouragement I would have floundered. I owe him so much. But I must also thank the Revd Alistair Ross, Head of Counselling Training, The Institute of Pastoral Counselling, University of Birmingham, who has ably guided me through the complex minefield of therapeutic process.

Kenneth and Alistair have also been supported by a range of friends who have dialogued the journey with me through my MA into my PhD. Among these are Dr Ruth Deakin-Crick of the Graduate Institute of Education, Bristol University, Dr John Jelfs in general practice, Dr Anne Murphy of Heythrop College, London University, the Revd Dr Adam Hood of the Queens Foundation, University of Birmingham, and the Revd John Harding, a lover of all things Biblical and Hebrew. Also, in the early stages of my MA and Susan Williams' MPhil., Dr Martin Stringer of the University of Birmingham,

But my intellectual journey has not been limited to the UK. A friend since 1980, the Revd Derry Long of Portland, Oregon, USA has continued to be an able sparring partner, as have Professors Mary Kate Morse, Larry Shelton, Steve Delamarter and Dan Brunner, all of George Fox Seminary, Portland, Oregon. Their wisdom and guidance have been invaluable in attempting a mid-Atlantic perspective. In addition, I would like to give thanks to the enduring patience of Merrill Johnson, the Librarian, George

Fox University, along with his very able team. I should add however, that none of these can be held responsible for the ideas expressed in this book.

But to return to home, I could not have done this journey without the huge support of the members of Christ Church Deal, especially the Leadership Team and those of the Academic Forum. They have all given me the gift of dialogue and trust, to implement many of the ideas I have been exploring. I must also mention Susan Williams, whose personal journey out of emotional illness began this whole current cycle in 1989.

I must also thank my son Christopher, on a journey of his own, who has so often been the victim of my errors, rather than of my wisdom. But finally, I thank Mary, my wife since 1975, from the Mid West plains of the United States. She has on more than one occasion had the opportunity to quit on me, but instead has stood by me and on occasions even given me back my calling. I owe her so much, and dedicate this book to her.

Peter R Holmes
Walmer, Kent, UK
June 2005

Chapter 1

Introduction

From the beginning

My personal journey

My father was a diesel motor fitter much of his life, so I grew up being fascinated by how things worked. Also, like my father, when things did not work I always wanted to know why. Throughout my life I have applied this same inquisitiveness to areas such as my Christian faith, and the challenges facing the Western Church.[1] I have been on a journey seeking explanations and exploring solutions.[2] This book is a snapshot into this continuing personal journey.[3]

One of my foci over the last 40+ years as a Christian has been an interest in mental illness, since undertaking chaplaincy duties at Crichton Royal Infirmary, Dumfries.[4] Returning to London I found myself deeply disturbed by what I had seen, having encountered large numbers of people with long-term mental illness. Among them were Christians, for whom religious symbols and experiences had become part of their pathology (Greenberg and Witztum 1991, van der Heyden 1999). 'If God is God, why can't He[5] help these people?' I asked. I found myself in the same place as Stephen Clark, conceding that the Western Church needed to find something new (1972:182). Though not consciously aware of this at the time, my mind was actually set. If possible, I wanted to understand more about emotional and

---

[1] In 'The collapse of the Western Church' (page 1) I explain my use of the term 'Western Church'.

[2] I have used an experiential approach where I reflect on my experience, finding in either the Christian walk, in Scripture, tradition or others' experience reasons and explanations for what is happening. But on numerous occasions I have had to take the risk and explore the questions first, before necessarily finding any satisfactory cognitive or theological constructs. I am aware that by acting this way, I find myself in the Charismatic tradition, where there is the danger experience can be considered more valid than Scripture. 'The safest way to prevent disillusionment is to ensure that one does not take on beliefs that are illusory' (Middlemiss 1996:xvi).

[3] In the debate about the place of personal religious views and experiences as part of academic work, Marsden (1997) suggested they can make a valid contribution. See appendix 1.

[4] Crichton was at the time, I believe, one of the largest mental hospitals in Scotland, with huge grounds and a traditional approach to treatment, including medication, lobotomy and ECT. I was on a summer placement as an Assistant Chaplain from London Bible College.

[5] Throughout this text when speaking of God I will be using the formal case, He or His, though not suggesting gender by doing so. When speaking of the male gender I will use he or his.

mental illness, helping people find healing in Christ.[6] In part, this book is about this aspect of my unfolding journey.

During the early 1970's, while seeking to help people in a lay pastoral capacity, I began noticing that many emotionally and mentally ill people often exhibit a reluctance to change, be they Christian or otherwise, even where positive personal change would probably help defeat the sicknesses in their lives. Often it is only when they are desperate that they will show this willingness. But I also began to realize this applied to most people, not just the sick. The majority of us seem reluctant to change, once we have decided on a matter or a lifestyle, regardless of whether it is good for us. Because of this I began to feel a growing personal despair, not unlike Keith Phillips, who at 25 wanted to quit the Church,[7] because all he could achieve was converts (1981:preface). The ongoing discipleship change necessary for Christ-likeness was elusive.

These issues came to a head for me while studying and 'church planting' in Turkey,[8] where I was forced to observe that many followers of Christ in this Moslem culture would need to make substantial changes in their lives and lifestyles. Not all of them were willing to do so. So toward the end of my first ten years as a Christian I began to admit I was unable to reconcile this human reluctance to change with Christ calling His followers to discipleship, transformation, personal maturity, and the learning of a life worth living. Larry Crabb would have comforted me in those early days with his insight that in the midst of efforts to describe the spiritual life, to live it, and to help others live it, there are some things we simply do not know (1999:3). However, at the time I did not give up.

Also, in spite of the bravado and triumphalism of my Evangelical background, I began to realise that the Western Church, particularly in parts of Western Europe, was in a sad state with numerous serious diseases, e.g. the toll of the Enlightenment with its apparent reductionism, collapsing numbers, personal and social irrelevance, and being 'one generation from

---

[6]   I see this as part of our duty in Christ: '……try to excel in gifts that build up the Church' (1 Cor. 14:12b (NIV)). Bible verses, where quoted or referenced, will be from the New Revised Standard Version (NRSV), unless otherwise stated.

[7]   In 'The collapse of the Western Church' (page 1) I explain my use of the word Church in this book.

[8]   My book focuses on the Western Church, but from the 1970s onwards, while serving the Lord, I travelled to over 70 countries in Europe, Africa, the Middle East and Asia. I have also lived in the USA. On many of these journeys I have stayed in the homes of Christians, and visited many congregations. Through these experiences I have been forced to conclude that basic human needs are frequently not being met in the wider Church in the lives of many Christians around the world, even among leaders. For a comment on the global Church in the context of the dying of the European Church, see Brierley (1998).

extinction' (Brierley 2000:27).[9] I was witnessing the Church losing its relevance to contemporary society.[10]

But despite these growing concerns, from the 1970s onwards a steady stream of people came to me seeking help.[11] Many of these had emotionally unstable backgrounds, had tried numerous therapies, but still needed to change.[12] I instinctively asked the Lord what was making these people unwell, and what I should do. Their need brought them to me, and the Lord helped me.[13] In time I found myself drawing together a cluster of heuristic concepts and practices from Scripture that helped individuals identify how to resolve major areas of conflict in their lives. These principles I also found helpful for 'normal' Christians in their search for maturity in Christ. I had inadvertently begun to identify aspects of what Grenz called a post-noeticentric (relevant) gospel (1996:172). For me, these concepts included recovering Hebrew ideas,[14] developing a clinical pneumatic model of human make-up, outlining my own 'folk psychology',[15] discovering the healing power of catharsis, and making numerous mistakes on the way.

But I also found in myself a growing unease over the conflict between pastoral care and psychology,[16] what appeared to me to be an absorption of psychology's therapies and self-help into soteriology. In this I felt the frustration of a Church losing sight of its distinctive appeared to me to be

---

[9] Not everyone would agree with my sweeping conclusion that the Western Church is sick, arguing instead, maybe, for exceptionalism. But for the purposes of this book I am assuming this sad state does exist, based on the extensive work of Brierley and others (Brierley 2000, 2003).

[10] A helpful illustration of this appeared recently in Time Magazine, '...unorthodoxy worries some church leaders, but it satisfies the yearning of millions of people who prefer to chart their own spiritual journey, getting help and guidance along the way from websites or the New Age shelves of the local bookstore' (Chu 2003:30). The cover story was 'Where did God go? Churches are half empty and God can't get a mention in the new EU constitution. But he's turning up in some of the most surprising places. A special report on Christianity in Europe.'

[11] In a lay pastoral capacity I frequently found myself committing to several months working with such people, meeting as and when we could. I never charged or advertised, but merely offered support when asked. It has been suggested I am 'liberal' as I appear to tolerate religious pluralism, and am too open to change in both myself and others. My response is that I honour others' choice of faith and spirituality whilst maintaining an evangelical perspective personally.

[12] In conversation Dr Anne Murphy (Heythrop College, University of London) reminded me of the obvious, that around 10% will quickly change, 10% will probably never change, while the remaining 80% either will or may change, but at their own pace, subject to exposure and need (30.12.03). This book is about Christ Church Deal, which has intentionally sought to create this change culture, able to facilitate personal positive change.

[13] I noticed early on that I had a natural ability to empathize, even though I only had modest pastoral psychology training. In chapter 4 I will be expanding on this therapeutic process.

[14] In 'Defining some of the terms' (page 1ff.) I explain my use of the term Hebrew.

[15] I use the term 'folk psychology' here to describe my practical common sense grassroots approach to human need. For an overview of this way of thinking, see Smythe (1998a). Some would suggest I am beginning to create a distinct field theory of human nature (Bloom 1997:8).

[16] I use the term psychology to describe that field of research and practice that focuses on human personhood.

an absorption of psychology's therapies and self-help into ability to offer a unique inheritance of authentic Christ-centered spirituality, with all its health and wholeness: a redeemed life lived in this lifetime. Looking back over those years I realize I had a dream growing in me, to see numbers of men and women walking with Christ, un-encumbered by their toxic pasts, having been able to positively change and consistently stand, with increased capacity to love Christ, themselves and other people, thereby helping to hasten the Return of Christ.

By the 1980s I had developed a model of therapeutic discipleship that was helping people.[17] Then in 1988 Susan Williams came to me seeking help. At 27 she was slipping into her second 'psychotic breakdown', with a cluster of other disorders including addiction to medication, depression, agoraphobia, chronic fatigue syndrome (CFS), and panic attacks. But unlike many before her, she vowed to the Lord that if she found genuine healing she would commit herself to teaching others those things that had helped her. She began to find freedom from her sicknesses in her healing journey,[18] appropriating wholeness with the Lord's, my wife's and my help, while also asking me to teach her *exactly* how it was we had helped her. This was not as easy as it may sound, as much of what I was doing was intuitive and I had already been doing it for a number of years. But I agreed, and began writing 'Bible Notes' as background material to help her teach other women how to find healing.

Such was the success of this 'team' that by 1998 we had a formidable waiting list, mainly women, seeking help. Susan launched *Rapha* weekend workshops for up to 25 women here in our home, Waterfront, in Walmer, Kent, UK. These women, mostly friends of those who had been previously helped, came from all over UK, and even further afield. I assisted Susan in writing the teaching scripts, and also did some of the teaching. By popular request, a year later, we were asked to launch similar workshops for men. People were also asking us to make more widely available the model we had developed and were now using. We were quietly intrigued at all this success and growth.

Here in Deal, Kent, there were also a growing number of people benefiting from my ministry, and in 1998 a group of these met with me, saying they wanted to plant[19] an independent congregation.[20] They felt the

---

[17] See for instance Trinkle (1986), though at the time I was not comfortable being seen as her counsellor or therapist, so she graciously kept my name to the minimum.

[18] Susan's personal journey was originally published as *Passion for purity: Principles from a personal journey into wholeness* (Williams and Holmes 2000), a book I co-authored now re-published by Authentic Media (Williams and Holmes 2004), entitled *Letting God heal: From emotional illness to wholenesss.*

[19] The whole field of church planting has a wide literature, but a place to start, outlining some of the problems and challenges, could be Snyder (1996a, 1996b).

need for a faith community that would be a safe place for the people we were helping while they were working through painful or tragic pasts, or needing to 'begin again' in their relationship with God. They invited me to join them and provide some of the pastoral care and teaching. Cautiously I agreed, and Christ Church Deal (CCD) was born.[21] For the first time my one-to-one model entered local church life.[22] Unknown to me at the time, it was about to go through its own transformation.

In many ways this book has not been easy to write. I have always been uncomfortable talking about myself, especially the work I have been doing with sick people over the last 35 years, and since 1998 in helping plant and lead a local congregation. My preference has always been to let the fruit speak for itself.[23] Also, I feared writing down my thoughts, believing the result would sound like self-propaganda. My grace is that the reader will already have noticed I have often had to learn the hard way, frequently stumbling en-route, and what I am beginning to understand still remains far less than there is yet to be understood.

Introducing Christ Church Deal[24]

Christ Church Deal[25] could be described as a community built on the 'solidarity of the shaken'.[26] It is an independent congregation on the east coast of Kent, UK, six miles north of Dover. Deal is a seaside town with a population of over 20,000 with a large retirement community. It suffers high unemployment and has lower than average salaries, partly because it is in one of the few areas of South East England beyond commuter distance of London. Also, not being on a trunk road it has little transit traffic, and only

---

[20] This was unthinkable to many of us, because we were all from mainline or new denominations, and felt committed to traditional Church, wanting to see renewal within its structures. By planting this new congregation we would be independent, and in a sense become outsiders.

[21] That was 1998. I have been married since 1975 to Mary from Minnesota, and have one son Christopher, now 25. Christopher completed his first degree in theology at Bangor, then did a Master's degree in philosophy at Birkbeck College, London University. He is continuing his studies in maths and physics.

[22] Much of my previous counselling work had been on a one-to-one basis, sometimes with a scribe sitting in and taking notes.

[23] In the wider field of psychological therapies the question of effectiveness is a hotly debated one. For a helpful introduction to this see McLeod (2001).

[24] I am using the proper name and address of Christ Church, to allow for comparisons and authenticity. In this I am following the precedent of Becker (1999). I also have permission from the Leadership Team of CCD to do so.

[25] The name 'Christ Church' was problematic for me. The 24 initial members chose it because it best described what they wanted the congregation to be. Although I tried to explain such a name might misrepresent the congregation, by sounding Anglican or Catholic, they did not listen.

[26] This phrase was first used by Patocka in the Czech Republic of the Charter 77 document which described those already shaken by their pasts, who now actively wanted to reverse this, especially by questioning the established order (Shanks 2001).

a modest holiday trade. It has been described as a 'sleepy town'.[27]

At the time of writing this book the membership of CCD has grown from 25 plus children to its current membership of over 150 plus children. Statistics[28] show that it has a higher than average proportion of men to women (one of our original goals). 19% of new members reported that they were not Christians when they joined, and a further 20% reported that although they believed themselves to be Christians, they were not attending a local church prior to joining.[29] CCD describes this latter part of its work as a 'recovery' ministry.

> *[Others] have called [CCD] a church and I have said that it is not a church. I have used the correct term, a therapeutic community,[30] not because it sounds posh. But it says what it means and does what it says (M9-2).* [31]

The congregation has a number of unusual features,[32] one of which is the migration of individuals and families to Deal to join the congregation,

---

[27] This 'sleepy town' proved to be an ideal 'laboratory' to test the ideas explored in this book. Previous congregations I have helped plant have mostly been in urban areas, with large transit populations and a fluid core membership. For more background to CCD see 'Introducing Susan Williams' MPhil' (page 1) and appendix 2.

[28] For further detailed information regarding CCD see Susan Williams' MPhil thesis at the University of Birmingham (2002). Some of her statistical data regarding the congregation is in appendix 2. Statistics refer to data collected in January 2002, unless otherwise indicated.

[29] At the planting of CCD two main areas for potential growth were identified; the un-churched that needed help, and those who had left the Church. The latter often retain a belief in Christ, but no longer feel able to attend a local congregation. A number of those joining CCD had left previous churches for a range of reasons. In 2002 only 12% of the congregation had moved from other local churches to join CCD and this percentage has since decreased, so we have seen little 'sheep stealing'. Many of CCD's members who were current or former church-goers moved to Deal to join the congregation.

[30] As this book will illustrate in due course, CCD and *Rapha* have a therapeutic focus, and doing research in such a highly dynamic environment is a challenge. See, for instance, Bloor, McKeganey and Fonkert (1988). For a review of research methods in therapeutic communities, see Lees (1999). Regarding the concept of CCD being a therapeutic community, this is a well-known model in the health care services. Members of the community have adopted it, calling themselves a therapeutic *faith* community. But it goes beyond this to an acknowledgment that we are all in need, and need to change. In chapter 6 I will be unpacking this concept in greater detail.

[31] The quotations are drawn from Susan Williams' research, for which she used small self-managed focus groups with members of CCD, to collect her data. She also produced a 'reflective questionnaire' that went to all members. Quotations will be drawn directly from her material, and are used with the permission of the participants. The data has been lodged with Christ Church Deal, and is available as evidence to any interested parties, via application from their research institution. For reasons of confidentiality, data will only be made available to those involved in relevant research. Applications should be made to The Leadership Team, Christ Church Deal, 3 Stanhope Road, Deal, Kent, CT14 6AB UK. Participants are numbered 1-15, and either M (male) or F (female). The number after the hyphen indicates the question number being referred to, e.g. M9-2 is male participant number 9, answering question 2.

[32] The 'model' of church CCD is following has been more by instinct than strategy, but is close to the Celtic approach developed by St. Patrick. Like the Celts, CCD has almost entirely abandoned the classic Roman model, largely because it is seen as a barrier to the contemporary un-churched.

usually after previous help from Susan or myself, or attendance at a *Rapha* workshop.[33] Membership includes retired ministers and missionaries, the emotionally ill,[34] and those merely tired of urban life. Alongside CCD, because of the success of the workshop programme around UK with 1,000+[35] attending in the first six years, we also have a network of 20+ *Rapha* support groups.

A book of several strands

My goals for this book

Although practical theology is at the core of this book, it is intended to be a landscape, marking frontiers where theology, social psychology and psychology's therapies all meet.

My recent academic journey began by my intending to write a theological book on the problems of the Church needing to change.[36] I naively believed at the time that by writing for the Church a 'theology of change' I would be able to contribute to a discussion on the need for change in the wider Church. I quickly learned that I could not say what I wanted to say in the language of theology. (See 'Defining some of the terms', page 1.) But another more compelling problem also arose. I was part of a faith community (CCD) that was speaking eloquently to anyone interested in listening, but to my surprise was expressing a range of different views to those familiar to me from my previous congregational experience. I found myself wanting to explore these 'new' ideas people were expressing, but

---

Hunter (2000) outlines the Celtic model as a group of Christians with useful trades, (in our case a therapeutic journey, life skills training and personal development), moving into an area, and over a period of time earning the right to be part of the community, thereby allowing the bridge of friendships to introduce Christ.

[33] Moving to Deal is one modern aspect of migration of identity, '.........the universal way in which human beings conceive of their lives in terms of moving–between identities, relations, people, things, groups, societies, cultures, environments as a dialectic between movement and fixity' (Rapport and Dawson 1998:33). 'Home is no longer a dwelling, but the untold story of a life being lived' (Berger 1984:64).

[34] Our health care programme is introduced in a pilot study we have completed, *'Developing a new model for care in the community* (Holmes and Williams 2002). It is available from Community, Therapy and Rehabilitation Ltd., 3 Stanhope Road, Deal, Kent, UK, CT14 6AB. Email: ctr@f2s.com.

[35] We also have over 300 people who have completed workshops in the USA and nearly 100 in Turkey.

[36] Traditionally anthropology has a negative view of change. Change is seen as problematic, imposed from the outside, forcing people to adapt or react to what they are refusing. Change is a negative external influence. A culture that celebrates change at its roots, as I will be illustrating CCD does, is therefore a very unusual culture.

they did not fit comfortably into the more orthodox theological treatise I was embarking upon.

In its present form this book now seeks a far more modest end. I want to share some of my experience on this long personal journey, along with some of the ideas being expressed by CCD, then ask in a synthetic academic way what the implications might be for myself and whether there are any for the wider Church. These ideas I will unpack throughout the book, then in the final chapter summarize some of them, not as a post-hoc justification, but in order to ask whether they could be of interest to the wider Church. In this sense the book does not end, since neither has my journey.

My 'confessional narrative'

This book is therefore made up of four strands, all interweaving within one another. These four strands are four complementary sources of data. As already noted, firstly I borrow from my own emotional perceptual world with all of its disparate experience.[37] This I call my personal narrative. But this personal dimension is also supplemented with my own clinical (mostly lay) pastoral experience in the field of spirituality[38] and mental health. These two threads form the basis of my 'confessional narrative' (Wengraf 2001:362), expressed as one in CCD, while making sense of much that the Lord has taught me in the past. For the third strand I draw from Susan Williams, now a friend and colleague on her own journey, and her MPhil research. As a fellow insider I believe she has successfully captured CCD from within, through her analysis of focus group data and her 'reflective questionnaires'.[39] But fourthly, I reflect academically in a multi-disciplinary[40] way on the three strands noted above, tentatively asking what a theoretical framework may look like were it to embrace the perception of all these strands. This book only reflects the beginning of this work. I do not seek to separate out these four distinct features in the writing of this book, preferring instead to move between them in an intuitive, or naturalistic way, as better reflecting my own narrative experience.

---

[37] For a range of comments on some of the problems related to interpreting subjective emotional lived experience from a symbolic interactionist perspective see Ellis and Flaherty (1992).

[38] I am using a definition of spirituality combining an acknowledgement of its reality as personal, transforming, therapeutic and corporate, but not necessarily Christian. Few definitions within the Church combine these. See 'Defining a transforming spirituality' (page 1) and appendix 4.

[39] For the complexity of doing research as part of a team see Erickson and Stull (1998). For the complications of doing insider/outsider team research see Bartunek and Louis (1996).

[40] I am using the term multidisciplinary rather than interdisciplinary. This is a personal value judgment rather than a methodological one, but in my book the various disciplines remain somewhat separate, while relating to each other through my work.

The first, second and fourth strands all focus around me, my personal experience, my lay clinical pastoral interests, and my intellectual journey.[41] I have continually needed to reflect back on the processes I have used, and ask why I used them. So although these strands are separate in my thinking, on paper they have a tendency to blur, migrating into each other. For instance, my personal experience is wedded to those I have sought to help. Also, my personal academic journey has frequently enlightened my view of human disorder and how to tackle it.

So reading this book will take some grace, particularly for theologians and their ilk, as I am unable to separate the four strands of data. Neither have I been able to avoid some of my own prejudices. So the process of interpreting the information in this book needs to be done with wisdom, bearing in mind that both the members of CCD, as well as myself, echo throughout its pages. But I hope you as the reader will find stakes in the ground as you travel with me, the sane voices of others who have walked and are walking the same footpath, with wise words that will hopefully allow you some respite from my own ramblings.

Introducing Susan Williams' MPhil

The third strand of this book is Susan Williams' focus group and questionnaire data from her MPhil. Twelve months after forming CCD the congregation had doubled in size. Following a visit from one of my lecturers, an empirical psychologist from Heythrop College, London University, the Leadership Team[42] became aware that much more was happening in the congregation than was immediately obvious. She drew attention to the unusual social process at work, and especially the 'social rules'.[43] As a result, we wanted to understand more about why the congregation was such a success,[44] and explore its 'social process'. We decided to do some research, focusing on the 'meaning' of CCD to its members.[45] This became Susan Williams' MPhil at the University of

---

[41] I recognise that Susan Williams' MPhil to some degree also focuses around me, as I am a leader in the community in question. However I have treated this as a different type of data. It reflects the ideas and thinking of others, and much of the research findings surprised me. (See appendix 5.)

[42] Christ Church has developed its own Leadership Team model (currently 12 men and 12 women), instead of having a more traditional pastor/minister. Details of how the Leadership Team operates can be found in appendix 6.

[43] When we first heard the phrase 'social rules' the Leadership Team's response was that CCD had no rules! She then read off over twenty 'rules' that she had noted in her interviews over the weekend: 'cut the crap', 'it will hurt like hell but is worth it', 'tell the truth (they know already)', 'drop the religion', 'do not judge', 'its OK to cry', etc.

[44] I would be the first to acknowledge that just because something works it does not necessarily make it true (Middlemiss 1996:178).

[45] Susan Williams' research comments on the question of meaning in congregational research. She quotes 'I am following the congregational research tradition of Hopewell (1987) and

Birmingham.[46] The results were surprising, especially to me.[47]

In writing up her data Susan Williams used a constructivist grounded theory approach.[48] In 2002 she conducted 6 self-moderated focus groups with, at that time, 28% of the congregation of CCD. She undertook line-by-line non-hierarchical coding utilising qualitative data analysis (QDA) software, to produce codes which grouped into 7 primary categories around a central category of 'journey'.[49] Many of these codes have become sensitising concepts in my own theoretical framework. Her focus group research was supplemented by a 38 page 'reflective questionnaire', completed at that time by 70% of the congregation. These she used as a confirmatory source. As mentioned, I have had full access to her data, with permission from the participants, and will use throughout the book these colloquial quotations, un-edited, from both the focus groups and questionnaires, to illustrate key ideas as I suggest them, e.g.,

> *My church background, it's been so crap (M13-9).*

I believe Susan Williams' work to be of a high standard, following classic research lines of inductive qualitative analysis.[50] It is ideal for my purposes, focusing as it does on CCD, and drawing on her collection of over 200 pages of typed verbatim transcripts from the focus groups she conducted, then supplemented by her 80 questionnaires. I am drawing from her raw data, and merely cite her findings occasionally. I have sought to select *illustrative* quotes throughout the book mirroring what I am saying, but I do not seek to critique either her content or her conclusions, being outside the scope of this book. This book is therefore not itself empirical, instead drawing on Susan Williams' own empirical data.[51]

Ammerman (1987). Guest et al.'s (2001) typology describes such research as an 'intrinsic' study. From an anthropological tradition, Cohen suggested "what does the community appear to mean to its members?" (1985/1992:20) is a helpful perspective, because of the symbolic nature of community' (2002:7 n.22).

[46] Susan is currently completing her PhD at the Graduate School of Education, University of Bristol, UK.

[47] I have noted in the past that there is a belief often shared by leaders of congregations that they know exactly what is going on among their members. When the Leadership Team began analysing the results of Susan Williams' findings, we realised the congregation was forging ahead, working as a group through issues and interests of which we were hardly aware. We were to learn in due course that a part of this was both the experience of disenchantment with traditional Church among the 'mature' Christians, and the new perspectives brought by the un-churched members.

[48] This book does not enter the Glaser (1992) and Strauss and Corbin (1998) debate on grounded theory. For a helpful summary, including the constructivist approach, see Charmaz (2000).

[49] These categories were 'community/family', 'change', 'different type of church', 'met emotional need', 'tell my story', 'being real' and 'journey'.

[50] For further detail regarding the methodology used by Susan Williams, see her MPhil (Williams 2002:11-17, 22-24, 149-155 and 169-174).

[51] For further discussion on my use of Susan Williams' data see appendix 5. On the question of the accuracy of both this data as collected, and this book presenting it, I see validation in four ways.

The impact of these findings on me

Susan's published findings noted three key areas of importance to the congregation, all related to the category of 'journey': the need for personal change, the concept of change in personhood expressed in terms of 'identity', and the significance of a community culture[52] to help facilitate this.[53]

These findings deeply impacted my own thinking, and some of their implications for me are documented in this book. An example of this was the community's deep appreciation of living in a culture of personal positive change (chapter 3), and my impression that much of the Church resists such change. I also needed to let go of my prejudices regarding the whole idea of 'community' (chapter 5). I was shocked by the extent of this prejudice. Reflecting now on these findings I see they were a significant turning point for me, as I questioned how these values could have been so important to the community, but so marginal to me?

Therefore at a personal, clinical pastoral and intellectual level I was changing with what I was being taught by the community. I now realize I was pretending, in some ways, to have laid down my own prejudices. After all, the majority of the congregation believed we were doing something new. It was a humbling time and has done much to shape my current thinking. So as I began writing this book, it inevitably focused around these findings and the upheaval it brought me. But I also found myself admitting, consequently, that writing in the way I am, I am no longer following a traditional sociological, anthropological, theological or even psychological academic format.

The selection of source materials

The fourth strand of data in this book is a continuing literature review. Any piece of academic writing needs a review of literature around the field being researched. But because this book is multi-disciplinary, seeking to be a landscape rather than a rigorous academic study focused around a single intellectual domain, the literature review is restricted and selective in its sources. References will either illustrate a point, or where necessary, extend the argument. At almost any key point in this book I could have taken more

---

Members of the Leadership Team have read this book in draft and confirmed its accuracy. Also Susan and I have reported back to the congregation on several occasions. In addition a substantial number of the congregation have collaborated in the collection and use of the data, and visiting outsiders have lived with us in the community and have verified its authenticity.

[52] Barnard and Spencer provided an ethnographic history of the term 'culture' from an anthropological perspective. The use of 'culture' in this book is broadly consistent with 'culture-as-symbols-and-meanings' (1996:136), rather than from a moral or pluralist perspective.

[53] Chapter 5 looks in some detail at the loss of community in modern times, but avoids the debate as to whether we are actually seeing such a loss.

time or offered more reference, texts or background. For instance, on the issue of spirituality and human spirit, I have over 550 reference texts on my database, but have only used a select few in this book. This selection has been done on the basis of scope, where I illustrate the diversity of views rather than merely selecting material that supports my argument.

So although mindful that in the social sciences the use of footnotes is not as widespread as it used to be, I have used footnotes more extensively than might be common to illustrate background evidence and academic thought. But even this continual review of literature makes no pretence to be either exhaustive or comprehensive. By its very nature it cannot be, restricted as I am by the length of this book.

I have found that my review of literature in these various disciplines has greatly increased my capacity to contextualise and interpret the other three strands of my data. It has added an invaluable breadth and depth, and enabled me to locate my own findings as part of a number of wider academic and intellectual discussions.

Definitions used in this book

Defining some of the terms

This book uses a number of familiar words in new ways, as well as borrowing words from various disciplines. On my journey I have sometimes been unable to find the words to describe what I want to say, while in other instances I have invested old words with new meanings, or taken words from one discipline and re-invested them with a new meaning for this book. So I am using some words outside the context of their academic discipline to help convey what I mean. Let me briefly outline some of these words.

The word **therapeutic** traditionally carries two meanings: 1) the branch of medicine that deals with the treatment and cure of disease, the art of healing, or 2) in a more general sense of a curative agent, a healing influence (Oxford English Dictionary). I will be using the term throughout this book in the latter sense, but equivalent in meaning to the word 'change'. The process for this *therapeutic change* is the letting go of the sometimes toxic painful experiences of our past, by a journey, that allows us to both become more human, who we were created to be, while also becoming more like Christ.

The concept of **'change'** was proposed by members of CCD as a key feature of community life. They used the word, but for years I have struggled for alternatives to describe, in a positive sense, this discipleship journey CCD and I have developed. Transformation, for instance, has too much prejudicial history. But the word change also has its problems, and is

Assumption

grossly over-used. For example, it is often assumed that church leaders are more Christ-like, so everyone needs to *change* to be like them. Change can therefore be associated with conformity, even compliance. Also, the word change is often suggestive of growth, leading me to choose between two other words to define the goal of this journey; 'maturity' and 'wholeness'. Chapter 3 explains how I resolved this. So I have conceded defeat and am using the word change throughout this book to explain the personal positive (change) experience[54] of moving toward maturity in CCD and *Rapha*. I will be suggesting that this could have been the experience of those in the Early Church[55] in committing to Christ and entering a 'counter-culture'[56] faith community. But I am also investing the word with a sense echoed by Quinn's (1996) concept of 'deep change', as being a helpful way to describe the experience of members of CCD, where change precipitates growth and maturity.[57] So the use of the word change in this book has a backdrop of personal positive change frequently associated with a 'therapeutic' process,[58] which I will be suggesting can and should lead to more maturity.

In its original form this book was a PhD dissertation. I have made a number of changes for publication, for instance, removing most of the anthropological and sociological debate about the academic location. These are now relegated to the appendices. Likewise, the original title was *'Becoming more fully human? Exploring the ecotone of human spirituality, salugenic discipleship, and therapeutic faith community'*. For the purpose

---

[54] This book suggests several aspects to this phrase, though I will not be seeking a precise definition. Susan Williams in her PhD is hoping to propose one.

[55] Dunn suggested we should not talk about 'the Early Church' but instead see a diverse range of types of congregation in this early period (1977 passim). I take his point, so throughout this book, when I speak of the Early Church I am talking about all those congregations and groups wherever they may be found, from the Ascension of Christ to the end of the first century. As I will note later, this latter period was a significant threshold for the Church. I at no time imply there was ever just one model of Church being explored or planted.

[56] The concept of CCD being a 'counter-culture' follows a long tradition. For a comment on this concept, and a helpful review of this idea among communities inside and outside the Church see Angrosino (2003). He focuses his paper around Vanier's *L'Arche* communities (Vanier 1979).

[57] Quinn (1996) has done a parallel journey to myself but in the field of corporate management, proposing that 'cultural change starts with personal change' (103), but that 'change is hell' (78). 'We can change the world only by changing ourselves' (9). 'We must reach a point of ultimate despair and frustration before we seriously think about initiating deep change' (86).

[58] This book, though focusing on several Hebrew ideas, does not consider the concept of change in Hebrew thought. Although the Hebrew language is rich in descriptive emotion words, it does not have a wide vocabulary to describe what today we see as internal reality e.g. the intrinsic or unconscious aspects of human nature. But this is the way I am using the word 'change'. For a range of Old Testament meanings of 'change' see van Gemeren (1996 (semantic fields 2200, 2736, 2722, 2739, 4710, 9455, 9101, etc.)). 'Repent' is probably closer to the 'positive personal change' I am describing. (See 1996 (semantic fields 5412, 5714, 8654, 8740, 8743, 8745, 8746, 9588, etc.) and volume 5:202.). You may also want to look up the semantic field references to 'turning, apostasy, returning, faithfulness, repentance', for further background.

of the book title I have dropped the words 'more', 'ecotone' and 'salugenic' from the title. But because I refer to these words at various stages in the text, I need to introduce them to you.

The word **ecotone** I have borrowed from the natural sciences[59] where it describes the meeting place of two diverse biospheres, e.g. forest and sea, desert and oasis, etc. The ecotone is the region of transition between the two ecological systems. From these origins I am using the word to describe the intellectual interface, especially theologically, psychologically and socially, where diverse concepts or experience meet, for example, where a personal search for spirituality can be assisted by community. Later in this book I will note some of the ecotones the Western Church and CCD are currently experiencing, illustrating that these can produce a third unique and novel type of intellectual praxis and its spirituality, mixing human relational experience and outcomes.

The word **salugenic** is commonly used in the sense of wholeness inducing, or to describe healthy religion,[60] as opposed to sick (pathogenic) religion (Seeber 2001). This is the sense in which I am using the word in this book.

The terms **spiritual and spirituality**[61] are used in the sense of human spirit and Holy Spirit, both in and around us, everywhere they might be perceived to appear.[62] This book takes a critical realist position,[63] assuming that there are such phenomena as spirituality and spiritual reality, whilst also recognizing that they are, to some extent, personal constructs. However, all expressions and perceptions of spirituality I see as equally valid in an exploration of the field.[64] Debating whether spiritual reality

---

[59] Professor Clarence Joldersma from Calvin College, Grand Rapids, USA introduced this concept to me at my home (April 2003), while talking through philosophy, and my struggle to find words and concepts to describe what I wanted to say.

[60] This book does not need a definition of religion, but were I to use one I would be inclined towards Geertz '(1) a system of symbols which act to (2) establish powerful, pervasive, and long-lasting moods and motivations in men by (3) formulating conceptions of a general order of existence and (4) clothing these conceptions with such an aura of factuality that (5) the moods and motivations seem uniquely realistic' (1966/1977:4).

[61] One of the ways the wider Church uses the word spirituality is to 'spiritualize' something, suggesting it is being internalized in the post-Reformation sense, becoming deeply personal and private. This is not the way I am using the word in this book.

[62] The complex issue of defining spirituality is addressed in 'Defining a transforming spirituality' (page 1). Comment is also included in appendix 4.

[63] The three ontological layers in Bhaskar's (1975) framing of critical realism allow spirituality to be treated as a 'real' but unseen causal power, a generative mechanism, also acknowledging the integrity of actual and empirical realities.

[64] As in Hebrew thought, I see spiritual reality all around us and within us. I conceive it interpenetrating all material reality. So every act is a spiritual act, and all acts are relational. Our nature was first spiritual and then embodied, so everything we do and are has a spiritual dimension. For a different perspective see Clark (1984:24ff.). Yet even in Hebrew thought one sees a distinction between the 'precious' and 'common' (e.g. Je. 15:19). Certain objects, locations and

exists is outside the scope of this book. Also, I do not seek to make distinctions regarding intrinsic and extrinsic aspects of spirituality. Instead, this book assumes the presence of spirituality in various ways, especially as it is expressed in contemporary literature and culture.[65]

At various places in this book I will be talking about **Hebrew ideas,**[66] speaking more specifically of the **Early Hebrew period**.[67] There is considerable debate in Hebrew studies today as to whether the Church can even talk objectively about these times. For instance, many scholars now question the Exodus as a real event, because we have no archaeological evidence for it. Others argue that we should not treat the early Old Testament books as history, since they were only written much later as propaganda pamphlets. Although I make some comments on this debate at various places in the book, to avoid this debate as much as I can I have instead turned to more contemporary sociological tools[68] to talk about this period, rather than use besieged traditional exegetical methodology. Likewise, in speaking of the *Early* Hebrew Period, prior to the Monarchy, I am suggesting this could usefully be seen as formative in Yahweh communicating some of His core values to newly-birthed Israel. Then, from the Monarchy onwards, Israel developed these early ideas by progressive revelation.[69]

Like many scholars before me, I have read the Old Testament and seen themes, concepts and ideas in the narrative of the text, interpreted them for myself in the late twentieth and early twenty-first centuries, then re-interpreted them to others. We all interpret, and we are all inculturated,

---

even people are set aside in some way for Yahweh, and I believe it is from this that we get some of the dualistic thinking regarding sacred and secular. But this should not be confused with the spirituality of all things. For a modern definition of *secular* see Volf (1998a:17ff., footnote 43).

[65] See 'Being human, and the search for authentic spirituality' (page 1) for a fuller landscape of some of the fields and disciplines where spirituality currently appears.

[66] Using Hebrew ideas in the contemporary Church is not new. For instance the Biblical Theology Movement, led by Cullman, Kittel, Wheeler Robinson and others in the 1920's rejected Greek ideas in favour of Hebrew. But this was not all good, these scholars being accused, for instance, of denouncing the immortality of the soul (Boyd 1996:24,95) and of influencing others to lose the concept of the soul (human spirit) from the modern Church (e.g., Brockway 1979).

[67] The Early Hebrew period extends from the Exodus through the Early Settlement period to the beginning of the monarchy, into Saul, David and Solomon. But in this book, although I see some important records of Yahweh's values in this early period, the outworking and applying of these does of course extend throughout the Old Testament record.

[68] For an overview of how sociology began to be used in the study of Scripture, see Lang (1985a, especially the introduction). A useful summary is that of Gottwald (1993:142-153). Also see Gottwald (1975/1979) for an outline of the general principles he used in his own major sociological study.

[69] I am very aware that some scholars would argue that it is not possible to have 'Early Hebrew ideas' at all, simply because these 'early' books were written much later, and the ideas read back. It is a matter of conjecture as to how much editorial control Yahweh Himself had in this process, therefore I use a range of Old Testament references to illustrate my case where helpful.

since all understanding is historically and personally conditioned. So the Hebrew ideas I draw out of Scripture, and my own reading of it, and the issues I have subsequently raised, must always be seen as deductive, personal and culturally bound. Some ideas that I suggest are supported by others whom I cite, while other ideas are my own. So in speaking of these 'Early Hebrew ideas' I make no substantial claim that I am tapping into a rich established academic culture, though in some cases I am. But instead, that they are ideas that have proven helpful to me personally, to clients over many years, and also to members of CCD, helping shape the vision and practice of the community. In the eyes of some I may be guilty of 'romanticizing' the Hebrew period, but this has not been my intention.

Also woven into this book is a dialogue between the more lively dynamic of **Hebrew ideas**, and the more passive, static ideas found in **Greek thought**. However, I am anxious not to over-emphasize any bifurcation. As I will be noting, both societies lived together for several hundred years and *together* offered useful frameworks for the Early Church, and even for today (Skarsaune 2002). In this book I do not seek to justify the existence of these two cultures. They are taken by me as given, though as I will be suggesting, some Greek ideas may be less useful to the Church today than they have been in the past.[70] Also, some readers may accuse me of making these two cultures and their ideas too simplistic. For instance, I could be guilty of using ideas in the Hebrew period without substantiation, and guilty of some reductionism in the Greek. I do not believe I have, but for those who believe I have, I apologize now.

I also speak of the **Early Church** By this I am describing the historic period from the time of Pentecost (Acts 2), to the end of the first century. This period includes the whole of the Book of Acts. I will be speaking of it in an evolving sense, so it is my intention to be as real as I can, but some may accuse me of romanticizing this period. This is not my intention.

The word **authentic** will be used throughout this book to describe something specific. I have found three ways of understanding this word; being true to an original prototype in character and purpose; describing sincerity; or in the Greek sense: real, genuine, being free from deceit. In this latter sense an authentic person[71] is one who is true within themselves to themselves. The word authentic is never used in the New Testament, but

---

[70] The substantial benefits of the Greek culture and its *pax Romana* aided the rapid growth of the Early Church (Stark 1996). It gave a framework through which the Early Church could communicate the Gospel, something Judaism resisted (Acts 15:1ff.). But what may have been helpful in the Greek culture, is not necessarily now suitable in responding to contemporary Western pluralism. From the Ionian natural philosophers, through Eleatic, Heraclitean, Platonic and Aristotelian philosophies, there is, as an example, an inheritance within the Western Church of a static, transcendent and immutable Being in God, which does not readily dialogue with contemporary spirituality. See 'The impact of Greek thought' (page 1).

[71] My use of 'person' is explored in 'Exploring personhood' (page 1).

in the context of discipleship Christ is the authentic original model, e.g. the Master, the model of excellence, a true correspondence to the original. For instance, His authority was His exercise of authentic power (Mk. 1:22), and His disciples were His authentic witnesses (Kraus 1979:19). In this book I am suggesting true authenticity is only found in knowing Christ, implying that an authentic spirituality[72] is one that is truly holistic, and must include a growth in knowledge of Christ, oneself, others and the created world. This 'authentic' process, I will argue, is what it is to become more fully human.

Many books have been written on the subject of postmodernity, even questioning whether a 'postmodern era' actually exists (Giddens 1991:27). In writing the first draft of my PhD I naively used the term to describe a set of characteristics of contemporary people, especially here in the Western world. But I became increasingly uneasy about this. In the culture of CCD members make a distinction between insider and outsider. For them outsiders fall into two main groups, those who would call themselves Christian, and those who would not. This latter group I call in this book 'un-churched'. They are perceived by members of CCD to have a different value system.[73]

In referring to characteristics of these contemporary un-churched people, I realized the term 'postmodern' was in fact broader, able to describe people both inside and outside the Church.[74] So I have dropped the word 'postmodern' from this book, instead I will be using the phrase 'contemporary un-churched' to describe those seen by the member of CCD as outside the Church,[75] on the whole having a post-Christian outlook.[76] But I also suggest that among these 'contemporary un-churched' is a growing interest in spirituality. I am aware I do not attempt to substantiate this, only giving a brief overview of this growing interest in selected areas. I make a

---

[72] Snyder took up this theme, that the Church of tomorrow needed to demonstrate an *experientially authentic* community, relationality and fellowship with God: a mysticism joined with relevant action (1975:189) (my italics).

[73] One of the surprising findings from Susan Williams' research was the extensive difference between the welcome on offer to those in need or who were un-churched, and the suspicion and fear towards the 'experienced Christian'.

[74] In conversations while writing this book I have been urged to step more into this subject of the Western Church and postmodernism. I decided not to, even though by doing so I may be missing numerous ideas relevant to me. This book suggests one of the reasons for the Church's lack of confidence in standing against postmodernism is simply that it is failing in being distinctive. See 'Theme one: The challenge of the post-Christian spirituality movement' (page 222) for a summary of some of these failures.

[75] Whether such a group even exists is outside the scope of this book, but some authors seem to think so (Drane 2002, Frazee 2001).

[76] See, for instance, from a Christian perspective, Grenz (1996) and Lakeland (1997), while from a social perspective, Dunn (1998).

more substantial case for this interest in a separate book.[77] But on the complex issue of 'postmodernity'[78] I keep an open mind.

The collapse of the Western Church

When speaking about **the Western Church**[79] I am not referring to the whole Western Church, but to the contemporary Church, both Catholic and Protestant, institutionally, as it currently exists across Western Europe and North America. I also include in this the new denominations and movements,[80] as well as the ongoing proliferation of independent churches like CCD. The reason I put them all together is simply because they follow what I will later be describing as Constantinian Christianity (see 'The impact of Greek thought' (page 1)). In this book I will be suggesting that any institutional change in the Western Church needs to be driven by personal intrinsic change, not new management structures and programmes.

The background to this book is the continuing devastation, or collapse in numbers of traditional Christian denominations,[81] especially here in Western Europe. My personal concern is that Western Europe could be only a couple of decades ahead of North America in this mass desertion from Institutional Church. The hegemonic, osmotic form of congregation is collapsing (Barrow 2003:9) despite many brave initiatives.[82] '…Sections of our church are virtually swimming in five-step renewal processes, natural development programmes, change consultancies, training packs, resource materials, growth manuals and analytic frameworks… If salvation by qualitative management really worked we would all surely be in an

---

[77] See Holmes *Trinity in human community: Exploring church in the image of the social Trinity* (2006b)

[78] Postmodernism and post-structuralism, according to Lather are refusing to settle on meaning and definition (2001:478 n.28), so we are now into a time where they are even being used interchangeably. For a view of how ethnography may fare in the 'postmodern' 21st century, see Spencer (2001).

[79] To avoid confusion I will be using the word 'church' in several distinct ways. I will speak of the Western Church or the Church, to describe the Church as it is experienced generally in our world. I will use the term 'congregation' or 'church' when referring to a local group of believers. The Early Church will refer, as previously mentioned, to churches from the Ascension of Christ through the first century to the rise of Constantine, while Christ Church Deal will be referred to as CCD. In all these I recognize that there are a wide variety of traditions (and numerous exceptions), so I am inevitably resorting in part to a stereotypical phraseology.

[80] For an overview of some of these, see Barrett (2001).

[81] For instance, over one million people left the Church in UK in the nine years between 1989 and 1998, with the Roman Catholic and Anglican attendance falling between 40-50% in the last two decades. One local congregation is closing every day. (For a more detailed comment, see Brierley 2000.)

[82] It is hard to choose one example of the numerous initiatives seeking to recover lost ground. One might be Hannaford (1998).

advanced state of sanctification' (Barrow 2003:11).[83] Such initiatives are on the whole clearly not working (Drane 2002). Part of this collapse, suggested in this book, is the Church's increasing disconnection with contemporary culture. The un-churched perceive few good reasons to be Christian, therefore less and less ecotone exists with contemporary society. But having said that, this book does not pretend to be a new model for the *whole* Western Church. What this book is suggesting is that the model being developed here in CCD may be one among many new initiatives that will help engage the Church in our contemporary society more successfully.

> *Most people have come [to CCD] because they couldn't find any place in the conventional churches that they attended. And many came with great disillusionment that the church hadn't lived up to the promise that it seemed to hold when they thought they met the Lord. I think that is true for most of us. We didn't find what we were looking for. We were promised much and didn't find that (M14-4).*

Susan Williams' findings outline numerous changes that any local church could make, to give un-churched people some good reasons to follow Christ. But much within the Western Church's traditions stands against these changes taking place. Therefore, throughout this book I am suggesting we need to begin building a *theology of change* to help facilitate relationship with contemporary people, and their existing spiritual journeys. To help redefine this problem, and to build such a case, at various points in the book I will be suggesting definitions of change in relation to God, people and the Church.

But first, let me provide some contemporary background and comment on life among the contemporary un-churched.

---

[83] For an overview of the Church flirting with 'modernity' symbolic of some of those efforts, see Guinness (1993).

Chapter 2

The remarkable contemporary search for 'authentic' spirituality; its change character; seeking this within Christian Trinitarian theology

Introduction

Change characterizes our contemporary Western culture.[1] Part of this change has been a unique search for human spirituality in a relational context,[2] a seeking to become more fully human by discovering one's spiritual nature. Spirituality in past centuries has always been the domain of religion, but not any longer. Outside established religion one is seeing a significant rise in interest in spirituality, not led by the fringe, but within mainstream academic and professional life. To respond to these megatrends the Church needs a greater understanding of both itself[3] and contemporary trends in the field of religion and spirituality.[4]

In this chapter I will briefly outline some of the features of this new interest in spirituality, then note some of its characteristics through adopting a contemporary definition of spirituality. I will then note that this new

---

[1]   Not everyone would agree. For instance, an Eastern Shamanistic perspective of the West is 'Our static view of the world abhors any kind of change, except perhaps economic and technological. In particular we resent any alteration of consciousness and ontological change' (Kalweit 1989:80).

[2]   For an alternative view of contemporary spirituality, arguing there is nothing 'new' in this 'new age' spirituality, see McCarthy (2000).

[3]   Some would argue that the Church should not even attempt to offer anything comparable to contemporary spirituality, but instead promote a spiritual 'faithfulness' where one 'preaches the Gospel', inviting God to bless this process. Christ is attractive enough on His own, without the 'baubles and trinkets' of psychology, self-help, wholeness, spirituality and/or modern ways of doing things. On this basis features like personal empowerment and psychological therapy should not be part of the 'Gospel'. For an example of this viewpoint, see Wells (1994). 'The New Testament never promises anyone a life of psychological wholeness or offers a guarantee of the consumer's satisfaction with Christ.... As being made in God's image we are fundamentally moral beings, not consumers. The satisfaction of our psychological needs pale in significance compared with the enduring value of doing what is right' (Wells 1994:115, quoted in Cray 1998:14). For some attending CCD and *Rapha* such a position has been hard to maintain.

[4]   An interesting illustration of these changes is the shift in contemporary people's views of therapists and the priesthood, where, ironically, the priest might be marginally more attractive (Schindler, et al. 1987).

'religionless' spirituality raises numerous questions for the Church, not
least its limited success in dialoguing with this new domain.[5] I will then be
suggesting that this difficulty is contributing to what some are seeing as the
Church's growing irrelevance within contemporary society.

At its heart this interest in spirituality is about personal change and its
progress, people desiring to explore more deeply themselves, relationships,
and the world they live in.

> *With a lot of people, that is what they are looking for, themselves really. They feel
> very far away, traveling to find themselves (W9-3).*

This personal positive change no longer characterizes much modern
Western Christianity.[6] For many years I have been asking why. One reason,

I have concluded, is that the Western Church is largely intellectually
located within Greek philosophical ideas. In the past this had not been a
problem, but gaps are now appearing with contemporary culture. One area,
for instance, is the traditional view of the Trinity[7] with what is now being
seen as problems with its immutability, and its inadequate pneumatology.
These intellectual structures, I have concluded, are contributing to a
resistance to a *theology of change.*

The use of Greek categories has been helpful to the Church in the past,
but times have changed, and contemporary un-churched people's ideas are
now challenging traditional values, especially within Western society.
Dualism[8] is giving way to holism,[9] relationality questioning individualism,[10]

---

[5]   I am not denying 'mature' types of spirituality exist in the contemporary Church, e.g.
Ignatian, Quaker, Celtic etc. What I am saying is that although the ideas and experiences are readily
available, and helpful questions are being asked, the Church does not seem to be successfully
repackaging this for the twenty-first century. Later in this chapter ('Christ Church Deal and its core
values', page 1), using the experience of CCD, I will suggest several possible reasons.

[6]   There is a basic cultural resistance to change throughout the Western world, perhaps because
'all change requires passage through chaos' (Rebillot 1989:223). These spirituality movements can
therefore be seen as reactionary. In Asia change is more widely accepted as part of the culture. (See
'The implications for authentic faith community', page 41)

[7]   For a helpful contemporary view of Trinity, see McGrath (1994:247-269). Giles (2002)
argues that the Church has hierarchical structures, but the Trinity does not. Others are also working
in the same areas as the ideas in this book regarding personal wholeness, Trinity and community.
See, for instance, Fiddes (2000).

[8]   By dualism I am thinking of theories or systems of thought that recognize two independent
principles, e.g. monism and pluralism, mind and matter, good and evil, etc.

[9]   I would be accused of being a modernist by Cooper (1989/2000:4) and others, simply
because I am holist. It is not that I am accusing substance dualism, or any other school, of
subverting Christianity, but that Hebrew thought was more holistic regarding human make-up, and
this is today conceptually growing more popular among the contemporary un-churched. Having
said that, Hebrew thought also had its dualism, focused around the sacred and profane.

[10]   Gorman (1993:36ff.) noted the difference between *individualism*: the self-sufficiency and
independent separation of an autonomous person, the fruit of the Enlightenment, and *individuality*:
being a unique person. Kraus (1979:84-85), like Gorman, saw individualism as a matter of
alienation and pride, the essence of sin. I will be using these words in this sense.

and change replacing conformity and compliance.[11] This is not a new problem. As I will be illustrating, numerous people in the 20th century have sought to respond to these changing ideas and values. Toward the end of the chapter I will outline a response to this Trinitarian problem through the use of Early Eastern Orthodox theology. But I will also be suggesting that Hebrew ideas have a contribution to make, and that together these can help provide the Church[12] with an authentic relational *pneuma*-psychology[13] within a theology of change. I will also be noting that some of these tools are already being used by CCD in its pastoral clinical work, in responding to contemporary un-churched people's search for spirituality.

> *No matter what [an outsider] had experienced and what they have lost, a comforting phrase would be that when I arrived [at CCD], I knew that a life-long search for something was over. I was so profoundly aware of it, that when I came to this church, I didn't know what that search was, but I was aware that whatever it was I was looking for had come to an end. It was here (M9-4).*

Contemporary spirituality, the Church and human personal positive change

Being human, and the search for authentic spirituality

While Western thought has tended to reify personhood, traditionally making it a static category, there is today an increasingly deep interest in the dynamics of human personhood, and especially its spirituality.[14] Belief in an authentic, tangible, spiritual reality is becoming more widespread outside the Church. Hay and Hunt (2000), researching spirituality among the UK un-churched, note a significant numerical growth in those who believe spirituality is grounded in their personal experience, from 29% in 1987, to 55% in 2000, while those admitting to an awareness of evil has risen from 12% to 25%.

---

[11] This book suggests that some people today are actively searching for something to replace religion. See Ferry (2002) and Vattimo (2002) on this point.

[12] Much has been, is and will be written on the subject of the Church needing to change. My own comments in this book are based on the empirical work of Susan Williams (2002). Others, similar to both Susan Williams and myself, also draw on their experience as insiders. See for example, Goldsmith (1991), Drane (2000), and Edwards (2002).

[13] In 'A pneuma-psychology within a discipleship therapeutic wholeness journey' (page 130) I develop this concept further.

[14] Schneiders cautioned that the longer she worked at the theoretical elaboration of this new field of spirituality studies the more serious and complicated the questions appeared (1993:10-15). I share her experience. Francis Schaeffer (1972) was for me one of the first Christian thinkers to put the subject on the modern map. For a typical landscape of the substantial range of books currently available on contemporary spirituality outside the Church, see the catalogue of 'the Inner Bookshop', run by Ruth Ashcroft and Anthony Cheke, at 111 Magdalen Street, Oxford, UK OX4 1RQ. They list over four thousand titles.

In our lifetime, for instance, in the sciences we have moved from a place where it was unfashionable to talk about spiritual reality ('what ain't seen, ain't real'), to the early 21st century where at least in non-Christian society, it is now increasingly acceptable to speak of one's spirituality, personal journey and experiences (Drane 2002). As noted by Susan Williams' participants, as well as many others in and outside the Church, the increasing interest is in *experiencing*[15] a more authentic personal and group spirituality. Consequently spirituality as an area of interest has now left the church, and is beginning to appear in most areas of human life and perception, be they personal or professional. But so far few have attempted to landscape this domain.[16] Let us note a few of these areas.

In psychology, spirituality is now a significant area (Young-Eisendrath and Miller 2000). A spiritless twentieth century psychology is now awakening to the fact that we are more than our biology (Purton 1998), having the capacity, experience, and hunger for supra-sensible reality.[17] In losing the concept of human spirit[18] we have lost in part the value of the sacred in human life (Christians 1998). Also, in psychology the measure of

intelligence quotient (IQ) birthed EQ (emotional intelligence) (Goleman 1995, 2002 etc.), which has now led into SQ, (spiritual intelligence) (Zohar and Marshall 2000, 2004). This book argues that all three are needed for us to become more fully human. Spirituality is therefore emerging from within both psychological therapies (Richards and Bergin 1997), the human potential movements (Puttick 2000) and the 'self-help' movement (Hanegraaff 1998:42-61).

Likewise, the rise of interest in spirituality in the health sciences in recent years has been significant, both in the United States (Miller 1999) and here in UK (Orchard 2001). Health care professionals are beginning to

---

[15] The growing research field of 'experience of God', since William James (1902/1928), has created its own literature as well as proposing its own measurement tools. For instance, 'Charismatic beliefs and experience must be assessed as a whole constellation [e.g. its own paradigm], by using a cumulative case argument' (Middlemiss 1996:155). In CCD we do not 'objectify' personal experience in this way. Instead, if the experience is 'authentic' to the person, then we do not question it until they do. In intellectually questioning another person's experience, one is in danger of judging or dishonouring them. In part we have adopted this practice because we do not want people to begin thinking dualistically, in having to choose between the authority of the Bible, other peoples' views, their personal experience and the independent 'facts'.

[16] I presented such a paper outlining some of the domains of spirituality, at the annual conference of the British Sociological Association's Sociology of Religion Study Group in March 2004. (See (Holmes 2006a).) Kidder suggested this search for spirituality is paralleled by a 'global breakdown in ethics and morality' (1994:xi).

[17] Advances in neuro-physiology can account for some aspects of the nature and function of human sense perception, but like many others, I see that it requires much more than this to offer a full understanding of human sensitivity and experience.

[18] Throughout this book, in speaking of mind, body or human spirit, I am not suggesting a priority of one over the other, but instead seeking a living balance when speaking of these characteristics in human nature.

argue that spirituality needs to become a key component in health promotion (Chapman 1987a, 1987b, Brown 1998, Thoresen 1999, Miller and Thoresen 1999, Swinton 2001),[19] and this is clearly beginning to happen (Bensley 1991) even in the area of serious mental illness (Lindgren and Coursey 1995), and fields like occupational therapy (Enquist, et al. 1997).

But this rise is not even across all fields of health care.[20] Nursing is one of the leaders, where there is a call for an awakening of spirit in clinical practice (Burkhardt and Nagai-Jacobson 1994), and a recognition of spiritual distress and how to work with it (Burnard 1987). There is also a growing body of evidence that spirituality is a key health contributor (Koenig 1999), which in some circles is becoming known as 'spiritual health'.[21] Psychological therapies are one example[22] where spirituality has become a key element (Clark and Thompson 1990, Fouch 1997, Steere 1997, Schwartz 1999, Izzard 2003). Likewise, the rise of medical-ethical holism, and its spiritual dimension, is now becoming a core part of treatment, for instance with dependency disorders (Miller 1998). The search is now also on for a spirituality suitable for those with learning disabilities (Swinton 2001). Such spiritualities are seen as having a transformative character, being personally experienced and relationally celebrated. But, sadly, very little of this is being driven by the Church.[23]

In the field of sociology one can too easily slip into social comment about spirituality, rather than commenting on the place of spirituality in sociology. Numerous social phenomena have contributed to the search for the spiritual, for example, the heartless sterility of technology, the breakdown of larger frames of meaning in people's lives, the loss of long-

---

[19] Swinton looks at a range of spiritual models of assessment now in vogue (2001:93ff., 179ff.) as well as offering a review of literature (64ff.).

[20] In this brief overview I am not addressing in detail areas like surgery and general practice, both of which warrant mention. For an introduction to spirituality in the mental health sector, see Gilbert and Nicholls (2003).

[21] For an overview of the whole subject of spirituality and the caring professions, from 1962 onwards, see O'Connor et al. (2002). For a helpful introduction to the question of personal spirituality and the need for it to be considered more seriously in the healing process, along with avoiding spiritual stress in patients, see Scott and Allen (1997).

[22] For an example of combining these interests, see Liverpool John Moores University, School of Psychology, who, along with others, run doctoral scholarships in the field of consciousness and transpersonal psychology, 'concentrating on spiritual practice and perceptual and memory functions. Assessing dimensions of spirituality and spiritual transformation' (British Psychology Society Appointments Memorandum 623, March 2003).

[23] Outside the Church there are a large range of books on the market of the 'self-help' and 'change' variety, many having an assumed spirituality in them. See, for instance, Myss (1996). One can further illustrate this point by visiting any good bookshop and comparing the 'Christian spirituality' section (if they have one) with the extensive 'self-help', 'mysticism', 'healing', 'wholeness', 'New Age' offerings of a 'non-Christian' variety.

held values, especially absolutes, and the creating of rootless cultures.[24] The modern failure of materialism and the rise of secularism also play their part.[25]

One of the biggest factors may be the breakdown of community (Etzioni 1993/1995). Society has been fragmenting socially and relationally for several hundred years or more. This may be why Wilber (2001) and others are proposing the development of an integrated spirituality, as part of a postmodern consciousness. Here one can detect a 'communal urge', seen by some as intrinsic to human nature (Shenker 1986:4).[26] Many believe that spirituality has a key part to play in this recovery process, as people find each other in common interests and purpose. But such movements are largely post-Christian, moving beyond the confines of the Church.

In educational discourse[27] the idea of spirituality has re-emerged as an important element in schooling. National Curriculum documentation in UK describes pupil attainment as consisting of *both* learning and achievement *and* personal development (which incorporates spiritual, moral, social and cultural development). Such statutory assessments of spiritual development are fuelling the debate about spirituality, calling for a new language, new methodology and a means of supporting personal and communal spirituality.[28] Fullan (1999), for instance, used the language of spirituality interchangeably with the language of 'moral purpose'.

Likewise, in the field of business we now 'talk spiritual'. On the American corporate scene see Mitroff and Denton (1999) who noted that most people have strong spiritual beliefs, regardless of religion. They also argued that where company and spiritual values coalesce, company

---

[24] Lyon, among others, proposes that accelerated globalization can lead to a renewed interest in religion (2000:147). For an earlier call in responding to this, see Covey (1970).

[25] Habermas (1986) helpfully outlined a framework for understanding and locating social science research through his use of strategic, hermeneutical and emancipatory human interests, accompanied by distinctive rationalities and ways of knowing. Of these three areas, emancipatory rationality is the least developed and understood, yet perhaps the most promising for spirituality research. Although the first two sets of knowledge and concomitant interests are fairly well established by Habermas, his claim for emancipatory knowledge and interests is little more than a promissory note, instead of a well-developed idea (Outhwaite 1994/1996, Brown and Goodman 2001).

[26] This 'urge' takes many forms. One of the most novel has to be online 'virtual communities'. One site can be a community talking about communities, e.g. {www.epinionsaddicts.com} or another the fans of the Honda Prelude, with over a thousand plus pages, complete with classifieds, event lists and a parts swop. For a brief review of this type of 'virtual community', see Kapelke (2001).

[27] Here I am focusing on current thinking in the field of the delivery of education. But spirituality also contributes to literature, poetry, fiction, and other writing, to the arts and creativity, including theatre, drama, the media, and the family, alongside developmental studies. In most of these areas a literature focusing on spirituality is beginning to emerge.

[28] In the field of education this call is associated with the teaching of 'core values' as part of the curriculum. For an outline of some of these, see McGettrick (1995:7).

performance is higher. Roof (1999) also noted that spirituality was firmly entrenched in the marketplace. Here in UK, articles on spirituality in business are common, as is the emphasis on ethical leadership (Covey 2001, Goleman 2002). But coupled with this is the advertising media where 'spirit' and 'spirituality' are frequently mentioned.[29]

Many other academic disciplines, like gender studies, theoretical physics[30] and even *Feng Shui* (Gunn 1999) and gardening design (e.g. the Chelsea Flower Show) are all 'talking spiritual'. Motor mechanics and fishing can now be spiritual acts, as can studying the biodiversity of the natural world. The construction of *Ground Zero* is being conceived as a spiritual place (Conran 2002).

Overall, several features of this spirituality emerge, especially its unevenness and unreligious pretensions. Yet amidst this enthusiasm we still have no unified understanding of what spirituality is,[31] especially its intellectual ownership and definition. Consequently, we have not yet begun cross-referencing the research tools from one academic discipline to another. Spirituality will probably be the first academic subject to appear almost everywhere, while defying one definition or domain.

Defining a transforming spirituality

The need for a definition of contemporary spirituality first became obvious to me some years ago when trying to define what it meant to be human and spiritual in the modern world. Although definitions of spirituality do exist in the Church (Armirtham and Pryor 1991), I decided to adopt one outside of the Church, with a more clinical paradigm.[32] There are numerous reasons for this. For one, I am still personally some distance from writing a definition adequate for my own work.[33] Also, the task of doing so is becoming increasingly more difficult, given that so little comparative work is being done between these growing spiritualities in Western culture and

---

[29] These comments on business should really be expanded to include issues of spirituality in finance, economics and politics, as well as the spirituality of teams, with its EQ, and social and group processes.

[30] Quantum physics, holography, synchronicity, and the role of mathematics are also helping to define spirituality. See O'Murchu (1997).

[31] Some have begun this work. See, for instance, Schermer (2003), who seeks to bring together much of the thinking in this field, while also reviewing the literature.

[32] I am in two minds as to whether we can achieve, or even need one definition. For example, when we recently explored at the University of Bristol the setting up of a National Centre for Spirituality, Social Values and Learning we agreed a definition of what we meant by spirituality would be helpful. After much effort it was finally decided, at my suggestion, to go with a 'landscape' of what may need to be considered in any final definition. This I drafted with Dr Ruth Deakin Crick. See appendix 3. For a similar exercise see Armirtham and Pryor (1991).

[33] Over several years I have drafted working definitions, frequently amended to take account of new developments or thinking in psychology, sociology, medicine and other fields. One was used in an early draft of this book, but I had to conclude it was inadequate.

the modern Western Church.[34]

So for the purposes of this book I have adopted Martsolf and Mickley's (1998) five central *features* of spirituality, which is not a definition as such. Neither is it specifically Christian, being instead a meta-analysis by the authors of modern theorists' ideas: a descriptive outline of features of contemporary spirituality that are broad enough to be a reference point for this book. But it offers a helpful place to start:

(1) MEANING: the ontological significance of life; making sense of life situations; deriving purpose in existence.

(2) VALUE: beliefs and standards that are cherished; having to do with truth, beauty, worth of a thought, object or behaviour; often discussed as 'ultimate values'.

(3) TRANSCENDENCE: experience and appreciation of a dimension beyond the self; expanding self-boundaries.

(4) CONNECTING: relationships with self, others, God/higher power, and the environment.

(5) BECOMING: an unfolding of life that demands reflection and experience; includes a sense of who one is and how one knows among other things.

Martsolf and Mickley were primarily focused around nursing clinical practice, and this is why I find their descriptive outline helpful. It evolved from within clinical practice. This 'hands-on' pragmatism regarding the issue of spirituality is something that can be lacking within Christian definitions. For instance, few even referred to the idea of personal change.[35] As I will be mentioning several times in this book, change is at the heart of the modern human search for both personhood and one's spirituality.

These five points form a landscape of key attributes of spirituality. They are practical, specific, and use a straight-forward language that can be easily understood and appropriated. A person is encouraged to think through their ultimate values, thereby growing in their own spirituality, identifying aspects of their life that lack meaning, or where they feel they may have 'lost' their spirituality. It is a broad 'working' model, not confined to a personal private spirituality. Instead it recognizes communal connectedness, a sense of that which is beyond self, tendering new learning and change, a sense of communal becoming of who one really is and could

---

[34] For some interesting comments on the question of the place of the Bible in relation to this new spirituality, see Ballard (2003).

[35] Some definitions of 'transforming spirituality' do exist, mainly in the Catholic and Eastern traditions. For instance: 'Spirituality is a lived experience, the effort to apply relevant elements in the deposit of the Christian faith to the guidance of men and women towards their spiritual growth, the progressive development of their persons which flowers into a proportionately increased insight and joy' (Ganss 1991:61). This comes close, but fails to mention any living intimacy with Christ, suggesting instead one is driven by learning the Church's traditions?

be. In this sense, this descriptive landscape suggests an implicit, intrinsic, authentic, relational and transforming spirituality integral to every person.

We have already noted that a megatrend now exists among Western peoples to develop spiritualities no longer defined in Christian, religious or theological terms.[36] In the past, 'spiritual' thinking was expressed in ecclesiastical science and dogma, but now it is being spoken of in terms of human personhood, wholeness, healing and the wider human community (Reuther 1972:2, quoted in McCoy 1980:24).[37] Commented McCoy, 'while the gods abound in our new global culture, a new pluralism has evolved that conventional theologies have ignored' (1980:69).[38] The rapid emergence of people's interest in spirituality has not been matched by the Church's capacity to lead such thinking, or even dialogue with these new expressions of human interest.[39] Many of these spiritualities are focused on a journey into personal change, so how does the Western Church find a framework to dialogue with these movements and their ideas of spirituality? Let us leave definitions of spirituality for a moment, and look at the Western Church.

Change: Seeking a theological framework within Church and tradition

The current change in the Church's fortunes has been blamed on 'secularisation' (Bruce 2002).[40] But I do not accept it is that simple. No one

---

[36] For two of the classic statements on this process, from a theological and social perspective, see Bellah (1970) and Smart (1971).

[37] Bonhoeffer, through his 'worldliness of the Word of God' theology believed that 'Wherever therapy is, theology is present. Helping which nurtures selfhood is Christian, regardless of whether or not the name of Jesus is mentioned', (Bonhoeffer 1955/1995:193ff., cited in Oden 1983:199ff.). Oden built an interesting thesis around these ideas of Bonhoeffer, noting as Bonhoeffer did, that a two-sphere thinking exists in the Church and psychological therapies. They suggested that all knowledge and healing is Christ-centred, whether we acknowledge this or not. It is interesting to tie this in with Rahner's concept of the 'anonymous Christian' (1969/1974:390-398). For a summary of Rahner's view of human personhood, in theological terms, see McCool (1961, 1970).

[38] The subject of pluralism is substantial. For a summary, see Cobb (1975). McCoy saw pluralism as a tool for the liberation of theology (1980:60). But some are beginning to question whether it is now outdated as a tool of interfaith dialogue. See D'Costa (2000) as an introduction to this issue.

[39] This tension is noted. 'We find groups of Christians who are "losing their faith". Giving expression to the faith is becoming incompatible with their real existence..... Today it would seem that among many Christians the process of growing into mature human beings is estranging them from their faith' (Segundo 1968/1973:vii).

[40] Bruce (2002) notes 'secularisation' has many different interpretations, calling it the 'secularisation paradigm', describing the various meanings from a sociological perspective. Secularization is today an emotive word. In using the term, I realise I am implying such a thing is and has been taking place. Some, like Cox (1965), who began the debate in the Church, suggest the process is not entirely negative, while others question its presence at all (Mellor and Shilling

single force can account for such dramatic change in the Church's fortunes, especially since the 1960's. The battle confronting the Church is far more complex. My observation, shared by McCoy, is that the new gods of spiritual pluralism are more invisible (1980:70), and far more aggressive. Modernity cannot take all the credit.

Instead, I believe we need to look within the Church for some of its current problems, especially its early history, where its theology and philosophy have formed the basis of its belief systems and traditions. If secularisation could be blamed for loss of interest in the Church, then the Church is relatively powerless in addressing these forces. However, if part of the problem is current ideas within the Church's own thinking, then the correcting of these could prove significant for the 21st century Church. In this section I will explore some of these concepts as they developed historically, illustrating their impact today by using some of Susan Williams' research.

Christ Church Deal and its core values

At the core of life in CCD is a belief of God being in our midst.

> *As I was a non-Christian before I came to CCD I had no relationship with God. I still would not say that I have a relationship with Him. However - I am beginning a relationship with myself and out of that will come a relationship with God. (04F-2.16).*[41]

This is grounded on an assumption of who the members of CCD believe God is, His nature, and His desire to relate to us.[42] This belief is a core value within a system of thought and understanding that helps centre CCD.[43] For instance, the concept that He desires to be present whenever we meet together, rather than when we are alone. Also, that He has the capacity to respond to our changing moods and needs. We believe these characteristics are fundamental to His nature. Therefore our journey of change in CCD is set within the context of relationship with the Trinity as divine community. This is one of the ways we as a community are seeking to become more authentic. These are simple ideas, but ones I have until

---

1997:188 footnote 2). Gill (1993) suggested that blaming secularization on falling Church numbers is far too simplistic.

[41] In addition to the focus group data, I also sampled the first 25 of the 'reflective questionnaires' that Susan Williams used as a confirmatory source. This source is extremely rich in illustrative material.

[42] For a helpful introduction to God's attributes, see Gunton (2002a). For a defence of traditional views of God, against modern trends, see Huffman and Johnson (2002).

[43] In later 2004 this was forcefully brought home to us in CCD when the Lord began to speak to us through several members of the community, saying we had grown arrogant and selfish, no longer valuing His smile on us. This led to a canceling of all Sunday meetings in early 2005, giving way to a 4 week 'retrospective', where we found ourselves agreeing with His observations, and needing to begin to say sorry to the Lord.

recently struggled to place within a Christian theological framework, because such a view of God needs a theology of change or adaptability in both Trinity and human personhood.

The impact of Greek thought

In Europe, Christianity enjoyed organized dominance by the fourth century, consolidated this in the Middle Ages, and maintained it in the Western world until the 20th century. But in the 21st century, in Europe particularly, Christianity is no longer dominant. The Church today finds itself among a pantheon of other gods and their vibrant spiritualities.[44] The Western Church is in competition with them, but still carries all its history, inherited ideas and traditions. Such theological systems, framed as they are by Greek categories, are largely rigid and non-relational.

The womb of Christianity was initially *both* Hebrew[45] and Greek ideas[46] (Skarsaune 2002 passim). But during the early centuries, with the help of Greek trained converts like Augustine, Christianity increasingly relied on Greek philosophical categories,[47] accepting the bifurcation of Western intellectualism into subject/object, essence/existence, substance/accident, noumenal/phenomenal and theoretical/practical (McCoy 1980:29). These classical Greek ideas were mainly static, essences, snapshots, or single pictures of reality, whereas in the 20th century contemporary philosophy and its 'postmodernity' have progressed to thinking in whole movies.[48] The Western Church has not moved on into such thinking, for instance, having the ability to see change as an asset, or see spirituality as a clinical reality. Instead, it has retained its classic ways of thinking, so it now struggles to dialogue with contemporary ideas.[49] Greek cultural thinking is the fibre of

---

[44] Books on this subject and the related area of the Church needing to re-invent itself are too numerous to list. But they could include Guinness (1993), Tomlinson (1995), Hunter (1996), Barrett (2001), and Leech (2001). Croft (2002), summarizes much of this thinking.

[45] I am assuming Hebrew Judaic influences remained in the Early Church up to the fourth century, with the presence of Jewish believers called 'Nazarenes' (Skarsaune 2002:203). Both Origen and Jerome sought instruction in order to read the Hebrew Scriptures (266).

[46] I am using these words, Hebrew and Greek, to talk about systems of thought that might inadvertently suggest one set of comprehensive ideas in both traditions. This is hardly the case, so at several stages I will be defining what I actually mean by Hebrew and Greek ideas.

[47] This process was gradual, as less and less Jewish believers were part of the Gentile Church. The watershed was probably Justin Martyr in the second century, where fewer and fewer Jewish believers were being added to the Gentile Church (Skarsaune 2002:267).

[48] I thank Dr Anne Murphy for this helpful illustration (30/12/03).

[49] See Rist (1985, 1996) for some of this Greek background. Merton, Macmurray, Lee and Come are some of the exceptions. In 'Being a person in Hebrew thought' (page 75) I propose a Hebrew alternative in the area of human make up.

the Church's tradition and theology,[50] whereas new spiritualities frequently do not accept the either/or of Greek thought, with its dualistic notions. Neither do contemporary people accept the dogmatism of subjects like good or evil, preferring instead a situation ethic or relativism. This creates conflicts of value systems and a widening of ideas between the Western Church and contemporary society.

> *[Maturity is] having an awareness that you are probably wrong, that the world is grey and there are no real black and white definitive answers and that which you may believe is right today will probably mature tomorrow and end up being wrong (M12-9).*

Through examining certain features of the Church's Greek heritage I will suggest that although it was helpful in the past, the Church needs to acknowledge that such Greek categories could now be a hindrance. But not everyone agrees on the timing of when such Greek dualistic influences took over the Church. McCoy did not accept this happened in the Early Church, but rather matured with the re-introduction of Aristotelian philosophy in Scholasticism in the thirteenth century, primarily through Aquinas. 'The epistemological bifurcation appears in the Thomist presupposition that there is "nothing in the mind that is not first in the senses", *nihil in mente non prius in sensu*. This formulation assumes a dichotomy between an inner or mental sphere and an external sphere' (1980:119ff.). He then suggested this was affirmed in Philip Melanchthon (1497-1560), re-appearing later in Descartes (1596-1650), Locke (1632-1704), Newton (1642-1727), Berkeley (1685-1753), Hume (1793/1888) and Kant (1724-1804), among others (1980:119ff.).

Gunton, however, saw this bipolar weakness beginning in the second century with Irenaeus (130-c.200 AD) (1991a:105), whose theology embraced Greek intellectual structures, that were later adopted even more enthusiastically by Clement of Alexandria (c150-c215) and Origen (c185-c254) (Farrow 2000). McCoy noted this method of doing Christian theology was 'successful' in becoming dominant by the time of Constantine. However, it also adopted an imperial mood, occupying a transcendent perspective, an ontological peak, outside and above the limited perspectives of historical and social location. This 'Constantinian' theology, as McCoy called traditional Western Christianity's doctrines (1980:14), has remained foundational,[51] formative to the way the Church now views reality and subjects like the Trinity.

---

[50] I am pleased to note that Ehrlich (2001) presents an extensive argument for the importance of Greek thought and culture as the womb for the Early Church. I do not dispute this, but want to balance it with some Hebrew ideas.

[51] 'By accepting this trinity of bifurcations (metaphysical, epistemological, ecclesiastical), Western theology has gradually withdrawn from the larger cultural arena, into sectarian communities, retreated from the wider intellectual market place into academic enclaves' (McCoy 1980:123).

While the Church remained dominant and fashionable these weaknesses have not been obvious, but when competition arose in the 20th century, flaws in its structures have been exposed. Conventional theological forms here in the West, having assumed the inherited Greek academic traditions of Europe and North America, have consequently found themselves unable to respond to the pluralism Western culture is now creating (McCoy 1980:56).

> *[In other churches] you become a Christian after a year from a very damaged background and you are expected to follow all these rules precisely, you have to read your Bible for an hour and you have to – It is all implicit rules that is expected of you and you can't keep up with it. I found it impossible to live what I thought was a good Christian life (M10-4).*
>
> *If they are a non-Christian they think they would have to put on a whole face and churchianity before they come [to church]. And know they can come [to CCD] as they are, to speak in any way they want or behave in any way they want and they will still be accepted... (W2-2).*

Although I would not wholly agree with McCoy's suggestion that this is the lone reason, it is true that firm intellectual structures, philosophical or otherwise, cannot respond to new thinking without themselves having fluidity of ideas. Greek structures do not readily allow us to 'imagine' a living, salugenic spirituality[52] or an immanent personable God.

So the Church continues to lose ground by insisting on repackaging and repeating certain theological formulas developed within the Greek tradition over its long history. Consequently, McCoy sees the era of the Constantinian Church, and its Greek theoretical framework fast drawing to a close (1980:110). Contemporary thought is constantly evolving and changing, but the Church, with its mainly Greek philosophical theology, shows little sign of being able to address these new challenges. In the Protestant tradition especially, action follows belief (Pocock 2001:61),[53] and if the Church believes it already has all the 'correct' beliefs, there are few reasons for change, or even dialogue.

Introducing the Trinitarian problem[54]

What I am suggesting is that the task before modern theology[55] is not to

---

[52] De Certeau (1992) suggested this barrenness began within Catholicism in the 16th century, with the loss of the mystery of faith. If this is so, then the Reformation merely quickened this loss, though Shelton would argue that the Reformers sought to reject the sacramental aspects of penitential ideas, while holding onto the language of substitution (Shelton publication in process, used with the author's permission).

[53] Pocock's materials are self-published, but available through myself.

[54] In speaking of the Trinity I am aware we are not dealing with a concept that is implicit in Scripture, but actually a second level reflection. See Burrell (1986) or Lee (1997:191).

[55] In this book I am not attempting a new definition of theology. One may be needed, but that is the task of others. However, one helpful recent definition is Grenz: 'The purpose of theology is to

defend past beliefs, but identify the uniqueness of the Christian God in a world of competing religious pluralism. Jenson argued that the Western Church must either renew its Trinitarian consciousness, or experience increasing impotence and confusion[56] (Jenson 1982:ix, quoted in Gunton 1991a:18). Gunton[57] reinforced this idea, seeing one of the two main categories needing to be reconsidered is the problem of Western 'Theism' (1991a:1-2). For it is only through an understanding of the kind of being that God is, that we can learn what kind of beings we are (Gunton 1991a:vii). But if our image of deity has been formed by Greek philosophical structures of either/or, dualistically, then we must be hindered in our understanding and experience of both a personal God and our own relational personhood. Ideas within the Church on such subjects as Trinity personhood are largely built on Greek categories and separation, not holism. Alongside contemporary people's spiritual searching, the Church will therefore struggle to deliver a personable deity[58] living with humanity, in whose personable image we are all created.[59]

> [God] was some distant figure who we ought to love and know and we should have relationship with but who was probably dead and gone a long time ago (M13-1).

For most of my life I have not questioned a traditional view of Trinity, but in recent years have conceded that Church dogma, and its inadequacies in describing God[60] may be obstructing helpful new thinking.[61] The

---

serve the Church and its mission by engaging in the constructive task of setting forth a coherent model of the Christian belief-mosaic that is faithful to the biblical narratives and teachings, is informed by the trajectory of the Church's theological reflection, and is relevant to the contemporary setting' (2001:9).

[56] See Pinnock (1994) for a similar call. The Institutional Church is not faring well, on the basis of data, but it is probably true to say that the more independent fringe faith community movement, especially in the USA, is gaining health and becoming more robust.

[57] For an overview of Gunton's thinking regarding Trinity and personhood, with a call for a theology of relatedness, see Gunton (1993).

[58] In using the word 'person' I am implying 'relationship', rather than using the word 'individual', which suggests isolation. See 'Struggling with the term person' (page 70).

[59] Exceptions, like the mystic movements within the Church have always sought a redressing of relations with the Living God (Butler 1922/1986, Underhill 1964). Likewise Calvin and Luther emphasized a living Union With Christ (Lull 1989:165ff., 314ff.). But the need for such an emphasis merely illustrates the overall view of a static God.

[60] For some of the background books to this section on Trinity, see Fortman (1972), taking a classic viewpoint, and A.J. and T.F. Torrance (A.J. Torrance 1996, T.F. Torrance 1996) seeking a personable view of the Trinity, while avoiding the 'open Theism' of Pinnock (1994). Pinnock has come under heavy criticism for his initiative. 'The 'openness of God' theologians are being criticised for their uncritical use of existentialist process theologians, and postmodernist philosophy'. (Bennett (personal correspondence April 21st 2003) reviewing Gray and Sinkinson 2002). For a more sympathetic review of Pinnock (2001), see Fackre (2002:319-323). Moltmann is also helpful (1974, 1991). I will be suggesting in 'A Hebrew perspective on change' (page 53) another, maybe 'safer' way of achieving what Pinnock sought to achieve. See Pinnock (1994:194ff.) for his definition of purpose regarding a more relational God.

Constantinian paradigm is restraining new theological thought. Rahner noted how serious matters really were[62] in his seminal book *The Trinity*, '...should the doctrine of the Trinity have to be dropped as false, the major part of religious literature could well remain virtually unchanged' (1970:11).[63] At a clinical pastoral level this suggests the Church has few ways of describing how our lives are impacted by immanent Trinitarian relations. The Church cannot offer the contemporary world what it is not itself first enjoying. For instance, the human soteriological experience of accepting Christ is not currently dependent on meeting God, but making a decision to follow Him. Likewise, we worship Him, but do we ever meet Him?

> *[Until Christ Church] I didn't know that God could be that close and that people could be that sincere with the Lord. It was shocking. In fact I never knew the Lord was real until then (M13-6).*

However, when speaking about God in Trinity[64] in immanent reality, caution is necessary. It is a perilous task, though not, I believe, for the traditional reasons suggested by Greek categories, that we are unable to penetrate the veil of His being. Instead, there is always a danger of what Gunton described as 'objectifying' Him, 'of turning Him into a static and impersonal object, to be subjected to our unfettered intellectual control' (1991a:162).[65] This objectifying of God is something the Church seems to have done throughout its history.[66]

To illustrate this problem I will now outline some aspects of the Classical[67] (Augustinian/Constantinian) view of the Trinity, showing how it

---

[61] For a review of some of the recent authors sharing this view, see Gunton (1991a:14 especially footnote 1), Bracken and Suchocki (1997b passim) and Cobb, who admitted he knew of no currently convincing or adequate doctrine of the Trinity (1997:2).

[62] 'It is commonly held that Rahner has done more than any other Catholic theologian to revitalize the theology of the Trinity in the twentieth century' (Ormerod 2003 passim).

[63] Not everyone agrees with the key centrality of the Trinity. T. F. Torrance (1975), for instance, argued that it is not divine personhood, but worship that should be the starting point for any new thinking regarding God. These same themes are further developed by A. J. Torrance (1996:262ff.).

[64] Trinity has always been a key topic in the Church. Schadel (1984), for instance, listed some 4,656 titles up to 1984 on the theme of Trinity, but even he missed the likes of Hartshorne (1948) and Ogden (1967).

[65] Gunton was referring to Whitehead's observation that all Western philosophy is merely a footnote to Plato (e.g. Eleatic and Platonic metaphysics), meaning that we are all imprisoned by a static view of being (both Divine and human), together with what Lee calls its static ontology (1979:12). Lee (1974) also suggested the idea of possibility in God, the idea that God can experience suffering, which would be offensive to the Greek mind (Skarsaune 2002:310ff., 335).

[66] For a more detailed critique of the legacy of the Enlightenment focused on a Trinitarian theme, see Gunton (1985). For a Trinitarian treatment of modernity, see Gunton (1993).

[67] The transposing of terminology and concepts within Greek and Latin, particularly the differing understandings of personhood and essence, is complex. For instance, the Latins think of

has structured our view of God's nature, especially His pneumatology. Also, how this in turn has contributed to the loss of lived spirituality and community in the contemporary Church. I will then consider three 20th century responses to the problem of this Greek legacy, before outlining an alternative model of Trinity, more able, I believe, to support a theology of change and relationship as it is sought in CCD. Finally, I will suggest a Hebrew perspective of change to help further support what is being sought in CCD.

The classical Western view of Trinity

Any theologizing about the knowledge of God is necessarily carried out in the context of the philosophical teaching and cultural assumptions of its day (Gunton 1991a:33). Therefore, the philosophical outlook of the wider culture at any one time or in any one place becomes the landscape for Christian theologizing.[68]

In speaking of the Classical view of Trinity, I mean the view of God reflected in the Nicene Creed, which focused on *homoousios*, 'of the same substance', a oneness and indivisibility of the Godhead. Likewise, the Athanasian Creed affirms God is triune, not only in His activities, but in His essential eternal nature. We can summarize this consensus, the Western or Augustinian view, in one simple phrase, 'one God in three persons'.[69]

In time this traditional thinking divided into several 'schools'.[70] Cobb saw four Trinitarian theologies. The first Eastern, secondly Augustinian, thirdly a non-metaphysical view that used the horizons of human language and experience, and fourthly an 'economic' Trinity, where the discrimination of three functions did not necessarily imply much about differentiations within the divine life itself (Cobb 1997:2ff.). But within all these schools one theme emerges - God's being is defined by God's relationality.[71] Yet the way this is expressed in each school is different.

The classical Western Trinitarian approach, following the Augustinian school, states that God's essential 'sociality' is defined within God's self,

---

personality as a mode of nature, the Greeks think of nature as the content of the person (Collins 2001:117, quoting de Regnon 1893:365, quoted by Meyendorff 1974:181).

[68] Wolfson cautioned us that the Church should not be dogmatic regarding any single influence or type of cultural background. It is rarely only one factor. He cited Augustine as an example, who was himself a complex figure, with numerous influences shaping his experience and ideas, no just Greek ideas (1956:358). Throughout this book I am assuming a great number of factors make up an intellectual landscape at any one time.

[69] Giles argues that the Early Church had a developed Trinitarian theology that has been lost today (2002:32ff.).

[70] For a recent overview of Trinitarian theology East and West, see Collins (2001). His book seeks to follow the ontological implications of Barth's enterprise, in terms of personhood and relationality of God.

[71] In 'Recovering Cappadocian thought' (page 48) I expand this concept as *perichoresis*.

and His relationship with the world becomes contingent, a matter of divine whim. This is my point of concern. In Western Trinitarian theology there are few constructs capable of carrying the concept of the sociality of God within both material reality and personal relationality. Jesus is the traditional contact point, but He came, then went. Here in the West the Church has therefore inherited, primarily through the guidance of Augustine of Hippo, a static transcendent Trinity.[72] Such a Trinity offers little point of connection with a personally experienced God, or one's own spirituality in relationship to Him.[73]

> *[In my old church] there was this bloke standing there between you and God, at the end, who didn't appear to have a relationship with God and said a lot of stuff about things and some about God (M13-11).*

So how has this come about? One explanation is that Byzantine or Eastern Orthodoxy began with an affirmation of belief in the Father, Son and Holy Spirit, according to Scripture, with a focus on *hypostasis*[74] (personhood), whereas Augustine of Hippo, McKenna suggested, thought it better to begin with the unity of the divine, as this was a truth that could be demonstrated by reason (1963 Introduction, quoted in Gunton 1991a:55,n.3). Augustine, though African, is today seen as a Western man, since his ideas were constructed by Greek categories.

Gunton built on this philosophical observation, proposing that we need to go behind Augustine's thinking, to his inevitable (Greek) suspicion of material reality, seen in his Christology (1991a:33). Gunton suggests Augustine was reluctant to give due weight to the full materiality of Christ's Incarnation[75] and despite Chalcedon, John Owen and Scot Edward Irving, among others, Western theology has for the most part failed to develop adequate conceptual tools to ensure due prominence to Christ's full humanity.[76] To illustrate this, Gunton referred to the numerous Old Testament *Theophanies* of Christ, suggesting Augustine appeared to be

---

[72] Having said that, Augustine does seem to be blamed far too often, maybe even in this book. For instance, it is Tertullian, not Augustine, who is generally accepted as the father of Latin theology, borrowing as he does from the legal language of Rome.

[73] In Church history it is not difficult to see counter movements reacting in every age to these types of problems. Take, for instance, the practical mysticism of the Shakers, who 'experience and recognise the mystery of Christ-in-us our hope of Glory (Col. 1:27) travelling from gift to Gift, and glory to Glory' (Whitson 1983).

[74] The word *hypostasis* is used here by me in the theological sense of personality, personal existence or person, as distinguished from nature. When referring to Christ, I am speaking of His complete nature, part of His hypostatic union, as found in human personhood.

[75] Dr Kenneth Wilson comments, 'God by becoming Incarnate in Christ makes plain the true nature of God's continuous involvement in creating by 'committing God's self' to make a success of the process'. (Notes of a conversation on 31/10/02).

[76] 'The revelation of God in Christ is the foundation for what it means to be human. This implies, secondly, that the true humanity of Christ is understood as the paradigm for true knowledge of human being' (Schwobel and Gunton 1991:145).

rather embarrassed by too close an involvement of God in matter. Augustine's problem has become our problem, as it lets slip the mediatory role of the Word in material reality. Such a position distances God from the world,[77] re-emphasising Greek dualistic separatism, suggesting a static deity remote from His creation.

Gunton further noted that Augustine seems either not to have understood the Trinitarian theology of his predecessors, both East and West, or that his perspective was distorted by neo-Platonic assumptions (1991a:39).[78] Augustine's brilliance seems to have hidden, until now, these deep flaws in his thinking. For instance, his firm stress on the mind, following Greek thought, has had unhelpful consequences for the Western Church, encouraging ideas that a knowledge of the experience of God was to be found primarily, and adequately, in the mind alone.[79] Augustine lost sight of God-in-man-in-Christ-on-earth, and focused on Christ's transcendence and Deity. He looked at God from his Greek perspective, not from the perspective of nature of Deity itself.

Augustine's thinking has significantly influenced the Western Church's doctrine of God. But if we follow Augustine's perspective we will find ourselves believing that when we know ourselves correctly (intellectually) we will also know God in the same act, 'the man who knows how to love himself, loves God' (Gunton 1991a:48). Gunton, following Nicholas Bradbury, called this a 'decadent mysticism' (1991a:57, foonote 18), a degrading anthropomorphism that fails to place God's nature, on His terms as God, within human experiential reality. Instead, it flatters our intellectual capacity for a self-knowing of our nature, and God's. McCoy called this a metaphysics of divine stasis (1980:32). Put in contemporary language, it is a cognitive knowing about a God who is static and distant, rather than a personal knowing of God that is relationally authentic and dynamic.[80]

What I am suggesting, instead, is that the being of the visible Church should resonate with the *dynamic* of the relations between the three persons, who together constitute Deity, that the sociality of the Trinity should in some way be able to suggest or allow the eternal God – the eternally inter-animating energies of the three – to provide the basis of the

---

[77] For an interesting comment on the idea that because the concept of Logos was stolen by Greek thought the Church needed to return to the Old Testament to fully understand what God was saying. See Lee (1997:191ff.).

[78] Where neo-Platonism is influential, there is a temptation for us to observe reality in terms of degrees of a hierarchically-structured world (Gunton 1991a:60). This can place God far away.

[79] Gunton also suggested that Irenaeus (c.130-c.200) is the earliest source of this thinking within the Western Church. 'In Irenaeus' famous distinction between image and likeness there began the process of making reason both a chief ontological characteristic and a criterion of difference between human and non-human. By the time of Aquinas the tendency has hardened into a dogma' (1991a:105). In Protestantism, by returning to Augustine, we see the replication of his weaknesses in the Western Church (see the next section).

[80] On the idea of bringing metaphysics and theism together, see Kretzmann (1997).

personal dynamics of human/divine relationship (Gunton 1991a:81). This would allow the Trinity to be more 'involved' in both Church and contemporary society. Let me illustrate what this could mean by looking more closely at one person in the Trinity, the Holy Spirit.

Pneumatology,[81] a personal Spirit?

Gunton suggested that Augustine's treatment of Spirit[82] was used more in terms of substance, rather than being personal and relational. He saw it as the Achilles' heel of Augustine's theology (1991a:47). 'The overall result is that because the doctrine of the Spirit has inadequate economic hypostatic weight in Augustine, the father of Western theology also lacks the means to give personal distinctiveness to the being of the Spirit in the inner Trinity' (51).

Augustine's failure to develop a full pneumatology has other implications, especially for us today. With no recognition of the role of the Holy Spirit *spirating* within the whole Godhead, it is then not easy to conceive of the Spirit constituting the Church dynamically. By the Church placing great importance on the next life, it can inadvertently suggest a limited experience of God being available here and now.

> *If I carried on going to [my previous church in London] (which I wouldn't) I would have believed that God was dead and in wasting my time with Christianity. Reality - here / death - there (06M-7.8).*

Without a pneumatic theology of a *personable* Spirit, the Church will struggle to create a taste *now* of this life to come, suggesting instead that the experience of Christ-centred authentic spirituality is not available until after death.[83] The Church has often blamed sin and the Fall, and our running from God, for this breakdown in relations (Steele 1990:20), rather than its own theology.[84]

---

[81] In this section we are looking specifically at the Holy Spirit. In 'Theologising on personhood' (page 73) we look in a similar way at the absence of a human *pneuma* in the Church and in psychology.

[82] Gunton suggested the doctrine of the *Filioque*, that the Spirit proceeds from the Father *and the Son*, has been the source of a number of weaknesses, particularly the tendency in the West to subordinate the Spirit to the Son (1991a:168). Regarding the Greek background to the idea of *pneuma* see Tanner (1985).

[83] In looking at most eastern religions one quickly notes that unlike Christianity in this area, Eastern thought has much mature practice currently available, like meditation, mystic experience, developing and using one's inner strength, finding one's 'subtle energies' and harnessing them, seeing auras and understanding one's chakras, to name but a few. The Western Church seems to be frightened by much of this, thereby allowing other spiritualities to develop them. Some Christians seem to live as though there is some hidden spiritual power able to ambush them if they move into such spiritual reality, rather than believing the Lord has the power to keep and protect them when they explore these realms.

[84] Fiddes (2000) seeks to begin answering some of these problems.

But its failure at a clinical relational level, Gunton suggested, has given birth to both a seriously deficient pneumatology and its ecclesiology here in the West (1991a:65). Cobb and Griffin concurred, in calling for a new ontology for the Church (1976:71ff.). Collins is also thinking along similar lines, describing the need for a new *ousia* (Gk. = being or substance, Latin = *essentia*, or *substantia*), where the three divine persons share in the common *ousia*, creating a structured relational ontology (2001:143). In essence, these and numerous others writers[85] have all, one way or another, acknowledged that a Spirit that is not active in Trinity, and also living in the world now, has no mandate or ability to create either a vibrant relational spirituality or authentic divine-human community.[86] At best, such a Spirit might help assist individuals with their private 'faith', but not facilitate a lived reality *now* of Trinity-in-humanity-as-community.[87]

One further point needs noting regarding this underdeveloped pneumatology here in the West.[88] Within the Trinity it is the Spirit that effects change and conversion (Eph. 4:6) as an event or a journey, suggesting that the Spirit has the ability to connect with the deepest core of human interiority. Lee developed this point. 'We are conditioned by God's Spirit in the valuational structures of our own spirit. We are transformed in our appetitive faculties to feel things accurately with the feelings of God, and to yearn for them. Put simply, God's Spirit is where God's deep story is. Our spirit is where our deep story is. Through the immanence of God's Spirit in the human spirit, the deep story that is intended for history is transmitted' (Lee 1997:195).[89] What Lee is suggesting is that an inadequate Trinitarian pneumatology leads to an inadequate Atonement and its transformative relationality, both in Trinity and humanity. It separates

---

[85] Spence suggested others, like Owen (1862), have been working on the problem of the full humanity of Christ. See Spence (1991:74-97), for an echo of Eastern Byzantine theology of person, cause and relation, which we shall note later in the chapter. Also, Collins noted that Illingworth in the late 19th century taught the social implications of divine fellowship within the Trinity (Illingworth 1894:vii-viii). For other comments on and by Illingworth including his view of personality, see Schwobel (1991:1ff.).

[86] One illustration is the modern interest in the human side of Jesus, seeking out the humanness in God, and its parallel interest within the self-help movement of becoming more fully human.

[87] For a recent echo of a similar theme, arguing the Church must keep the developing of the doctrine of Trinity alongside hands-on pastoral experience, see Fiddes (2000).

[88] One does not have to go far to see this historic imbalance. Berkhof's systematic theology (1939/1963) has over 100 pages devoted to the Person and Work of Christ, but no section specifically devoted to the Holy Spirit. Likewise, Strong's systematic theology (1907/1962) devotes over 110 pages to Christ, but again has no specific section on the Person and Work of the Holy Spirit.

[89] Human make-up is a huge subject, and for many years I have suggested that one of the main reasons why the Church has failed to offer a relevant spirituality, is that it has no pneumatic model of human make-up on which to base it (e.g. Williams and Holmes 2004:32). In 'Exploring personhood' (page 68) I will be confronting this issue in more detail. For a similar conclusion to mine, see Schwobel (1991:9).

Christ's finished work from ongoing personal moral transformation.[90] Salvation is seen as an experience of a moment of enlightened belief and declared allegiance, not a lifetime journey receiving more wholeness through a relational Trinity that moulds us into Christ. Views of the Trinity colour our expectations of spirituality, transformative change and Christ-likeness.

In response to this in CCD we have been seeking to develop a participatory involvement of Trinity within the life of our community, an experience of ongoing participatory union between God and humanity, in faith community. I believe that what we are seeking to harness and experience is part of what contemporary un-churched people are also looking for, the engaging of Martsolf and Mickley's definition of spirituality, an ongoing transformative relational experience.[91]

> Here [at Christ Church] it is just a reality, and people saying 'well this is where I am at', and you are given space, you are not expected to conform to a whole set of rules (M10-4).

The implications for authentic faith community

We have already noted that relationality is important in contemporary spirituality. However in looking at Augustine of Hippo we are near the beginning of the era when the Church was being conceived as an Institution, mediating grace to the individual, rather than as a community formed on the analogy of the Trinity's *interpersonal* relationships (Gunton 1991a:51). This process alone has led to a number of contemporary losses. From Constantine onwards the Church was no longer individual households, or small communities of believers with a communal God. Tertullian (c.160-c.220 CE) in his *De Pudicitia* (1993) had earlier seen this danger, arguing that the Church should not consist of its Bishops, but of a Trinity, a community of faith and its free act of congregating (Gunton 1991a:63).[92] Augustine gave us little reason to believe in a God who can be known, since his desire was to create structures of human intellectuality, toward a singular deity for whom community was epiphenomenal or secondary. It is now accepted that Augustine's deity is less than fully personal, in part because He was conceived as immutable. If something other than Father is the ontological foundation of the being of God, the

---

[90] 'Counter culture' movements within the Church have at all times challenged such generalisation, for instance the Pietist or Holiness movements, who typically demand a comprehensive change of lifestyle. A contemporary illustration of this is the *L'Arche* movement (Vanier 1979, Angrosino 2003).

[91] Professor Larry Shelton argues that conversion is traditionally seen in Western tradition as a legal transaction, substitutionary in nature, whereas Paul, as a Rabbinic Jew held a covenantal view of law that emphasised maintenance of relationship, rather than a once-off forensic act (Shelton in personal conversation 15th January 2004).

[92] See also Gunton (1991a:84 footnote 11).

world and everything in it derives from what is fundamentally impersonal (Gunton 1991a:54) .

The combination by Augustine of the lack of appreciation of the subtlety and importance of Eastern Greek terminology (see 'The importance of Cappadocian thought', page 50), together with the predominant influence of Neo-Platonism, has meant that the Western tradition continued to see the question of 'being' in terms of core personal ego (Collins 2001:191). Such a position denies a personal God and His power to both personally transform, and corporately create community. God is not seen being able to offer authentic spirituality, is unable to engage in change[93] either in Himself or us, and has none of the attributes able to restore to us now the experience of a fulfilling life-giving authentic community. Faith communities like CCD have therefore struggled to find a theological framework to describe what they are seeking in Trinity relationality within human community.

Some 20*th* century responses to this situation

We have noted so far that the being (*ousia*) of God needs to be more than mere relations. Instead, it needs to be described in concrete particulars of relation to one another. As Rahner noted, there must be no distinction between the dogmatic loci *De Deo Uno*, the One God, and *De Deo Trino*, the Triune God, if we are to be true to the being of God (1970:15ff.). But it also needs to be relational *toward us*. Trinity must be seen and experienced in more than transcendent ineffable terms if it is to contribute anything to contemporary spirituality either inside or outside the Church. Numerous thinkers have sought to move toward this in various ways. I will focus briefly on a representative three; Karl Barth (Reformed theology), Alfred North Whitehead (Process thought), and Young Jung Lee (Hebrew and Far Eastern thought). I will then offer one further alternative model from Cappadocian theology, which I believe helps address some of the problems raised, with the ease others do not.

KARL BARTH

Karl Barth sought to redress some of the flaws noted in Augustine's Christology and pneumatology. Collins, in his helpful study of the Trinitarian thinking of Barth, the Cappadocians and Zizioulas, focuses on three forms of expression; movement (Greek *kinesis*= motion, change), energy (Greek *energeia*)[94] and becoming (Greek *dunamis*) (2001:25). He

---

[93] The issue of the uniqueness of God and His freedom to respond to human need, while being Himself, needs further comment. In our spiritual nature we must all change in order to *become*. But I am assuming that it is in God's nature and power to be God's self, and to share that nature with whomsoever He will, without it in any way diminishing His capacity to be Himself.

[94] The understanding of *energeia* as active being in the Christian tradition, is originally found in Gregory of Nyssa (331/40 – c. 395) (1857-1866:1.19).

notes that implicit in the concept of event are notions of temporality and change, what Barth called the 'self-moved being of God' (1956:2.1:268)[95] conceiving this as 'being-in-act'. Barth, following Scripture, sought to replace the static being of God with one that is dynamic.

In his *Church Dogmatics* the notion of divine event as movement and change has led to its interpretation by a number of commentators as God's being as *becoming*,[96] the notion that '*Gottes Sein ist im Werden*', the being of God is in becoming. This had promise for me as a way of describing Trinity as continually becoming. Unfortunately, Barth's use of 'becoming' related primarily to the Incarnation and the self-revelation of God,[97] implicitly to His *being*, rather than carrying any suggestion of ongoing change in God. For instance, the Incarnation of the Word is a becoming: the Word *became* flesh (Jn. 1:14). Therefore I doubt that Barth intended this concept to open the way to God's *becoming* in the world, and especially in the Church.

Revelation, according to Barth, is His revealing (Collins 2001:28). In revealing Himself as a repetition of God ('*eine Wiederholung Gottes*'), God is revealing Himself again and again, as a continuing process. God takes form in revealing Himself (Barth 1956:1.1:316). So for Barth Christ is the continual becoming in God: it is not the whole Trinity becoming in human history. Barth sought to redress the Western stasis in God by proposing His becoming *moves*. For some Constantinian scholars this would be an offence, suggesting the possibility of change in God.[98]

As already noted, Augustine actually took a step backwards from Eastern Byzantine Orthodoxy when he ignored the true meaning of *hypostasis*. This tradition of not using *hypostasis* when speaking about the Trinity continued in Barth, who preferred the terms 'three' and 'one' to describe the relationship. He did not suggest intermingling within the persons of the Trinity. In doing this he helped perpetuate the failure of Western tradition.

---

[95] For the purpose of this study I will be referring to the standard English texts of Barth's 14 volume *Church Dogmatics,* edited and translated by G W Bromiley and T F Torrance, and published from 1956 onwards by T and T Clark. The first reference is to the volume, the second to the section and the third the page number.

[96] For instance, see Jenson (1969), Jungel (1976) and Gunton (1978).

[97] I am aware that to be theologically correct, any talk of Trinity should be preceded by an analysis of the understanding of the concept of revelation that we are using. Barth and Collins, following the notion of 'unveiling' (*Enthuellung*), recognize that the doctrine of the Trinity is rooted in the event of God's self-revelation (Collins 2001:31), and this self-revelation in God is something that happens (Collins 2001:7). All revelation of God is self-revelation, revealing Himself through Himself. But as Collins notes, any suggestion that the Church has a consensus concerning the meaning of the concept of revelation is still illusory (2001:34).

[98] But not all: 'Contrary to the concept of the immutability of God in philosophical theology, the Biblical notion of the constancy of God, which underlies his faithfulness, presupposes God's free intentional agency which includes his capacity for change' (Schwobel 1992:53, quoted in Collins 2001:93).

Barth remained within Greek tradition. The terminology of personhood in antiquity offered three main alternatives: *prosopons, hypostatis and persona* (Collins 2001:115). Augustine, Gunton suggested (1991a:41), did not understand the Eastern distinction, and as a result there is in Augustine (1968) and in most Western theology since, including Barth, a tendency toward modalism (Gunton 1991a:42), that there are merely three different modes or aspects to the one nature. What the Western Church is left with, because it lacks an adequate theology of co-inherence within the persons of the Trinity, is a view suggested by Augustine of an unknown substance *supporting* the three unique persons, rather than three persons *being constituted* by their relatedness (Gunton 1991a:43). For Augustine, the Holy Spirit does not constitute Trinity community. Instead, some ill-defined force does. This has become a weakness in the Church's pneumatology, and Barth's problem.[99]

Barth appears to have failed to redress this fault in his *Dogmatics.* Collins suggests part of the reason was that although Calvin, a key influence on Barth, was himself clearly influenced by the Eastern tradition, it was not enough to correct Barth's thinking. Barth did not carry a bias toward Trinitarian *communion* and *becoming* (2001:139ff.). Collins notes 'despite his attempts to employ some of the methods and terms of the Eastern tradition, he remained locked into the influence of Augustine and Hegel' (2001:156). Barth's 'becoming' in God had some potential to help me usher in a personable God able to respond and adapt to human action, but in some ways, notes Collins, it was conceptually more similar to a dialectic Trinity found in Hegel's concept of the self-repetition of *Geist* or spirit (Collins 2001:29). This leads to the inevitable under-characterization of the third person of the Trinity, because the Holy Spirit is conceived not as personal and cohering, instead reflecting the Greek idea of thesis and antithesis.

In summary, Barth did seek a correction in Constantinian theology, but his understanding of *person* remained inadequate and individualistic, rooted in the concept of both self-consciousness (the Greek idea of person), and freedom (Collins 2001:223). Consequently Barth resisted the language of persons and personability, and this limited his ability to personalize the Holy Spirit. Jungel, in seeking to paraphrase Barth, focused on the notion of the doctrine of the Trinity as theology's interpretation of God's self-interpretation. The rejection of some Aristotelian metaphysics finds its apogee in Jungel's writings (1983:214-215, 1989), especially his essays

---

[99] I am not downgrading Barth's achievement, for he insisted on the world's dependence upon God for its nature (1956 4.2:345), as well as God's *voluntary and trustworthy* graciousness as the ground of the world's opportunity of real and full life. But he did not develop this thinking or seek to explain how theologically this might work.

'*Metaphorical Truth*', and '*The world as possibility and actuality*'.[100] However, Barth's work, or his disciples', is not enough to give us personability in God, something I believe the contemporary un-churched expect.[101]

ENTER PROCESS THOUGHT

The idea of God *becoming* was hopeful for me, but Barth did not develop it as far as I needed.[102] In process theology[103] and philosophy however, I believed I had found a system allowing me to argue Trinity is able to be both the Church's example of harmonic relationship, and the model for us in relationships.

Process thought was an inevitable response to some of the problems we have already noted. Contemporary science, from Einstein's relativity, to Planck's quantum theory makes the world, time and space, interdependent and complementary. This new type of thinking in the human sciences has made traditional Western static views of God and the universe untenable. Whitehead (1861-1947) took up this challenge. He was a physicist and mathematician, whose process thought was a reconceptualizing of the structures that account for existence. These structures were thoroughly relational, and consistent with the discoveries of modern physics.

Whitehead's impact on Christian theology has been significant, especially in respect to the doctrine of God. If relationality is the *sine qua non* of all existence, as process thought argues, then the tension between God and the world is resolved (Bracken and Suchocki 1997b:viii). What Whitehead gave the Church is a relational metaphysics, through which to reinterpret creation, providence, redemption and eschatology an entirely new and novel relational paradigm. I found this promising.

Hartshorne, a disciple of Whitehead, created a series of axioms, whereby both proof and concept follow logically from the basic insight that reality can be understood panpsychistically as interrelated process. Gunton

---

[100] For a helpful summary of Jungel (2001), see Gunton (2002b).

[101] O'Donnell, in summarizing Western Trinitarian thought, saw three main views of God's relationship with history; (1) God's being does not become (classical philosophical theism); (2) God's being is in becoming (Jungel); (3) God's being becomes (process theology) (1983:87). It is interesting that in looking at Western ideas, like Augustine's, O'Donnell missed what for me is the most promising next stop - the recovery of Byzantine Orthodox Trinitarian theology, focused on the Cappadocians.

[102] Gunton argued that the concept of the *becoming* of God is something Barth shares with process theology (1978:137). Also, in his comparative work on Barth and Hartshorne, Gunton noted they both acknowledge God not as being, but as *becoming* (1978:215). He suggested the Church's concept of God is logically dependent on the way it perceives His existence, the form of the proof. Since the Middle Ages this has focused on the cosmological proof of His existence.

[103] Process thinkers have been prolific over the years, even having their own journal, *Process Studies*. For a helpful introduction to some aspects of process theology and philosophy from a range of viewpoints, but mostly a traditional theist perspective, see Nash (1987).

described this as a rationalist metaphysics (1978:216).[104] Ogden, within the liberal Protestant tradition, began the dialogue between process philosophy and the Christian faith (1967 passim). He now leads it, along with John Cobb, a disciple of Hartshorne. Whitehead's thinking has a compelling, attractive edge for contemporary society. But unfortunately, as I discovered through further reading, it also has several weaknesses that basically makes it unhelpful to me. I will note three of them.

Firstly, there is no unanimity in developing a process metaphysics from Whitehead's writings. Bracken and Suchocki's book (1997b) illustrated this for me, having a profusion of differing opinions about how Whitehead should be interpreted and applied. Feuerbach (1841/1956) cautioned us that the Church has a penchant to conceive God in our own image, and this seems particularly true in process theology, with its profusion of interpretations. Also, as Clayton noted, Whitehead's doctrine of God has meant a gradual shift in Whiteheadian scholarship away from interpretation, toward a fundamental rethinking of numerous points (1997:120). Aware of this fragmentation, Kelly (2002) argued that a synthesis of Trinitarian theology and process metaphysics can be achieved, but using Whitehead alone it is inadequate (1970 passim). What became obvious to me is that Whiteheadian process thought raised as many diverse problems as it resolved, so using his metaphysics, with little unanimity regarding its implications, is not easy or helpful.

Secondly, in my reading I have found some disturbing aspects to Whitehead and his disciples. For instance, by using the analytic method, Whitehead presupposed the exclusive way of thinking, based on Aristotelian logic (Lee 1979:17). This meant that while recognizing God and the world are interdependent, he also insisted they are *concrescent*, that the world *requires* God for its order, while God *requires* the world for its experience. This is how Whitehead made his philosophy cohere[105] (1929/1947:3). However, this creates an essential God-world relationship, whereby God's sociality is world-dependent. To suggest that for God to be God He needs a world, somehow reduces something in God as God. Could a loving God ever be without a world?, asked Faber (1997:149).[106] The

---

[104] For a more detailed critique of Hartshorne, see Gunton (1978:215ff.).

[105] The Whiteheadian sense of the term 'cohere' suggests that fundamental ideas presuppose each other, so that in isolation they are meaningless (Whitehead 1929/1947:3). This creates what is now described as panentheism, defined by Bracken as the three divine persons and all creation sharing the same divine life (1997:102).

[106] Bracken concluded his article with the idea that 'the field of activity proper to creation is seen as a semi-autonomous reality governed by its own empirical laws of development even as it is included within the all comprehensive field of activity proper to the divine being. The three divine persons, accordingly, can be at work in creation to achieve their own designs without interfering with the freedom of their rational creatures or with the laws governing the evolution of the cosmos. Only in this way, as I see it, can we consistently espouse a process-oriented doctrine of panentheism without inadvertently collapsing the world into God or God into the world'

response of process theology would be an emphatic no! This is problematic for traditional Western Christianity, in making God dependent on the world He has created.

Finally, much of what is distinctive in Constantinian Christianity is adversely affected when one abandons the self-sufficient sociality of God. For instance, it becomes more difficult to maintain the traditional view of creation, salvation by grace, the Incarnation, and also the ability of God to answer prayer, or for us to believe the supernatural can intervene without constraint in human history.[107] It also brings into question God's final victory over Evil, and whether God's sociality with the world is a matter of metaphysical necessity (Boyd 1997:74).[108]

In summary, process thought shows much promise, but because it does not seem to have a coherent theoretical framework, and also has ideas offensive to traditional Western theology, for instance, requiring a dependent deity, it is incapable of offering me what I need.

LOOKING TO THE FAR EAST

Lee, in his short but significant book *The theology of change: A Christian concept of God in an Eastern perspective* (1979), has followed a similar journey to mine. He looked for a way of theologically expressing the basic ideas of God and of change. But while I have spent much of my time within the Western tradition, his book suggested a new theology based on both Biblical interpretation and Far Eastern thought.

One of his key proposals was that at the heart of the Trinity is 'change' (1979:115, 117). He introduced the ancient Oriental book, the *I Ching: the Book of Changes*,[109] focusing particularly on *yin yang*. Since change (*i*) is

---

(1997:109). O'Donnell summarized this by proposing that it is impossible to conceive of God existing in isolation. It is argued He is God precisely by being in relation to a world (1983:190).

[107] This latter point is particularly disturbing, as process thought has no place for an actual personal existence beyond this life. This precludes any possibility of monism, an expectation of the melding of personal life into the divine. See Grenz (2000:584).

[108] Boyd would seek to reconcile these differences by arguing that even within conventional thought, sociality requires something outside of itself as its content (1997:75). He also argued that Hartshorne was mistaken in his assumption that he needed to attribute contingent features of experience as a necessity. 'My proposed revision avoids the difficulties that surround the process view of the abstract necessity of the wholly contingent actuality of the world and of God' (1997:88). A similar comparative piece of work has been done by Faber (1997:147ff.), but none of these efforts seem to adequately remove this fundamental problem that Biblical theology has with process thought. In order to have a social Trinity, one must have co-dependency. Bracken and Suchocki suggested only an artful combination of insights from a number of theological schools will produce a system of thought truly responsive to contemporary desires for ultimate meaning and value (1997a:223). They proposed an eclectic cocktail of ideas and concepts, in order to respond and attract 'postmoderns' to Whitehead and his disciples. I believe they are missing the point, that few of these ideas have helped us in an authentic way so far.

[109] The *I Ching* originated in early divination in China. The present text is attributed to King Wen, founder of the Chou dynasty. Although Confucius had little to do with the text, it was

responsible for the changing world, it is the ultimate reality, which is also known as *t'ai chi* (the "Great Ultimate"). In Eastern thought the process of change takes place through the two primordial forces of the receptive (*yin*) and the creative (*yang*). Without *yin yang* there can be no change (1979:4). Whereas process thought, as Lee saw it, even at its most creative, remains static and linear, the use of the *I Ching*, Lee believed, gives the theology of change a new foundational logic, and helps it sit more comfortably with Einstein and Planck. Like me, he noted that the simple message of Christianity was transmuted into the metaphysical dogmas of the Church, primarily through the intellectual apparatus of Greek philosophy (Lee 1979:11). He argued, using Gebser (1970), that the Church needs to move away from Aristotelian logic, toward a model where matter is temporal, and dualistic thinking does not exist (Gebser 1970:10, quoted in Lee 1979:16).

Although Lee was writing to help build a foundation for a Christian dialogue with Far Eastern religion, he did so by arguing that Christianity was unable to exist easily among these nations because of the profound inseparability of Christianity from its Hellenistic Greek philosophical roots (1979:11). His Eastern ideas were helpful to me, but more significantly, throughout his book he used Hebrew ideas to parallel those of East Asia. He noted several times that Hebrew ideas complimented his Eastern understanding of change and reality.[110] He suggested that both world-views sit well together, while Greek Christian thinking does not.

Lee's conclusion was that the weakness of the Western Trinitarian position could be answered from the East, and that this would be more compatible with Hebrew traditions. I will return to Lee and Hebrew thought in 'A Hebrew perspective on change (page 53). His struggles, though not his answers, helped authenticate mine. But this led my thinking to another Eastern tradition, Byzantine Orthodox Trinitarian theology, focused on the Cappadocians.

Recovering Cappadocian theology

As I have noted above, Augustine appears to have failed to appropriate the ontological achievement of his Eastern colleagues, instead allowing into his theology traditional Greek categories, in which being is not communion but something underlying it (Gunton 1991a:10). Augustine was a man of his time, so he embraced the dualistic tension of which Barth and Rahner, among others, have now made us aware, between God's being and God's

---

canonized and became one of the Confucian classics. Some see the *yin yang* echoed in Hegel's thesis and antithesis (Hegel 1807/1977).

[110] For example, the Hebrew God is not limited by Aristotelian either/or logic (Lee 1979:25). Like Eastern thought, the Hebrew way of perceiving reality is a changing, moving, affective, and dramatic whole (37). Also, the *image of God* is the analogy of relation, not unlike in China where the heavens, earth and humanity form a trinity (77).

becoming, between the one God and the triune God.[111] Augustine failed to observe that God is wholly in relationship within Himself *and by implication, the created world*. As relational, if He chooses to create, He is necessarily related to what He creates, and what He creates also has some of this potential relationality. This is why we all realize ourselves primarily in and through others. This weakness in Augustine, Zizioulas suggests, has led to misconceptions about God and His relation to material reality.[112]

While noting Gunton's caution that we should not romanticize the Eastern tradition (1991a:viii), the achievement of the Cappadocian Fathers in the 3rd century was significant.[113] Basil the Great, Gregory of Nyssa[114] and Gregory Nazianzus, while having some abstractions themselves, borrowed from Athanasius (Collins 2001:136), and achieved several steps in the development of a view of Trinity that the Western Church, until recently, has largely ignored. In Cappadocian thinking there is no 'being' of God except the dynamic of persons in relation. The two aspects, person and relation, are one and the same. The consequence of this is that if becoming is more fundamental than being,[115] then God must be the perfect instance of becoming (Ford 1997:56).[116] At this point I found myself thinking that if God is Trinity by His nature, He is therefore becoming in His nature: could this be mirrored in human community?

The Cappadocians created a new conception of the being of God, seen to consist in personal communion. God has no ontological content, no true being, apart from communion (Zizioulas 1985/2002:17).[117] God is 'a sort of

---

[111] I am aware that in making this distinction I am also suggesting a claim that could appear dogmatic. I use the distinction introduced by Collins (2001:26ff., 96ff. etc.).

[112] Zizioulas noted Augustine differs from the Cappadocians in two significant ways. Augustine remained individualistic, and secondly also denied that the being of God 'unfolds' in the relations of the divine persons. Zizioulas commented, 'in identifying a particular thing we must make it part of a relationship, and not isolate it as an *individual*' (1985/2002:9). McFadyen suggested we cannot achieve this alone, 'As the (divine) Persons are what they are only through their relations with the others, it must also be the case that their identities are formed through the others and the way in which the others relate to them' (1990:28). In some ways he is reflecting Jungel, 'God's self-relatedness is based on God's "Yes" to himself. In this "Yes" of God, God himself sets himself in relations to himself, in order to be who he is. In this sense being is in becoming' (1976:102-103).

[113] A helpful introduction to the Cappadocians is Young (1983:92ff.).

[114] In some ways Gregory was the key Cappadocian. For a critical introduction to his thinking, see Coakley (2002).

[115] The philosophical question is 'which is more basic, *being* or *becoming*?' Responses relate to views of how God, history, human nature, and non-human nature are conceived. Contemporary process philosophy, as we have noted, stresses *becoming,* whereas classical views argue *being* is primary (McKim 1996:27).

[116] Perfect becoming must also require a new conception of creation, essentially involving the activity of the creatures. See Ford (1983).

[117] Cappadocian thinking was not entirely original, but grew out of the work of other early Greek theologians. See Collins (2001:134ff.). We can easily trace the concept of communion, for instance, through the work of those like Ignatius of Antioch, Irenaeus and Athanasius, into the Cappadocians (Zizioulas 1985/2002:16). Zizioulas' own life illustrates what my book is suggesting:

continuous and indivisible community' (Basil of Caesarea 1975:34-35, quoted in Gunton 1991a:9). Rather ironically, the Western Church now describes this concept as a 'modern' doctrine of God: a communion of three persons – not individuals – in mutually constitutive relations with one another.[118] The person (*hypostasis*) is both constituted by and constitutes the ontological category of communion (Zizioulas 1985/2002:18). Two people are a relationship, three a community.[119] I began to think the Cappadocians could offer me a way of seeing Trinity in relationality, as mirrored in contemporary faith communities like CCD, and also for those seeking post-Christian authentic spirituality.

The importance of Cappadocian thought

The initial insight of the Cappadocians was to distinguish between two ordinary Greek words, which until then were virtually synonymous: *ousia* (being) and *hypostasis* (Gk. *prosopon* or person). In this they anticipated the modern concept of persons in their position of logical priority, and this observation has been developed in modern times by, for instance Macmurray,[120] and Strawson (1959) (Gunton 1991a:96).

When this distinction of being and person is applied to the Trinity, each person is only what they are by virtue of what all three give to and receive from each other. Yet through these mutually constitutive relations, each remains distinctive and particular (Gunton 1991a:11). Such a Trinitarian theology allows us to develop an ontology of the personal, both for the Trinity and for human nature, with all of its relations.[121] The Cappadocians saw that the way we view God is the way we view everything else, including creation, human nature and redemption. God is a society of three beings, in *perichoretic* relationship.

But God is also seen as Creator, Redeemer and Transfigurer (Sanctifier).[122] Most Western theology focuses primarily on the second,

---

he has an Eastern Orthodox background, is publishing here in the West, and is helping to reconstruct the Church's thinking.

[118] For a comment on the subordination of the persons to one another within the Trinity, see Gunton (1991a:165ff.). It is also interesting to note that the Fourth Lateran Council, 1215, sided with Peter Lombard against Joachim of Fiore in emphasizing that God is one reality shared equally and totally by the three persons and also that human beings ought to be 'one' as the Son is 'one' with the Father (Jn. 17:22). But we see little fruit within the Church today of these important observations. (See also Faber 1997:151.).

[119] For the modern articulation of this thinking see Grenz (1996/2000, 2000).

[120] Two significant books this last century went against the prevailing Constantinian individualistic tide, both by Macmurray (1957/1991, 1961). See 'Enter John Macmurray' (page 169) for an enlarged comment on the importance of Macmurray.

[121] I am not abandoning Aristotelian logic, merely accounting for the 'person in relation' with some new thinking based on contemporary experience.

[122] From Cobb (1997:4), quoting one of his doctoral students, Lynn Lorenzen.

Redemption, largely ignoring the first and the third.[123] Lee noted Western theology's failure was to stress God's redemptive aspects at the expense of His creative ones (1979:80), while largely ignoring God as Sanctifier. If God is relational He therefore cannot be static, but in constant harmonic change (Gk. *kinesis*). The loss of both these emphases, God as Creator and Transfigurer, has been profound, because they carry key ideas that we now need in Western theology, e.g., capacity for relationships, like our Creator, continual positive change promoted by Him, and the innate capacity for *Theocentric community*[124] etc. These Cappadocian ideas suggest a repositioning of soteriology within a larger framework of both Father Creator and (Holy Spirit?) Transfigurer. Creation and Sanctification become an ecotone of continual change, encircling a fence of inter-relationships within the Godhead, capable of being mirrored in human community.[125] Restoration of all human damage therefore includes estrangement from God, others and creation. This is our redemptive task, with Him facilitating this entire process.

> *It has made me feel that God and I are working together on [my healing] - no quick prayer and sitting back and waiting for a miracle to happen (01F-8.35).*

Building on Cappadocian thought Zizioulas[126] captured in his concept of 'an event of communion' (an event of *koinonia*) the essence of what these men were describing: a social Trinity (1985/2002:18).[127] Zizioulas argued that God *knows* through communion, and *the event of communion* rests on the concept of divine rationality, divine self-knowledge and divine love. God knows by relational love. Likewise, God has no true being apart from communion (Zizioulas 1985/2002:17), for true being comes voluntarily only from a free person, and such a concept moves personhood into post-Enlightenment thinking, with echoes of both Idealism and Existentialism (Collins 2001:179). 'The ground of God's ontological freedom lies not in His nature but in His personal existence, that is, in the "mode of existence" by which he subsists as divine nature. It is this that gives people, in spite of their different natures, hope of becoming authentic persons' (Zizioulas

---

[123] One can always find exceptions within the Church that went against prevailing tides. Wesley is a good illustration here, who sought to avoid the forensic rationalism of the Constantinian Atonement, by emphasising that 'regeneration and sanctification had to do with actual transformation' (Collins 1997:16).

[124] See 'Introducing *Theocentric* kinship community' (page 170) for a building of this concept.

[125] Barth confirms his view, agreeing with the Cappadocians, that the relationality of the Godhead is the basis for the divine relationship with the world, and for the workings of analogy. The relationality of the Godhead to the creation was a central theme of Barth's *Church Dogmatics* (Collins 2001:11).

[126] For a critique of Zizioulas, see T.F. Torrance (1996:283ff.).

[127] For a comment on the various meanings of social in this context, see Ford (1997:41). A social Trinity implies all parties benefit from the others, and all have the capability of being so enriched. 'To say the Godhead is three persons in one substance immediately raises the question of how many consciousnesses are to be attributed to the divine life' (Collins 2001:140).

1985/2002:43). Put another way, it is the freedom of the Father who chooses in love to live as Trinity, a mutually constituted communion of three persons. Zizioulas moved this Cappadocian idea of communion from person in being to event of relationship. Prestige noted that with this 'new' way of thinking the Church needed to look at God, 'regarded from the point of view of internal analysis, as one object, but that, regarded from the point of view of external presentation, he is three objects.... 'God + God + God = God' (Prestige 1936/1952:169).[128] As O'Donnell commented, God is one object in Himself, and three objects to Himself (1983:41).

Zizioulas suggested the Cappadocians developed an ontology of divine being by employing the Biblical rather than the Greek view (1991:40), focused on an ontology of love, rather than an ontology of *ousia* (being). As Richard St Victor has exquisitely noted, if it is truly love, the two will seek a third in order to share their love: '"Shared love is properly said to exist when a third person is loved by two persons harmoniously and in community"' (Richard of St Victor 1959:7-9, quoted in Gunton 1991a:92).[129] What we also see in Richard is an approach to the doctrine of the Trinity that has great possibilities for developing a relational view of the person. Richard developed the idea of the unity of the divine persons as *ex-sistentiae*, as beings who are intrinsic to one another, so that they are continually emerging out of one another. His now famous definition of person in this context is: *persona est divinae naturae incommunicabilis existentia:* each divine person is essentially only out of, and in relation with the other person (Faber 1997:150). God can remain God's self, while also being available, and having the capacity, for dynamic loving relationship.

Not everything the Cappadocians developed is being eagerly accepted as the final word by the Western Church (Tuggy 2003).[130] Such a theology is still evolving, it is not yet mature. But we have so far made enough ground to be able to distinguish between being and person,[131] which then allows us to move further by adopting the Greek term *perichoresis*. This is used by the Cappadocians in two senses: 1) that of reinforcing the unity of the Godhead, and 2) as the centre of consciousness in the Godhead, an interpenetrating or co-mingling of the persons wholly within one another. The word *perichoresis* has been used differently in the East and the West, since it had two equivalents in the Latin, *circumcessio* and *circumincessio*.

---

[128] Collins also suggests Maximus the Confessor (2001:189).

[129] See also Collins (2001:139).

[130] Tuggy (2003) argues that neither Social or Latin Trinitarianism have all the answers, nor have yet matured. He believes both are unfinished. He notes neither can yet support a full Trinitarian view Biblically. He supports this claim by noting a number of inconsistencies.

[131] In the next chapter I will suggest that the analogy of being has failed in Western theology. Instead the Church should be thinking in terms of the analogy of relation. It is not something in a person, but between persons. It is not their ontic nature, but the function of their relationship with God (Lee 1979:55).

Collins proposes the former has more a sense of dynamic, while the latter is more static (2001:209). The Cappadocians used the former and Western Trinitarianism the latter. Bracken and Suchocki described the term *perichoresis* as the inter-animation in relations within the Godhead, a mutual co-inherence (1997a:221), while Gunton described it as a vital device ensuring Trinitarian language does not lapse into tri-theism (1991a:167).

In summary I quote Collins commending Zizioulas. '[He] combines the radical outcome of the ontological revolution which is implicit in the Cappadocians' terminology, with a modern understanding of consciousness, *Dasein,* and freedom' (2001:144). In reading the Cappadocians and Zizioulas I felt I was beginning to move toward a *theology of change* facilitated by the Godhead, and also the beginnings of a new ecclesiology that is more in keeping with the thinking of Susan Williams' findings. The Cappadocians give me a helpful toe-hold, without the ambiguity of Barth and the difficulties of process thought. But doubt still lingered, for I could not shake off the idea that even the Cappadocians had a Neo-Platonist background, so we may yet find flaws in their thinking. Also, I still lacked the ability to say that to be fully human one needs relationships with non-personal reality (Gunton 1991b:60) that also incorporated an authentic personal and corporate spirituality. The Cappadocians help us build this, but do not give us the mature intellectual framework that I believe the Church needs today. We could still be hampered by Greek categories. So let us leave the Western culture, as Lee did, and instead look not to the East, but to Hebrew ideas.

A Hebrew perspective on change

As noted above, in CCD we have this notion that God is among us as well as in us, so we understand Him as being alive in our community, while also recognizing He has a wider kinship with His whole creation. Whereas *being* is basic to Greek, *becoming* (Hebrew verb *hayah*) is the basic category of Hebrew thought (Boman 1954/1960:27ff.). Along with Lee I believe the Church needs both *being* and *becoming* in order to describe ultimate reality (1979:19). In this section I will argue, with the help of Lee and others, that a traditional theology of being, with a contemporary theology of becoming, appears more achievable with the help of some Hebrew ideas.

In Hebrew thought change is the matrix of all that was, is and shall be, the ground of all being and becoming, as with God Himself (Lee 1979:30ff.). Long before Hellenization, Hebrew ideas and Christianity's original message were inclusive. This is illustrated in the teaching of Christ. But under the increasing influence of Greek ideas it became exclusive. The *tertium non datur*, "there is no third", only two (dualistic) ways of looking at reality, became the norm. No third alternative exists in Western Greek philosophy, so its dualism became Christianity's basic structures (Lee 1979:21). This made reality two dimensional instead of three dimensional, e.g. me and God, me and you, but not us in community.

In Hebrew thought we see Yahweh's vibrant presence among His people. This is especially evident in His calling Himself the *Living* God, *Elohim Chay* (Dt. 5:26, Jos. 3:10, 1 Sam. 17:26 etc.), the same root as living creatures (Gn. 1:20,24; 2:7), or living water (Je. 2:13; 17:13). The Hebrew verb *hayah* signifies 'to be, becoming', rather than being (Boman 1954/1960:38ff.),[132] describing becoming into existence, to keep alive, to be living (Bresinger 1996:18ff.). Within the root *hyh* is the suggestion that one cannot be alive yet remain the same.[133] To live is to continually change. We see this in His becoming incarnate among His people.[134] This is a process, a journey, not an instant occurrence. Even the name Yahweh itself is associated more with power or energy, than with mere structural existence. In Hebrew thought He is a dynamic God, ever active, ever promoting new things. As Van Leeuwen noted, the Hebrew conception of reality is 'a changing, moving, affective and dramatic whole' (1985:47). Yahweh is the source and being of all of this vibrant reality, and central to this is change as continual becoming.[135]

But Lee was not comfortable with merely proposing Yahweh is becoming. He suggested His nature is becoming, making continual change in Him the source of all creativity.[136] The ineffable nature of God is not limited by His "*I become who I become*". Lee suggested that Yahweh wants to be known, like His Name, as a God who is becoming (1979:32). I began to think what might happen were the Church to take this position, as Clarke Pinnock (2001) has suggested. In one step it removes the Western disjunction between creation[137] and salvation, allowing salvation to be a

---

[132] On the subject of the Hebrew ontology of being, see Zizioulas (1991:38ff.).

[133] Rev. John Harding, Hebraist and friend, pointed out to me that whereas *hayah* has the idea of becoming, *chayah*, 'to live', has no idea of becoming.

[134] I hesitate to even suggest it, but the fulfilment of Incarnation is seen in Christ, and Scripture suggests He took a body unfamiliar to us, into the presence of Father (Jn. 20:26; 21:12). So was Trinity changed by encounter with human reality? Did He have this body before Incarnation? Did this act somehow impact (change?) God, as well as us?

[135] I would not wish to brush over the substantial problems of both the distinctives and the harmony of the Old and New Testament God, as portrayed in Scripture. But for the sake of this book I am assuming we can see some continuity. For a recent exploration, seeking to reconcile Yahweh with God in Christ, see Peels (2002).

[136]'Supernaturalism', the affirming of belief in the supernatural, built on the concept that since God created the material universe *ex nihilo*, with all its design and structure, some would argue He must also be able to completely determine the events of the material world. See Griffin (1997:23ff.). Also, on the theme of Trinity and creation, see Finger (1997).

[137] The implications of this way of thinking for creation are significant. 'It is remarkable how little Augustine's doctrine of creation is informed by Trinitarian categories, in the sense that he does not articulate the doctrine Christologically and pneumatologically' (Gunton 1991a:160 footnote 12).

return (a process journey of change/becoming) within the wider arena of God's continuing full relationship to creation.[138] God's personhood is no longer related solely to His intermittent whim of contact with 'the saved'. But for such a shift to take place, as well as requiring we begin to consider old (Cappodocian) ideas that are offensive to Greek immutability and its penal structures, it also means we need to begin to conceive all aspects of reality conceptually as being in a permanent fluid mode of change. Lee saw Christ's work of salvation as an extension of the Father's work of creation.[139] Salvation becomes contingent on creation (1979:87), and a God whose nature is becoming. To my surprise I found myself resisting such a shift, even though I knew such a framework was necessary if we are to explain the perception of those in CCD.

What I was more comfortable with, based on a Hebrew perspective, was that change itself is the most meaningful way to describe God's *is-ness* in a modern world of constant change and becoming (Lee 1979:40). But taking it one step further, Lee suggested that it is not only God's nature that is in continual *perichoretic* change within itself, but that in changing Yahweh remains *changeless*. Lee achieved this by noting God's immutability, and also borrowing from the *Tao te ching*. He described His view of God being like the stationary axle of a moving cart wheel, where all the spokes are moving, but the spindle remains fixed. For Lee, the element of changelessness in God was His faithfulness to Himself, being found in change itself, in the 'living God' (1979:43).[140] Lee blends Hebrew and Eastern thinking with current Western realities. Yahweh has the capacity to respond to a changing world, for change is His familial nature, and Creation expresses and engages this. Continual change itself constitutes Covenant in process, and the Covenant in process makes possible creation in process. Thus the world is in process of becoming (Lee 1979:75). This perspective offers a useful foundation from which to respond to the modern spiritual search for transcendent relationship with God.[141] 'Oneness in three and

---

[138] Much is beginning to be written on the theme of creation. For an introduction, see Zizioulas (1985/2002). What I am suggesting as a background theme throughout this book is that creation first implies good order in both God and His created reality. Also, that God ordered material reality in such a manner that it allows us to discover, in an ordered way, our own nature. Creation precedes this, so that recreation (reconstruction/healing) is then possible. By suggesting such a process, I reflect Irenaeus, and more recently Lundensian theology. See Ferre (1939).

[139] 'Jesus' redemptive work was but an extension of his Father's creative work. Thus creation is the *a priori* category of redemption. Theology's proper subject, then, is divine creativity rather than divine redemptivity, because the former includes the latter' (Lee 1979:68).

[140] Not all Lee's arguments sit comfortably with me. For instance, I have a problem with his phrase, 'God must be the subject of this change' (Lee 1979:45), preferring myself to use a word like 'capacity', rather than 'subject'. Also, I see a need to emphasise God's immutability as both His faithfulness to Himself, and His consistency regarding covenant relationship with His people.

[141] Little is heard in the Church of that part of God's nature that has the capacity to be excited about events in human life. Hull suggested that when a couple have a child this is an event for God

three-ness in one' is the perfect symbol of divine nature, suggesting not only relationship, but an inner process of change (Lee 1979:115). In thinking this through I began to formulate an idea. What we might be able to say is:

> Within Trinitarian relations in local faith community, change is His endless capacity,[142] guided by His unchanging Covenant commitment, to support our continual becoming through both the *Rapha* principle ('Introducing the *Rapha* concept, page 89), and His facilitating this in our life in Christ.

Put another way, the Hebrew way of living could be described as continual becoming in ourselves and in and through others.

Testing my idea

The idea of sin being an unwillingness to change is a key concept in CCD. But another is the idea of *imago Dei,* the image of God. So I believe it would be helpful to explore these two ideas alongside a 'theology of change', borrowing Cappadocian and Hebrew thought.[143]

THE CONCEPT OF *IMAGO DEI*

God's goal for every believer is maturity in Christ (Eph. 4:13), conformity to His image (Rom. 8:28-29; 12:1-2, 2 Cor. 3:18), not merely happiness, or self-realization, but holiness, likeness to Christ (Grogan 1995:477). Therefore the concept of the image of God is important to CCD, as both a theological construct to help explain human particularity (see 'Introducing personal uniqueness, page 65), but also as one of the chief goals for the *Rapha* journey (see 'Introducing the *Rapha* concept', page 89). But its foundation in CCD is also as a giver of faith community, a vivid vibrant presence of God in our midst.[144]

---

as well (1991:222ff.). So in this sense, as we go through life we delight God by our integrity and love for His Son, and so He, along with us, moves from knowledge to more knowledge about us. To learn is to change, for to be surprised is part of the phenomenology of spirit (223). Such a view of God appears to fly in the face of an 'omniscient' God. My response in the past has been that He knows the chessboard we are on, but not necessarily what move we will make next?

[142] I am not suggesting God needs to change, in the sense of evolve, but be seen to be able to change, e.g. adapt, in response to the Church, the individual, prayer, etc. This approach honours the essence of relationship.

[143] Another idea could be the Enlightenment concept of individualism and the Hebrew idea of corporate personality. In Hebrew Semitic thought one can easily move from the 'one' to the 'many', and vice versa. Hebrew Biblical thought introduces this paradox, which we find difficult to grasp with our Western Trinitarian mindset. (See Zizioulas 1991:39.)

[144] I do not want to pretend CCD has something special going for it. We are no different from most other churches in wanting to seek after corporately His anointed presence. In the past, to our shame, the opposite has been true, where our community ceased being a special place where the Lord rests. In fact He has even accused us of not noting when He was not among us.

The image of God[145] for most of us in Western Christianity is individualistic – a private inner quality - our human spirit mirroring His Spirit.[146] The Church usually begins with the idea that some part of human nature is divine, having a supernatural quality (cf. 2 Pet. 1:4, 1 Jn. 3:2 etc.) (Murray 1977:43ff.). This was also my view for many years, seeing no reason to question it. But A.J. Torrance proposed that the *imago Dei* in humanity needs to be interpreted in terms of the participative life of the Body of Christ,[147] the manifest creating anew of humanity in the image of God. He did not believe it should be interpreted as a natural 'state', possessed exclusively by individuals (1996:368). In taking this position he highlighted a weakness in the Western view of *imago Dei* (see 'Spiritual growth, maturity and community in Paul's writings, page 187). I am comfortable with this observation, but Torrance's solution to this observed failure is to suggest that we should only see people as *imago Dei* when they are restored humanity (1996:368). Here I am uncomfortable. Human spirit, quickened by Holy Spirit, *in communione*, in worship to God, may complete the personal image, but does not necessarily initiate the image in the first place. Instead, I see this image already in all of us, regenerate or not.[148] For me, being human is being spirit, and being personally spiritual is only truly *personal* when it becomes *public*.[149] Let me explain.

Outside of Christianity all humanity seems to have a drive for life, and many have experienced spirituality (Hay and Hunt 2000). This I see as a 'base spirituality',[150] something that every human being has,[151] and to

---

[145] An extensive literature exists on the theme of *imago Dei*, and continues to be published. See, for instance, Orr (1906), Barr (1968, 1971), Clines (1968), Snaith (1974), Borresen (1995), Grenz (2001) etc.

[146] On the question of how creation of human beings in the Image of God can be made specifically Trinitarian, see Smail (2003).

[147] A body of literature is building on this subject. See for instance, Grenz (2000) and Volf (1996, 1998a, 1998b).

[148] This is not my original thought. See, for instance, Gunton, 'To be a person is to be made in the image of God: that is the heart of the matter. If God is a communion of persons inseparably related, then surely Barth is thus far correct in saying that it is in our relatedness to others that our being human consists' (1991b:58).

[149] 'To be a person is to be constituted in particularity and freedom – to be given the space to be – by others in the community. *Otherness* and *relation* continue to be the two central and polar concepts here. Only where both are given due stress is personhood fully enabled' (Gunton 1991b:59).

[150] I am aware I am moving toward Brunner in the Barth-Brunner debate. Like Brunner, I believe that fallen humanity somehow retains part of the created image of God, identified as humanity's ability to be addressed by the Gospel (1947 passim). Barth's response to Brunner's suggestion was scathing (Monlar 2000:85ff.), forcing a lifetime separation between them, by Barth's insistence that the possibility of revelation is entirely God's.

[151] The question of when spirit co-mingles with matter, thereby creating human personhood, is an open one. Is it when the sperm and egg meet, or is it several days later when the egg beds itself in the wall of the womb, so-called viability? This is one problem. But I am also aware that in

which we can appeal as the essence of being human. It distinguishes us from the natural world of which we are a part. We are all spiritually-embodied beings. This image may be tarnished, undeveloped and out of harmony with God, creation, itself and others, but it remains a sustaining presence in every one of us on the face of the earth (Jn. 1:4). To be human is first to be a spiritual being, to have a 'base' spirituality. This is our *imago Dei,* suggesting that all humanity, at its core, has the same basic needs[152] regardless of the veneer of culture.[153] Holding to such a position is important to the members of CCD, as it allows them to be able to appeal to anyone, regardless of how 'godless' they may be, without first having to make them Christian. Newcomers can enjoy discovering this image in themselves, at their own leisure.

> *Hearing about my human spirit opened up a whole new world for me that will take me a lifetime to explore (04F-5.3).*
> *[CCD is a] community of people allowing each other to become who God created them to be in a safe place (02F-4.19).*

So they are not judged, put under pressure, or treated as an outsider, just because they want to take their time thinking about the 'God bit'. God has created in all people this potential of relationship with Him, which when quickened by the Holy Spirit brings more alive what is already there.

I accept from Scripture that God holds material reality together (Col. 1:15ff.). He is Creator, Sustainer and Transformer. But I am also suggesting we see evidence of this in our own self-transcendence, our *imago Dei.* As Schwobel noted, it is the capacity for all of us to go beyond the given-ness of the natural in the instinctual equipment of humans and their relations to their biological environment, or to transcend[154] the immediacy of the present (1991b:6). However, I sense that the modern emphasis in the Church on personal salvation can have the tendency to blur this image of God in all of us corporately as community.[155] So in CCD we see *imago Dei*

---

suggesting the Holy Spirit through human spirit is present in all humans, *before* allegiance to Christ, I may be suggesting a new idea to some.

[152] It is interesting to note that many un-churched people today will see their spirituality contributing to this balance of all things in their lives. 'People who are involved in the process of spiritual emergence tend to develop a new appreciation and reverence for all forms of life and a new understanding of the unity of all things' (Grof and Grof 1989a:235).

[153] Research is beginning to support this position. Travelling around the world showing various cultures photographs of faces and asking what the expression means, has shown significant correlation. Most people recognise anger, a sneer, laughter or a smile (Gleitman 1995:443).

[154] Here I use the term 'transcend' in a non-supernatural sense.

[155] What I am describing is two in-dwellings. The first is through our conception, the *imago Dei,* the quickening of the Spirit creating human spirit, giving us our 'base spirituality', while the other is the indwelling of Christ through the Holy Spirit as we invite Him. This latter I see as a 'quickening' of this base spirituality.

as kinship becoming, in Christ in community,[156] and I will later be suggesting this is a Hebrew way of viewing life, where becoming is becoming in community ('Introducing *Theocentric* kinship community', page 171).

But what I am suggesting here is that *imago Dei* is only fully possessed in us when it is lived relationally, corporately, by example of *perichoretic* Trinity. This is what Volf called 'the sociality of salvation' (1998a:188). Grenz describes the Christian 'soul'[157] as 'the communally constituted self of the people who by the indwelling Spirit find their identity in Christ to the glory of God' (2001:20). The whole thrust of Grenz's recent work (2000, 1996/2000, 2001) has been to develop a social or communal understanding of the *imago Dei*. This view of *imago Dei* requires substantial change in the Church's current thinking,[158] and calls for a model of 'Church in community' authentically demonstrating corporate *imago Dei*.

What I am suggesting is that there is a sense in which to become more fully human, to become our real selves, we must learn to be at ease as a public relational self, rather than confining *imago Dei* to its traditional private personal expression. God created man and woman (Gn. 2:18ff.) so they could be community with Him. As CCD demonstrates, contemporary un-churched people find this way of thinking attractive, a 'living community in Christ'. Such a communal *imago Dei* also sits well with both Susan Williams' findings and the post-individualism of the contemporary un-churched. An *imago Dei* community brings together both Trinity *communio* with human intentional community, forming a *Theocentric* 'Christ among us' divine-human community.

> The normal church experience would be that yes, we are all one in Christ Jesus, those of us who are saved, but then there are the others, the unsaved. But within Christ Church there is no us and them. And our theology is different, not taught but just how I have perceived it, that we are all one in Christ Jesus because we are all made in God's image, which is the community of God and we don't need to be saved to be in that community. We were created to be in that community (M12-3).

In summary, Bonhoeffer noted in his *Creation and Fall* (1959), that *imago Dei* is *analogia relationis,* an analogy of relationship. This idea was similarly taken up by Barth in his *Church Dogmatics* (1956). Also, along

---

[156] In using the term 'kinship' I am recognizing that much Christian theology and its thinking is built on a separation of God from the world. With this term I am suggesting that God always wills to make God's self available to the world. My use of the word kinship suggests He desires to be *manifest* to us, among us and within us, He who is already wholly present in the world. See 'Introducing *Theocentric* kinship community' (page 170), where I develop these ideas.

[157] For a traditional view of the human soul as distinct from human spirit, see Boyd (1996:73ff.).

[158] Personhood does have a metaphysical claim built into it, but I am taking up Zizioulas' point (1991:33), that this is not nearly so apparent in Augustine.

similar lines, Lee noted it is by the 'analogy of relation' that God extends Himself to humanity (1979:77).[159] This requires the Church respond to His Divine initiative, seeking to harmonise with Him, others and creation. What we are noting is that human personhood is a unitary organism, related inextricably with other persons in community (Whitlock 1960:12), not merely a description of an individual (Gunton 1991a:106). In CCD we see *imago Dei* as both the capacity to have relationship with God, but also to experience authentic relationship with one another and our true selves. But we also recognise that much of this, because of the damage and its baggage in our lives, remains little more than potential. As to how we deal with this, we need to return to a Hebrew idea.

A HEBREW VIEW OF SIN

In CCD we equate sin with a refusal to change in the way that God requires we should: our resistance to both His will, and our own best interests. On my personal journey I have lived believing this, though it took several years for me to consciously realise it, and CCD has helped me take up this concept and link it with both Scripture and the wider Church's traditions. In CCD relationship with God means being called to personal change, in order to become like Christ. Without personal change none of us can be more Christ-like.

> *I never really thought about changing, I've pleased others all my life. I've never really thought about me. CC is an amazing place; you see change in others and want it for yourself (09F-2.19).*

Kiefer suggested that there was probably only one element of Jewish religion that was really unique, the idea of sin (1988:35). This unique Hebrew idea has also given Christianity a unique feature. In Hebrew Scripture, on most pages, we see a record of Yahweh requiring change from Israel. His self-disclosure as the Living God meant His people had to choose His ways, or suffer the consequences of the sin of not changing (e.g. Lv. 26:1ff., 'Reward for obedience', 14ff., 'Punishment for disobedience'). These choices are seen in the Hebrew Scriptures from the beginning of history (Gn. 17:9ff.; 22:15 etc.), for all positive learning requires a change of mind and lifestyle.

Today the traditional view of sin (Gk. *hamartia*), 'missing the mark', is 'the lack of conformity to the moral law of God, either in act, disposition, or state' (Strong 1907/1962:549).[160] This definition suggests it is possible to see all actions as either sinful or righteous. But borrowing from Hebrew thought, sin could be seen, by deduction, as our personal stubborn

---

[159] Covenant makes creation possible, the internal intra-trinitarian relationship, as Grenz called it (2000). This alone makes the external relationship possible (Lee 1979:75).

[160] I am not the first to call for 'a restoration of sin as a concept to the Church'. See, for instance, Menninger (1988).

unwillingness to change (Ps. 55:19b), to refuse to authentically seek to mirror Him and His will for us, by conforming both to His moral character and a life of love. In responding to Greek constructs, it is humanity's desire to continue to *be*, to refuse to change, rather than to *become*, e.g. becoming like Christ, who said Himself that we must all change to be like Him (e.g. Mt. 5:1ff.).

Along similar lines, the Church's concept of 'Original sin'[161] could also be seen, not as a substance of being, but as the power of disinclination, or refusal to harmonize oneself with this Christ-centred sanctifying process of ongoing change. Sadly, the human inclination to oppose any process of change is in all of us.[162] Free will and its rightful exercising, on the other hand, can become the spontaneous inclination to seek to harmonize the self with Christ and others in the process of positive change. When we want to become more Christ-like, to be more authentically human, mirroring the vibrant *perichoresis* of Trinity, we will need to be in a permanent state of becoming, experiencing continual positive change within a learning relationality.[163] At the opposite end of the spectrum, our base spirituality will desire a quiet life, and by its nature and in its baggage, will resist change.[164] This contrasts with a 'quickened' spiritual nature, either through need or allegiance, that begins to increasingly mirror Christ more, by seeking a Holy Spirit led continual personal and corporate positive change.

In Susan Williams' findings, one notes the strong influence change has as a drive in both the members' and the community's life.

One of the biggest adverts about Christ Church is the way we are all changing and people can see it and they say 'we would like some of that' (M5-2).
Nothing is set in concrete in Christ Church, it is always changing (W15-11).

Emotional illness is often associated with isolation, incapacity to take on anything new, an inability to learn and an unwillingness to change.[165] The

---

[161] Fall theology is beyond the scope of this book, but contemporary thought outside the Church seems to be looking at human nature less as sinful and more as flawed. In other words none of us are in fact who we could or should be. See Wiley (2002).

[162] In 'The darkness in all of us' (page 120), I expand this idea, suggesting we all have a dark side that stands against our best interests, including our need for positive change.

[163] A classic example was the refusal of Solomon to conform to Yahweh's wishes by separating himself from the kingdoms and gods around him. Uxoriousness was the pattern of Solomon's life, conforming with the kingdoms around him by taking foreign wives and their gods. This refusal to be different, to be willing to change, ultimately caused the downfall of his kingdom (1 Ki. 11:1ff.).

[164] Some would argue this 'base' spirituality is in fact the soul. The problem in using this word is its multitude of meanings. See Boyd (1996:73ff.).

[165] This is not always the case, since some do not have the inner resources to promote or even allow inner change to take place. The concept of human 'will' suggests rational cognitive processes, and this is not always initially accessible in the person. Though having said that, cognitive behavioural therapy (CBT) for instance, is about changing behaviour, not changing the person. It seems to work best with those who are unhappy with the state they are in. For an introduction to this significant area, see Garfield and Bergin (1994).

sicker a person is, the more isolated and resistant to change they normally become.[166] In CCD, some of the time, we do not see mental illness as sickness, but instead as stubbornness, arrogance, and other inflexible human qualities, a refusal to take responsibility for needed positive change. Our companionship with our sicknesses is far too comfortable. This same stubborn unwillingness to change is also seen in a Hebrew perspective. It is our resistance to the wishes of Yahweh, as well as against our own salugenic best interests. But where the image of God is being restored by learning God-centred relations, all other relationships which exist in humanity are capable of being restored as well (Schwobel 1991a:153). Thus, to always be changing is to be wholly alive. As Lee observed, according to a theology of change, salvation becomes a process of God's continual redeeming creativity (1979:123) within a vibrant community of relationships. Therefore, in CCD it is assumed that to be authentically more human one needs to learn a perpetual state of becoming, experiencing positive relational change.

Summarising the rift

A rift is in process, in fact almost complete, with a Western culture seeking what it means to be human, especially what it is to be spiritual, and a Church that largely is not. The term 'spirituality' is today pregnant with a host of meanings, both Christian and otherwise. But it is now broader, as noted earlier, than the religious roots it has largely come from.[167] Yet whilst this interest in spirituality continues to widen and grow within society, the Church continues to see itself a victim of secularization that is making it redundant,[168] with a 'spirituality' that remains largely static and historic.[169] It continues to appeal far more to *being,* (e.g., our sense of unchanging

---

[166] We will come back to this key theme in 'Seeing sin as a refusal to change' (page 127).

[167] For a different view, arguing 'religion is the instrument, spirituality the goal', see Hull (2002). He commented: 'religion represents the most highly developed form of spirituality. Whatever you take as ultimate will become your religion' (175).

[168] However, the Church was not blameless in its own stripping of spiritual reality. For instance, with Ockham's 'razor' in hand, furnished by the Church, 'Enlightenment rationalists shaved off the embarrassing whiskers of supernatural beings from the modern cosmology' (Grenz 2000:216). Attributed to William of Ockham (c. 1285 – c. 1349), but never actually stated in his writings, this methodological dictum, referring originally to angelology, states that 'entities are not to be multiplied beyond necessity' (216). Our Western Church culture has seemingly lived this into the 21st century.

[169] As a young Christian in the early 1960's I was impressed how people changed when they began attending Church. But before long I suspected much of this 'change' was expectation to conform, to 'be one of us' (the 'one size fits all' mentality), rather than wholesome positive unique change away from past baggage and sicknesses. Susan Williams' conclusions were that mandating such change leads to compliance, not personal transformation (2002:78).

history and tradition) than seeking to meet more vibrant contemporary needs.[170]

---

[170] One example of this is the form and structure of institutional Church's worship, which like its spirituality, remains largely unchanged over the last 200 years. The need for change, to adapt to contemporary needs outside the church, is now beginning to generate its own literature. See for instance, Hunter (1996), Moynagh (2001) etc.

Chapter 3

Defining personhood; proposing personal change and wholeness as a therapeutic discipleship journey

Introducing personal uniqueness

Underlying the 'must fit me' culture of our 21st century is a belief in the uniqueness of human personhood. Likewise, in CCD there is a belief in personal uniqueness in Christ.[1]

> *Here in Christ Church everyone matures together, everyone in their own uniqueness (W12-2).*

Susan Williams' findings note this sense of uniqueness is associated with a discontent with one's lot, admitting the need for personal change,[2] and committing to a journey to break cycles of self-harm and defeat. Likewise, among the contemporary un-churched, their search for personal spirituality, for meaning and significance, for wholeness and identity, are all associated with being a unique person.[3] As contemporary literature illustrates, they are seeking out *how* to become more fully themselves.

> *This is going to be the place where I am going to find the answers (M7-1).*

Here in CCD we are seeking to develop a model of Christ-centred personhood, with a clinical 'how to' application, that can empower our and future generations with the answers they need in becoming the person God created them to be.

---

[1]   This belief in personal uniqueness is interesting to me, as nowhere in recent years can I find myself referring implicitly to this in either my counselling or teaching. What seems to be happening is that members of CCD have themselves quite naturally concluded their own uniqueness in Christ. Rahner commented, 'God of course wills precisely that each should be a unique individual and this personal uniqueness he not only received at his creation but is free himself to achieve throughout his life' (1963:19-20).

[2]   I would readily admit not all change is good. I am here speaking about positive transforming change, describing, for instance, the type of change outlined by Jung's individuation (Perry 1991:71).

[3]   This is not a new idea, for instance it was the subject of the Terry Lectures in 1954, given by Gordon W. Allport, published as *Becoming: Basic considerations for a psychology of personality.* He stated, '...for it is the knowledge of our own uniqueness that supplies the first, and probably the best, hints for acquiring the knowledge of others' (1955:backcover).

Zizioulas suggested that in the history of philosophy we do not yet have a consistent ontology of human personhood,[4] arguing that nothing else is 'me', nothing else can *ever* be 'me' (1991:37).[5] Typically in the past, particularity[6] of being in a metaphysical sense is annulled when we use the classic Greek categories, which most often imply the replaceability of one by another. In Greek thought no one is perceived as 'unique', so such a Greek view of personhood is unhelpful for both contemporary people, and Susan Williams' participants.

> *The thing is, we don't have a package. Everybody is taken at their individuality (W15-8).*

What is needed, suggested Zizioulas, is the ability to attach fixity to the 'many' as if they were the 'one', thereby creating a concept of absolute uniqueness[7] and irreplaceability (1991:34ff.).

To this end Zizioulas tabled an ontology of particularity of personhood by appealing to the Cappodocians, while also seeking a new Christology. 'In Christ the general exists only in and through the particular; the particular is thus raised to ontological primacy....for man to acquire this ontology of personhood it is necessary to take an attitude of freedom *vis-à-vis* his own nature' (1991:43ff.). He then went on to suggest that human personhood needs a 'new birth' in order for this process to be possessed and that only relationality, in the Trinity and in human personhood, can offer personal unique ontology. Expanding on this, he has commented, 'In the West the starting point of Christology is found in the concept of the "nature" or "substance", whereas the Greek Fathers, for example, Cyril of Alexandria, argued the starting point was *hypostasis,* the person' (Zizioulas 1985/2002:55). Ferry (2002), along similar lines notes that starting from God, in an Augustinian sense, has proven problematic, so a fresh approach is needed.[8]

---

[4] In talking about personhood I will not be making a distinction between male and female, even though some argue, when talking about people, one is more likely to think of male (Hamilton 1991). In our therapeutic practice in CCD, however, we make a number of distinctions between male and female. See 'Gender and marriage' (page 159) for further comment.

[5] We should note here that because of the uniqueness of divine personhood itself, human particularity in Christ (e.g. Christ-likeness) at both a philosophical and theological level, also implies absolute uniqueness.

[6] In using the word 'particularity' I am not wanting to confuse it with the philosophical sense of 'particularism', in making our philosophical opinions agree with what we necessarily believe at other times.

[7] I have had an extended discussion with myself asking whether I should use the word 'unique' or 'original'? In settling for the former, unique, I adopt the word used by Susan Williams' participants.

[8] As we noted in the previous chapter, Augustine thought it best to begin with the Unity of the Godhead, rather than begin with personhood, as the Cappadocians did. Also, Augustine never applied the concept of *hypostasis* (personhood) to the Trinity, as the Cappadocians did. '...The Cappadocians (cf. Basil, Ep. 38, 8, Gregory Naz, or 31, 14) tried to express the unity of the Trinity:

In CCD our search for this personally unique human spirituality blends with the idea of a 'transcendent humanism' that emphasises a particularity that needs to be possessed. While this is under-girded by Biblical anthropology, it contrasts with Greek thinking.[9] Such a position is not always accepted in the wider Church today.[10] But exploring this personal uniqueness is clearly part of the goal of Susan Williams' participants: discovering how to be more fully human, through a journey to mature unique personhood.

I don't think there is a better reason to live your life than to find out who you can be (M7-2).

In the previous chapter I noted that traditional Trinitarian structures are inadequate to support what we are seeking to do in CCD. Also, that change needs to be at the heart of any new thinking. To respond to this need, in this chapter we begin with a brief overview of the state of personhood studies in psychology and theology, noting some of the problems. This is followed by a focus on a Hebrew perspective of personhood, following which I will explore a definition of personhood as Christ-likeness,[11] arguing this is consistent with both Hebrew ideas and in some ways the journey of the contemporary un-churched. To explore the therapeutic dimensions of this growth in personhood I then note the *Rapha* promise of Yahweh, tracking this Hebrew change concept of relational discipleship through the New Testament, Early Church and into the 21st century. Throughout this chapter I am describing a personal relational journey, which I search for in both psychology and theology. Toward the end of the chapter I explore a definition of wholeness that offers a framework of therapeutic discipleship and particularity in wholeness for the 21st century. Then in chapter four I outline the process of this journey as I have developed it, possessing Christ-like personhood as an authentic self in relationship.

But first we must enter the complex world of human personhood studies in psychology, looking for both a model of person to support Susan Williams' findings, and also its theoretical framework.

---

each person carries the full, undivided nature, and co-inheres in the other persons...' (Zizioulas 1991:40).

[9] For an overview of 'being human', noting some of the Greek Christian aspects of this, and how it impacts us today, see Macaulay and Barrs (1978).

[10] A typical recent example is the Right Reverend Doctor Rowan Williams, the present Archbishop of Canterbury. Marsh, commenting on Williams (2000) says; 'Williams' distrust of interiority and depth and his attendant rejection of all notions of an 'authentic self' as a 'therapeutic fiction' require him to question the self's integrity as a formful unity created in the image of God....a theological revivification of personhood is thereby frustrated from the start. Williams imagines the self to exist 'without interiority, with no deep psyche, no buried emotional truths longing to achieve authentic expression' (Marsh 2002:265).

[11] I am not suggesting my approach is unique. See Tyrrell, who goes some distance down the same path, describing the 'psychotherapeutic dimension of the healing event that is Jesus Christ' (1975:xiv).

Exploring personhood

Personhood studies in psychology today

The discipline most devoted to exploring personhood today is psychology,[12] a burgeoning academic and therapeutic industry, which claims to be 'the science of the nature, functioning, and development of the human mind (formerly the soul), including the faculties of emotion, perception, communication, etc. (Brown 1993).[13] '*Personology* is the branch of psychology that studies individual human lives and the factors that influence their course over time...emphasising the importance of the person's history for understanding the person' (Carver and Scheier 1996:116). It is a high calling indeed, but in focusing on the mind, as psychology has, from the perspective of CCD such research now lacks numerous elements we are calling for, especially its relationality and an authentic spirituality.

In 1979 Sigmund Koch asked a number of fundamental questions about the goals and purposes of psychology.[14] Along with many others since, he proposed that psychology exists in an atmosphere of disarray, because, somewhat ironically, it has lost its focus on people, thereby also losing its reason to exist. In sympathy with this perspective, Van Leeuwen saw psychology having three main problems: it legislated itself into existence, unlike other 'sciences' that evolved naturally over hundreds of years; in its wholesale pursuit of scientism, psychology has cut itself off from any help from its historical antecedents like philosophy, religion and the other humanities;[15] and thirdly, in its quest to be scientific it has failed to develop the capacity for meaningful [relevant] thought (1985:244ff.). This third point, Van Leeuwen suggested, has brought psychologists to the dangerous place of being mere research technicians, increasingly out of touch[16] with the real world of personal human need. Over the last hundred years

---

[12] The debate continues as to who first used the term psychology. See Lapointe (1972).

[13] For a modern search for the soul, see Crick (1995).

[14] Koch is generally accepted as the premier philosopher-historian of psychology in the English-speaking world. His six volume (1959/1963) *Psychology: A study of a science,* is still considered a seminal work. But it is an address that he gave to the American Psychological Society at its centenary meeting in 1979 that helpfully reviewed the first one hundred years' history of psychology, and asked where psychology is actually going (Koch 1981).

[15] As Oden noted, most of psychology's ideas have come from the previous twenty-six centuries of philosophical thought, and the last three thousand years of theology. All of this has preceded psychology's nineteenth century bid for independence (1992:137ff.). However, as I will be noting later, the failure of fields like philosophy and theology to develop ideas of personhood and personal change, make it even less likely psychology would succeed in doing so.

[16] The growing debate that psychology is 'out of touch with reality' is uniquely illustrated, argued Rogers (1998), in his survey, a 'visual rhetoric', looking at cover art on psychology textbooks. His survey revealed an abstract modernist genre that presents a person-less view of personhood, representative, he believes, of the discipline of human psychology today.

psychology's research, like much science, has become increasingly 'reductionist', raising the question of whether a constructionist approach would be more suited to studying and helping people (Schwandt 2003).

A loss of focus on people will inevitably hinder psychology's capacity to offer an effective theoretical model of human personhood. Dunn, in his helpful work *Identity crisis: A social critique of postmodernity* (1998), noted that this is one of two distinct problems related to personhood within psychology, that human identity has been dehumanized by the depersonalizing of personhood,[17] so that people become objects of scientific research - mere organisms (as psychology has described them in the past). Dunn's second problem, though outside psychology, is also worth noting, being the growth of postmodernism and the 'destabilization of identity' (1998:107ff.) through the fragmenting of personhood (Smythe 1998b:ix).[18] I see these two problems acting like a pincer movement around traditional psychology's practices. At a time when contemporary society is calling for a deeper holistic understanding of personhood, psychology is increasingly looking at people in discrete, fragmented terms, mostly following medical (spiritless) models.[19]

But the deeper problem is not the absence of models of personhood, but that there is no general agreement on human make up. Loptson, for instance, listed 45 models in his book (1998 passim), while Wilber's 'universal' model of human make-up (2001:67ff.)[20] is one example of a contemporary attempt to find an all embracing model. But it was Kohut from a psychoanalytic perspective who admitted we are still some distance from psychology having a useable model of human personhood. His book *The restoration of the self*, in noting this absence, proposed new thinking for new times (1977/1988 passim). Some 22 years after Kohut, Barresi, working along similar lines, again noted the need for a review of the concept of personology. Instead of the current reductionist approach, he suggested human nature needs to be looked at as a complete whole (1999:79).[21] Yet no model seems to have emerged. Because of this and numerous other reasons psychology cannot yet answer the basic question of what human nature is. We find no consensus. Likewise, it has been unable

---

[17] The western world's plunge into what is being called *ethnopsychology* (Furedi 2002 passim) suggests that some psychological therapies lead not to a development of unique individuality, but the danger of standardization of personality (23).

[18] Indeed, all the 11 authors in this recent book, edited by Smythe (1998b), are united in their dissatisfaction with the *status quo* of depersonalized psychology.

[19] The stigma of labelling is also part of this problem. See 'Where has the therapist gone?' (page 150) for a further comment.

[20] Wilber credits his model to Huston Smith (Smith 1992, cited in Wilber 2001:66-67).

[21] I am in danger of making the debate too simplistic, since the absence of a personology is only part of the problem. For instance, Barresi also noted that we must first overcome the 'hard' issue of what we mean by *consciousness* (1999:84). A literature is beginning to emerge on this theme. See for instance, Dennett (1991) and Cornwell (1998).

to deliver models of human personhood that are clinically constructive. The Church also seems to be a victim of these failures.

But perhaps the core problem that psychology brings to this exploration of personhood is its rejection of the spiritual, being rooted as it is, in empirical traditions. In the development of the field of psychology 'soul' became absorbed into mind, or rejected totally, thereby strengthening the centrality of cognition. As noted above, it is only recently that we are beginning to see a ground-up interest in spirituality in psychological therapies. But this loss of a *pneuma*-psychology[22] alone does not explain psychology's inability to build a holistic model of personhood, or why it is making a *pneuma*-psychology an oxymoron alongside psychology.

Struggling with the term 'person'

In its discussions about personhood, the preferred term in psychology has been 'self'.[23] Not everyone has accepted this term,[24] but it has, nevertheless, become commonplace.[25] However, matters may be changing, for psychology is beginning to acknowledge that 'self' has an unfortunate modern meaning of 'individualism',[26] and this is hardly acceptable in a contemporary age (Shotter 1998:246ff.).

But the obvious alternative term, 'person', has also fallen on hard times in recent centuries, for numerous reasons.[27] Paranjpe argued that the modern demise of the term person was initially its entanglement with

---

[22] For an example of this viewpoint see Boyd (1996).

[23] A search on Psychinfo {www.apa.org/psychinfo}, the main database of psychology and psychological therapies maintained by the American Psychological Association, easily demonstrates this focus. In a search of the database on 9th April 2004, there were 61,639 references to 'self' in the title of articles and books, compared with only 4,372 references to 'person'. See also Hoskins and Leseho (1996), or Weber (2000) etc. For a helpful review of modern theories of the self, see Mann (1996).

[24] See, for instance, Wilkes, commenting on Strawson (1959), who acknowledged that although the idea of the self is initially attractive, it is not ideal. He perceptively comments that what psychology wants to do with the 'self' can equally well be done with 'I' (Wilkes 1998).

[25] We should note that within a Christian context some work has also been done on the concept of the self. See Fairchild (1978), Ellens (1992) etc. For a helpful analysis of the self and the problems of Cruciform theology, see Clark (1990).

[26] In talking about 'individualism' I am taking the normative view that the first stream in psychology was Freud and psychoanalysis, the second behaviourism and the third cognitive behavioural schools, promoted by Rogers (1946, 1951) and his disciples. This third movement is committed to 'self'-actualisation at an individual level, which Crabb defines as self-preservation, or enhancement of the self. Most psychologists believe this is good. Like Crabb, I see some aspects of this as being un-helpful. Although Fall theology agrees that all people are committed to their own self-actualisation, seeking their own security and significance, this can create a problem, since in living for ourselves we are unable to live for community (1999:51ff.).

[27] For a helpful, though now somewhat dated introduction to the need to recover personhood, from a Christian perspective, see Evans (1979). For a general introduction to persons and personality from a broad Christian perspective, see Peacocke and Gillett (1987).

Enlightenment philosophers, and the trilogy of mind/cognition, affect and volition (1998:49ff.).[28] Allport further undermined the term with his landmark book in 1937, *Personality: a psychological interpretation*, that launched modern personality theory. In much psychology today 'personality' has been the focus of 'self'. This has led to more than half a century of literature on modelling human personality, epitomised in the human potential movement (e.g. Rogers, May, Maslow (1964/1970, 1970), etc.). However, on this journey the term person has had imposed on it a specific viewpoint, a spiritless[29] Cartesian tradition. Smythe (1998a) argued that this line of enquiry, treating human personhood individually in a Cartesian fashion, epitomises individualism, but its usefulness is now exhausted. So in using the word person today, we have a problem divesting it of its baggage. Although I still prefer the word 'person' to 'self', during this half century of 'progress' psychology has moved no closer to a unified psychology of persons. A mature personology still remains a distant objective.[30]

Smythe suggested we need to understand persons as both socially and historically constituted beings, rather than as autonomous sterile selves, the way much psychology currently does (1998b:xxii). But seeing personhood in relational social terms is a major problem for psychology, since it moves the task outside of psychology's comfort zones, into the discipline of social psychology.[31] The science of psychology currently has little theoretical capacity to see persons in relation. So, not only has psychology failed to develop a 'personology', a fully fleshed model of human make-up,[32] but it is also failing in developing a psychology inclusive of a public personable self.[33]

---

[28] This process has been further accelerated by naturalistic scientific *zeitgeist* (a spirit of the age) that swept through psychology in the first half of the twentieth century. See Paranjpe (1998).

[29] My use of the term 'spiritless' does not imply all subsequent philosophy and psychology is spiritless. For instance, the notion of 'spirit' is explicit in disciplines like transactional analysis e.g. Trautman (2003).

[30] In writing this book I came close to proposing that the phrase 'mature personhood' could include the meaning of relationality. Personhood, unlike the word person, is a word that is not used a great deal in a defined sense in modern textbooks, but does have dignity and stature. But I finally concluded the word 'person' was preferable for this book, though I use the term personhood numerous times, hinting at this added relational meaning.

[31] The whole field of social psychology with its group and family process, should not be overlooked, especially marriage and family therapy and the systems theory movement. But even in these fields of research one often sees a focus on the *individual in the group*, not necessarily focusing on the group first. Also, because social psychology straddles the fields of psychology and sociology, one often wonders where its allegiances are?

[32] For an introduction to the idea of human make-up, see Stevenson (1974/1987, 1981) and Loptson (1998).

[33] Vitz (1987) argued that modern personality theory cannot describe or make a person, only create an individual. He proposed, therefore, that publications like Carl Rogers (1961/1995) *Being a Person* are false advertising.

Barresi, in exploring the issue of personology, asked the question 'how does an entity become a person?' (1999:79). Bruner was thinking along similar lines, suggesting that it is the defining and articulating of the processes, the transactions involved in the construction of this meaning, that is now the central challenge of psychology (1990). The 'making of meaning' of one's personhood throughout life is a need unique to humans and is considered by many as the essential quality of personhood, defining what it is to be fully human;

> *to start to possess some kind of meaning in my life and find out what is really going on in my life, in myself and in the world around me (M7-1).*

Martsolf and Mickley linked the journey of meaning-making to their definition of spirituality. But modern psychology, on the whole, is not addressing this need, lacking as it does particularity of personhood and the concept of *imago Dei* as a meaning behind human life. Morris (1991) inadvertently exposed this failure by surveying all the main schools of psychology in a fairly comprehensive way on the theme *Western conceptions of the individual.* He does not note one school making any attempt to answer questions related to meaning-making in our lives.[34] One of the few exceptions, along with Foskett (1990), is Victor Frankl (1963), whose Logotherapy specifically sets out to focus on bringing meaning to one's past. Likewise, but more recently Wong and Fry (1998), in their edited work of over 20 essays, is helping redeem this sad situation, by covering diverse aspects of the human quest for meaning in life.

So having noted that we do not have within psychology a developed view of the person (including human spirituality), nor an emphasis on human particularity, or a relational psychology, we now need to note that on the whole psychology has not responded to the human quest for why we might exist, or our innate desire to find meaning in our lives. Some would accuse me of being too hard or dogmatic on psychology, but the ideas I am seeking are basic for most contemporary people, like those in CCD, and along with other enquiries form the package of ideas being expressed by Susan Williams' participants, as well as many outside the Church.

The failure of psychology to develop mature pneumatic models of *social* or *relational* personhood, at a theoretical and/or clinical level, has to some extent been the result of its own insular 'scientific' nature. Psychology, like many modern academic disciplines, shows reluctance to dialogue with other disciplines, or be open to new thinking. For instance, Greek thought and its philosophical systems gave us a pneumatic but fragmented view of personhood, while the Enlightenment gave us individualism, and modern-society personology, but also selfism. Theology, yet another academic

---

[34] A number of books have looked at the more general subject of human personhood. See, for instance, Stevenson (1981), Pervin (1984), and Smythe (1998b). Loptson (1998) is a helpful introduction.

discipline, with its anthropology and philosophy has done little to correct these imbalances. The challenge before us, then, is to begin the process of drawing together some of what each of these disciplines has to say about personhood, especially its relationality, gathering them into an holistic interdisciplinary approach to personhood for the 21st century.

Theologising on personhood

In CCD to be human is to be in a perpetual state of relational becoming. The expectation among members is this will always be the case. This viewpoint is in contrast to some in the contemporary Western Church, where the intensity of personal growth can be inversely proportional to the length of time you continue as a Christian. The longer one is a Christian, the less one sees the need to either grow or change.[35]

It is ironic that only now is Christian theology beginning to awaken to its potential contribution to this debate on personhood. The three *persons* of the Trinity are a plenum, a permanent meeting at which all persons are always fully present (Creel 1986:68-79), an authentic social Trinity. Therefore, being in His image, the Church should reflect this Divine inspired sociality. Additionally, in both Creation theology and Christ's Incarnation and Ascension a unique value is placed on human life.[36] Christ Himself held a 'high' view of human personhood as good, but damaged (Mt. 18:6,8-9, Jn. 8 - 11 etc.). So any model of human personhood should include this moral value. Likewise, Paul,[37] taking up a Hebrew model of human personhood, conceived the person as a synthetic psychical whole, an embodied spiritual being (Rom. 8:16, 1 Cor. 7:34, 2 Cor. 7:1, etc.), and sought to interpret this into his contemporary Greek Roman context.[38]

Numerous modern thinkers have also sought to interpret Christ's, Paul's and other New Testament writers' ideas regarding human personhood and its spirituality. This has mainly been through a theological and sometimes anthropological and philosophical framework.[39] For many centuries theological scholars have been developing concepts of personhood, divine and human, so one would think theology could have given psychology some support in developing models of human pneumatic personhood. But sadly, in Biblical anthropology, as well as in practical and pastoral

---

[35] When recently chatting with a newcomer to CCD, I asked them what the main reason was for them coming to Deal. His reply was quick and clear, he had been in his previous church for eighteen years, and had not changed much at all in that time. He felt a deep need to change.

[36] See di Vito (1999) for a Christian perspective.

[37] Throughout this book I am assuming all the Letters and Pastoral Epistles of Paul normally attributed to him are his authorship. Recent questions of authorship and date I leave to others.

[38] See 'The darkness in all of us' (page 120) where I look at certain aspects of this.

[39] See Robinson (1952), Stafford Clark (1956), Van Kaam (1972, 1975, 1983), Hill (1984), Macquarrie (1987), Thiessen (1987), Ware (1987), Kenny (1988), Norris Clarke (1993), Yale (1993), etc. to name but a few.

theology, little is available to halt the advance of psychology's 'depersonalized person'.[40] After two thousand years of thinking about human personhood and persons-in-relation, the Church still does not even have a widely accepted model of human make-up (Schwobel 1991b:9).[41] This is a serious setback in our efforts to help build a redemptive model of personhood, since one cannot fix what one does not understand.

However, there has been extensive effort or debate, over many years, on the borderland of psychology, anthropology, philosophy and theology. Indeed, whole journals are devoted to cross-disciplinary dialogue,[42] as well as a continuing substantial flow of published literature. More recently other disciplines, like sociology, are beginning to look at human personal formation on the borders of theology (e.g. Beaudoin 1998). So with such a wealth of knowledge and inter-disciplinary dialogue one would have expected much more from theology. But neither within theology, nor at its frontiers with psychology or even sociology do we see much mature thinking regarding models of human make-up,[43] personhood, particularity, meaning or the clinical aspects of corporate human spirituality.

In the previous chapter I suggested that personal transformation is facilitated by a God who through the Holy Spirit has the power to co-inhere all things in heaven and earth, and requires positive change in all of us. Also, we have agreed this should be a lived reality within a social corporate spirituality. What we are beginning to think is that one reason why this may be is because of the Church's own transcendent Trinitarianism, as there is

---

[40] In 'Being a person in Hebrew thought' (page 74) I will be proposing that an alternative model of personhood has existed since long before the time of the Early Church, but has been largely ignored.

[41] Some books have been written on personal spiritual nature during the 20th century. For instance, Come (1959) is a theological study of the Holy Spirit and human spirit, focusing on the immanent significance of our spiritual nature. It is helpful, but now long out of print. Rahner's *Spirit in the world* (1968) was part of his doctoral work, seeking through Kant, Heidegger and Marachelian Thomism to recover personal spirituality, but it suffered from Rahnerian density, Greek philosophical roots and sometimes an unhelpful translation. It is not for popular reading. His 1994 book *Hearers of the Word* (1994) built on the same theme, also stays largely in the language of Neo-Scholasticism. Goldbrunner (1966) is again a Catholic, but used a Jungian model as his framework, thereby limiting its helpfulness. Brown et al. (1998) struggled with the issue of spiritual reality from a scientific perspective, mostly written from a non-reductive physicalist viewpoint, where soul is part of physical make-up rather than something distinct.

[42] For instance, *The Journal of Psychology and Theology,* and *The Journal of Psychology and Christianity.*

[43] Some would argue that H. Reinhold Niebuhr in his *Nature and Destiny of Man* (1943a, 1943b) sought to take the idea of man outside the framework of idealist and naturalist philosophies. Others would argue that Grenz (2000, 2001) was seeking to do this, but neither of his books are informed by a model of human make-up, Biblical or otherwise, and neither book seeks to dialogue outside the domain of theology.

little evidence that the Church is yet extending its thinking into human personhood in any way.[44]

Having said that, we are acknowledging that in Scripture, theology and the traditions[45] of the Church we do see numerous concepts able to help us construct a theology of human personhood, and its spirituality. But no common model that will suffice for the task we have before us. However, matters are not as grim as they might at first appear. In the early chapters of the Hebrew Scriptures one finds a model of human personhood that I believe might be helpful to us. It can potentially support contemporary transformative spirituality and relationality, within a context of personal uniqueness, a *pneuma*-psychology for today.

Being a person in Hebrew thought

What I am suggesting is that in the opening chapters of the Hebrew Scriptures we see a model of human make-up that may be of help to us today. People work especially well with visual aids and clear ideas, and the Early Hebrew view of human make-up is, I believe, one such helpful tool.[46] Hebrew thought introduces us to a concept of human make-up described as a body spirit unity model.[47] It precedes all 45 of Loptson's (1998) models, and in its 'primitive' simplicity follows Huston Smith's example (1992, quoted in Wilber 2001:66), rather than following more complex 'postmodern' models.

In the Early Hebrew Scriptures (Gn. 1:26-27; 2:7, etc.) human personhood was seen by the young Israel as both spiritual and physical, two aspects of one reality, not unlike two sides of a coin. Hebrew thought 'shared with other "primitive" pre-logical and non-analytic modes of thinking, which conditioned their understanding of themselves as an

---

[44] Grenz believes this process is beginning, because of the renewal of Trinitarian studies in the last twenty years or more. He believes this is leading to a renewed interest in what it is to be a person (2001:4).

[45] Such thinking has not been entirely absent. A number of authors have sought to connect liturgy and the healing wholeness journey. See Nichols (2003) for a recent example.

[46] This model was first introduced to me in 1968 by the Old Testament scholar H. L. Ellison, Senior Lecturer at Moorlands Bible College, Devon, UK. I was attending the college at the time and am greatly indebted to him, especially for teaching me to understand and love Hebrew thought.

[47] Judge commented that seeking to go to the *roots of ideas* may not be enough, since a word or phrase inevitably means whatever the writer meant it to mean (Judge 1960b:9). But in hearing or reading a matter one automatically invests it with one's own perspective. Therefore, in using the term 'model' and speaking of 'body spirit unity' I am aware I may mean something quite different, depending on whom I am speaking to. Unfortunately, it is a complex issue of how we give meaning to language, how language speaks to us and what it communicates. Also, how we might bring any consistency to our communication as we speak to one another.

indivisible unity, body and spirit' (di Vito 1999).[48] In CCD personhood is viewed as an un-differentiated psycho-physiological oneness, whereby body and spirit co-mingle, interpenetrating within one another, in the same form – two aspects of the one nature, an amorphous wholeness.[49] Both aspects, spiritual and material, give form and expression to each other, the body the domain of human spirit, the human spirit[50] the domain of the body. Physical and spiritual co-mingle within one another, a seamless reality, a perfect harmony and continuity.

This simple model helps visualise how we are spiritual creatures.[51] Gotz suggests that material reality is fixed, solid, operating within structured pre-determined parameters (e.g. an acorn grows into an oak tree), while spirit is *capax infinite,* of infinite capacity, able to pass beyond itself, and in a permanent state of becoming (1997:2).[52] Hebrew Scriptures see human make-up as one irreducible whole (van Peursen 1966:100, 103) combining both these qualities. It is these two qualities, and their co-mingling within one another that makes us persons. In CCD this model of body spirit unity is key, for we do not treat discretely any disorders in our lives, e.g., medical from emotional, psychological from physical etc., but in an holistic way. Therefore, from a Hebrew perspective we are incorrect in speaking of people having psychological and/or emotional or spiritual problems.

---

[48] There is no systematic theology of the human spirit in Scripture. This interpretation is proposed on the basis of Genesis 2:7, and I have found it to be consistent with subsequent usage in the Early Hebrew Scriptures.

[49] On the complex issue of where the body ends and the spirit begins, Rahner suggested body needs to be conceived as 'solid' spirit (1958:57). The concept of body spirit unity, it is argued by some (Cooper 1989/2000:xxvi), is actually a 'holistic dualism', though John Kok suggested in a personal conversation with Cooper, that it might better be described as 'dualistic holism'. I personally prefer 'two aspects to the one nature', thereby avoiding suggestions of dual-aspect monism or its dualism. Also, I see monism and holism as the same, though I am not comfortable with idealistic monism or panpsychism, the view that humans consist of just one sort of metaphysical element – soul, mind or spirit – and bodies are manifestations of that element. See Cooper (1989/2000:20, footnote 36) for further comment on this.

[50] When teaching this model I am often asked whether spirit and soul are either synonymous, different, or somewhere between. My own tentative conclusion is that the concept of human spirit in the Old Testament is greater than soul, for in Biblical etymology 'soul' is the forerunner of spirit. Also, soul is generally recognised to encompass human personhood, but not specifically either our spiritual nature or spiritual reality.

[51] Not everyone agrees with this perspective. '....there is such variety in the ways the terms are used that it is impossible to arrive at a single, theoretically clear model of human nature from the Old Testament' (Cooper 1989/2000:37-38). My response is to emphasise the Hebrew model I am using, prior to other influences on Jewish tradition, like Hellenistic Judaism and the Church Fathers.

[52] Gotz (1997), in his essay on *Spirituality and Teaching* further suggested the idea that our spiritual nature is in need of permanent change, 'spirit becomes', while material reality all around us is fixed, merely *being*. On this basis, a life of positive personal change engages spirit.

Human personhood is seen by us in CCD as a single, seamless fabric,[53] where any form of change impacts the whole.[54] The early provenance and profound simplicity of this Hebrew model allows it to be used widely by us, across religious and cultural frontiers,[55] as well as being helpful to the contemporary un-churched.

> *...the huge impact of the teaching that I have a spirit, and all that that entails. Heard it first at the Intro Workshop - it was life-changing teaching and understanding (01F-9.2).*

But this same Hebrew model gives us much more, by suggesting that as spiritual beings we also all live in spiritual reality. Paul suggests that earth is the first heaven, where we as human spiritual beings dwell now, with a second heaven comprising all spiritual beings surrounding us, and the third heaven where Yahweh resides (2 Cor. 12:3, Thwaites 1999:142ff.). In CCD we have found this kind of thinking helpful, allowing us to visualize being spiritual beings within spiritual reality. As well as conceiving at a practical level our own spirituality, it also helps us bridge this difficult rift in relating to a 'spiritual' Trinity.

In this body spirit unity model spiritual reality co-mingles with physical reality, and this co-mingling is true of both the physical and spiritual worlds, and also our own human make-up. The shape of our body is the shape of our human spirit. No one organ, or one location or part of our brain's architecture is spirit. We are all spirit just as we are all body. With a body spirit unity model of this type the Church can speak legitimately of the redemption of the whole person, whereas with Greek categories, and

---

[53] The New Testament, when speaking of human spirit, gives us mixed signals. For instance, see 2 Corinthians 7:1 for a bipolar view, and 1 Thessalonians 5:23 for the trichotomous view. There are numerous complex theological and exegetical problems. For instance, although I am assuming we can speak of human spirit as an entity, some would argue we cannot, except when also speaking of the body: 'without the body there is no self' (Via 1990:70). Others argue that what Paul is saying is that the human spirit is merely the Holy Spirit indwelling the human (Jewett 1971:179, 183-185, 197-199). Jewett acknowledged that in 1 Corinthians 2:11 Paul makes a rare distinction between human spirit and divine spirit, but he denied that Paul here makes the human spirit the seat of self-consciousness (1971:187-189, 194, quoted in Via 1990:154, footnote 71). Such diverse views may explain why the Church is still so confused regarding human make-up, by speaking of tripartism, the terminology of mind, body and spirit, or bipartism (See, for instance, Clark, (1977:183ff.). Cooper noted that the Greek Fathers are normally trichotomists, while the Latin Fathers dichotomists (1989/2000:9). Such debate makes Christian spirituality confusing to the layperson, highlighting the need for the adoption of one simple model. Most models are based on Greek categories, obscuring the real point we want to make, that we are spiritual beings.

[54] There is, of course, a long-standing debate regarding the monist-dualist issue. For a comment on Hebrew personhood, see Whitlock (1960), and Boivin (1991). On the complex ongoing debate as to what happens when the person dies, when presumably the human spirit must experience the after-life, see Cooper (1989/2000). .

[55] In all my years of perusing books on human make-up, only one or two have ever made any reference to this Hebrew model.

their modern sciences, we are in danger of speaking of redemption, medically or therapeutically, only in terms of parts of us.

From God's perspective, all humans are seen as spiritual beings, though embodied.[56] In Scripture humans are considered part of the hierarchy of all spiritual creatures (e.g. Heb. 2:6b).[57] 'So, for Paul, while *pneuma*, spirit, when it is used of man, is that in virtue of which he is open to and transmits the life of God (Rom. 8:16)' (Robinson 1952:19). For the glory and authentic basis of human spirit is Holy Spirit (e.g. Rom. 8:10, 1 Cor. 2:12-16; 12:1-11 etc.) (Meye 1993:765). In the words of Irenaeus of Lyons, the true Glory of God is the human person being fully alive in Christ (Fink 1993:132).[58] We are spiritual beings in consequence of divine creative initiative.

When New Testament authors (e.g. Christ Mt. 26:41, Paul Rom. 8:10, Peter 1 Pet. 3:4 etc.) used the word *pneuma* they did not mean what the Greek-speaking world meant by it. Instead, imparting into the word the meaning of the Hebrew *ruach*. Stated Isaacs, 'what is far more apparent is that Hebrew ideas have been introduced into the Greek concept of *pneuma*' (1976:15). She proposed the New Testament writers did not borrow the Greek concept of *pneuma*, just the word. The *ruach*[59] of the Hebrew Scriptures was invested in *pneuma*, a Greek term, speaking of spirit, wind or dynamic movement of air. '[*Pneuma* is] the most significant word employed in the New Testament to bring into focus what being human "essentially implies"' (van Peursen 1966:99). *Pneuma* is used over 40 times in the New Testament to describe that power which we experience as relating us to the spiritual world and wholely to one another, through human spirit. God most immediately encounters us through our human spirit (Rom. 8:16, Gal. 6:18, Phil. 4:23, 2 Tim. 4:22, Phil. 4:23, Heb. 4:12, Jas. 4:5). *Pneuma*, therefore, is that aspect of our one nature most immediately open and responsive to God (Mt. 5:3, Lk. 1:47, Rom. 1:9, 1 Pet. 3:4). It is, also, that area of human awareness most sensitive to matters of the spiritual realm (Mk. 2:8; 8:12, Jn. 11:33; 13:21, Acts 17:16, 2 Cor.

---

[56] Commented Davidson, 'there is nothing very difficult in the phraseology in the Old Testament for the parts of human nature. The material part, spoken of in itself, is *dust* from the ground; the spiritual part, spoken of by itself, is *breath* or *spirit*. When united to the spirit, dust becomes *flesh* which may be defined *living*, or *ensouled matter*; and spirit when united to the dust, now flesh, becomes *soul* which may be called *incarnate spirit*' (1961:203). (Note: I have edited out the Hebrew font.).

[57] By using this verse I am not suggesting that matter is lower than spirit, only that it is distinct.

[58] For an introduction to Irenaeus of Lyon see Farrow (2000).

[59] '*Ruach* is not an immaterial substantial soul, but a vital force, the power of life, externally conferred on human material by God...empowering humans to do whatever they were created to do....both "spiritual" and "physical" organs have both "spiritual" and "physical" functions....*basar, ruach, nephesh* and *leb* are often used to refer....to the whole person' (Cooper 1989/2000:40-44).

2:13). The Hebrew model of body spirit unity continued within the New Testament concept of *pneuma.*

But Scripture can be ambiguous (Mk. 14:38, Lk. 1:17), unclear whether it is speaking of human spirit or Holy Spirit.[60] Said Isaacs, 'In both Paul and Philo, *pneuma* even when referring to the spirit of man, is never free from its divine signification....so much so that it is often difficult to determine whether the spirit of man or the Spirit of God is meant....the true *pneuma* resides in Christ and his church' (1976:81, 143-145). So *pneuma* is always more than *nous* (Roberts 1967:157, footnote 15) by speaking of our wholeness, focused on human spirit. 'The Bible does not provide us with either a philosophical model or concept of man....its language is performative rather than descriptive...the crux of the matter, therefore, is the *unity* of the total man...it is only on the basis of *prior cohesion* between them that any distinction between them can be made' (van Peursen 1966:100, 103). The Hebrew body spirit unity model offers to both theology and psychology a practical model of human make-up that is pneumatic yet simple.[61]

I am aware that stating the case in these terms I am making huge claims. But here in CCD we have assumed there is an aspect of reality that is spiritual, and that we can speak of a *pneuma*-psychology both in Scripture and personal experience. But some would say I am on weaker ground suggesting the Western Church has failed to develop such pneumatic models of human make-up. The evidence speaks for itself, for if the Church had developed such a model psychology would probably have not gone unchallenged in the twentieth century in making the soul the mind. For neither the Church nor psychology have developed credible clinically helpful models of spiritual personhood, nor models of human particularity, or a relational psychology, or begun to answer why we exist in the first place.

However, this Hebrew model of body spirit unity gives us some of these tools, allowing us to think clinically about our nobility of unique personhood in Christ, our spiritual nature, and the fact of our dwelling in both spiritual and material realities. In CCD we have adopted these ideas as foundational to our approach to formative personhood, thus allowing us to speak of a transformative relational spirituality like that being sought by the contemporary un-churched.

---

[60] Come had hoped that the rising interest in the person and work of the Holy Spirit in this last century would lead to the developing of a doctrine of human spirit (1959:140, 179). Sadly this has not yet happened.

[61] Merton commented: '....the only way in which we can become "spiritual" in the true sense is to possess within us a *pneuma* or spirit which is formed by the coalescence of our spirit and the Spirit of God in one principle of supernatural action' (1961:199-200).

The benefits of living with the idea of human spirit

By discovering more of my own spirit it allows more of God's Spirit to dwell in me (21M-3.2).

Within the Church there is no doctrine of human spirit, and its lack I suggest inhibits our visualizing and practicing spirituality as a valid relational aspect of our faith. For instance, in relationship to one's self, the Hebrew concept of body spirit unity suggests an holistic view of human make-up, though damaged and fragmented by baggage[62] and its sin.

The body spirit unity model suggests a spiritual side to our personal human nature. It is important to argue for this, as an alternative to traditional mind-body dualism. The Hebrew approach suggests an equality, a balance, in the two aspects of our one nature, rather than suggesting a spiritually good 'core' to human nature, as the Greeks saw it. Among others, in CCD this model enables all of us to look beyond our physical nature to our spiritual nature for the possibility of additional, though more subliminal answers, to the damage in our lives.

Also, the concept of human spirit and its image of God in us sets humanity apart from other species. There is an implicit deep value suggested in our being in God's image, having spirit-body uniqueness. This in turn suggests the possibility that we can all be greater than who we now are, helping release us from the constraints of our material circumstances. This encourages us to seek out the blockages, and the 'tarnished image', with all its potential for relationship with others and God.

But human spirit also reaches beyond us, suggesting not only the possibility of a supernatural life for us personally, but also the possibility of our being able to connect with others at more subliminal levels than mere words and body language. It suggests, especially, that as we relate to others at least two stories exist between us, our physical communication, and a more subliminal spiritual emotional communication. We have found this idea to be particularly important in relationships between the human male and female, often explaining sources of conflict as well as a common spirituality. We are all much more than our biology.

In relationship to the Trinity the idea that we are spirit allows us to believe in the possibility that we can hear and know God, a spiritual being. This helps us visualize a 'platform' of our human spiritual nature being a 'contact point' with the social Trinity. Also, for many of us, human spirit 'after the image of God' suggests a prehistory where He has a part in giving

---

[62] Within the culture of CCD, as mentioned above, we use the term 'sin' as the refusal to change, and baggage as the medium. By baggage I mean 'the old determinants called tapes, programmes, or scripts, from which we derive all our values and heritage from childhood' (May 1982a:51). In Christian circles, as in CCD, we extend this specifically to refer also to toxic past experiences from childhood, parents, people, life and church.

us this image, willing us to be born, and this in turn suggests the potential of a forthcoming eternity engaging this God, whose image we mirror.

> *[Since joining CCD my view of spirituality] has attached spirit firmly (and divinely) into reality. This reality. My idea of spirituality before was that it was 'otherness' - it happened elsewhere. Now I know I am spirit, here, now (13M-9.2).*

To be fully human is Christ-likeness?

In CCD, as well as seeing human make up in this spiritual way, we also equate personal maturity with Christ-likeness, and see this as the ultimate goal in our personal and corporate journey. Attached to this idea are a number of values and practices that we believe are necessary if we are to live this way in a consistent honouring manner. So in CCD we live believing we need to positively change in order to become more like Christ.

> *I never understood before CC why so many Christians were hurting. It's a relief to know that God can meet you in your place of need, in your deepest pain, and that journey is the beginning of being Christ-like (04F-8.36).*

The Hebrew model of personhood as body spirit unity gave me part of the answer of what it is to be more fully human. But it also led me to a more important question: What does it mean to be Christ-like?

A traditional definition of Christ-likeness is given by J. Oswald Sanders: 'We are as mature as we are like Christ, and no more. He was the only fully mature man. His character was complete, well-balanced and perfectly integrated. All His qualities and capacities were perfectly attuned to the will of the Father, and this is the model, the standard God has set for us' (Sanders 1985:21-22). The Greek word *teleiois* can suggest perfection (Brown 1971:1031), but is also used by Paul to describe one's objects or goals (2 Cor. 12:9), completing one's course (2 Tim. 4:7) or being a mature adult (e.g. 1 Cor. 2:6; 14:20, Phil. 3:15 etc.) (Schippers 1971). This is helpful as far as it goes, but how does the individual attain this? The first principle is that change is an imperative. Many Christians seem to believe they undergo some mysterious personal change through reading the Bible, attending meetings, talking spiritual or becoming pious. This model of Christ-likeness is a passive one, where it is hoped that in practicing these disciplines alone one ends up being both more mature and Christ-like. But my own observation is that deep positive permanent change rarely occurs through such mind-focused disciplines alone. So I wish to table a radical practical alternative: Living in personal positive change is a path to personal maturity, and when we acknowledge Christ's Lordship and act on His voice, we are then able to move toward authentic Christ-likeness. To seek to be more fully human, *becoming* a whole unique mature person, is becoming Christ-like.

> *Surely the closer you get to God, the more you become you (W4-10).*

I see particularity of personhood is most fully expressed and then possessed when maturity in Christ is being sought and lived. To be unique is to be like Christ, especially when one adds the idea of *imago Dei* in ourselves (e.g. our spiritual nature) as the gateway. The human spirit by the Holy Spirit is the medium, and our maturing in Christ the end goal. Mature uniqueness of personhood is to be like Christ. Here we see a paradox, for the more like Christ we become, the more unique we become.[63]

Using Christ-likeness as our aim also allows us to tie in our new understanding of social Trinity, giving us a relational understanding of pneumatic personhood. The Persons of the Trinity, and a human person, can both in a certain sense become *perichoretic,* having the capacity to interpenetrate into each other and bridge both realities, material and spiritual, within numerous other love-centred relationships. This I believe is authentic Christ-likeness. But in this process of becoming more like Christ, individuals also become community (1 Cor. 12:27, Rom. 12:4-5, Eph. 4:25 etc.), drawing others into themselves and Christ. Community becomes an essential part of personal (private) wholeness.

> *It feels a bit like Christ Church is a place where you don't find God, but in a sense God finds you, in that you meet people around you who carry the Lord and you see the Lord (M4-1).*

To be Christ-like is to be more fully a person, with increased capacity, also, to embrace relationships. Therefore, when you welcome the Trinity, other people, one's own self, creation and the natural world, one begins to be fulfilled in both humanness and spiritual potential, becoming complete as much as one can in this life.[64]

Combining a body spirit unity model of personhood, with Christ-likeness, as a goal of what it means to be more fully human, offers the Church a strategic advantage in the 21st century. For it provides a framework of hope to better one's self, and also a place to dialogue with the contemporary un-churched. We are living in an age of the authority of experience, and this clinical practical model and its salugenic outcome, gives the Church a unique platform. For it combines a practical issue-by-issue application of letting go the baggage and sin of our past, alongside the experience of how this unique personhood as Christ-likeness can be achieved. Contemporary people outside the church, demonstrated in numerous, often professionally-based spirituality movements, clearly want to know about both spirituality and how to become more fully human. Such a model gives them these.

---

[63] Such a concept is vital in contemporary society, as it highlights our particularity, while beginning to suggest a theology that in becoming Christ-like we do not all become clones.

[64] The Jewish perspective of pastoral care highlights that Jewish pastoral theology is based on imitating the Almighty (not unlike mirroring Christ), who shows care for us in times of illness and bereavement (Ozarowski 1992). This follows the *Theocentric* perspective noted in this book. See 'Introducing *Theocentric* kinship community' (page 171).

[In other churches] it is quite easy to lose your faith really, because the excitement and the reality of it quickly fades away, if you think of it as a fairly passive faith. But the fact that [in Christ Church] you encourage people from the start to take personal responsibility for the journey, to actively seek or make your own decisions really, is really important (W13-4).

Introducing a Rapha discipleship journey

Discipleship in an indifferent age

The subject of Christ-likeness and discipleship studies is vast, and like Volf, I see myself as no more than a pilgrim on a journey through practical theology (1998a:5). This book merely reflects my current position in forming these ideas. But as early as the 1970s I was aware that both my practice and intellectual journey needed more solid theoretical frameworks. It has taken a long time to develop this. Such an admission would be a relief to Firet (1986), who believed that trying to develop such models as I have been seeking to do since the early 1970's, is actually an impossible mission.[65] But this has not stopped me trying, and the fruit so far is in CCD and the *Rapha* movement, not at present in my 'mature' theology. But I have reached a place in my thinking where growing in Christ-likeness, based on a body spirit unity spirituality, and seeking to achieve this through a journey of positive change in our lives together, begins to offer us a therapeutic discipleship model.[66]

A Christian disciple is assumed to be someone growing in Christ-likeness.[67] Numerous authors have built on themes similar to J. Oswald Sanders' definition of Christ-likeness, as a basis for their understanding of discipleship.[68] Though Scripture does not define *discipleship or discipling*, a substantial number of modern writers have sought to do so in various

---

[65] 'Orientating itself to the praxis and the word of God which applies to it, it must begin to formulate theory on behalf of that praxis. In the nature of the case, it is impossible for the practical theologian to do all this alone. He would have to be at once an exegete, a systematic theologian, a psychologist, and a sociologist – to say nothing of the historical research which needs to be done in practical theology' (Firet 1986:10). He is right.

[66] The Greek word for disciple *mathetes* denotes the pupil or apprentice in relationship to the master. It is also often used as a synonym for a *believer*. See for instance Massie (1898).

[67] As will become clear, I see this process as a journey, not an event. So I would want to dissociate with what Middlemiss (1996) described as 'enthusiastic' or 'impatient grace', common in the Charismatic movement (19). I expect both personal transformation and a sense of well-being on this journey in time, but not necessarily social, mental and emotional prosperity for all *now*, as though it were our right from God. For a deeper criticism of such teaching see MacArthur (1978).

[68] See, for instance, on the theme of discipleship, Weatherhead (1934), Philip (1964/73), Sanders (1965/1971), Pratney (1975/1977), Eims (1978), Hanks and Shell (1993), Sanford (1979), Briscoe (1995), Sugden (1981), Watson (1981), Baumohl (1984), Sanders (1990/1994), Wimber (1990), Sanders (undated c.1945), to name but a few.

ways.[69] Willard noted that a disciple is an apprentice of Christ, and that by
being with Christ one becomes like Christ (1998:271ff.). Bonhoeffer (1959)
explored discipleship in theological terms, but did not actually define it so
others could usefully implement it. But I have frequently wondered if the
terms discipleship and Christ-likeness could be something much more,
since defining the idea as the Church has done, has not given us the clinical
path people are now seeking.

Collinson[70] commented on one aspect of this weakness: 'most writers
assume that their concepts are understood by their readers within the
Christian community and immediately launch into describing the life of
discipleship, or methods of discipling. Only a few attempt to define *disciple*
(1999:263). Hadidian is one of the few, 'The process by which a Christian
with a life worth emulating commits himself for an extended period of time
to a few individuals who have been won to Christ, the purpose being to aid
and guide their growth to maturity and equip them to reproduce themselves
in a third spiritual generation' (1979:29, quoted in Collinson 1999:264).[71]
But Hadidian's attempt merely illustrates the real problem I have had. By
seeking to define discipleship in journey terms, he defines a *type,* or aspect
of discipleship, in this case a coaching or mentoring type, but not the
needed clinical process I and others are looking for.[72]

For many years I have sensed that one of the major crises for the Church
in the 21st century will be to fulfil the command of Christ to '*go and make
disciples'* (Mt. 28:19), to become *Christ-like* in an age when people are
increasingly, politely, indifferent to God. The Church needs disciples to
make disciples, but increasingly most people on any kind of a spiritual
journey are bypassing the Church. So it seems to me that becoming Christ-
like, if it is to be attractive to contemporary people, must also include the
belief that one is also becoming more fully human, and part of this is
learning about our spirituality. But in addition it also needs to include the
actual *experience* of meeting and knowing Christ, rather than merely
staying the same after making a decision to follow Jesus.

So we are noting that definitions of Christ-likeness and discipleship that
include this issue-by-issue process of maturing and 'meeting Jesus' do not
currently seem to exist. In my early Christian life I read anything I could

---

[69] In addition to the substantial number of books, one could also add the endless definitions
through Bible dictionaries, journals, Christian monthlies, the weekly press, plus endless private
publications and Church and para-church literature.

[70] Many thanks to the author for her personal permission to quote her PhD dissertation, which
has now been published in the Paternoster monograph series.

[71] The obvious criticism of Hadidian was pointed out to me by Prof. Mary Kate Morse
(15/1/04), that in the Early Church we see little evidence that discipleship was separate from
evangelism.

[72] The Renovare movement is one of those seeking to be this. See their website,
{www.renovare.org/index.asp}.

find related to Christ-likeness. 'Just tell me what to do!', I shouted. Little existed, or seemed helpful in guiding me into how to change to be like Christ, though many books told me how I should be when I have finished. To me it seemed obvious that in order to become like Christ I needed to go on a specific type of Holy Spirit led journey promoting positive personal change. Modern definitions seem to fail,[73] while Scripture gives us little help.[74] No issue-by-issue clinical models seemed to exist.

What I am suggesting, therefore, is that the discipleship journey of becoming more fully human, becoming Christ-like, requires a process of positive personal change. This is implicit in the command of Christ to make disciples, and become Christ-like (Mt. 28:19, Rom. 8:29, 1 Cor. 15:49). As with the concept of sanctification,[75] I am suggesting that enshrined in such concepts is the idea of continuing change, a journey.[76] So from now on, in this book, I will use 'disciple' to describe one who is committed to this journey of discipleship change.

A generic interpretation of a disciple is someone who attaches themselves to another in order to learn from them. Scripture records that Christ required from His disciples a clear break from their past (Lk. 9:57-62), leaving everything (Lk. 5:11), sharing poverty and adopting an itinerant way of life (Mt. 8:20). From the evidence in the Gospels, the experience of growing into these values clearly brought a deep positive therapeutic[77] dimension to the disciples' growing up.[78] We see change in all of them by being with and being instructed by Jesus, although some of this growing up was probably subliminal, unrecognised and little understood by them at the time. It was only later that writers like Paul put this change in terms of transformation (Rom. 12:2, 2 Cor. 3:18 etc.). But for the Church today I believe these concepts together offer a framework for a contemporary therapeutic discipleship.

Spirituality, with its self-help culture, is thriving outside the Church, with numerous therapeutic change dimensions. Yet within the Church Christ-likeness and discipleship as concepts are still separated from an

---

[73] Of the few books in this area, see Freeman (1984), Kvalbein (1988), Houlden (2002).

[74] Although Scripture does not give us a precise issue-by-issue therapeutic process to becoming a disciple, two books, particularly, are helpful in drawing out from Scripture some of the groundwork. See Wilkins (1988/1995, 1992).

[75] I interpret the term 'sanctification' as the change maturing process, toward more holiness and wholeness as Christ-likeness, through the discipleship journey.

[76] This is not a new idea. Foster (1978) for instance, suggested this is achieved by spiritual disciplines, whereas I am suggesting it can be achieved, in part at least, through a therapeutic discipelship journey.

[77] In chapter 4 I describe in greater detail what I mean by therapeutic and its process.

[78] An interesting hint of this can also be seen in Luke 17:19, where only one of the ten lepers returned to Christ to thank Him. Christ's reply, suggesting a further stage to healing, was that he could now rise up and be made whole, Gk *sozo*, since He was willing to acknowledge and give glory to God.

ongoing commitment to *therapeutic change.*[79] It took me several years to
see this. Traditionally, within the Church, the only ones who are treated
therapeutically are those who admit they have pathological illness,
therefore need to change to get well. All other Christians normally stay
outside this therapeutic framework, never feeling any conscious need to
change. Therapeutic change, Christ-likeness and discipleship have rarely
come together.[80] So when I use definitions of personhood as discipleship
Christ-likeness, are there any grounds for reconciling these three worlds?

Personal therapeutic change, Christ-likeness and discipleship

We have recognised the centrality of *becoming* and *change* in Hebrew
thought, and also the suggestion that to be changing in a positive way is to
be more wholly alive. We also defined sin as a way of describing resistance
to change. In addition we have concluded that personal transformation is
facilitated by a God who, through the Holy Spirit, has the power to co-
inhere all things in heaven and earth. This view of Christ within Trinity, the
lived reality, requires change in us, in order for Christ-likeness, being in
Christ, to become our lived reality. Extending these Hebrew perspectives of
a body spirit unity model of personhood, with Christ-likeness as an
expression of becoming more fully human, offers a framework for personal
therapeutic change as discipleship.

In seeing these ideas for the first time a quantum leap confronted me. In
the 1970's I concluded that to become Christ-like and more fully human,
the type of change needed is in part therapeutic. I found myself practising
this in response to human need in those who came to me for help. Even
with those wanting to know Christ better, I found myself suggesting they

---

[79] The stark separation of the idea of discipleship and therapeutic change is easy to
demonstrate, by reading almost any book on the subject of discipleship, and noting the absence of
therapeutic comment (see footnote 69 above for some of the basic texts). But it is even more
apparent when one reads books on healing in the New Testament, where such a link is not even
made. See for instance Wilkinson (1998), who acknowledged health is maturity (29), but did not go
on and make a connection with the need for a therapeutic model to gain such health or maturity.
See also Carroll (1995).

[80] Many in the Church, particularly in the charismatic traditions, would argue that God has
called the Church to the Great Commission, not 'navel-gazing'. Some in the Church seem to be
suspicious, even alarmed, at the danger of therapeutic introspection. John Wesley was an exception,
with his band and class meetings (Henderson 1997:102). In his day, with Wesley's support, people
enjoyed nothing more than the pursuit of spiritual conversation and moral personal growth, to
'speak without reserve' (Henderson 1997:119). These meetings combined the Protestant doctrine of
grace and the Catholic ethic of holiness (Henderson 1997, quoting Davis and Rupp 1965). For
evidence of the therapeutic nature of these 'class meetings', see Henderson (1997:103ff.).
Traditionally, the origins of group psychological therapy is traced to Dr J.H. Pratt's work with TB
patients in 1905 (Drakeford 1967), but a century and a half before this movement Wesley was
doing the same thing (Henderson 1997:119). For a general introduction to this movement see
Church (1949). For the using of some of Wesley's principles in the modern Church, see Snyder
(1996/1998).

needed to change therapeutically, for instance beginning to see God as a *good* Father. As I helped these people, to varying degrees, I observed what I was doing, while also browsing through Scripture, seeing if these ideas and practices were part of the human experience of Biblical personalities. To my great surprise I noted this transformative 'therapeutic' change was the experience of many Biblical characters. I began to make peace with therapeutic positive change as a pathway to Christ-likeness. This process, created by my bringing these two ideas together, Christ-likeness and therapeutic change, has now travelled with me, and matured, over 30 years.

However, at no time, until I began my MA in pastoral psychology in 1997, did I seriously study any psychology, or psychological texts.[81] When I did I was surprised (and humbled) to discover that much of my therapeutic practice was already part of the body of knowledge and therapeutic processes within psychotherapeutic psychology.[82] I concluded that even though it does not offer me a model of personhood, or a direct path to Christ-likeness, therapeutic process within psychology is a helpful facilitator of the kind of change I have both observed, and have needed personally in my maturing in Christ. An integral part of modern discipleship is, I believe, to be able to live as though our toxic pasts never occurred, to see all the symptoms go once and for all. By this I do not mean living in denial, or repressing pain, but no longer carrying the drives at all, having given them to Christ. Being free in this way permits us to 'grow up' in body and spirit, that in turn matures us and gives us greater capacity to live Christ.

For many, as we teach this possibility, to be free from their pasts sounds unbelievable to them. Modern biomedicine or psychological therapies cannot offer this. Only Christ can. This therapeutic process, led by Christ, is intended to bring everyone to a point where only the empty lifeless memories of their toxic pasts remain. This is the therapeutic journey of owning and giving to Christ all the stored up toxic pain of our past[83] that holds us back, together with our redeeming the shame and stigma of its lost years. We allow Christ to take not only our damaged pasts, with all of its painful experiences, but to redeem the years in such a way that we not only

---

[81] In saying this I am not denying we are all passive absorbers of the 'folk psychology' so popular in our culture. We are saturated in it. For a comment on this psychologizing process of our culture, see Chriss (1999) or Furedi (2002). On the whole I see psychological therapies in a positive light, though merely as a servant to assist in the journey I am here introducing.

[82] Some have asked what would have happened to previous generations who did not have this therapeutic aspect available to them? My response is that the practices I use in therapeutic process have always been around, as one can easily see from Scripture and men like Wesley (see footnote 80 above). However, during the 20th century psychology has owned, labelled and expanded many of these emphases. For a defence of this viewpoint, see Oden (1992).

[83] In order to do this journey, 'we therefore have to let go of the prejudices we have held for generations and our pessimism toward pain and suffering' (Kalweit 1989:81).

recover lost ground stolen by our pasts, but with Christ's help we live as though they never occurred. We experience a re-creation, a transformation, of our person.[84]

> *People don't want to put up with all the shit that has been thrown around, they want to get rid of it. Here is the only place that I have been able to find that can help you do it (W10-1).*

This, I believe, is part of our becoming more fully human, becoming who God created us to be, rather than remaining the person we now are. In this sense, my definition of 'therapeutic' is unlike any in psychology. In CCD we live the possibility that everyone, if they so wish, can be free from their pasts rather than, as in much psychology, merely learning to manage it all in a repressive way, or by cognitively seeking to rewrite histories. This, for me, is the message and hope of the Gospel of the Kingdom in this life. I believe it is what Christ means when He says we must be 'born from above' (Jn. 3:3) (Peterson 2002:1920). A transformation focused on Christ through the Holy Spirit through our human spirit flowing into all our relationships. This is Redemption through transformation led by Christ. In approaching the promises of Christ in this way, I was better able to reconcile what He taught and lived with what needs to happen to every one of us today, not just the emotionally ill. We are all in need of change. It therefore ceases to be merely a faith claim, little experienced.[85] Instead it becomes a lived reality.

> *I did a lovely bit of homework[86] the other night with someone and I felt it was, my description of it would be going into a situation of abuse with a helper, meeting myself, meeting the perpetrator and meeting the Lord, dispelling the poison and the impact of the abuse, and welcoming what the Lord really had for me (M13-10).*

Therefore my goal and definition for change in people, is:

> the harnessing through Christ of the human capacity for personal positive transformative change, toward Christ-likeness, by owning our dark side and letting go our toxic pasts.[87] This is a gradual salugenic discipleship journey,

---

[84] One movement with a similar emphasis is Dr Ed Smith's Theophostic counselling movement, {www.theophostic.com}. But he remains para-church, and would not see himself forming therapeutic faith communities.

[85] Within my charismatic tradition there is the danger that for 'faith' to be truly effective it must also be as unquestioning as it possibly can be - 'blind' faith. The danger is that when one begins to think this way all views that differ from one's own can be put down to doubt or even 'attacks of Satan'. Questioning becomes the antithesis of faith, a powerful resistance to assessment and intellectual enquiry (Middlemiss 1996:42).

[86] The concept of homework will be explained in 'Introducing diagnostic counselling' (page 140).

[87] I am suggesting that Christ-likeness correlates with possessing more of our potential within faith community, and our becoming personally significant rather than merely successful. But we are also looking at a scale. Over the years I have noted that the more successful a person feels they are, the less likely they are to perceive they need salugenic discipleship change. They are OK, they

within the womb of faith community, possessing together the fullness of who we all might become. This is our personal journey, realizing our full creative potential as part of *imago Dei*, no longer wishing to remain individually the person we now are.

In the next chapter we will look more closely at this process. But what is my Biblical framework for offering this discipleship model of freedom?

Introducing the Rapha concept

Change, or even people's physical healing, has never been my goal. Meeting and becoming like Christ is my focus. But I realised theology alone would not give me the intellectual framework I was looking for, for theology alone does not change lives.[88] When people said 'tell me what to do', I found myself talking *therapeutically* in the language of psychology, not theology. For several years, in various lay pastoral settings I felt myself in the wilderness, almost outside the Church in some ways. Then Scripture came to my aid.

The two verses, Ex. 15:25-26, close with the phrase 'I am Yahweh, your healer'. Regardless of their continual use by Christians, these verses seem to play scarcely any part in surveys of Old Testament theology (Lohfink 1994:37).[89] But I see these verses are a unique self description of Yahweh as physician of Israel' (Lohfink 1994:61). He is the one who cares for Israel's health (36), which Lohfink, Luther (Hempel 1957:809-826, cited in Lohfink 1994:37) and Preuss (1996:144) translate as 'I am the Lord your physician' (*Ich bin der Herr, dein Arzt*) (37). Like Lohfink, I see this moment as more than just a single passing incident in Israel's unfolding history. Instead, this is a profound declaration of the type of God Yahweh wanted to be to His people. Traditionally, within a Hebrew context, sickness and efforts at healing and recovery primarily all took place in the family sphere, but this passage, instead, moves healing into the sphere of Israel's national religion (Lohfink 1994:70).

---

do not need to change. So inevitably, a model like mine, by its nature, will be more attractive to those who have not yet achieved (e.g. the sick, the poor, the mentally ill and the under-privileged etc.), but who now either want or need to experience change towards wholeness in their lives. Also, in due course, on this journey they will decide whether to invite the fullness of Christ into all areas of their lives.

[88] In saying this, I am not denying God's initiative in conversion, conviction of sin and the journey of sanctification. All these happen to us in the Christian life and are God's initiative, especially through the use of Scripture. Also, although theology as an academic discipline does not change lives, 'telling a story' and the thinking of it theologically (e.g., narrative theology), *cf.* the conception of life as a pilgrimage, does allow theology that possibility. My preference in using the language of psychology, as I have from the 1970s, was simply because it was more flexible, descriptive and understandable to my clients.

[89] I agree with Lohfink. In perusing some 40 introductions and commentaries on Exodus, I have found few that even comment on these verses.

Exodus 15 begins with a hymn of praise (1-18) of the deliverance of Israel from Egypt, a way of putting Egypt behind them, ending this part of Israel's history. At Marah we see a whole new drama unfolding that puts Israel to the test (Lohfink 1994:41ff.). These verses are pivotal, beginning a new phase of Israel's life, with a test that is to be fundamental to Israel's future success. Verses 25-26 read:

He said,[90]
If you will listen: Listen to the voice of the Lord your God,[91]
and do what is right in His sight,
and give heed to His commandments
and keep all His statutes –
of the diseases that I inflicted in Egypt,
none will I lay upon you.
For I am the Lord, the one who heals you (is your physician)
(Lohfink's translation, 1994:44).

Yahweh is imposing on Israel the rule of His social will, but is also promising that if they live by His will, He will not inflict sickness on them, as recorded in the plague narratives (Ex. 7-12). The Hebrew is in the language of high historic prose,[92] whereby a conditional promise of blessing is founded on a divine self-presentation (Lohfink 1994:45). He is saying to Israel they can be healthy if they live His way.

In Exodus 15:26 the Hebrew semantic field of 'heal', *rapa*, or *rp*[93] is normally translated *heal, cure or physician*. The traditional use of these verses in many Christian circles is to make the claim that God wishes to instantly heal someone. This is not the case based on the context. So although I am not denying such healing[94] takes place in the contemporary

---

[90] Moses is the speaker, but the passage slips into the first person of Yahweh (Childs 1974:267).

[91] There is a sense throughout the Old Testament that one hears the voice of Yahweh by reading His words (e.g. Dt. 28:15., *cf.* 45), but what I am about to suggest, based on this passage, is more radical than Dt. 28:15-61. Alongside this traditional view, as we practise it in CCD, exists the possibility that we can still hear His voice for ourselves about ourselves.

[92] On the question of the authenticity of these verses, and the possible scribal layering of them, or whether they are a late gloss, merely taking up one of the later key prophetic themes, see Lohfink (1994:35-95).

[93] 'The use of the word (*rp'*) is explained by the fact that sin was regarded as a spiritual disease so that *rp'* is to be understood as healing of the soul (as Ps. 41:5) or the transgression (Ho. 14:5, Je. 3:22)' (Keil 1872:465, cited in Brown 1995:331). Put another way, 'man is a sin-sickness bearer' (Lambourne 1963:58). Benner, among others, made the same point (1998:159). For a helpful comment on the Atonement of Christ as our healer from sin and its sicknesses, based on the Fourth Servant Song (Is. 52:13-53:12), see Reichenbach (1998). Adams called this condition *hamartiagenic*, sin-engendered sickness (1970:105).

[94] Miracles and 'signs and wonders' are welcome of course, but I am concerned that many people chase these experiences, ('have you had a miracle today?'), rather than take responsibility for their personal, damaged and baggage-ridden states. Power evangelism and healings clearly have a place in the Church, but over the years I have observed that for some this is not enough. They

Church,[95] (we have experienced it in CCD), the actual verses in context promises something much more profound, far more specific, and more remarkable.

Consistent with Akkadian, Old Aramaic and more recently Ethiopic, the root *rp'*, to heal,[96] originally meant 'to patch or sew together, to unite or make whole', usually explained as mending or stitching together a piece of torn cloth (Brown, et al. 1907/1962:950, Brown 1995:26ff.). This interpretation is more consistent with other Old Testament uses of *rp'* (Lv. 14:48, 1 Ki. 18:30, 2 Kg. 2:21-22, Ps. 103:3-5, Je. 19:11 etc.) rather than the contemporary claim of instant healing. Here, at the heart of the Pentateuch and at the beginning of the wilderness journey, one sees a new phase of Israel's history, where Yahweh is seeking to build a unique relationship with His people, focused on a promise of freedom from disease through 'therapeutic' positive change, initiated by obedience to Him. '....In the Old Testament, the usage of *rp'* is decidedly holistic (cf. the similar usage of *sozo* in the New Testament), where the range of meanings includes deliverance from sickness, demons, death, and sin, sometimes within two chapters of the same book (cf. Lk. 7:50; 8:36,48,50)' (Chan, et al. 1996:1165). Yahweh offered to help them toward mature healed personhood, a spiritual psycho-synthesis (Assagioli 1989:47), offering to tell them personally what they must do to be free from sickness.

But this Exodus 15 promise is subject to several preconditions. If a person is to be 'repaired' and be free as Yahweh intended, they must listen to His voice,[97] do what is right from His perspective,[98] live in obedience to

---

need much more than just the 'miraculous'. For a critique of charismatic theology by American Fundamentalists see, from an outsider's perspective, MacArthur (1978) and as an insider here in UK, Middlemiss (1996).

[95] For instance, among the Berbers of the Kabyle mountains in Algeria, it has been recently reported that a number of Moslems have experienced instant healing, often prior to salvation. Through such divine manifestations the region now has about sixty churches, with virtually no Western help and influence.

[96] Lohfink found 80 references in the Hebrew Scriptures to the root *rp'*, 'heal' in the Old Testament, excluding divine names. 42 belong to the category of Yahweh the healer/physician (Lohfink 1994:69, n. 104).

[97] I am aware I am beginning to speak in contextual language, from a culture with which I am familiar, but many others will not be. In Christian theology the Church speaks about God talking to us, while in psychology we speak of an 'inner voice'. Throughout this book I will use these two concepts interchangeably. See 'Listening to God's voice' (page 123). I follow Wittgenstein's observation, 'Meaning is located in the function words have as signals passed between people in the course of purposeful and shared activity....only in the stream of thought and life do words have meaning' (1953:180).

[98] Throughout this book I will be speaking of 'God's view' or 'perspective' on both our world, and particularly our human nature. In doing so I draw on ancient Christian tradition. See for instance Ware (1987 passim). But I am also noting the existence of a universal 'fallen' human state, denying us all full restoration and wholeness without *knowing* Christ's personal perspective and intervention. See 'The darkness in all of us' (page 120) and 'Listening to God's voice' (page 124).

His Law (submitting to it) and keep the spirit of the Law as they learn it. On this basis none are promised instant repair, e.g. being healed physically instantly, but must instead undergo a process that sews back together their fragmented selves, whilst also sewing them into one another and Yahweh. Body spirit unity is restored in divine human relationship. His initiative, not theirs, is the start and finish of this process.[99] Yahweh clearly saw this process as ongoing. This transformation, as well as its physical protection and healing, is the person allowing God to draw them to Himself, which then exposes their own fragmented view of reality, showing them their sin,[100] which He sees as disease.

My own contemporary transliteration of the *Rapha* promise reads like this, 'I am the mender, the one who sews you together, into Christ' (Ex 15:26). What this passage seems to propose is that we are all under the threat of sickness, from Yahweh's perspective, just like the Egyptians were, so we all need to change to avoid this, by going through a process that brings us healing.[101]

> *In one sense [healing] is the process of seeing what stands between you and God from God's viewpoint and taking responsibility for it, and choosing to do something about it (M2-10).*

Yahweh puts the promise of healing within the context of His testing our faithfulness to His wishes. The question always is whether we will seek to live His way, or live for ourselves.[102]

The *Rapha* promise is described as a learning process of hearing His voice and then acting on it.[103] I describe it simply as a discipleship journey,

---

[99] The process of hearing God's voice can easily lead to what Middlemiss described as a 'degradation of reason' (1996:21). Christians see listening to God as a noble task, but it can lead to a dependence on immediate revelation that can fuel a departure from reason. To counter this in CCD we encourage questioning and intellectual debate. For example, we have a seminar programme with visiting national and international speakers (e.g. Professor Clarence Joldersma (USA - Philosophy), Professor Elisabeth Donaldson (Canada - Education), Dr Viv Thomas (UK - Leadership and Spirituality), Professor Richard Flory (USA – Sociology) etc. Appendix 1 includes statistics on the significant proportion of the membership returning to formal education.

[100] This is a controversial word, but one Willard gave us some help with, in that we should see sin as distinct from the person. He suggested sin is the incapacitation of the soul to co-ordinate the whole person, internally and externally. By spiritual disciplines, Willard proposed, the person is able to progress toward wholeness, an integrating of these by His Spirit and their own (1998:35-59).

[101] For a Hebrew comment on this, see Erland (1984) and Wells (1996).

[102] In teaching this journey one of the most common accusations I hear from Christians is that they have been seeking God's help for years, but have not yet been helped by Him. The *Rapha* model implies that He may well have been talking to them, but they still need to tune in to His frequency, then be mentored as to how to interpret and apply this clinically.

[103] Other modern authors have taken up the idea that Hebrew therapeutic ideas were not about healing, but hearing God's voice and acting on it. See, for instance, Thompson (1984:33) and Fitzpatrick (1984/1987). I am also aware that by speaking this way I am placing myself firmly in enthusiast, Pentecostal and Charismatic traditions. But I would not want to proliferate what

becoming like Christ. It resolved for me what Volf called social dissonance (1998a:18), the irreconcilable gulf between what I saw in the Church regarding *discipleship* and *Christ-likeness,* and what I believe God wants to give. Yahweh, speaking to the Hebrew assembly, assumed every one of them needed this lifestyle change and its healing protection. He did not appear to define it just for those who get ill. I believe, instead, Yahweh gave His people in this passage a vision of wholeness that all of them could possess.

It was a whole range of people that this worked for, it didn't matter what baggage or what you had, anything could go (W10-5).

The Early Church and personal change

In CCD we believe that everyone is sick. Even the strongest, healthiest and most successful people need this *Rapha* healing, because sickness is defined from God's perspective, not ours, or the health care services. So in practising the *Rapha* journey we have over many years learned to adapt it to each individual's personal needs and circumstances. We believe it can work for anyone who really wants it.

Jesus' practice was His message (Twelftree 1993). His healing ministry demonstrated His heredity as God, so during His ministry Christ demonstrated two ways to heal. The first was instant, no doubt followed by a period of rehabilitation.[104] But secondly there was His work with His disciples, being 'disciplined' by Him. In this process, from the record of Scripture, everyone around Him was either showing signs of growing up (getting more whole) or leaving Him. The defining issue in this second model appears to have been the followers' willingness to learn and change on His terms.[105] Christ required significant change from all of them, expecting them to become like little children (Mt. 18:3). He both healed people and gave them spiritual restoration, by drawing them into Himself (e.g. the *Rapha* principle, becoming like Him by being near Him). The clear inference is that all followers of Christ are unfinished, needing ongoing personal positive change.[106] It is this 'hidden' journey process into Christ-

---

Middlemiss described as the bifurcation in the Western Church of existentialism v. rationalism, experience v. theology, subjective truth v. objective, knowing a person rather than knowing about a person, or I thou as opposed to I it (1996:61). I believe we need to strive in such matters for the middle ground.

[104] There is a substantial literature about Christ's healing ministry. Wilkinson (1998) is a helpful introduction.

[105] 'Like the prophets of old, Jeremiah in particular (Je. 7:26), Jesus seems to have thought that Israel misused the sacrifices in the temple to make them a substitute for this inner repentance and purification' (Skarsaune 2002:142).

[106] For an illustration of some aspects of this process of change to become Christian, based on the Epistle of Barnabas, see Skarsaune (2002:350, 363).

likeness that I will now focus on, proposing we call it the *Rapha* discipleship journey.

Paul, taking up the themes of Christ the disciple maker, speaks of *maturity* in terms of *union with Christ* (Col. 1:28, Rom. 8:29) and *moral stature* (Eph. 4:13, *Williams New Testament*). Commented McGrath, 'the New Testament suggests that salvation is inaugurated, but not completed, in this life, but it is clear that a decisive transition is envisaged' (1995:28). This therefore begs the question, is the Church to assume that *Christ-likeness, making disciples, union with Christ* and *moral stature* when practised, should lead to what is often described as spiritual maturity? I believe they should, and furthermore, I am suggesting this is the 'healing' envisaged in the *Rapha* concept of Exodus 15:26.

Paul's writings, particularly, illustrate the extent of the change expected.[107] At no time in the New Testament does this change appear to be optional, or only for those in desperate sickness or need. Instead, I believe this expectation of change, at both a personal and group level, was a pattern of discipleship foundational for the first three centuries.[108] It would seem the Early Church developed whole programmes intended to 'perfect' new converts.[109] For an outsider's perspective of this process see MacMullen (1984), and for an insider's see Field (1978/1997). Both books illustrate the stringent changes expected of new converts[110] which Field suggested meant a minimum of 3 years of 'training and exorcisms', before being baptized into the Christian community (19ff.).[111] Discipleship was inevitably 'therapeutic', in the sense of bringing about positive change by separating a person from their (pagan) past.[112] But such practices, and their importance promoting personal positive change clearly did not survive the heavy

---

[107] For a helpful description of migrating religions and the Roman response at this time, see Nock (1933/1972).

[108] 'Catechesis was only half the battle, and "battle" is the correct word: The purpose of the catechumenate was literally to "reform" the candidate.... Thus, as the catechumens' convictions changed from old values to new, their conduct had also to change from old ways to new' (Finn 1992:5-6, quoted in Skarsaune 2002:229).

[109] By convert, within a Christian context, I am speaking of a person who changes their belief and lifestyle by accepting the reality and supreme power of God in Christ, and are subsequently determined to obey Him (adapted from MacMullen 1984:5). Judge suggests this change was taught in a formal way (Judge 1960a).

[110] The radical nature of this change cannot be over-emphasised, from a pagan to a Christian culture. But it was clearly both attractive and successful, as is seen by the numeric growth in the Early Church and boldness in martyrdom.

[111] This has many similarities to the stage development model I have produced. Its first stage is the person working through issues and damage from their past, which, interestingly, I have noticed, typically takes between 2 to 3 years. See 'My stage development model' (page 138) for an introduction.

[112] The change would be dramatic for both Jew or pagan who chose to follow Christ. (See Skarsaune 2002:354, 229.)

waters of Christianity becoming the official religion of the Roman Empire.[113]

Enter Constantine

It is thought the time of Constantine saw the first major shift away from a personal change discipleship model. From this time, to be a Christian no longer meant one necessarily needed to be a disciple. The two concepts of being Christian and being a disciple began separating. Conversion for many was a political necessity, not so much a personal spiritual and/or moral choice.[114] From Constantine onwards, one could be a 'Christian' without experiencing the rigorous demands of discipleship, when moving out of a pagan culture. Evangelism began separating from change through discipleship, becoming the central thrust of the Church. This emphasis has continued into our times in some traditions. Even during the Middle Ages, although discipleship was still alive, change was no longer the imperative for everyone joining the Church, as it had been in the Early Church period. The Church's own internal culture no longer demanded radical change from its members, unless they joined, say, religious orders.

But other shifts were also taking place. For instance, into the third and fourth centuries the Church began writing its most significant theology, much of it in response to the threat of heresy, so requiring a more systematic way of talking about Christianity. Theology, like the Greek culture of which it was now part, became more and more intellectual/academic. Within the Church we see the beginnings of a movement away from a 'lifestyle Christianity' of personal change out of paganism, toward instead an intellectual maturing of one's beliefs as a cultural distinctive. But as theology matured it had a tendency to separate people from lifestyle change. Conversion was learned rather than experienced. Sapiential experience of union with Christ gave way to the Biblical authority of theology (Stevens 1999:11).[115]

Moving on into the Middle Ages, Aquinas, more than others, helped make theology a speculative science, thereby finally ending the 'agreement' or understanding that theology was in essence practical (Stevens

---

[113] Skarsaune suggests that the womb of Christianity was no longer Judaism, with the arrival of the Greek/Latin Apologists (from 120 CE onwards) (2002:226ff., 231).

[114] Illustrated in Tertullian (190 CE), 'I renounce you, Satan, with all your pomp and splendour', meaning the abandonment of all former religious loyalties and obligations, seeing them as slavery to the devil (Skarsaune 2002:60).

[115] 'By the third or fourth century the Church was failing to hold onto this *mystery* of personally experiencing the therapeutic atoning of Christ's death and resurrection. Instead it was embracing a theology based on Liturgy and formal structures, drawing away from personal encounter' (Regan 1994:31).

1999:13).[116] Put another way, theology became, more than ever before, an academic pursuit that anyone could study, rather than being a spiritual discipline that required a changed life.[117] The study of theology separated from spiritual disciplines, was no longer being supported by discipleship change. Aquinas dissolved Augustine's distinction between knowledge and wisdom, setting subsequent study on a path that allowed academic theology to be objective knowledge, independent of the knower's disposition.[118] Interestingly, this was not the case in Eastern traditions, which as recently as the 19th century held together these two aspects, until it began contacting Western university theology. Instead, theology remained more integrated into lifestyle, linking monastic practice and disciplines with the daily experience of faith (Schmemann 1979:129-144).

But such *phronesis,* the use of theology as practical wisdom, saw its last death-throes here in the West with the Reformers' supernaturalism, which focused on the redemptive power of Christ (Porterfield 2002:233), moving away from experience of relationship with Christ. Salvation became an objective fact that we believed in, rather than a journey of change we learn through. Scripture was exegeted, instead of lived. The learning of *knowledge about God* replaced a *knowing of God*, as the hallmark of Western Christianity.[119] This shift meant it was possible to be a theologian without any need for personal change, Christ-likeness, or the holiness of a life moving toward maturity.[120] Academic life within theology has remained that way ever since.[121]

What I am suggesting is that Christianity over time lost much of its transformative content, seen first in Hebraic tradition, then in the Early Church. In doing so it also lost its advantage in the quest to become more fully human. The potential of offering a transformative *Rapha pneuma-*

---

[116] For a modern review of Aquinas, see Kerr (2002). I would be the first to note Aquinas spent a lot of time thinking about Jewish, Greek and Islamic traditions, pastorally.

[117] The birth in the Early Middle Ages of universities in France and Italy, no longer part of monastic life, helped facilitate this process. Before this, to study theology meant one had to live in community, usually for life, and this required distinct personal change (though not necessarily therapeutically healthy change). Before the 1100s, theology was more tied to life-style and holiness.

[118] Bornkamm remarked that between the 17th-19th centuries both Catholic and Protestant churches were losing hold of faith and healing in the person of Christ, against advancing scientific reductionism (1969:2).

[119] The spiritual intimacy of knowing Christ even became suspect, particularly from the 1750's onward, when the revivals of Whitefield and Wesley only confirmed the establishment's fears about enthusiasm (e.g. affect) being akin to madness (MacDonald 1990:64). For a modern comment on this, linking this enthusiast movement with modern Charismatic Christianity, see Middlemiss (1996:1-31).

[120] For a helpful introduction to the concept of gaining personal maturity by joining holiness with the psychological concept of wholeness, see Steele (1990).

[121] All of the humanities have suffered the same fate, e.g. history, philosophy, literature etc. See Hadot et al. (1995).

psychology to the contemporary world became increasingly unlikely. Somewhat belatedly numerous people are now beginning to note the profound damage done by the absence of placing emphasis on experience and its change. Gelpi, with a Roman Catholic background, saw the need for a 'return to experience' (1994 passim), that seeks an authenticity in Christ. Regan (1994) expressed similar concerns. Jungel proposed that the taking up of humanity into the event of God's being is humanity's salvation, and this has to be experienced, not just learned like mathematics (2001:75). Also, Gerkin noted that in order to function properly clinically any theory of pastoral counselling has got to come to grips with the problem of change (1984:21).

Discipleship as a journey

The watershed for much of this loss was the Reformation, where both Protestants and Catholics were experiencing great change. Commented Byrne, 'Post Reformation Catholic spirituality tended to lose sight of [discipleship as a journey] in its emphasis upon a static ontology of grace.....' (1993:565). Reformed thinking, likewise, saw salvation as a choice of trust or belief, a static once-off, personal, even private justification, requiring little ongoing effort or commitment on the individual's part.[22]

> *That was when my Christian life went down the pan, because there was nothing to do anymore, nothing to find, because you had everything in Christ (M10-4).*

Christianity was increasingly learned rather than experienced, theological rather than therapeutic, requiring a high degree of conformity and compliance in belief and practice, not so much an emphasis on particularity and a journey seeking it out.

Over the centuries, within the Church, we have increasingly seen theology and the teaching of it as the core of Church leadership training. But its teaching, on the whole, was not intended to be at the level of personal change. Instead it was merely the accumulation of more religious knowledge, to be able to talk more accurately and skilfully about God. To be a church leader one needed to be professional, demanding academic training in both theology and the Bible. So congregational life increasingly reflected the weaknesses as well as the strengths of its leadership and their training. Members were required to learn, submit and conform, but were not necessarily required to go on a journey of personal transformation toward Christ-likeness.

Instead, change meant adapting to being part of congregational life, rather than firstly being an apprentice in the presence of the Master.

---

[22] Roger Hurding (1995b) helps redress any extremism I may be proposing, by noting that all five basic types of pastoral care are still seen by many as a journey.

Hierarchy in the Church placed the professional Christian 'closer to God', becoming the main channel to and from God. So for many the experience of Christ increasingly became second-hand, lived vicariously through Scripture, books and others' experience. It could even be argued that in some parts of the Church such personal encounter with Christ was positively discouraged, for it challenged the leadership's powerbase. Church life could become untidy if everyone started hearing from God independently, creating a 'third front' in congregational life. My observation is that the consequential loss of experiencing Christ through a transforming discipleship journey of personal change, has been tragic. But in some ways the more serious loss was that of the personal goal of Christ-likeness.

In the Church's long history, going back to earliest Hebrew traditions, life and wholeness was a journey everyone was expected to experience (e.g. Abraham, Moses, Peter and John etc.). This is clearly seen in Christ's command to 'follow me' (Mt. 8:22, Mk. 2:14, Lk. 5:27, Jn. 21:22). Commented Leech, 'in the New Testament we find a view of spirituality as progress toward maturity' (1986:9). This is also seen in subsequent Christian traditions, in that most spiritual masters and classic authors in the recorded tradition of spirituality, outline a progressive movement (Byrne 1993:569).[123] A typical early example is John of Climacus (c. 570-649), *The Ladder of Divine Ascent* (1982), where he saw Christian faith as a journey, the ideal of holiness, focusing on several of the themes we are noting here. Other classics include Augustine's *Confessions* (1997),[124] and Bunyan's *Pilgrims Progress* (1656/1987).[125]

In a more contemporary vein, spoken articulately, and authored by Lois Dodds, is the story of twelve Christians' personal experience on their 'journey' to maturity, noting particularly the role of the Holy Spirit in this process (1999:129ff.). Similarly, a modern challenge to see change and develop a journey approach is Scripture Union's *Christian life and Today's World: Not conformed, but transformed* (2002), highlighting some of the aspects of contemporary life, where change needs to take place. Other

---

[123] I need to distinguish here between my observation that spirituality in the church is not clinically applied, and my suggestion here that it is a progressive journey. The distinction is that within Christianity we have an emphasis on journeying, of maturing, but not so much on its practical spirituality, therapeutic process or its relational dimension.

[124] For an interesting comment on Augustine's *Confessions*, and the principles we can draw in seeing it as a therapeutic journey, see Sisemore (2001).

[125] Some of the other authors could include Irenaeus of Lyons (c.130- c.200CE), Clement (fl. c.96CE) and Origen (c.185-254), the Cappadocian Gregory of Nyssa (331/40-c.395), The Rule of St. Benedict (480-c.550), Bernard of Clairveaux (1090/1-1153), William of St. Thierry (c.1085-1148), Guigo II (1978), Bonaventure (c.1217-1274), the Spanish School including Ignatius Loyola (1491/5-1556), John of the Cross (1542-91), Teresa of Avila (1515-82) and Therese of Lisieux (1873-97), to name but a few.

modern authors speaking of a journey include Underhill (1936), Pennington (1988), Haughton (1967), Keating (1987) and Benner (see Moon 2002) etc.

The idea of a journey is still present in the Church, though no longer implicit in joining a faith community. This is evidenced in one recent piece of research by the Religious Education Association in the USA, who interviewed 1200 people and 23 religious organizations, seeking to understand relationally the changing dynamics of adulthood, and a person's developing faith. Two out of three persons interviewed believed that faith should change and develop throughout life, although *fewer church members* than non-members held this view (Religious Education Association 1987:Foreword).[126] It would seem being in the Church one is less likely to find a spiritual journey of change.[127] Susan Williams' research indicated that one of the significant factors in CCD was the journey concept, which participants hadn't found in previous church experience.

> *Our journey into maturity in Christ is a journey, and not just an event (W2-1).*
>
> *There is a real emphasis on discipleship [at Christ Church] and on our relationship with Christ being something that grows and develops and it is a journey (W13-2).*

Heelas notes Madeleine Bunting, observing that the Church has moved from the Early Church traditions of spiritual journeying, to an individual life journey with self knowledge replacing knowledge of God as the ultimate objective (Bunting cited in Woodhead and Heelas 2000:471).

Somewhat ironically however, therapeutic psychology has recognised the need for a journey. Claxton noted the idea in the title of his book, *Live and Learn: An introduction to the psychology of growth and change in everyday life* (1984). A more recent contribution is James Fowler's *Faithful Change: The personal and public challenges of postmodern life* (1996a). One of the themes of Fowler's book is a call for a return to a journey approach to maturity.[128] Another obvious modern example is Alcoholics Anonymous, where everyone must go on a journey, initiated by an admission that they are alcohol dependent. Similarly, the Mental Health Foundation's *Taken Seriously: The Somerset Spirituality project* (2002),

---

[126] This blindness to the need for a journey toward mature faith appears more the case in Protestant than Catholic traditions. Let me illustrate: Atkinson and Field (1995) claims to be a modern, 'new', psychologically informed Protestant *Dictionary of Christian Ethics and Pastoral Theology*, containing some 900+ pages, with a whole section on 'Sin and Salvation', but with no entry on journey. This is in marked contrast to its Catholic equivalent, *The New Dictionary of Spirituality* (Downey 1993), where Byrne devoted twelve pages to 'Journey (Growth and development in spiritual life)' (1993). Both reflect their Church cultures. Likewise, Vatican II saw the Church as a 'pilgrim people' (*Gaudium et Spes I*) (Flannery 1988).

[127] This would be especially true in Institutional denominations, where Word and Sacrament (e.g. Lutherans) will normally not promote inner conflict or a desire to change inwardly.

[128] We will be looking at *stage development models* in 'Exploring maturity' (page 100) and 'My stage development model' (page 138).

identifies the 27 interviewees throughout the text as being on a journey, in a chronological and spiritual sense. These, and numerous other illustrations within our Western culture demonstrate that the concept of a journey toward maturity is well-established in society generally, outside the Church.

At least two main outcomes emerge from this. The Church has not on the whole developed therapeutic discipleship models, so in some ways has forfeited its birthright from the Early Church. Instead, psychology has taken up the therapeutic journey idea (albeit mostly devoid of spirituality), which now challenges the Church to learn from it as a way of living. Some would counter this within the Church by arguing there is much evidence in the contemporary Church that many people are doing a journey. But this is not my point. The journey concept, so central to the transformative spirituality being sought by the contemporary un-churched, has not been adapted from the traditions of the Church so that it becomes attractive to contemporary people. So how do our contemporary society, and especially psychological therapies, see the idea of a journey toward maturity?

Exploring maturity

In the context of theology and psychology the concept of journeying has a number of implications which I have needed to explore in trying to build a clinically applicable *Rapha* journey model of therapeutic discipleship.

STAGE DEVELOPMENT THEORY

Psychology has always seen therapeutic change as a journey, one way or another, from the time of Freud onwards.[129] For instance, Freud's *Theory of the Unconscious* stressed the hidden *id,* and the need to know oneself by passing through stages of psychosocial development (1905/1965 passim). Likewise, Jung (1933/1973) saw everyone pushing toward more complex stages of development or individuation, and Erikson, in the field of developmental or ego psychology, also saw everyone moving through stages (1950/1963, 1959/1980, 1968).

Most of the time stage development is associated with the word maturity, with classic texts from Erikson (1997), Allport (1961 passim), Piaget (1926/1956, 1970, 1977), Conger (1973) , and Gilligan (1982/1993), among others. As Benner and Ellens have noted, we are all historical creatures, and can only begin to understand our human condition when we view it through a developmental perspective (1992:251ff.). Therefore, what all of these models have in common is a longitudinal approach to the subject, in most

---

[129] The reductionism of psychology may seem to conflict with the obvious assumption in most psychologies that one is on a journey. I guess it is part of the ambivalence of modern life that even a journey can be 'reductionist'.

cases from birth through to death. In essence they see a complete life cycle, based on the process of maturing through growing up.[130]

> *That is what I always thought, yes, [maturity] is out there, for me it was when I am 60 (W12-9).*

But behind much of this thinking is also the presumption that as we grow older, we also grow wiser and more mature. Few such models include a process for maturing, or ways of plotting this progress. For these reasons, and others, developmental models are not that helpful to me, as many of them do not include a *Rapha* journey, due to a lack of a direct therapeutic dimension.

MATURITY

Like Rahner, I take as given that maturity in Christ is the full blossoming[131] of intellectual, emotional[132] and spiritual virtue in one's life (Rahner 1978b:135), the maturely-developed capacity of one's intellectual, spiritual and emotional self. Rahner, like John the Apostle, treats love (1 Jn. 4:7-10 e.g. *selfless love*)[133] as the key virtue, for you cannot live well if you are not first loving well.[134] Other virtues must follow in our journey of maturation.

This need for a supernatural capacity to love is important in CCD, for it is assumed that as we mature in Christ on this journey we are able to love more spontaneously and consistently.

But another aspect that is important in CCD is the ability to discern what is good and positive, and what is dark and unhelpful in our lives. This is explained in Scripture: 'For everyone who lives on milk, being still an infant, is unskilled in the word of righteousness. But solid food is for the mature, for those whose faculties have been trained by practice to

---

[130] Change does not equal 'development', neither is 'older' the same as 'better', or 'more mature'. Scott Peck sought to combine the best of both worlds with his own four stage model that begins with a selfish chaotic spirituality, through conversion and joining the Church, followed by sceptical individual departure, leaving institutional life and moving into atheism or agnosticism, then finally finding a mystical spiritual path (Peck 1987:186-208). He based this on Fowler (1981).

[131] This hints at the theme of Christian perfectionism, which though I do not deny is mentioned in Scripture (e.g. Heb. 6:1), is something I have steered away from as a concept, on the grounds that it is not defined in measurable terms. A life of love, or the exercising of spiritual gifting can more easily be seen, quantified and tested.

[132] I comment in 'Feeling is healing' (page 144) on my view of emotion, focusing on abreaction or catharsis, both theologically and clinically. The Church is slowly coming around to a modern (and Hebrew) view, that emotion is an ally, not necessarily an enemy of the healing process. See Passons (1975), and more recently Allender and Longman (1994) and Bassett and Hill (1998).

[133] The theme of love is extremely important among Susan Williams' contributors, and is also central to Christian maturity. See, for instance Vanstone (1977/1993) and Newlands (1980).

[134] Many people over the years have asked me why we need to do this journey. My answer is simple. To be fully human one has to be able to love well. This will involve loving oneself, others and God, a precondition to experiencing Trinity (e.g. Jn. 15:22-24). For love comes before the full indwelling of the Trinity. Most people have to let go of a great deal of baggage before they have the capacity to love unconditionally in this way.

distinguish good from evil' (Heb. 5:13-14).[135] On this basis all must *practice*, *train themselves* and seek to *distinguish* whether what they observe is the work of God or evil.[136] Any mature Christian, this passage states, should possess such abilities. Their growing up trains them in this. My response is that these abilities are clearly rare.[137] The passage suggests people can be at ease in both spiritual and material realities, while also being able to discern what is righteous and unrighteous in both their own lives and those of others. The contemporary un-churched people's search for spirituality is clearly seeking some of this type of maturity. But such a definition of maturity is also disturbingly experimental, implying all of us are going to make many mistakes on the way. So what has the Church done with this faith[138] maturity idea that emphasises love, and requires such discernment?

Working within the discipline of psychology, Benson, Donahue and Erickson, have proposed a type of meta-analysis of what *faith maturity* is, noting its complexity and diversity, while themselves proposing a *faith maturity scale* that could be used as the basis of further research (Benson, et al. 1993:23-24). A number of other authors have sought to define maturity and faith maturity, but none has yet proposed, to my knowledge, a clinical process (and relational) model of how to gain this maturity, despite the promise of some titles, e.g. Wiersbe (1978).[139]

In reading literature in this field what has also become evident is the confused use of terms like 'maturity', 'wholeness' and 'faith', and the

---

[135] Within the Church today such matters are seen differently. In a contemporary charismatic meeting someone seen thrashing around the floor in anguish would be seen as demonically distressed, whereas in the times of Wesley, with its more enlightened view of God sometimes being the giver of sickness, they would be seen to be experiencing the deep anguish of sin (Middlemiss 1996:169). A vast body of informative literature awaits us from the 17th and 18th centuries involving some of the finest minds of the day, e.g. Edwards, Locke and Leibniz observing the enthusiast phenomena (Middlemiss 1996:218).

[136] In the next chapter we will be looking in more detail at the issue of both Evil, and the dark side in all of us ('The darkness in all of us, page 120).

[137] For an example of its use, see our book Williams and Holmes (2004:133ff.). One of the numerous concerns expressed by Christians in trying to use such gifting is the possibility of spiritual abuse. For a comments on this danger, see Hunt and McMahon (1985), Johnson and Van Vonderen (1991), and Beasley–Murray (1998), etc.

[138] In this book I will not be defining the term faith, though it should be noted, as Halmos has already, that both spiritual directors and psychotherapists, Christian or otherwise, live by faith, believing in the ultimate capacity for all of us to work through our disorders and thereby mature (1965 passim). This book suggests that maturity in Christ must also produce some of the benefits that are so valued by the contemporary un-churched, that of being capable of living well, and honouring and contributing toward interdependent relationships (Covey 1989).

[139] '*Be mature: How to break the mould of spiritual immaturity, and grow up in Christ*' (1978).

diverse ways they are used.[140] Little consistency seems to exist. Also, I find it disappointing that there should be so many authors within Christianity who have tackled this subject, and how to deal with various problems standing in its path,[141] but with virtually no *process journey* of how to achieve this maturity or its goal, Christ-likeness.[142]

But this fact is hidden below a substantial literature outside the Church, much of it being on the borderlands of psychology, spirituality and comparative religions, seeking to combine faith with maturity, from a psychological perspective.[143] Similarly, a glance at the broad range of Christian titles quickly dispels the fiction that the Church is not addressing this issue of maturity.[144] So although much has and is being written on faith maturity, few seem to be helpful tools in building a *Rapha* model. Seeking to use the concept and define maturity from a psychological perspective has been a dead end for me.

THE FAITH DIMENSION?

Much like Collinson's comments on the term discipleship, it seems to be assumed that in Western Christian culture there is someone out there somewhere who does actually know what these terms 'maturity' and 'faith' really mean, and how this can be achieved. [145] 'As we sort through our ideas about Christian counselling and the Church, as we debate the differences between psychological therapies, spiritual direction, lay counselling, and discipleship, we really should admit that we don't quite know what we're talking about. Neither the goal toward which we're aiming (exactly what

---

[140] Some writers, including Larry Crabb, go even further and argue that Paul and John taught that no-one can see exactly what true maturity looks like (1 Cor. 13:12, 1 Jn. 3:2-3) (1999:4). In this book I want to argue otherwise.

[141] Over the last 20-30 years a plethora of titles have been published on various aspects of this journey, addressing such diverse issues as rape, abortion, forgiveness, emotional, verbal, physical, sexual and spiritual abuse etc., but none draw these together. Also very little of this literature suggests that dealing with such issues is an essential part of Christian discipleship. I am arguing it must become so.

[142] For instance, Benner and Ellens (1992) made the point in the conclusion of their book that they both co-edited with Aden (1992), that their contribution to the science of human development is an *initial* contribution (253). This book is a useful introduction to the subject.

[143] See, for instance, Fowler (1974), Aden (1976), Aden et al., (1992), Groeschel (1992), Wilhoit (1995), Fowler (1996b), Wilber (1999), etc. to name but a few.

[144] Some are Merton (1951, 1961, 1963/1996), Philip (1964/73), Adams (1976), Levinson (1978), Wiersbe (1978), Bright (1982), Haring (1983), Van Kaam (1983), Fowler (1981, 1982), Sanders (1985), Keating (1987), Jacobs (1988), Kao (1988), Conn (1989), Young-Eisendrath (2000), Thomas (2002) etc.

[145] Some would argue working definitions do exist, but none incorporate all aspects of the journey the way I am suggesting.

does it mean to be whole, or be mature?) nor the process of getting there is clearly understood by anyone' (Crabb 1999:3-4).[146]

As we have noted, psychology normally sees maturity as the inevitable consequence of growing up, while within Christianity it does not seem to have one consistent meaning. This problem, coupled with its association with psychology's stage development models, as well as the much abused but still undefined word 'maturity', has forced me to abandon the use of faith development models,[147] and the word 'maturity' and the use of 'faith maturity' as concepts to build a journey on. Such confusion of baggage that comes with these words does not serve the Church well, nor begin to meet the demands of the contemporary un-churched. Susan Williams notes that the therapeutic process of becoming mature is one of the most useful benefits of the CCD model.

> *[I like] the willingness to explain to people how they work, the whole teaching on the human spirit is so – I know the response from the non-churched is that it makes perfect sense, they are hungry to hear it, want to hear it. Now it gives me something to think about, something to work on (M2-3).*

It is this 'hands on', 'how to' aspect that is missing in the Church today. The word I finally turned to in my quest to describe what we are doing at CCD and in the *Rapha* movement, used in both psychology and Christian literature, was the word wholeness.[148]

Wholeness as a concept for change

Human existence is inexhaustibly complex (Cobb 1977), which makes any effort at a definition of human wholeness almost impossible. So in looking at the idea of wholeness it would be helpful to see how psychology and Christianity use the word.

---

[146] Dr Larry Crabb is Professor and Distinguished Scholar in Residence, Colorado Christian University, as well as one of America's leading Christian authors, and a trained psychotherapist. Over the last few years I have watched his journey, from being a conventional writer of counselling books (1975) to a growing conviction of the need for mentors and therapeutic relationships (1997), to a full commitment to the need for therapeutic community (1999).

[147] Not everyone would be pleased with this move. See, for instance, Fuller (1988), who argued that religion is a fundamental part of personal development, and can enrich all stages of one's life. On the positive side he did echo many of Susan Williams' findings, and my own personal experience, but only within the framework of Allport's (1950) seminal work, *The Individual and His Religion: A classic study of the function of religious sentiment in the personality of the individual.*

[148] Not everyone shares my interest in using the term wholeness. See, for instance, Gay (1979). He challenged the psychoanalytic tradition of seeking wholeness as an integration of self from its former fragmentation. '...This ploy is altogether wrong....the ego-syntonic drive towards feelings of wholeness, are functions of the ego's obedience to repetition compulsion' (from Gay's abstract). Pannenberg noted it was Luther who first stated that the power of faith places us outside our old 'self' (1984:99), therefore suggesting a true and false self.

Within psychology it is a term that is implicit in the journey, but one struggles to find even a reference to it in most psychology textbooks. An illustration of this is its complete absence as a concept, or even as a subject, in the recent tome focusing on the clinical aspects of spirituality by the American Psychological Association (Shafranske 1996). Not even the Shorter Oxford English Dictionary has a full reference to it, instead slipping it under the term whole, as a one-liner, 'as a whole, with respect to the whole' (Brown 1993).[149] Likewise, when we move onto the fringes of psychology, for instance into the field of self-help books, the word is only slightly more common.[150] Probably because it is not a keyword in psychology no consistent definition seems to exist, though when applied to human personhood would probably have a core meaning like *to be whole*.

Within Western Christianity some writing does exist using the term or concept of wholeness. But any attempt to define the word would need to include a number of domains,[151] beginning with Scripture. As Popkes (1992) proposed, the Church must recognize God as 'whole', suggesting we also can be. This in turn suggests a process of growth and change in people, bringing to an end selfism and fragmentation. This should lead to numerous qualities, including the fruit of the Spirit (e.g. love), an ability to teach others, a growing ability to hear God's ways and will, know what is righteous and unrighteous, and demonstrate likeness to Christ. Beuchner (1993) proposed that for wholeness to be complete it should also include a capacity to see all reality from God's perspective, while Goldbrunner (1955) defined wholeness as a journey possessing holiness. But Benner reminds us that well-being and wholeness is not the hope or goal of the Kingdom. Union with Christ is (Moon 2002:68). While noting his comment, I would want wholeness and well-being, like maturity, to be an essential part of Christ-likeness. In CCD we do not separate them.

These ideas of what wholeness should be have appeared to me to be far more complementary to a model of personhood based on Christ-likeness, and to discipleship as a journey. But the idea of using the word in this way is not mine. Thinking along similar lines, Roger Hurding has done a great deal of work on the idea of wholeness as a therapeutic journey, from his

---

[149] A search on the PsychInfo database on 27th September 2003 showed only 116 articles referring to wholeness in their subject, compared with 1,440 referring to healing and 4,609 referring to maturity. On the more extensive ISI Web of Science database (incorporating the social sciences, arts and humanities and general sciences) on 23rd March 2004, out of a total of 33,401,199 items stored, only 472 had 'wholeness' in their title, subject or abstract. The comparable figure for 'healing' was 43,449, and for 'maturity' 26,599.

[150] For example, on the website of the Inner Bookshop at {http://www.innerbookshop.com/}, whose description of stock is 'Books for mind, body, spirit, health and the unexplained', there are 69 books with 'wholeness' as the keyword, in comparison with 2044 with healing as the keyword.

[151] For a helpful background article to this section, see Gibson (2000).

early article (1995b) to his more recent book on the subject (1998).[152] Many other Christian authors have also made wholeness a theme,[153] though none to my knowledge the way I am suggesting.

Defining wholeness as I intend to use it

At a personal level wholeness can be seen as either a journey toward a destiny we are seeking to attain, an identity in process, or as an end goal in itself. As a journey, it can describe a bringing together of our inner fragmented selves toward the restoration of full personhood. On this journey we could also be seeking to develop our 'base' or 'quickened' spirituality, engaging with our spiritual selves, or finding deeper meaning for our lives. Wholeness can describe all of these within a *pneuma*-psychology. For others, this journey could mean developing one's IQ, or learning a positive EQ or SQ. For some it will mean making peace with or beginning to enjoy one's gender,[154] a problem for many. Our definition of personhood as body spirit unity requires we seek to achieve this 'wholeness' or oneness, while also offering a completeness that we earlier noted as particularity, or uniqueness. The word wholeness can also acknowledge that we may be young or even immature, but still 'whole' for our age. Behind all of this, at a personal level, will be the challenge to begin loving one's self,[155] and the capacity to love others and God.

At a relational level, since it is relationships that have made us sick, it needs to be relationships that help give us our wholeness. At the heart of this word, then, could be the suggestion that we all need to be more whole, to increase our capacity, to extend our frontiers, in order to be whole. In this sense wholeness is also a journey to become whole in our public selves as well. One aspect of this wholeness journey is that when relationships begin

---

[152] Hurding has also written a helpful introduction to the Bible and counselling (1992), as well as a summary introduction to the domain of pastoral care and psychological therapies (1995b).

[153] Wholeness is a common theme in recent Christian writing. Clinebell is interesting in that he compared the traditional psychotherapeutic 'pathology model' with his own 'growth model' (1979:182ff.), while also acknowledging that 'facilitating wholeness is a shared and reciprocal responsibility' (136). Flory also took the idea of wholeness outside the context of a personal one to one journey, seeking to combine theology from the New Testament with psychotherapeutic practice, with a similar goal and outlook to myself (1983:105). McGarry (1996) proposed a clinical psychotherapeutic model combining many of the features of my own. Other Christian writers focusing on wholeness include Guttmacher (1979), Howe (1980), Haggard (1983), Lambourne (1983), Malony (1983), Huggett (1984), Thompson (1984:7), Maddocks (1986), Booth (1987), Bakken and Hofeller (1988), Kelsey (1989:30ff.), Moseley (1991), Aden et al. (1992), Clinebell (1979/1995), Benner (1998), Kornfeld (1998), Ford (1999), Hindman (2002) etc.

[154] On the question of links between gendered personality development and mature personhood, and some of the current models of pathology, see Kimmel (2004).

[155] I am pleased to see that the need for a healthy self-love is recognised. See Osborne (1976), Bauer et al. (1992), Halling (1994) etc.

to be seen as a positive experience, leading to a greater sense of freedom, the pathology of illness that so isolates us is broken.

Hurt people tend to withdraw and build walls around themselves and those walls need to be demolished (W2-11).

As we achieve this new freedom and its wholeness, it will also help us to re-conceptualize our personal experience, a re-writing of our history, so we can let it go. All of this has to be done in relationship.[156] But as an additional bonus to this effort on our part, we will also find ourselves with the capacity to live at peace with ambiguity, lots of contradictory loose ends, especially in the area of human relationships. For maturity means we accept we will never have all the answers the way we want. This is the experience of many on this journey.

What I am proposing here is that wholeness should be considered much more widely than its use in psychology, biomedicine or health care. Neither is it restricted to a stage development framework.[157] Also, within a Christian context what I am describing is broader than most other definitions, since it includes not only the spiritual aspects of relational maturity, but also a therapeutic dimension.

Earlier in this chapter I suggested that becoming more fully human is moving toward greater Christ-likeness, developing a mature unique personhood, but I would now like to add to this that being like Christ also requires a sustainable level of wholeness. To be Christ-like is to be consistently knowingly enjoying wholeness. At this stage the phrase describing what we are developing here does become a little cumbersome: to be Christ-like is to be experiencing through a therapeutic discipleship journey a mature, unique wholeness in oneself, and in all of one's relationships, spiritual and material.

[Maturity is when] you have the capacity to basically be as Christ-like as possible in whatever situation you are faced with, with whoever you are in contact with (M7-9).

I am proposing that becoming more fully human means being Christ-like. Wholeness in Christ is living more fully as a human, living within God's continual redeeming salugenic creativity, by a therapeutic wholeness discipleship journey. But in coming to the end of this chapter, and before

---

[156] Lambourne argued that 'to be made whole' in the Old Testament sense was the ability to live in harmony with all those who followed Yahweh (1963:103). See 'Maturity plus community as wholeness in Christ' (page 188), where I develop some of these concepts as part of my therapeutic process.

[157] 'But there is no guarantee that the biological development of the human being will bring all of these modes of human functioning into play.... But as spirit grows strong it does not have to continue its tyrannous rule....the full ideal for Christian existence is neither a strong spirit at the expense of wholeness nor wholeness at the expense of spirit, but an inclusive wholeness centering on spirit' (Cobb 1977:28).

we apply this idea clinically, we have one substantial practical roadblock in our path, in the path of anyone who wishes to walk this road this way.

The hurdle of taking personal responsibility

To accept and commit to a wholeness discipleship journey of the type I am describing will require a shift in most people's thinking, because we all now live in a culture where healing people has largely become the responsibility of others.[158] On the whole the therapeutic process is something done to us by others, be it the clinical psychologist, therapist or counsellor.[159] In contrast, in traditional Christianity discipleship is something one works at one's self. However, when one brings in a therapeutic dimension, liability can be seen intuitively shifting onto the shoulders of others.[160] We look to doctors and therapists, and they tell us what to do, because they have the expertise and they therefore become ultimately responsible. So becoming whole in a therapeutic sense is most often something someone else is paid to do to me for me.

[Taking responsibility] was one of the hardest things... I was quite happy giving [others] responsibility so I could give them all the blame (W6-12).

What I am proposing is a radical shift in mindset, both inside and outside the Church. I have suggested that Exodus 15:26 presumes everyone is in need of freedom from the damage of the disease called sin. But I see little evidence that merely having faith in Christ removes this sin and its damage.[161] So what I am suggesting is that we all need to stop looking to others, blaming everyone else for our damage and sicknesses, regardless of their nature. Experience has taught me that this shift is essential, and material to the success or failure of any discipleship journey. Behind this belief and practice is a trust in what God is doing in the individual, and His ability, whether we are Christian or not, to empower us for this change. Here in CCD we take responsibility to teach others how to do the journey, but it is they who accept personal responsibility for their own journey. We believe and experience the initiative of God taking every opportunity to

---

[158] For a modern comment on responsibility see Cole (1995). More dated, but still helpful, see Niebuhr (1978) and Jonas (1984).

[159] Likewise, within the Charismatic tradition of the Church, a person may be encouraged to relax, open their hands to receive from God but do nothing more, while they are prayed for by others. They are not to strive, but to accept passively from the Lord or from the prayers (Middlemiss 1996:245).

[160] This is always interesting to see in our community, especially to newcomers with a user background in the health care services. One newcomer asked one of the leadership team, 'which ones are the doctors and nurses?', as she expected white coats and uniforms. It was politely explained to her that in our community, with the Lord help, she is the doctor and nurse.

[161] Theologically after choosing Christ I see our sin being 'covered' by Atonement, but its permanent removal as if its symptoms are gone forever requires either our death or our ongoing confession.

teach them, once the person has given Him permission to 'meddle' in their lives.

I still struggle with the reality that God's perspective is so different to mine. Much of the time God surprises me with what He says and how He sees things. More often than not when He says nice things and doesn't condemn me for my sin but shows me the way out of it, and towards Him (04F-6.13).

In giving responsibility for our disorders to others, we deny ourselves the gift and opportunity to advance (May 1963 passim). Therefore, in adopting the concept of wholeness in this way, I am proposing it is something we must do *for* ourselves *to* ourselves, not have others do to or for us. No one, not even God, can ultimately take away from us the whole of our personal responsibility for ourselves: our health, well-being, relationships and wholeness. No one else can acquire our wholeness vicariously for us (e.g., Jn. 1:12-13, Phil. 2:12-15, 1 Thes. 2:13 etc.). Not even Christ can take upon Himself all that is mine, until I first choose to take upon myself all that is mine.

I see this unwillingness to emphasise personal responsibility as one of the great failures of psychological therapies, especially within the Church and the human potential movement, by implying others (e.g. therapists) can give us healing and wholeness. As I will be noting in the last chapter, I see passivity as one of the diseases of both our society[162] and the Church.[163] Our Western culture,[164] the Church included, is now saturated with the 'helping professions'[165] mindset (Chriss 1999:3ff.).[166]

Instead, for CCD, and those following a *Rapha* journey, wholeness is something we personally take responsibility for, to live and experience. It is

---

[162] [In a USA context] 'The mental health movement has turned us into a nation of victims. If we aren't victimized by abusive parents or spouses, we are victims of cognitive impairment, attention deficit, economic plight, guilt inducing religion, or subtle discrimination of people like us' (Boyd 1996:50).

[163] Furedi (2002) offers some disturbing observations here in UK of the subtle but persuasive growth of this 'health' culture and its passivity, observing that work is seen as stressful, examinations and competition as 'child abuse', and all decision-making as a possible health hazard.

[164] Our whole culture is now characterised by what Herbert Hoover famously called 'rugged individualism' (cited in Gorman 1993:70). For a reader on individualism, see Lukes (1973).

[165] My own observation is that psychological therapies can at times actually promote feelings of helplessness, victimisation and dependency.

[166] Chriss (1999) is a particularly interesting book, as it exposes in a multi-disciplinary way, some of the concerns in educating our culture toward a psychotherapeutic world-view. We now 'assume counselling is the appropriate avenue for ameliorating all sorts of disturbances in people's lives' (iix). From a slightly different perspective, arguing that we have fabricated fragmentation by our 'enlightened' culture, but are now moving toward a 'holistic' way of thinking, see Miles (1996). Some are now beginning to call for reconstruction. For instance, Johnson and Sandage (1999) suggested that postmodernism, having aided the demise of grand narratives like religion, now needs to put counselling in a wider context or story than the one-to-one therapist-client relationship. Psychological therapy needs to respond to the vacuum the failure of religion has created.

not vicarious, instead it is us learning to acquire a completeness of personality that is flexible, able to live life carrying a heavy load with a light touch and a well-rounded integrity. It is our living well, having found a fullness in our self with others and with God, who is Himself the only wholeness any one of us will ever truly know. Wholeness becomes a matter of right thinking, right feeling and right living. A journey. Wholeness will never mean being fully complete or perfect, but will always give us the capacity to live fully, while living Christ.

> *If you are on the journey, you are more mature that you have ever been and less mature that you should be (M4-9).*

In God, this wholeness can continue to be tested, while also being drawn upon. It can never be diminished, for it is found in Christ, through the help of Trinity (e.g. Ex. 15:26). Anything less than God Himself cannot be this wholeness, or give us fullness of humanity. But the *Rapha* journey and its salugenic discipleship can only begin as we take responsibility for who we now are. With Christ as our wholeness, we are able to become *imago Dei*, for ourselves, others and Him. I now turn to how this process actually works in CCD and *Rapha*.[167]

---

[167] A note of caution. I have been concerned about the practice of unjustified certainty in the Evangelical tradition, so would not want to imply that because a thing works it is valid, nor that because it is successful it is true and its theory valid. Instead, I would prefer to see anything that works as neutrally valid, thereby seeking to avoid building up rules for everyone from any one person's experience. Fluidity is essential. One illustration of this in practice is that in CCD we refuse to write down a list of the social rules, as they are changing all the time. 'In epistemological terms …there are no grounds yet discovered which would justify a claim to know about absolute truth' (Middlemiss 1996:210).

Chapter 4

Some of the processes of salugenic discipleship

Seeking a way forward for the Church

I was so ill before arriving in Deal, I had ceased to function even on a basic level, e.g. washing, dressing (10F-2.6)... Having done lots of homework [I am] now finding a level of peace and having a purpose and goal for my life (2.7)... I don't feel so anxious any more, also I don't feel so tired, heavy, drained and lethargic. I have more energy (2.10) ... People have told me that the change they have seen in me is a miracle (2.12).

Setting the landscape for my therapeutic process

What we have noted so far is that the upsurge of interest in spirituality, alongside the increasing interest in self-help therapy, could allow the Church, if it wished, to re-focus on both a Christ-centred *Rapha* wholeness, as well as develop models of personhood that included human spirit (Steinhoffsmith 1995:148ff.). This chapter outlines some aspects of this model, developed first by me, then within the social process of CCD.[1]

We have already noted that spirituality is on the map outside the Church. Commented Lonergan 'the spiritual dimension cannot be ignored, for it is what makes us human' (1967, cited in Frankl 1965/1973:9). Puntel, likewise, took up a similar theme, 'Being can be understood only in the spirit.... man is only what he is by being thus "greater than himself"' (1970:143). Whitlock, also from a Christian perspective, brings these themes together: 'The primary function of the Church in the area of psychology of religion is not to concern itself with the psychological services which will provide self-understanding. The primary vocation of the Church is to understand the nature of the person in relationship to both God and his fellow, as well as his relationship to himself' (1960:13).

But other forces besides the lack of pneumatic or therapeutic models of personhood, also divide Church from society. Over the last 100 years especially, we have seen a separating of the Church from most forms of human healing. Although modern psychological therapies have not been able to heal all those who have come to them (Engel 1977:134, Pattison 1989:113, Pilgrim and Rogers 1993:250), neither has the Church. So at a

---

[1] However, I would not want to give the impression that in our emphasis in CCD on therapeutic process we have abandoned more traditional forms of Christian disciplines, like prayer, meditation, Scripture reading, exegesis, fasting, service and worship etc.

time when it needs distinctives more than ever, the Church has forfeited much of its unique wholeness/healing role (Atkinson 1993:29).[2]

Because this person has so much troubles, I can't bring them into the church I was going to because they won't know what to do with them (M10-2).

In the UK much of this health care responsibility is now in the hands of the state. The UK National Health Service (NHS) now makes statutory provision for psychiatry and counselling, while voluntary agencies' support is often focused around specific issues. General Practitioner (GP) services, subject to Primary Health Care Trusts, can also offer a range of therapeutic alternatives. But psychological therapies are currently dominated within the NHS by Cognitive Behavioural Therapy (CBT) and its spin-offs, like Cognitive Analytic Therapy (CAT) (Ryle 1995a). This is because these psychological therapies, usually through short course one issue programmes (e.g. 6-12 sessions), lend themselves more easily than others to the 'evidence-based' practice now dominant in the NHS.[3] Therapists are required to prove positive results. There are significant time pressures, with many clients not getting therapeutic help, while those that do are more likely to be taught to 'manage' their disorders than become free from them. Therefore, the 21st century sees many people with mental and emotional illness either taking medication to 'manage' their disorders, or going without any treatment, hoping time will heal. Some do explore allopathic alternatives, and increasing numbers find their way into a range of private counselling, though few would look toward the Church for help unless they were already members.

This separation of health care from the Church is now almost complete. James Barr noted 'In general, Biblical scholars have not gone in a psychological direction in their scholarship. And someday there is going to be a terrible price that will have to be paid for that failure' (quoted in Boyd 1996:111). This is one of the reasons, no doubt, why we have seen so few initiatives toward a *Rapha* approach to wholeness. Instead, within the Church, psychological therapies and becoming Christ-like are seen as two different worlds. I now realise this is one of the main reasons why I chose not to study psychological therapies before 1997, instead focusing more on Scripture and its discipleship journey, alongside traditional pastoral practices like prayer, meditation and confession. It was not that I disliked or distrusted therapeutic process, but rather that I wanted to help people on their journey toward wholeness in Christ, not necessarily break self-harming cycles of emotional illness. Naively, because of this cultural bifurcation in the Church, I believed for a number of years that therapeutic process outside Scripture and the traditions of the Church had little to offer

---

[2]   In 'Rediscovering a relevant Church' (page 232) I explore some aspects of the contribution of pastoral care and its theology.

[3]   Some are even suggesting we adopt this in a pastoral setting (Stone 2001).

me. But I also I believed, and still do, that hearing Christ speak to us about ourselves is preferable to any therapist.

However, as I began studying modern psychological therapies academically, to better understand the location of the therapeutic discipleship process I was using, I began noting two key things. First, that I had already absorbed some of what 'secular' psychological therapies taught, (e.g. the Freudian concept of a human unconscious, or Janov's revival of therapeutic interest in catharsis (1970, 1972/1975) etc. But I also began to note, secondly, that many of the principles and concepts I was using were in fact already well known in psychology's therapies, e.g. cognitive dissonance, dream interpretation etc. These observations caused a profound shift in me, illustrating to me that human nature was the same, whether seen from Scripture, the Church or outside the Church. We are all in the same place, with the same deep human needs. But this also prepared the ground for me to understand better the contemporary search for spirituality, helping me see that contemporary people are on a similar spiritual journey. In addition, as Creator, God has given human nature a journeying instinct, seeking out the knowledge we need to be more than we are. I began to see that all such knowledge, regardless of origin, is God's knowledge.

So I borrowed what I needed from psychology, while maintaining *functional control* of its practice through the guidance of Scripture. My borrowing from psychology[4] is not because of inadequacy of Scripture, but to honour people seeking help by offering them best practice and the most effective clinical method. This is not something in which Scripture claims to have expertise. In this I am speaking in contemporary language about the timeless promises of knowing Christ.

However, it has also become clear to me that the therapeutic wholeness discipleship model in CCD and *Rapha* offers a distinct Christ-centred alternative to traditional psychological therapies. There are several reasons for this. Many in therapeutic schools would resist what I am proposing and practise. For instance, human spiritual nature is not widely recognised,[5] and

---

[4] On this long journey finding my place I have now come to see psychology as a servant, not a rival to Scripture or my Christian integrity. The 'them and us' mindset of some Biblical schools, birthed initially in the 1960s by Jay Adams, has been a constant cause of concern to me. I would prefer a rapprochement of mutual honour, along the lines of Hurding (1992, 1998). For the integration approach, see Collins (1972/1975, 1988) or Jones (1996). Adams' seminal works (1970, 1973, 1974) are outside this tradition, alongside MacArthur and Mack who would label my model as 'foolish or wicked', by not believing Scripture is intrinsically adequate on its own for the task (1994:89).

[5] Most current models of psychology, even phenomenological traditions, fall short by denying human spirit (Norris Clarke 1993:5). Some have sought to correct this by arguing they are the same (Helminiak 1986, 1996:6ff., following Lonergan 1957). 'There has also been a rather comical effort to find a part of the brain that could be identified as the "seat of the soul"....this anatomical figment

the principle aim of psychological therapies is still recovery, not necessarily a new wholeness. There is also a substantial reliance on medication that in certain cases can permit denial and control of emotion. Also, power in a one-to-one therapeutic relationship usually rests with the therapist,[6] whereas in CCD's therapeutic community model all can potentially become skilled helpers to each other.[7] Finally, in psychology a wide range of models of human make-up exist, many denying holism. These, along with numerous other differences, have led me to accept that what I am proposing must live separately, but alongside traditional psychological therapies.

Although my model is synthetic, I have also sought to make it plastic enough to adapt to personal need,[8] regardless of damage and how people perceive themselves. This, I believe, is essential to any Christ-centred model, since every person is unique and begins their journey from a different place. Also, every human act draws on how we perceive ourselves, and this is particularly true in the field of healing where one's model of personhood dictates both the client's and therapist's approach. In addition, like Faber, I have many years of evidence that within all of us, waiting to be called out by hope, is an inherent power to regain health and personal wholeness (1988:39). This capacity I partly equate with human spirit and the help of Christ. Finally, the Church needs God's *Rapha* view on our disorders rather than the therapist's, regardless of how skilled they might be.[9]

So in bringing these elements together, we have the beginnings of both a distinct *pneuma*-psychology of human make-up, and the clinical journey that we all need to make to change towards becoming like Christ. My own observation is that without such distinctives, like the *Rapha* promise, the

---

has not been discovered' (May 1982a:23). It has even been proposed there is a 'God spot' in the brain (Begley 2001).

[6] The issue of power within the therapeutic relationship has been addressed over the last decade by its focus on issues of difference and equal opportunities (e.g. Gugenbuhl-Craig 1985).

[7] I am suggesting that the Church, as it takes responsibility in this way, has much to offer psychological therapies, not least the 'lay' movement of those within the Church who, though not qualified as therapists, love people enough to give them their time and seek to help them. For a comment on this, see Collins (1987) and Ganje-Fling and McCarthy (1991). Conflict over who is the best healer, professional or lay person, is an interesting one. For a recent summary of this debate see Crabb (1997 appendix 1). On the downside of professional training one should note Crabb's comment: 'I sometimes think five years of graduate school trained me to shrink the questions people ask down to a size I can handle' (1997:24). For the view that lay counselling has a key contribution to make, see Tan (1994).

[8] Every person is first loyal to their own needs, and all human perspective begins from a place of loyalty to one's self. I have found the accepting of this focus essential, for everyone begins this journey as we offer it at CCD and in *Rapha* from selfish, sometimes desperate motives.

[9] The perceived advantage of God being involved in the process is a source of some debate. I find it a positive gain. See Houston et al. (1999) for a summary of some of these benefits. In saying this I do not dismiss Susan Williams' and my own role teaching diagnostics, though even this is done more and more by mentors.

support of Christ, and body spirit unity in personhood, one struggles to find good reasons for being Christian[10] rather than just being spiritual.

I have got to have the reason [to come to church] and [Christ Church] is what provided the reason. If the men and women of the church didn't provide me with a reason to pursue that faith even further, then I would have given up and I would have nothing to say about this church. It wouldn't have just been this church I would have walked away from every church (M9-4).

The Church needs such distinctive models if it is to respond to the 'must fit me' culture we are now all part of, for they are personally empowering, ideal for our psychologically informed generation, and offers the hope of the change many are seeking. Where a model of personhood incorporates human spirit, such a journey of wholeness also offers the potential of the 'working model' incorporated in Martsolf and Mickley's description of spirituality. Finally, the journey of wholeness we are clinically practising makes change a process rather than an event, incorporating the Hebrew becoming, rather than the Greek ontology of being.

To my knowledge no such model has yet been proposed outside Scripture, *alongside* yet distinct from psychological therapies.[11] Contemporary people are seeking to be fully human by living, as Robb describes, on the frontier of matter and spirit, time and eternity, to journey through matter toward a fulfilment beyond matter (1974:51ff.). The Church is well placed to offer such a distinctive alternative to people. But I have struggled with a way of describing this journey, choosing to use the term 'soul care', mirroring as it does a holistic view of the process.[12] Let me outline some of the distinctives in the model as we have developed it so far.

---

[10] I am not discounting the role of the Holy Spirit in calling people to Christ, merely emphasising the finality of the human will.

[11] Having said this, several aspects of solution-focused brief psychological therapy echo mine (de Shazer 1979, O'Connell 1998). For instance, brief therapy requires the person be willing to change (O'Connell 1998:3). Brief pastoral counselling also has similarities (Stone 1994, 2001).

[12] My reason is that the term pastoral care brings with it more theological historic baggage. Along with Benner I see soul care as personal support and restoration of our spiritual and physical well-being, in its depth and totality; a healing, sustaining, reconciling and guiding, sometimes called soul shepherding (1998:23). Put another way, by the Jungian Goldbrunner, soul care is the encouragement of the incarnation of divine life in us so we can participate in divine nature (1966:19). It is a therapeutic spirituality flowing from relationship to Christ, requiring that pastoral office point towards a therapeutic relationship with Christ (Oden 1989:7). Bruner spoke of this truth as encounter, the Word of the Thou which opens the self-enclosed self (1990 passim). However, I will continue to refer to pastoral care as a term, because I am addressing some of the current problems I have with its character and practice.

The importance of 'mystery' of Christ

In essence, what I am proposing is that the Church must now dig deep for a recovery of the healing mystery[13] of relationship with Christ, at a time that the modern world, epitomised in the sciences, seeks elimination of such mystery.[14] A number of factors in the 20th century contributed to the loss of mystery in our culture, even though Aristotle left us a semi-biological, semi-mystical model of human make-up, whereby stellar energies are involved in human coition (Clark 1975:205). But human spirituality remained ill-defined, so even Aristotle's slight hope has been abandoned in modern times, giving way in the view of many, to the Freudian *unconscious,*[15] the inner world now claimed as the domain of psychology and its therapies. The analytic process has been eliminating the mystery of our spirituality and our meeting God.

Although the New Testament emphasises the mystery of union with Christ (Col. 1:27), and its therapeutic gain (1 Pet. 2:24), by Medieval times the Church saw conformity to Jesus Christ's love as active and contemplative (Raitt 1988), rather than the engaging of such mystery.[16] Likewise, the Reformers viewed relationship with Christ as surrender to Him, and the goal as one's interior (private) spiritual development (Wolski Conn and Conn 1990:12, Calvin 1960:Cover Page, Teresa of Avila 1958). Communal *imago Dei* was no longer central in the way it had been. Throughout Church history the mystery of Christ has survived one way or the other, especially through the mystics themselves, but it has become less associated with personal transformation, and the *Rapha* and Christ-centred wholeness principle. Instead, it has focused on specific types of human experience, most often devoid of a therapeutic dimension.

---

[13] The word mystery is used in numerous ways within Christianity. See, for instance, Tuggy (2003:175ff.). Like many New Testament concepts, mystery has a Semitic background. See Brown (1968 passim).

[14] I am not tabling an either/or, mystery or science position. Instead, I see the need to live the mystery of knowing Christ, while appropriating all the knowledge to achieve this through modern ideas and clinical practice, much the way the Church has in the past (e.g. the medical missionary movement).

[15] Sinnot (1955) suggested this is a force called 'biological purpose' or 'entelechy', underlying the activity of all protoplasmic forms. He sees this same force behind human motivation and purpose. But instead of a biotic process there is in human make-up human spirit, our human principal of self-organisation, which by its action brings spirit out of matter, which is considered by Sinnot an aspect of God. 'They may say that the concept of the body as a mechanism, operating by known laws of physics and chemistry, is the only one a biologist can profitably use. The "psychical" aspects of this mechanism is something that can be studied as process and behaviour, but such inner feelings and experiences as it has, and especially its sense of purpose, are facts beyond the competence of science' (1955:171). For a more recent comment on the same theme, see Trevarthen (1993).

[16] I am speaking here of something much wider than the apophatic tradition, suggesting instead that for all of us this loss of mystery of knowing Christ is greater than the knowledge of God gained through negation.

It is therefore not surprising that the twentieth century Protestant theological hermeneutic has proved unable to recover a *knowing* of Christ beyond an emphasis on loving relationship, and a fidelity to one's personal call and gifts (Wolski Conn and Conn 1990:6).[17] Today some believe we are seeing a restoration of the mystery of spirituality or spiritual direction within the Church, and its affective renewal may be underway in some parts of the Church (Barnes 1990:30, Schneiders 1986:253-274), especially since Vatican II. But on the whole this has not translated into models of salugenic change by a deep corporate knowing of Christ.

Other complications have not helped. For instance the field of Christian metaphysics,[18] Owen suggests, is itself in chaos (1963:1ff), making it difficult to say 'what the Church believes', especially in the field of psycho-pneumatics (Noffke 1993:908-910). This, along with numerous other failures, has helped deprive the Church of its possibility of being clearly distinctive. But one specific further loss needs to be reversed if the Church is to begin offering a distinct therapeutic model for contemporary people.

Recovering a lost language

Language is one of the ways identity is formed.[19] So helping damaged people towards a therapeutic knowing of Christ is one of the distinctives of this journey, as is the importance of the language used. Sadly, as the Church has become more psychologically informed, it has also largely abandoned traditional pastoral terms describing human nature and its condition. The use of such 'old fashioned' language, I am told, is offensive to contemporary people. Susan Williams' research however, suggests this is not the case.[20]

[Homework] is cleaning yourself from sin and taking hold of the things that we have discussed, maturity (M10). Growing up (M3) acknowledging sin really... It

---

[17] Some argue the final shift that drew Protestantism away from Christ as healer and under the new science of therapeutic psychology, was probably in 1905. Elwood Worcester and Samuel McComb, with a group of Episcopalians at Emmanuel Church in Boston, birthed the pastoral counselling movement, embracing the new science of psychological therapies (Brooks Hollifield 1983:201).

[18] Bertrand Russell contended that philosophy died with Aristotle and was not resurrected until the 17th century (1946/1979:173). The reluctance in much philosophy to recognize the role of philosophy of religion and its metaphysics has kept it off most agendas. Some suggest spirituality is a modern word for the field of metaphysics, traditionally defined as the study of features of ultimate reality. (See for instance Norris Clarke 1994, or Honderich 1995:556ff.) The full blossoming of the study of metaphysics began in the early Middle Ages through Scholastic philosophy and theology (Kenny 1972). Outside the Church it is still very much alive as seen in Loux's (2001) two volumes, *Metaphysics: A contemporary introduction*. However, today it seems disconnected from the numerous contemporary spirituality movements.

[19] The field of how language shapes our identity is substantial. See for instance Wood (1992).

[20] I am aware one cannot make such claims from a single case study, but at this stage of the book I need to note this point in building my case.

is quite humbling to admit sin to yourself, to admit that you are where you are (M14-11).

In fact, such terminology is welcomed as a way of 'being more real'. As an example, I have already noted one of the most contentious of these terms, sin. Other terms are avarice, pride, idolatry, hate, contrition, repentance, suffering, sacrifice, arrogance, and eternal hope (Erikson 1968 passim). Each is pregnant with a rich Christian tradition and its theology, carrying a view of human nature that I believe is key to both *Rapha* healing and wholeness for the contemporary un-churched.

Take for instance pride, or arrogance, which psychology recognises as a *self-serving bias* (Gleitman 1995:436ff.). Another is unrighteous hate, which is considered a pathology (758). They are not considered within psychology as 'roots' or primary drives themselves. In fact, psychology will often see them merely as symptoms within the *Diagnostic and Statistical Manual* diagnoses (DSM) (First 1995), rather than as the sin CCD would see it to be.[21] Similarly, in soul care such qualities, often described emotively, are attributive primary *drives* that fragment our lives and poison our whole nature if they are not removed by Christ (Tit. 1:1). They are the energies or underlying pathologies that are part of our nature, but largely hidden to us.[22]

Baggage was a driving force behind my state of mind, it wasn't so much weakness, it was unrighteous. It was more my state of mind in my sin would be unrighteous (M9-9).

Modern psychology recognises stubborn pride as a problem, even in the youngest of us, but it does not see it as *sin* (Festinger and Carlsmith 1959, Aronson and Carlsmith 1963), the way God describes it (Pr. 8:13). From a Hebrew perspective pride blinds our judgement, so allowing us, in our arrogance, to refuse to change. These hidden contrary drives, described as sin, arrogance and lust, are at least in part woven into the fabric of our

---

[21] For the definition of sin often used in CCD, see 'Seeing sin as a refusal to change' (page 127).

[22] The term 'drive' in its earliest form probably comes from the Greek concept of 'entelechy': 'a striving force inherent in the essence of all things' (Ganoczy 1964:208-209). The first use in psychology was probably Freud, but his daughter developed the idea in her *Theory of Instinctual Drives* (1953). The German *Trieb* when used by Freud is translated *drive* (Bettelheim 1982:103ff.), describing an inner propulsion, a basic urge, an impulse. Some drives are good, some toxic to us. I now use the term slightly differently, to describe not just the libido energies, but all those psychic and spiritual energies that are our nature. Unhelpful drives are formed by the toxic build-up of human experience and emotion that accumulates in all of us over the years. (See Lampel-de Groot 1985.) For a survey of the Freudian development of these ideas see Bibring (1941) or Bateman and Holmes (1995). For an overview of drives related to the self and ego, in a psycho-analytic context, see Kernberg (1982:893-917). I teach that these drives or energies are one of the principal causes of much psycho-physiological disorder. For a modern discussion of drives as spiritual energy, see Goddard (1995). For the concept that 'the radical drive of the human spirit for self-transcendence unifies every dimension of the developing person', see Conn (1994).

nature, even into our spirit (Gal. 5:17, 2 Cor. 4:16). A traditional psychologically-driven approach however, will not confront such disorder in the direct way Christ wishes to (Jn. 5:14; 8:34 etc.).[23]

Instead, modern psychology examines us not as God sees us, but as others or we ourselves see us. Therefore sin has been largely replaced by pathology, forgiveness by insight, grace with unconditional acceptance, sanctification with growth, and holiness and its wholeness with healing (Barnes 1990:35, Benner 1998:221). Psychological therapies see sickness in some of us. God sees spiritual disease in all of us, requiring everyone to focus on Christ's view of our disorders and seeing the continuing presence of such disease as sin. Consequently, my goal is not to return someone to their normal level of 'healing', as Freud and others strive for (Vitz 1977/1994:124), but instead to seek transformation into Christ, a begetting of wholeness of personhood.

Within CCD every person, as part of their therapeutic discipleship journey, will need to acknowledge personal complicity in this *autogenic* (self-engendered sin/sickness) process (Adams 1970:29-31), and its subsequent toll in their lives.[24]

We are all damaged and we admit and discover how damaged we really are (M6-5).

Susan Williams' participants found it a relief to admit *'we are all sick'*. While it is true everyone is a victim of external forces, most of us will discover over time that from God's perspective we, rather than others, have brought most of the disorder into our own lives. We are our enemy, we need no other. This reverses the typical therapeutic scenario where the client normally blames everyone else, and looks to the therapist (or God) for 'healing'. By adopting traditional pastoral language one allows the person to admit that sickness occurs in part at least because they remain unaware of their true motivation and fears (Davison and Neale 1998:494).

---

[23] I am aware it may sound as though I am speaking in moral terms about psychological therapies, for instance in speaking emotively about unrighteous hate. One of the areas of greatest distinctiveness I have noted over the years between a Biblical and non-Christian approach to psychological therapies are the moral aspects. See, for instance, Kugelmann (1997), and Vitz and Mango (1997), who all look at different aspects of the moral issues raised. On the issue of whether it is possible for psychological therapies to discover moral norms, see DuBois (1997:101-128). Lambourne argued, when speaking of the pastoral counselling movement, that through it a 'new soteriology was born, which in truth does not have the authority of the natural sciences, but which can still scorn ethics, philosophy and theology because it claims to belong to the field of clinical practice' (1983:139). Such movements, he suggested, reduce Christology to anthropology' (150).

[24] It is interesting to watch some people discover this early in their journey, while others will deal with many issues before facing this personal responsibility.

My experience is that the use of an appropriate language, telling-it-like-it-is, is essential.[25]

> *People are real about how they feel. We could try anything. Every week it was changing. Freedom to do what you want (02F-4.4).*
> *You can be honest about how you really are and people still care about you anyway (W6-1).*

It is my personal observation that the greater the level of sickness we admit to, the greater the potential we have for wholeness. So in losing the language that allows people to own their sickness by being real about their condition, we actually steal from them the possibility of *Rapha* wholeness. This loss of a distinct language, I believe, is partly why the Church no longer finds its place in fields like the philosophy of language, or sociology, because it no longer insists on using its own distinct language to describe honestly its view of the human condition.[26] At various stages in this chapter I will be using some of these terms, seeking to recover some of their meaning, while also investing deeper contemporary meaning into some of these words.

The darkness in all of us

Before the Church can offer an appropriate language to describe human nature and its condition, it must first be clear about its view of human nature. I have already suggested adopting a model of body spirit unity as the foundation of personhood, but there is another strategic contribution the Church can offer once it recovers its lost language. Our view of ourselves determines our attitude to ourselves. Likewise, our sense of how responsible we are for our condition determines how we feel about remedying it, and about whether that remedy is our own or another's responsibility.

> *One of the things for me is to realize that when people back away from me, it is not because of them but because of me. So the majority of what happens around me – it is personal responsibility again – is because of what I am, my wall, my barriers, whatever, rather than what other people are doing (W5-12).*

Also, our view of our own nature will guide our view of God's part in our condition. How much is *He* responsible? Unless the Church gets the foundation of human personhood right, I would suggest, it will be unable to grasp that everyone needs to do a journey toward wholeness. Is human nature mostly good, or basically evil at its core?

---

[25] In his 'grounded therapy' Simmons has noted the importance of 'grounding the operative side of therapy in the client's everyday life, values, interpretations, understandings and meaning systems' (1994:24).

[26] Numerous other reasons exist, including a weakening of traditional language through familiarity of ritual and liturgy.

Like Via I have come to the conclusion that human nature is in a permanent place of self-deception,[27] whereby we conceal the real narrative about ourselves with a 'cover story' which we choose to let others believe, while we ourselves only half believe (1990:32). For most of us, the blind arrogance of our nature is to think outwardly more highly of ourselves than we should (e.g. Rom. 12:3), while denying the true darkness in all of us, described in Scripture as evil (Gn. 3:1-4, Je. 2:10-13; 17:1,9-10).[28] This distinction is likely to break down as we become emotionally or mentally ill, to a place where we may see ourselves as dark, sick and useless.

I think when I first came to CC I had so closed down to how I felt I didn't feel anything towards anybody, myself or God. I knew underneath that what I thought and felt was not nice. So I think the change for me has been to acknowledge how I really feel, with all its messiness, see the sin of it and repent and let it go. It is a huge relief to be in a place where you are allowed to say how you feel and you don't have to put on a nice smile on top of it all (04F-6.25).

The term Evil is used intentionally by Lee and myself. He notes that in Hebraic thought Evil occurs when we choose to live in disharmony with the processes of change in our lives (Lee 1979:63).

[Healing is] discovering that a big part of you doesn't want to change (W1-10).

My own pastoral experience persuades me of the existence of some-one or some-thing greater than personal sin, negatively exploiting and enlarging our disorders, while also being beyond them. This I term Evil. Yet in my counselling practice I also find myself veering conceptually away from personal Evil toward the more traditional Catholic view that Evil is a force rather than a person, since clinically, within us, we all have a dark side to

---

[27] Via's work (1990) contrasts Paul and Matthew's view of wholeness, and so goes beyond my own use of his work in this section. He used the two New Testament authors to demonstrate there is more than one way to be self-deceived (137). My main reservation with Via is that he does not take the idea of wholeness far enough. Salvation for Via, like for so many Christian authors, remains a personal experience with no corporate dimension.

[28] This is a far more complex matter than I might appear to be suggesting. Within the Church there is little consensus on the current condition of human nature. Being 'totally depraved', as in Reformed theology, brings little hope, while the 'new man' theology of modern Pentecostalism argues that once we are 'in Christ', every aspect of our old life is gone. We are a 'new creation'. According to this view, every time we are sick it is assumed we either lack faith to remove the sickness, or are not yet 'converted'. With a proliferation of such theologies it is understandable why the un-churched find Christianity confusing, and even offensive. To experience God's grace, any understanding of our dark side must be set alongside a redemptive hope that can be experienced, and is tangible.

our nature[29] that cannot be directly credited to a personal Satan or his angels.[30] What I am saying is that I find both helpful.

Paul, like many others, recognised we all have an evil or dark side to our nature (Ross 1997:103).[31] He suggested we all need to positively change, exposing our own hidden/unconscious self, its sin(s) and disorder (1 Cor. 14:33, Jas. 3:16). Our lifestyle of self-deceit is, I believe, a violation of God's intended humanness for us all. In this sense, I am suggesting that part of our own nature resists our becoming more fully human. This combination of self-deceit, our gravitation towards the darkness within us, as well as our ignorance of our true nature, means much of the time we are more likely to harm ourselves, making the wrong decisions and actions, than to do ourselves good. It is not until much later in our journey that we often see exactly what we have done.

The reality of the presence of this dark side, what Jung called 'the shadow' (Greene 1988:167ff.), needs to be at the core of any model of human make-up, and any concept of wholeness.[32] The mystery of our own spirituality, both its righteous and dark side, together with the access it gives us to spiritual reality[33] in Christ, allows us to acknowledge that there is much of our nature that we do not yet know, but which is working against our best interests (Gn. 6:5; 8:21, Rom. 7:14-20 etc.).

Such a view of human nature is in marked contrast to person-centred psychological therapy (typical of modern psychologies), seeking good in all

---

[29] According to Duck this is not a much researched subject, especially the dark side of relationships (1986/1998:212, quoting Cupach and Spitzberg 1994). He comments, 'despite their frequency in social life, there is no deep understanding of flirtation, forgiveness, regret, remorse, disappointment, polite refusals, impolite requests, or 'needing' and bullying' (212).

[30] The metaphysics of Evil are outside the scope of this book. But I have adopted a view that Evil can be personally experienced and is mirrored in the dark side to our nature. For a comment on the Christian idea of evil, see Wright (2003). For a comment on evil as a force rather than a person, see Duffy (1993:361ff.).

[31] We are stepping into the duality of the 'two worlds'. Gundry had some helpful comments (1976 especially 135ff.). In this book I will be following his lead, seeing the problem of duality in, say Paul's theology, not as a body spirit issue, but 'the real conflict occurs between the inner man and *sin*, with the body caught in the middle and dominated by sin rather than the mind' (Gundry 1976:138).

[32] Because we are not perceived as spiritual, we deny ourselves the possibility of becoming aware of our dark *spiritual* side. As an example, when speaking with the guest speaker at the Bishop John Robinson Annual Conference on Religion and Psychiatry, at the Institute of Psychiatry, (23/11/00), he stated 'There is no such things as a negative spiritual force'. Similarly, in Gleitman; 'The demonological theory of mental illness is a thing of the past' (1995:716). Such an attitude within psychology is not helpful. To balance this see Rebillot (1989). He adopts the idea of a Jungian Gestalt ritualizing of discovering this dark side, a mythological journey, playing out the heroic demonic in all of us. For a Christian challenge to the imperialism of modern psychopathology in rejecting such key concepts, see Gleitman (1995:760), Vitz (1977/1994), or Hobart Mowrer (1961).

[33] In this I am thinking of Berger *The Sacred Canopy*, (1969/1990). For a comment on this spiritual presence in psychological therapies, see Steere (1997).

of us, while not acknowledging either darkness or its sin. Humanism, along with other cultural ideologies, has given us an unrealistically optimistic view of ourselves. Likewise, some modern positive based therapeutic schools allow us to believe we are fundamentally good, though maybe needing a therapeutic tune-up. Modern psychological therapies, without the language or the model,[34] can struggle to expose our darkness and its self-deceit. When psychological therapies ignore this concept of Evil and its darkness in every one of us, we are left with all the carnage of Evil, yet stripped of the equipping of emotional and spiritual tools to diagnose and reconstruct the person's broken life.

Pastorally, humanly-caused evil does not so much reside in a person, though it may, but is usually perceived as someone else treating us as though we carry evil power (Duck 1986/1998:105). For power and its evil are relational concepts.[35] So without a concept of Evil internally standing against personal wholeness, much damage cannot be seen for what it really is. The condition I am describing, borrowed from both Scripture and my own experience, I call *sin against ourselves*.[36] By not acknowledging this gravity and its cycles of self-harm in us, we permit ourselves to prolong self-deceit, while blaming everyone else for our plight and its condition. This in turn, inevitably, negatively impacts all our relationships.

Martsolf and Mickley in their overview of spirituality focus on the importance of finding meaning in our sicknesses, assuming the spiritual dimension is a key aspect to this quest. By not allowing the client to see their own dark contribution to their sicknesses I see them being denied some of this meaning. Alternately, by allowing the person to see how they have sometimes made matters much worse is actually the beginning of hope, for if they are willing to change, these things will not continue to happen. Without owning our self-deceit in denying the dark side in our own disorders, we have little hope of making the changes we all need to make.

---

[34] Some would argue this is not entirely true, as some psychological therapies are familiar with the language of self-hate or loathing, self-harm and self-murder etc. (e.g. Winnicott 1965, Mann 2002), suggesting psychology has re-written some of the language. However, it has been my observation that psychological therapies are reluctant to use language focused around the individual's dark side, e.g. arrogance, pride, selfishness, unwillingness to change, etc., because of the 'client' aspect. Some therapists seem comfortable implementing others' blame culture, but are unwilling to help the client recognise their own complicity in their disorders.

[35] The prevalence of relational power issues is now being widely recognised in research practice (Lincoln and Denzin 2000).

[36] The concept of *sin against oneself* is central to my work, but one struggles to find a specific concept close to it in contemporary psychological therapies. See 'How do we get sick?' (page 154), where I expand this idea.

Listening to God's voice

Paul taught that all human beings are enmeshed in a self-deception that promotes a cover story of righteousness in order to conceal a real story of unrighteousness (Mt. 23:25-28, Rom. 9:30-10:3, Gal. 6:3, Phil. 3:6-10) (Via 1990:133). But this remains theoretical for most of us unless the Church can find a practical therapeutic change process to expose it. What is needed to break this self-deceit is the disclosing of the secrets of the heart (1 Cor. 4:5; 14:25), and the bringing of this unconscious state to our consciousness, where it can be personally owned and dealt with.

It is here that I believe Paul comes closest to Freud and modern psychologically-informed thought regarding human nature. Both recognize a dark side to our nature,[37] a hidden self that is not readily, consciously available to us. For Paul it is accessed by the Holy Spirit, for Freud via the analytic relationship. In both instances, it is believed by faith, through an 'inner voice'.[38] The access, in both instances, is an act of faith, trusting the authenticity of this 'voice'.

Through the birth of modern psychological therapies and their concept of the unconscious the Pauline centre of self-deception has not been entirely lost. It has been identified in many schools within psychology, with concepts like the unconscious, the subliminal self, and generic concepts like the id and the shadow etc. All of these concepts suggest a 'counter-voice' to our cognitive nature. Paul regards wholeness as correspondence or harmony between inside and outside, between faith, intention and act (2 Cor. 8:1-15, Gal. 5:6,25),[39] calling for harmonic obedience in both heart and act (Rom. 2:25-29; 6:17). God's sovereign grace, His love in desiring to want to make us more human, holds back the full consequences of this darkness in us, until He and I together agree I am willing to see it and take responsibility for it. Then having seen the carnage of it, I begin to confess it and let it go.

Following Exodus 15:26, and the *Rapha* promise, I see this process initially triggered not by a therapist, but by God talking to us[40] about how

---

[37] Staub noted that Freud suggested man is basically wicked and selfish (1978:1, 2003).

[38] Some would argue this is not the case, by suggesting it is the counter-transference feelings evoked in the analyst.

[39] Erikson called wholeness 'the lower totality', suggesting it is the affective sense of being able to tolerate ambiguity in one's life (Josselson 2000:97). Modern psychology is also grappling with the inner and outer selves. (See the Psych-Info database as an example.)

[40] I agree it is a quantum leap from a therapist telling a client what they see, to a claim that God is telling them what He sees. But this is not a new problem, if we go back to the *Rapha* principle in Exodus 15, or take note of Christ diagnosing the real issues for, say, the woman at the well (Jn. 4:6ff.). I have known no-one who comes to us for help stumbling over the concept of God's voice speaking to them, if I introduce it initially as an 'inner voice'. See Perry (1991:68ff.). Many people are plagued by voices in their heads, so it is a relief for them to begin distinguishing their own and God's from others'. We never teach people to distinguish the two. This inner voice is also inner feelings. See 'Feeling is healing' (page 144).

He sees us. Susan Williams' findings support the importance of this concept.

[Homework is about] letting God talk to you about who you should have been and who you really are, [and] who you have become (W1-11).

In hearing from God about what stands between Him,[41] myself and my wholeness, I then consciously choose to separate myself from my own darkness or self-deceit, by either giving it to Him in words, or cathartically engaging it, letting it go. This is the essence of the journey being mapped by Susan Williams' research.

I find these great big gaps where I stopped growing, quite often at [age] 6. There are these great big holes where I stopped maturing as a person in that area, only there are lots of them. So once I go back to where the damage was, get it sorted and give that area of damage to God, then I can learn how I should have been, put that in place, rewrite those scripts and then become mature in that area, so it is like as if the damage wasn't there (W6-9).

'Wholeness is the actualization of a consciously understood connection between my flawed finite concreteness and God's sovereign and gracious freedom' (Via 1990:133). To be more fully human requires we fully own our dark side. 'God can only make us whole if we accept the dark side of our nature, firstly making peace and possessing our sinful nature, then confessing it and giving it to Christ. Maturity must follow as we discern good and evil in ourselves' (Raub 1992:53ff.).

If we allow Yahweh to talk to us, as the *Rapha* principle suggests, we can enter levels of truth about ourselves that we can experience in few other ways.

[Homework is] an engagement of your true feelings, confronting those things in your life that you would rather not know about or see, grappling with the new truth about why you have become what you are and starting to declare that you need to change. Prepared to listen to Christ (M9-10).

I see this inner voice within a personal therapeutic change context, as the Father telling the Church what it must do to know His Son, and be whole by becoming like Him. In our ministry we describe this inner voice as we touch our chest, suggesting it comes from the core of our being, not our intellect or brain. We also teach people it is not the voices they hear talking to them in their heads that we are talking about. Instead it is what we feel 'in our heart', at our centre.

---

[41] For a helpful overview of 'hearing God's voice', see Deere (1996). For the suggestion that this inner voice is our moral conscience, see Butler (1922/1986:59, cited in Schrag 1997:96). For a narrative account of how hearing God's voice can have a therapeutic benefit similar to that experienced by Susan Williams' contributors, see Cowper (1817). Cowper's is an interesting account of this well-known lawyer and hymn writer's journey out of mental illness, by hearing the Lord speak to him through Rom. 3:25. Following this reading he began to feel some peace, and his melancholia lifted (intro.). (A copy of this book exists in the ML Special Collections: rPR 3383. A2. 1817, ref. 0043239, University of Birmingham Central Library, UK.)

One of the useful tests for many learning this process, is that it is more likely to be something they initially feel, that they then have to interpret. It is not so common that it is something they just hear. It is often felt, not thought (see 'Feeling is healing', page 144). Such an approach avoids the minefield of questions as to whether it is God's voice that has been heard. Our approach is to teach people to test it in practice.[42] If it is authentic, it will bring about authentic change. Using this approach also does not discriminate between those who are Christian and those who are not. We are either hearing God's voice (as a Christian), or we are choosing to listen to our inner voice (as an un-churched person). Both are effective. In time un-churched participants naturally begin to see God in the process, if they wish to.

> *[To someone who wasn't a Christian] I would say you can miss out the God bit if you like and then let them find God for themselves if they do their journey (W6-4).*
>
> *[To someone who wasn't a Christian] Don't worry about not being a Christian. It will happen anyway (W1-3).*

In addition, the idea I have already suggested that we all have a 'base spirituality' means almost anyone can do this journey in connecting with God, whether committed to Him or not.[43] Finally, once someone has learned to hear God speaking to them about themselves, and begins to implement the change He requires, it equips them to begin hearing God for others, and for the Church as a whole. The wholeness journey with all its positive experience replicates itself as it has done through several generations in CCD.

The Church does not have a good record encouraging people to hear God's voice for themselves.[44] In fact, part of the culture of some modern churches is that the leader hears God's voice through Scripture (Johnson and Van Vonderen 1991:81ff.) for the members. Such situations can become power, abuse and control issues. I would be the first to agree that when a whole congregation begins to hear God speaking to them individually, it can feel like chaos. But it is also strangely liberating in shifting the power back to the place where it should be, with the members

---

[42] As a young teenage Christian I learnt to fear the possibility of 'the devil' talking to me. I was taught the most reliable way of determining God's voice was by its content. If it was nasty it was assumed to be the 'enemy', if it was good it was God. We all need to mature from such thinking. In some ways I now see it the opposite way round. The *Rapha* principle suggests God wants to expose our dark side to us, showing us what we do not want to see about ourselves. This is always a very painful process.

[43] Some Christians may object to the idea that God can talk to people without the 'quickening conviction' of the Holy Spirit. We do not raise such issues because in Scripture one sees numerous occasions when God uses unorthodox means to talk to people, e.g. a bush, donkey, cloud, heavens and pagans etc. So why not someone open to letting Him, that does not yet know Him?

[44] Having said that, within the Church there is a focus on learning to hear God's voice (Fitzpatrick 1984/1987, Huggett 1986, Deere 1996 etc.).

of the congregation. The pastor is no longer responsible for everyone and their spiritual well-being. When such knowledge is accurate, as it is much of the time, and is delivered with maturity, it has great benefit to all, and is well worth the risk. Here in CCD I personally rely heavily on the community hearing God for themselves, then themselves testing and filtering out any error. For instance, one simple rule is that if it leads to healing, and promotes relationship and affirmation, it will certainly be of the Lord. If it does not, then it will be looked upon as suspect. God rarely speaks against His own best interests, especially regarding His Son.

Listening to God's voice for one's self about one's self is part of the 'mystery' of learning to know Christ. This practice also emphasizes God's perspective, unveiling the 'mystery' of our nature and His helping us engage it. In this I am echoing Brunner (1964), who spoke of 'truth as personal encounter'. Learning to hear God's voice promotes our meeting Christ in a place of truth.

hearing God's voice makes you not give up (19F-8.36).

I [now] find it much easier to hear the voice of God and in most instances I can feel his presence immediately following my invitation (23M-6.12).

Seeing sin as a refusal to change

Within CCD listening to God's voice forms the basis of a journey of therapeutic discipleship. The *Rapha* promise makes it clear that God expects us to listen to Him and respond. Contemporary spirituality likewise places strong emphasis on wholeness change. So, it seems, does Yahweh (e.g. Ex. 33:5, Ps. 32:8-9; 55.19, Acts 11:5ff.). When Christians refuse to change in response to God's voice, they are refusing to harmonise their lives with Christ, with *imago Dei* wholeness. In CCD and *Rapha* we believe this to be sin.

In seeking to restore the concepts of Evil and sin to the therapeutic journey,[45] I am drawing on a long tradition in the Church (Haring 1974) and Scripture. But my suggestion that sin can be seen as a refusal to change in a way that God requires, is admittedly different to more orthodox views of sin. I am not suggesting I would want to replace this interpretation with a more traditional one, but draw it out as a distinct idea. In taking such a position I am borrowing from Boman's Hebrew perspective, suggesting sin against God and ourselves is in essence our unwillingness to change (1954/1960:27ff.). But also, as I have already noted, such a view of sin is implicit in many of the Old Testament stories, being grounded in Hebrew history. This is the case whether we look at the role of the prophets calling Israel back from sinful ways, and the people's resistance, or look at any of

---

[45] Working with the un-churched we find the term 'baggage' less offensive to begin with than 'sin'.

the narrative of how Old Testament personalities resisted change being required by God, e.g. Moses, Jonah etc.

This attitude of refusal can be in our opinions ('I tried it before, I can't change'), or our lifestyle ('It won't hurt me, my dad smoked till he was seventy six'), even where such change is required both for our own good and in our obeying Him.[46] In both my teaching and practice, sin is no longer a 'static ontology' (Lee 1979:13), but a wilful chosen existential estrangement, our suspension or disruption of the natural ongoing change processes in our lives. As I have noted, this 'sin' is humanity's desire to *be,* rather than to *become* (Lee 1979:93).

So in essence, our self-deceit is a chosen blindness to our true condition, our personal refusal to change.[47] In Hebrew thought *becoming* is the basic category of both reality and personhood, rather than *being*. To change, we stop trying to establish our security in *being*, fighting to hold on to what we have and are. Instead, we choose to be willing to change under Yahweh's *Rapha* guidance. Wholeness, I would propose, is our committing to a needed journey of continual positive personal change. This viewpoint is echoed by Susan Williams' participants.

> Doesn't the vision get bigger all the time, we are not so limited in what we think is going to happen anyway. So you are always, when you get towards something big, there is always something bigger beyond you that you never even dreamed of before (W5-12).

Moving on into the New Testament, no author directly addresses the issue of sin seen from this persective. Paul helps us more than most, seeing the beginning of our personal journey as our admitting our personal need and condition (2 Cor. 3:18; 4:16, Rom. 7) (Via 1990:49). Change is necessary in order to dispel our deceptions.

> Having the hope of what I could become has given me the courage progressively to be able to face more and more truth about myself (M15-1).

Faith in Christ, for Paul, releases the potential in all of us for a new self-understanding in this present life (Rom. 10:5-21, Gal. 2:20, Phil. 3:7-11 etc.). This is the beginning of finding much more of our humanness. Paul sees salvation beginning in this life, and as Ford suggests, it can be health

---

[46] Lapierre noted six factors or dimensions that help us experience life as a spiritual person; the journey, transcendence, community, religion, 'the mystery of creation' and transformation. He went on to describe evil as a lack of progress and/or regression in any of these six dimensions (1994:153-161). Davis put it in a slightly different way, suggesting Satan is a symbol of what we disown in ourselves (1976:118), while Ling pointed out that Satan ultimately derives his power from us because of our chosen ignorance (1961:83).

[47] In speaking this way I am in good company. See for instance, McFadyen, 'Sin is the resistance or opposition to the energies of God's dynamic order, the disorientation of personal energies in an alternative dynamic, a distortion of the conditions of genuine joy' (2000:220).

for all of us now (Ford 1999:1).[48] This new understanding, having God's perspective, gives us a 'single-mindedness' that helps us focus on what stands between God, ourselves and others, namely our self-deceit and its sin epitomised in our stubborn and deceived view of ourselves. Without this more realistic understanding of ourselves we have no reason to change. God, through the *Rapha* promise, is volunteering to be our diagnostician.

One aspect of original sin,[49] therefore, could be seen not as a substance of being, but our disinclination to harmonize ourselves with the change God wishes to talk to us about, which He desires for us. Jesus' redemptive work is part of the Father's creative work, making creation an *a priori* category of redemption (Lee 1979:68). A full return to a prelapsarian state is not what I propose, but instead our willingness to identify with the Father's help, a life in more harmony with Christ, ourselves, creation[50] and others, within an environment of permanent, positive, creative change (2 Cor. 3:18). It is this letting go of our pasts and its darkness, and moving into permanent positive deep change (Ps. 85:8-9), that guarantees we can sustain it. In seeking to live such a life, while still holding onto our psychic and pneumatic debris, we are in danger of continuing to harm ourselves if we refuse to change.

In Chapters 5 and 6 I will explore the community context for the *Rapha* discipleship journey at CCD. But like Lambourne, I now believe such wholeness can only occur in relationships that include God, my own personal and spiritual natures (1983:98ff.), and other people.[51] Let me now outline some of the emphases of this therapeutic discipleship journey, the way we currently practise it in CCD.

---

[48] Robinson stated 'the Gospel is the gospel or good news of the Kingdom, of the reign of God breaking into, transforming and renewing this world-order of sin, decay and death' (1960:121ff.). He went on to state that wholeness in a perfectionist sense is unobtainable in this life (126-127).

[49] In saying this I am not expressing an opinion whether 'original sin' actually exists, or is merely a figment of theologian's imagination. However, what is clear, and this is the point I am making, is that one way or another we all have varying degrees of fascination toward darkness, suggesting none of us are all good.

[50] It was Francis Schaeffer, I believe, who was one of the first to note that in the Protestant tradition one of the consequences of putting redemption before creation is the subsequent appalling capacity we have to abuse the created world. Western Christianity, driven by capitalism and 'getting people saved', has failed to develop a mature Creation theology or its ecology (Schaeffer and Middlemann 1970, Clinebell 1996). It is interesting that contemporary people, especially those in the New Age movements, have beaten the Church in this area also, e.g. Greenpeace.

[51] Nouwen (1975) also saw these three dimensions. However, throughout this book, as you will note, I am drawing in a fourth, creation, its order and ecology.

A *pneuma*-psychology within a discipleship therapeutic wholeness journey: some of the distinctives of the *Rapha* model

Where I locate my model

Like Clinebell, I work from the basis that to be a whole person includes one's social (relational), psychological, intellectual, physical, ecological and spiritual functioning (1988:8ff., 1996). Each of these domains are included in the integrative[52] model that I have developed, treating people as one irreducible whole. But I also recognise that all of us have a profoundly deep inner yearning within us to be more than we are, to be psychologically and even physically more whole as persons. So I believe that every one of us must also discover our own 'ground of being' (Tillich 1952:153ff.),[53] adopting a willingness to change, and embracing personal wisdom from Christ within our own nature, which with the *Rapha* principle, is able to empower us to pursue our personal wholeness. Sanford recognised that because we are all sick, failure to pursue a wholeness journey means we continue to be adversely possessed by what we have chosen to ignore (1978:101). So people are drawn into their futures, but are still hounded by their pasts (Phares and Trull 1997:373). The goal of my *Rapha* model is the person's positive personal change,[54] by meeting Jesus, letting go of their pasts,[55] and being able to extend their capacity to become full members of Christ, community and society. Such a task I find clearly resonates with contemporary people's spiritual quest.

Although in the past some have described me as a pastoral counsellor, like Hand (1978) I now see my task more as the practice of theology in the quest for wholeness as Christ-likeness, a process journey for the person, with myself and others facilitating this as spiritual director or teacher. I am now more comfortable speaking of my own role as diagnostician, or even in a new sense, as a metaphysician. My work and responsibilities in the

---

[52] My model is integrative rather than *eclectic* because I not only already have a clinical practice, but a theoretical rationale behind this practice. It is also true that the process of integration produces something new, generating its own relational perspective. See, for instance, Mitchell (1988) and Pelham et al. (2001:117).

[53] See also Tillich (1948, 1955).

[54] Psychology has always recognised the need for change, but it is probably true that it was George Kelly and his *Personal Construct Theory* (1955/1963), that was one of the best early examples of psychology's recognition of the need for healthy people to be in a permanent process of change, 'new constructs' as he called them. 'Man looks at the world through transparent patterns or templates which he creates and then attempts to fit over the realities of which the world is composed' (1963 edit.,8-9).

[55] I am not suggesting this is only possible with Christ. It is already a common theme in psychological therapies (Haaga and Davison 1991), but what I am suggesting in this book is that to be fully human must include a mature spirituality focused on Christ and lived out in faith community. See chapters 5-6.

community are distinct, but how I would describe them I am still unsure. Lambourne saw pastoral counselling as heretical when using the one-to-one model, because it weakened the Church when practiced outside the local congregations (1983:138). In CCD we have sought to avoid this by setting up diagnostics and mentoring within the church and *Rapha*. I have a part to play in this, but it continues to lessen by the year, as people mature and carry more, and the social process and SQ in the community continue to grow, giving greater capacity to help others.

What this section describes is not a theoretical model, though I have begun building one, but a much-used clinical practitioner's model refined over many years. It is already, *a posteriori,* a lived reality in the lives of many hundreds of people in both Europe and North America. Also, I would need to include those hundreds I have 'counselled' in a lay pastoral capacity, while I have been developing this model. Those coming to me for help have been my teachers, guiding me in what has been most helpful to them. As God speaks to and heals them, He also teaches me, as I watch the way the Lord unpacks the person's disorders, layer by layer. So my approach has been relationship building, an integrative *skill set,* based on people's deep personal needs. Many of the features of my approach are noted in Collins (1988).

Giving hope

We have to begin the journey at the same place with everyone, Christian or un-churched. We need to give them hope, so help them begin finding both meaning and reasons for past toxic experiences, damage and failure.[56] Our observation is that such hope enables them to both engage their personal spirituality, while releasing a belief in them that they can change. This hope comes primarily, initially, from a combination of teaching and personal encounters. Newcomers will have a series of meetings with folk in the community, who will 'tell their story'.

> *The testimonies are very important for these people, like non-Christians coming in and getting healed, going through their crap, trying to explain that to them (M8-3).*

We specifically seek to create a 'narrative culture'. This gives people a sense of perspective that they too have a personal destiny, they too can begin their own journey, find wholeness, and discover *imago Dei* in becoming the person they were created to be. By listening to how others have succeeded, they begin believing that they too can discover their personal uniqueness. In these early stages everyone in the community has a therapeutic pastoral role to play with these newcomers.

---

[56] As we all have to learn, much distress is the failure in our lives to secure meaning behind sickness (Boivin 1991, Burnard 1987).

Another early means of giving hope is to introduce to them the reality of their spiritual nature, by teaching them the concept of their 'spiritual house'. (See appendix 4.) This metaphor of the human spirit as a house has a long tradition in the Church (Teresa of Avila 1958) and in Scripture (Ps. 127:1, Mt. 7:7-8, Lk. 11:24-26, Acts 7:49, 2 Tim. 2:20-22, Heb. 3:6 etc.). It describes the person's spirit as their God-given house, which has become over-run by the debris and damage of their personal histories. None of us feel we are fully masters of our own house (Norris Clarke 1993:60-61), so our whole house is waiting to be cleaned and possessed by us. For those who have invited Christ into their 'house', this probably means He is still waiting in the hallway for them to invite Him to help them clean up and occupy the rest of the property.

Many find it helpful to think of areas of damage in their lives being like different rooms in their spiritual house. For instance, they may feel the door to a specific room is locked, until they choose to recognise the name on the door, perhaps a person (e.g. mother, father, sibling), or issue (e.g. sexual abuse, failure, shame). For many, although the door may be locked, its windows are open for both others and evil to enter and abuse them, making them vulnerable. We teach people they can make choices to step into these rooms, inviting the Lord to help them open and clean the room by clearing out its baggage, closing its windows and fully recovering that part of their lives.

We introduce the concept of sin by describing this as unwanted 'baggage' in many rooms of their spiritual house. Although often hidden to them by them, their deep story, the impact of this baggage or psychic debris and its emotional and spiritual dimensions, will have been felt in numerous areas of their life, because of our holistic nature. In due course they will be willing to recognise this baggage as sin, but we never press the point, leaving it to the Lord.

The concept of the 'spiritual house' gives them hope that they can systematically, clinically, issue-by-issue, (e.g. room by room) remove the baggage in their lives. At last they can do something about the problems they have. They do not have to rely on others any more. But this also requires they acknowledge their growing self-awareness of all they do not yet know about themselves. We work on the assumption that one insight about themselves and its damage will naturally lead to others. Having found wholeness (e.g. fully occupancy) in one room, they move on to another. Each person's journey is unique, and this model is highly flexible in allowing them to see their house in any way they wish.[57] This metaphor

---

[57] Many do personalise this concept in unique ways. Some talk of feeling they had lived in the under-stairs cupboard, thinking this was all they had in their spiritual house. Others camp in the grounds, never believing the house they were looking at every day was really theirs. Yet others start

also links them in a practical way with their spiritual nature. With the use of the spiritual house their journey comprises many steps into wholeness, rather than one mega event.

As in human nature's entelechy, we teach a person that all their human baggage is wholly theirs, affecting their whole being (1 Cor. 11:27ff., Jas. 3:14ff.). The one aspect often missing in previous counselling experience, and their personal understanding, is their hidden unconscious spiritual nature.[58] Here lie hidden many of one's sicknesses. So since Christ demands integration from all of us in wanting to bring wholeness to all our members (Benner 1998:161), we must enter these hidden areas of our lives with Him. The idea of the spiritual house helps this process to begin.

Therefore the goal of this journey, therapeutically, is that it will be for the person as if the toxic events of the past had not occurred. They are able to live without the ongoing symptoms of their disorders. Only the empty memories will remain.[59] I am not describing therapeutic containment or sublimation, or the managing of baggage, but the removal of all the encumbrances that stand in the path of living and loving well.

Making a choice to change

We noted earlier the huge obstacle of taking responsibility for one's own life (page 108). We have also noted the idea in CCD that sin is perceived as a refusal to change (page 127). So taking these on board, the whole tenure of the early stages of a journey of wholeness requires that the person needs to make the choice of positively changing. This happens as their hope grows and they begin either to hear the voice of the Lord, or their inner voice speaking to them, about the damage and its baggage in their lives. The shift will begin to happen as they admit they 'do not want to live this way anymore', or 'I have to change, I cannot stay this way'. Implicit in this process is the person's acceptance of their need to deal with their own historic baggage.

Realizing how sick I really am is the beginning of getting healed (02F-5.3)

---

their journey with a modest bungalow, but then find whole additional wings to the building. For others, the Lord gives them architect's drawings!

[58] Viktor Frankl, a Viennese analyst, father of existential therapy and founder of Logotherapy, insisted that psychological therapies needed to move beyond the dynamics of the neuroses, to look at distress in the human spirit. He was critical of those who 'take refuge in psychology by pretending that the spiritual distress of a human being who is looking for a meaning to his existence is nothing but a pathological symptom' (Frankl 1965/1973:9, 10, 14).

[59] This is not loss of memory, or just forgetting, though over many years this can happen. What I am describing is that the person will go through the process of engaging the pain and giving it to Christ. Although the memories will remain, without the accompanying emotional toxicity they will naturally fade over time. In the past the toxic emotion, especially trauma, will have kept the memories and this pain alive. For a recent comment on the 'healing of memories' movement, see Garzon and Burkett (2002). See 'Introducing scripts and schemas' (page 156) below, for a further comment on scripts and their schemas.

In a more traditional therapeutic setting people seek out therapists because they need to change in one area of their lives. But therapists know all too well that because of the complexity of human nature, bringing about change in any client in any area is much harder and more complex than people assume. The first thing that needs to change is the person's perception and attitude to themselves, and this alone in a one-to-one setting can take several sessions, and will be a slow process. Yet within a community where they are learning both to hear their inner voice and learn hope from others on a daily basis through the social process,[60] this process will normally be much more rapid.

> *Before I came to CCD I was terrified of any change, however small. I have been learning that it is your approach to change that determines whether you benefit or lose from it. Having hope that you can see change is essential. It is very exciting watching others changing for better around you and watching them grow into who they were created to be, as it gives you hope for your own transformation (04F-2.19)*

Within the community of CCD the process of positive change is compressed. It takes on a psycho-kinetic nature. The key issue here is that none of us know instinctively how to change, so it must be 'caught' from others. Therefore, a narrative culture within community that contains this knowledge, a group IQ, EQ and SQ, allows the person to learn at their own pace, and by learning, change. In this sense, I am harnessing people's need to change, using psychodynamic insight and behavioural change, within the social process of community.[61] Such a hope-centred culture makes positive change contagious.

> *Because you can see people changing around you all the time and it is such an obvious change in so many people, you can't stay still yourself (W9-2).*

This process will in turn teach the person how to work systematically through the typical 8-12 major issues that most people have to deal with. The concepts learned in these early stages also teach the person the long-term principles needed for their continuing healthful journey into wholeness.[62] Such a journey becomes a way of life, in possessing all they

---

[60] This social process will be explained in more detail in 'Introducing therapeutic communities (page 202).

[61] What we ask newcomers, or those considering beginning the journey, is whether they are 'hungry' or desperate for learning and its change. Those who are not desperate are not ready to start.

[62] One of the many interesting observations made by us since 1998, when we began using my counselling model within CCD, is that with each generation the length taken to work through the first part of one's journey is reduced. It took my colleague Susan Williams some eight years to work through the basic issues, the generation she first taught around five, the next, assisted by the social processes of CCD around three and it is now coming down to two, though beginning to level out.

are becoming.[63] This journey, once learned, is not for a season, but for a whole lifetime.[64]

Initially I almost needed a little guidebook really, I would keep going back to it thinking, am I doing this right, and so I did it in a fairly clinical way. ... Its not clinical anymore, but part of my everyday lifestyle (W13-9).

Like Kornfeld we see in CCD two levels of change, first order change is one of adjustment; the second, often after several months in the community, will be the beginning of transformation (1998:7). During the early stages in the community we help teach and support people to build relationships. Although they may often feel they have begun their journey, and tell us so, there is usually a clear point at which a deeper layer of change is initiated by the individual.

One of the other interesting patterns to have emerged over the years is that this choice to change is made many times over. Many folk, having benefited from an initial stage of healing, then take a break in their therapeutic journey. They will feel a need to '*live again*', to '*enjoy what they are possessing*'. This particularly applies to those who have contacted us during a period of crisis. The break takes many forms. They may leave the community for a period of time or 'take time out' from their journey, while remaining part of the community.[65] A person comes to Christ for healing, which He gives them unconditionally. But, as in the Gospel record, He then waits to see if they will come back and follow Him, or just enjoy the healing they have received. Do they really want to become a disciple? We have found this a healthy pattern, since when they do come back, as most do, they commit themselves to becoming full members of the community. They begin to be givers, no longer just takers.

For me there has got to be a tipping point, like whereby I know that there are still issues that need to be dealt with, but [I] start putting other people first and where my desire to serve other people becomes much greater (W13-9).

---

[63] 'I believe that it is only in a reconciliation of will and spirit that we have any real hope for wholeness.... something else is needed: some source of inspiration, some reservoir of power and wisdom beyond that which is provided by our personal wills...but spirit and will do not come together easily in the life of this modern world' (May 1982b:vi).

[64] One disturbing aspect of this need for change is that people who join the congregation but who do not want to change, find it increasingly difficult to remain. Change is the expectation and norm in the culture of CCD. Such an environment is not what everyone wants, and Susan Williams' research indicates that the congregation accepts that those who are not seeking personal change may find a different congregation more suitable.

[65] Pingleton has noted that temporarily taking 'time out' from Church can be healthy (1992:111).

Learning to be Christ-like?

Aquinas,[66] despite his intellectualizing of theology, would still argue that for us to be fully who we can be, this desire, the spirit and likeness to God [to *know*[67] Jesus] needs to be the deepest, most authentic longing of our spiritual human nature (Robb 1974:20).

> *It is becoming that close, so that you can hear Jesus' heartbeat, that close to Him that instinctively you know what He is thinking, feeling, doing (W10-9).*

Here lies an important aspect of this discipleship model, my suggestion that Christ-likeness can be learned. For me Christ-likeness is no longer some mysterious 'spiritualizing' of one's life over an extended period of time, becoming more 'other worldly'. Instead, much of it is a learned wholeness journey, the goal of which is Christ-likeness. Christ-likeness and wholeness should be synonymous. Teaching,[68] therefore, features highly in my model, for it enables the individual to learn to *become*. But what I am speaking about is not traditional learning about God, but a transformational learning. This is something we can all do for ourselves to ourselves with the help of Christ, within a faith community. Learning also, in a range of ways, becomes an outcome of one's healing, a means of achieving wholeness. So we will often describe our model as a learning journey toward Christ-likeness.[69]

Initially we introduce enquirers or new members of the community to our model through weekend workshops, teaching them about 'the journey'[70] in separate male or female groups, usually between 25-50 in

---

[66] See Pasnau (2002) for a recent review of Aquinas' view of human nature.

[67] Biblically, I see the term *knowing* Christ as a description of personal relationship growing out of regular intimate encounters with God (see Botterweck, et al. 1974:478, or Fretheim 1996a:413). Both Hebrew and Greek liken this *knowing* to the profound and deep intimacy possible within sexual union.

[68] I am not talking only about lectures, in speaking about teaching. Throughout the community, not only in *Rapha* workshops, we use a diverse range of ways to communicate and encourage ownership of new transforming knowledge, e.g. a narrative culture, mentoring, testimonies, catharsis, friendships, etc. CCD is both a learning and teaching culture. So I fully concur with Kraybill, 'Lectures are the worst medium......the most effective teaching methodologies are based on case studies, group discussions, role play exercises, low cost audio visual and multi media presentations' (2001).

[69] The longer I do this journey myself the more I realise the closeness that learning has to spirituality. Much learning is the changing of our minds, and experiencing spirituality is about undergoing change, seeing beyond ourselves. The learning experience can be a spiritual experience, especially when we are learning about ourselves. For example, 'Growth orientation' was one of the most significant components of an individual's learning power in Broadfoot, Claxton and Deakin Crick's (2002) ELLI research. 'The soul is so powerful, so actual, so close to divine, that it engages in an action on its own, independently of the body. This is all it means to say that the human soul is spiritual' (Pasnau 2002:71).

[70] In the early stages of a person's journey, we rely heavily on our workshop programme, as this allows the person to grasp quickly the basic principles of the journey. We now hold around 20 workshops a year somewhere here in UK, Europe or the USA, and they are becoming more

number. In the first workshop we teach them about human make-up, and how we all get sick. We introduce our 'Baggage List' (appendix 5) and how to 'undo' these different types of baggage. This is all done at a group level. A number of those attending these workshops have no Christian background. Toward the end of the workshop we suggest they can take personal responsibility for their journey. We then send them away, asking them to consider whether the approach we have introduced is something they can work with. If they can, as most do, we begin to support them. We 'listen actively', giving them an initial appraisal and diagnostic session to help begin their 'homework'. We have sought to design our workshops, models and programmes to be learned by anyone wanting to do such a journey, regardless of age, background and culture.[71]

We welcome everyone equally, but initially do not focus on relationship with Christ unless this is what the person chooses. Most begin their journey with historic baggage as their priority. They may have no faith background, and merely come with therapeutic need.[72] Or they may feel betrayed by God and/or a church.

> *I told one [person] the other day that it was OK that he hated God and God understood (M13-4).*
>
> *[The] provision of a sound basis from which they can recover gradually [is important] and they aren't forced into something they are not ready for (W2-5).*

We always allow the person to choose where they want to start on their journey. Many times this means focusing on building trust and giving hope. We have observed that contemporary people need time to think things through, not wanting to be intimidated into quick decisions. This way of living has required in me and in many of the more mature Christians in our community that we make a significant shift in our thinking regarding 'evangelism'.[73] Over the years of the journey, though, we see almost

---

popular. They are a major source of growth in CCD. The subjects covered in the workshops include Jehovah *Rapha*, human spirit and personal spirituality, emotion, ways of hearing the voice of God, spiritual surgery, relationships and differences between men and women, revenge and forgiveness, sin against oneself and taking responsibility.

[71] For instance, several of those recently seeking help have had Moslem, Buddhist, Hindu and animist as well as un-churched backgrounds. Also, at several workshops we have had groups of deaf people and at most workshops several with serious mental and emotional illness, churched and un-churched alike.

[72] I am aware of the complex ethics of working with the un-churched, while using a model that has a Christian dimension. The principle of respect of client's autonomy over religious beliefs is a matter that has been considered often by authors, e.g. Hiltner (1949), Wise (1951), Foskett and Lyall (1988), etc.

[73] CCD has a specific approach to 'evangelism'. Instead of an emphasis on conversion, it seeks a reputation in the local community for making available support in times of need. Most local people joining the community do so in recognition of personal need. Some people do a journey 'meeting Jesus', while others have a dramatic conversion. We let the Lord lead this. The congregation also has a high profile Christmas and summer carnival programme, with an open-top

everyone naturally moving into relationship with Christ, becoming more Christ-like, as they begin to find wholeness. A typical comment toward the end of this first stage of their journey is, 'Now tell me more about this God that's been helping me'. We see this approach in Christ's life; He healed people unconditionally, then waited to see if they would return to become disciples. It was then that He gave them the Great Commission.

My stage development model

People quickly learn that they have a lot of baggage. Each issue becomes a stepping-stone on the early journey. Following the idea of stage development theory,[74] I began configuring my own description of the journey, and this model has proven robust over many years of testing. It is in three stages, beginning not at birth, but as a person makes a deliberate choice to begin their therapeutic journey. Many discover this journey had begun before they ever met us, but proved to be unsatisfactory, or had even led to a worsening situation. The model looks like this:[75]

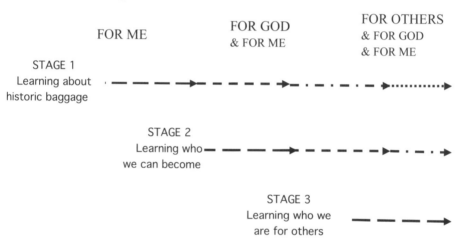

[When I talked about homework] I said it was like a journey, in three parts, three stages. To start off with you have to learn to honour yourself and when you start to do that you can start to honour other people and when you do that you can start to honour God and then you start to become a bit more mature (W4-2).

Stage one of the journey sees the person dealing with issues from their toxic past. This will normally end with a time of profound self-awareness of the

---

bus, live music, giving out sweets and invitations to special events. Members actively resist allowing anyone in the community to put pressure on folk to 'become a Christian'. It must be at the individual's initiative and in their time, if at all.

[74] For the idea of stages and learning socialization, see Kohlberg (1969).

[75] Although I use this model illustrated this way, I agree with those who would rather see this as a circle that grows ever larger.

dark side of their nature, and the need to be free from its gravity to self-harm and failure. Support at this stage can be psychological, dealing with matters like verbal, spiritual,[76] emotional, physical and sexual abuse. Or it can be practical, helping them manage their debt,[77] resolving lingering bad relationships, or parent-child issues etc. Some who come to us have little immediate need or any serious emotional damage. Yet during this stage of their journey, they too will discover areas of damage and self-deceit they didn't realise they were carrying, e.g. disappointment, fear of intimacy, anger from a betrayal etc. For most people this period of their journey will last anything from one to two years. We will often see this time come to an end as they show signs of 'brokenness'.[78]

The second stage, often overlapping with the first, is a growing awareness of their uniqueness and gifting, and may be accompanied by psychometric tests and an identifying of their natural skill set which we will help them interpret and pursue. They will often begin redeeming their education or careers, restoring broken relations (especially with family), and start to believe in themselves. The first stage of their journey is for them, but this second stage includes an awareness of obedience to God, moving toward a deeper intimacy with Christ. During this time they often begin benefiting from the simple truth that the Lord wants them to live free from their pasts. They begin to experience the reality of the wholeness of the *Rapha* promise. Relationships begin to be valued and go deeper. A number of them will end up getting married, or seeing family and friendships restored. This is always a priority area for us, when the person is ready.

This stage will blur into the third stage, 'for the Church and the world', as the person begins to mature in their knowing of themselves and God. During this stage they will be hearing Christ in a consistent way, and will begin moving in gifting and anointing. They begin having a deepening capacity to love people and to be loved, as they learn to love themselves.

---

[76] A literature is beginning to emerge on the issue of spiritual abuse, putting this issue on the agenda of the Church. See Johnson and van Vonderen (1991), Beasley-Murray (1998) etc. There is less on abuse as a broader subject.

[77] We make it clear that we are not financial advisors. But we offer some introductory teaching on managing a household budget, together with a simple budget sheet that the individual can complete, to help them identify what financial commitments they can or can't meet.

[78] This is a time when an individual truly begins to own their 'sin', to see their own complicity in their sicknesses, and their stubborn refusal to change. This profound shift is noticeable, and an essential step on the path to wholeness. By brokenness, I am describing that profoundly deep moment in our lives, sometimes several moments, in the presence of Christ and others, when we allow ourselves to acknowledge our dark side, our self-harm and the utter despair of our fragmented lives. We say sorry to ourselves, others and God. Many joke to me that they have already been there, done that, but when one authentically does this it leaves its permanent mark, sometimes a new meekness, sometimes a 'knowing' that allows us to personally see our arrogance, pride and self-possession in ourselves and others.

They naturally begin to serve others.[79] They have begun a discipleship journey that will continue throughout their life.[80]

Introducing 'diagnostic counselling'

Once an individual has made a decision that they want to change, and have begun hearing from their inner voice about the 'dark side' of their nature, they are ready to move on in their journey. CCD has developed its own version of my earlier one-to-one model, which is now a key feature of community life. We call it diagnostic counselling, but I do very little of it myself these days. It is now part of the group IQ within the social process of the community and its narrative culture. Most of the time it is one of the mentors assisting the person to identify specific areas of damage in their life, with their contributory drives. Once this is agreed by the person as being true, they subsequently begin to dismantle this damage emotionally and cognitively, giving it to the Lord, so that its consequences are no longer present, and the person is free to live as though it had never happened. The diagnostic idea is based on the principle that you need to be able to recall, in order to remember, in order to let go.

So in referring to part of our therapeutic process as diagnostic 'counselling', I confess my continuing unease with the term 'counselling', as in every case the whole community is involved. But I have not yet found an alternative. No-one involved in this model takes a traditional counselling role. In some ways this term applies better to the Holy Spirit (Is. 9:6, Jn. 14:6,26; 15:26) in bringing God's perspective to us. But God as counsellor is also God as diagnostician, giving each of us the initial knowledge, often experienced as wisdom, that helps unpack what has been said. The individual chooses their mentor. It is also important to note that anything that anyone says is open for questioning and discussion by the individual. For instance, one of the unwritten social rules in the community is our ban of '*thus saith the Lord*' type statements, as potentially abusive and misleading. Also, such a social process breaks the power relationship of counsellor-to-client, and makes the whole journey more relaxed, fluid, flexible and open to change. Telling people what to do is rarely helpful for them.

The underlying principle we are speaking of here is that the individual focuses on a single issue, usually the biggest or heaviest one, that they already know is contributing negatively to their lives. This issue will often

---

[79] During the first year of CCD we saw ourselves as a field hospital, where we were the wounded. In time the Lord expected us to get out of our beds and become the nurses and doctors, making way for the next waves of people.

[80] When we do workshops, or even where we do not, we will support people doing the *Rapha* journey. In 2005 we will be sending teams to the United States, Germany, Turkey, Egypt as well as throughout the UK.

be seen as a locked room of their 'spiritual house'. They learn from both others and the Lord to differentiate between the symptoms of that issue and its underlying drives.[81] They reach a 'diagnosis' when they can identify these underlying issues.[82] For example, they may discover their anger toward a work colleague is a symptom of the pain they are carrying from the betrayal of a sibling in their childhood. Or they may realise that their fear of intimacy in marriage is a self-protection they instigated instinctively after earlier relational abuse.

Achieving the actual diagnosis often proves to be significant for the individual. So when it is achieved it brings meaning to both their current difficulties and their troubled history. Articulating the underlying damage is the beginning of an empowering, which allows them to declare, '*I do not want this anymore.*'[83] By knowing what it is they do not want, they are able to take responsibility for it and separate themselves from it. All sessions, and many of the other meetings within *Rapha* and the community are taped, or have a mentor or 'scribe' write notes. It is very important that nothing is lost of what might be declared or said by the Lord during the session. The person must subsequently be able to think through carefully and accurately what has been said.

In the first few months many are still learning how to trust their inner voice and the best way of taking responsibility for their own therapeutic process. Sessions are always available, and arranged usually within a day or

---

[81] In speaking this way I am not describing the therapeutic process of 'labelling', the defining of mental and emotional illness as discrete disorders, using the DSM (First 1995). The concept of labelling, essential in organic medicine where disease can be seen, does not transfer well to psychiatry, where one can only see the symptoms and can rarely talk of one drive or single 'cause'. Many people come to CCD with the stigma of these labels, which have added to the fragmenting of their lives. I can understand why some feel it necessary to use labels, but I see the whole system having major flaws simply because no emotional or mental illness will have one 'cause'. Such an approach to human disorder is naïve. Human nature at every level is far too complex for that, and the neuro-psycho-physiological aspects that respond to medication will be only one part of the disorder. Pharmacy, long term, will often do nothing more than dull extreme mood swings, the managing of symptoms. (See 'An example: lifestyle disease and iatrogenic illness' (page 236).

[82] In this diagnostic process I am borrowing the Johannine picture of darkness and light, whereby in exposing ourselves to the Light, we are able to seek the authenticity of our own nature (Goldbrunner 1966:62) as God sees it. The interior world of our unconscious is the focus. As Cassell observed, people suffer from what they have lost of themselves (1982:642). He gives us an interesting list of such sources of loss, including our pasts, family, bloodline, forebears, culture, society, personal role, emotion, relationships, our bodies, unconscious, secret life, perceived future and our human spirit.

[83] Many of those who come to us will already have lots of ideas about their problems, having experienced counselling and psychological therapies, Christian or otherwise. They may be familiar with such diagnoses already, and be ready to move on to the next stage. But we will always require they tell us what they think the key issue is, rather than repeat what a counsellor might have told them. They must own the area as theirs, at both a cognitive and affective level.

so, at the person's discretion.[84] The focus of a diagnostic session is primarily teaching, as the person learns how damage in one part of their history might be leeching into many other areas. They are often given a series of suggestions about possible contributory factors, and are invited to reflect on which might be the most significant or toxic. They are always able to book further session at their own initiative whenever they and their mentor feel it is most appropriate.[85]

A key feature of the diagnostic process is the individual's personal responsibility to undertake *'homework'*.[86]

> *Homework is hearing from [the] God that you perceive that you love, to discover that He tells you that you don't love Him. And you possess that and you realise you are talking to a God you hate, who then tells you how to be healed. And who then begins a voyage of relationship with you, and you discover finally that you meet your true self, and then have life, and then choose to want a relationship with the God that you have met (M4-10).*

We encourage people to do a little homework every day, for up to an hour. We stress this is time devoted to themselves, not for meditation, devotions or Bible study. During this time, while alone, they reflect on what they are learning, work through session notes and listen to God's voice. It is important they consider what they believe, and what is not true of them. Homework, therefore, is at the core of our work and its journey, as it both places the focus with the individual and allows them to set the pace. Each person chooses their own unique style of homework, adapting it to their work and family commitments, their personal strengths and weaknesses, the priority of issues, and their level of sickness, etc.

> *I think there are principles [for doing homework] but there are as many different ways of doing homework as there are people (M12-10).*

---

[84] Such an approach, where the client sets the appointment, avoids the difficult and complex problem of getting stale or stuck with a client in the therapeutic process. Most people doing this journey will follow a major break-through by a period of rest, while adjustment and integration takes place. For a helpful comment on the 'stuckness' in the therapeutic process, see Mearns and Thorne (1988/1999:153ff.).

[85] We practise a 'quick response' culture, where sessions are no more than 2-3 days notice. Susan Williams and I have done most of these in the past, but have noticed over the last two years a dramatic fall in demand as the mentors have increasingly carried this function. Most of our sessions now focus around newcomers who have not yet found ways of applying what they are learning.

[86] Homework is a common feature of some behavioural schools of psychological therapies. See for instance, the work of Wolpe and his followers (Wolpe 1958, Lazarus 1971, 1981). Ellis' *rational emotive therapy* (1962), and modern cognitive behavioural therapies taught by Aaron Beck (1975) and others all set homework. However, the homework we require is not just the relaxation instructions traditionally associated with these schools. It is similar to, but not the same as homework used in CAT (Ryle 1995b:41). Extensive work has already been done in therapeutic process and homework planning (Schultheis 1998), so we are merely adapting it.

We encourage people to identify their own heuristic shortcuts[87] in their homework journey, to let God teach them a unique way of pursuing their own therapeutic discipleship toward Christ-likeness.

In the diagnostic process, mentors also play a key role.[88]

> *My mentor is kind, caring, and friendly. I'm not used to this in my life, so when I see her and talk about absolutely anything, it's like a breath of fresh air. I don't talk that much to family and friends, as they seem to always knock me down, but my mentor lets me say whatever I like (09F-4.18).*

We prefer the word mentoring rather than 'coaching', as the latter suggests a hierarchy.[89] In CCD mentors are all members of CCD or *Rapha* who are pursuing their own journey, having themselves successfully worked through the areas now being tackled by the newcomer. These are the *skilled friends* (Egan 1975) who will meet as often as the person wishes as part of their homework programme. The mentor is chosen by the newcomer,[90] and will always, where possible, sit-in on the diagnostic sessions.[91] Many people will change mentors according to the issue they are dealing with,

---

[87] The field of heuristics, in both science and psychology is central to the generating of new ideas and knowledge. However, in this book I am using *heuristic* in a more narrow sense. I am speaking of aspects of our practice within the community in counselling and homework programmes that aid the client's release from sickness, finding ways to help them, and for them to help themselves, with the least additional pain. Much of the time these heuristics or *prescriptive therapies* are concepts and ideas that throw a profound new light for the person on their own disorders. But it must be noted the *heuristic value* of these practices are being tested within the community not just on outcomes, but also ethics and our developing psycho-theological framework.

[88] Although the *meta-analysis* of Smith and Glass (1977) (and Smith, et al. 1980) helped balance out the discrediting or the failure of psychological therapies, one interesting and robust finding is that 'paraprofessionals' (those not trained to practise psychological therapies) produce outcomes equivalent or sometimes exceeding those of trained therapists (Durlak 1981, Hattie, et al. 1984, Berman and Norton 1985, Weisz, et al. 1987, Phares and Trull 1997:309, etc.). In CCD these paraprofessionals are normally those who have themselves been helped, having *experienced* benefit. Within soul care this can be the best qualification to help others on the journey (Egan 1975:22ff.), as any soul carer must themselves also be continuing to achieve personal maturity (Cowen 1982).

[89] For some of the aspects of the mentor model we use, see Biehl (1996) and Wilson and Johnson (2001). The latter summarizes thinking to date, while noting some of the qualities needed in a mentor, namely integrity, courage, care and the ability and willingness to highlight ethical dangers. Mentoring, however, as we practice it, is more a passing on of personal experience, than the intentional building of life-long personal relations.

[90] Newcomers quickly find their way to suitable people who can help them. It is rare we assist them in finding mentors. They normally make wise choices. It is implicit in the culture of the community that as you get well you will be expected to take up a mentoring role if asked. Today, this 'mentoring group IQ' in the community, much wider than the Leadership Team, now represents hundreds of years of therapeutic success and failure.

[91] 'The relational approach anticipates that the client's problems will be re-experienced within the counselling relationship' (Pelham, et al. 2001:116). With the use of mentors we extend this process, so it is shared and carried by a larger circle.

and this practice is encouraged.[92] A person will also often choose a new mentor when they feel that they have undergone a significant personal change, wanting to deal with a new issue or explore new types of relationship. We expect the person and mentor to go through homework together. We find this relationship is key, as it breaks the dependency of the exclusive one-to-one counsellor approach, as well as the isolation and power issues of the counsellor-therapist relationship.[93]

The process of dealing with an issue we liken to 'major surgery', with a diagnosis, preparation, surgery, and rehabilitation. The difference is that this surgery happens in the person's own subliminal spiritual-emotional core, so we describe it as 'spiritual surgery'. The diagnosis is followed by this 'surgical' period of cleansing, removing the area of damage. This often requires repentance from the person, not because they are responsible for the damage, but to express their regret that the damage has been obstructive for too long. This process of letting go of pain, abuse or trauma etc., is a 'removing' of it, by an act of the will of the individual, coupled with God's co-operation and the affirmation of those supporting them. Sometimes this 'letting go', or spiritual surgery, will happen spontaneously as the person 'sees' the damage they have been living with, and chooses not to want it any longer. But more often, especially early on in their journey, there is an essential dimension of emotional engagement to the cleansing process.

> *When I first heard [about spiritual surgery], I thought, 'what on earth are they talking about?' I did not fully understand this until I went on a workshop. It took me a good year to say the words, 'Lord, I do not want this any more.' Amazingly, it worked. I could not believe it. My father's death, I thought was my fault, and I said sorry to him many times, but the feelings never went away. Spiritual surgery helped me to do this and now I can think and talk about my father and it doesn't hurt any more. Thank you, Lord (09F-6.13)*

Feeling is healing

CCD has developed a theory and practice of the benefits of emotion that borrows from both psychological therapies and Hebrew ideas, but has been developed over many years clinically through personal experience. This has given it a unique edge. Aspects of the 'dark side' of our nature are often most easily identified at an emotional level, whereas much of our self-deception is more often cognitive. For instance, we may have re-written our history so we no longer think of ourselves as abused, but emotionally

---

[92] One of the questions asked is: what does the mentor get out of these relationships? They benefit in a whole range of ways, in re-enforcing their own journey, thereby bringing added meaning to their own lives, but often it will give them significant encouragement when the newcomer goes through major change that is often called 'helpers high' (Kottler 1996:186).

[93] See, for instance, Guy and Liaboe (1985 passim).

continue to feel we have been. Therefore the retaining of an emotional dimension to our wholeness journey[94] is not just helpful, but essential.[95]

In traditional church you are taught to ignore emotion. To actually go into your emotion is paramount to your healing (07M-5.3).

It is our toxic pain that keeps bad toxic memories alive. Normal life will frequently trigger circumstances that continually draw us back into re-living our damaged pasts. All the while we carry this pool of toxic pain, we keep alive all the events that gave this to us in the first place. Like a hot air balloon kept aloft by the historic pain and its memories, we must own, engage and give to Christ, or put into the Cross, all that we have denied of this trauma, pain and shame from our past. In owning this emotion, by feeling it and letting it go, we deflate the balloon, leaving only the carcass of the fading memories. In time even these memories will fade. However, this can never happen at a cognitive level, but only by letting the emotion flood us. Repressing or denying it predicts it may psycho-physiologically come back and bite us one day.

The healing of our damaged emotion and its feelings will happen naturally on our journey, from a place of seeing our emotion as the painful enemy, to a place where through engaging it, and coaching it, we experience it being healed. This process allows our emotion to begin to become one of our greatest assets. Wholeness as Christ-likeness includes a process towards emotional maturity. This emotionally-experienced dimension of discipleship brings to the individual part of the authenticity they are seeking. The benefits of healed emotion is a key issue among the contemporary un-churched (e.g. Goleman 1995, Diamond 1985/1990). Outside the Church we are entering an age of the authority of the experience of emotion for both men and women. Expressing emotion, be it at the Rugby international, or a TV soap, is now becoming more widely acceptable among men and women.

The modern practice of engaging our emotion is often called catharsis or abreaction. In its original form catharsis seems to have had two meanings from Aristotle: that emotional tension is lessened by expressing it, and that emotion can be refined by its sharing (English and English 1958). Of these, the former entered psychology, suggesting that aggressive action can be temporarily reduced by feeling it, thereby removing some of the inclination

---

[94] None of us can learn without emotion. See le Dioux (1998).

[95] For me this is why the results of research on *desensitisation* is profoundly worrying, as we now know continued exposure to violence extinguishes emotional reaction and moral objectivity, whether live e.g. Baron and Kempner (1970) or symbolic, e.g. Bandura (1965), Liebert and Baron (1972). Observational learning will always occur wherever it can (Carver and Scheier 1996:382, Heller and Polsky 1975, Geen 1978). As people's emotional reactions to violence are extinguished, being victimised (and also victimising others) comes to be seen as an ordinary part of life (Carver and Scheier 1996:383). To repent, or to even change our lifestyle, we must all have the sensitivity to the wrong of harm.

toward aggression.[96] In the early days of psychoanalysis the term catharsis was used to describe the expression and discharge of both repressed emotion and ideas,[97] freeing psychic energy by converting these repressed ideas and their emotion into experiences of consciousness, so-called abreaction.[98] Emotion has had a chequered path in therapeutic psychology. Freud never developed a separate mature theory of emotion, neither have the modern cognitive psychological therapies offered a cogent and consistent view of emotion and its therapeutic use.[99] All schools of psychological therapy have to work with emotion and its feelings, but this is mainly in the one to one relationship. Others make it a key part of the therapeutic process, e.g. rational emotive therapy (RET).

Although most people would see expression of emotion, especially laughter, as therapeutic (Jamieson 2003:224), it is now beyond doubt that worry and stress cause a wide range of physical illnesses (Pennebaker 1995:5), while the clinical release of emotion produces striking reductions in blood pressure, muscle tension, and skin conductance (e.g. Reich 1949, Wolff and Goodell 1968, Pennebaker 1995:6 etc.). Despite these benefits, most psychotherapists still prefer to remain with ideation (Greenberg and Safran 1987, 1989), the world of ideas and mental images in a cognitive framework, since this is much less 'stressful' to all parties. Therefore catharsis or abreaction has never been mainstream in psychological therapies, and will probably stay that way until a clinical apologetic for its benefits is developed alongside, I would suggest, the writing of a needed Biblical theology of emotion.[100]

---

[96] For a fuller treatment of this view, see Berkowitz (1962, 1993). This is often described as the *Catharsis hypothesis*. It is still claimed today that there is insufficient empirical support for the therapeutic gain of catharsis (Adams and Bromley 1998:7), though not everyone shares this view (Stocker and Hegeman 1996).

[97] See Wolman (1973), referring to Freud (1893-1895).

[98] Primal therapy is probably the best-known cathartic school, developed by Arthur Janov (1970, 1972/1975), focusing on the concept that most of us have deep-seated trauma from our pasts, and the most effective way of releasing this is by reliving the experience as 'primal pain', out of the 'primal pool' in our psyche. The therapy is based on the observation that children who cannot be themselves, mainly through parental denial, suppress the frustration, trauma and its pain. Therapy begins with a 'major primal scream' which, after this 'flooding', opens the person to further 'primals'. 'Primal Therapy does not preach a system of rules by which to live. It is, instead, a process through which we may feel their pain. It is each man's personal revolution against the tyranny of his neurosis. As long as man is sick, the world will reflect his pain. Primal Therapy is an end to that pain' (Janov 1972/1975:234).

[99] Having said that, scattered around various schools of psychological therapy, emotion is being confronted (Arnold 1968). Likewise, various aspects of emotion are mentioned, for instance, grieving for all kinds of loss, a subject on which much has been written, e.g. Bowlby (1980), Kubler-Ross (1970), and Parkes (1972). See 'Borrowing a Hebrew view of emotion (page 232).

[100] It is interesting to see how the Church has diverse views on this point. See, for instance Allender and Longman (1994), who see emotion as a strategic tool for the Church, as I do, and MacArthur and Mack (1994:13, 96) who along with numerous others, saw emotion as

As we live we *feel*. Therefore, on the basis of my body spirit unity model, our sensibility, our human emotion, is centred in both our brain (our physical nature) and also in our spiritual and emotional natures (1 Sam. 30:6, Jb. 7:11; 17:1, Ps. 34:18; 51:12; 143:7, Ec. 7:8-9 etc.). Within CCD we see emotion[101] as one of the phenomena that transcends both aspects of our one nature, as well as spiritual and material worlds.[102] In support of this I follow the Hebrew Scriptures, which saw emotion as both spiritual and material, for Yahweh presents Himself as an emotional deity (Nu. 11:33, Ps. 136:1ff., Am. 5:21 etc.),[103] and we are made in this image. Therefore Hebrew personhood is seen as emotional.

This Hebrew perspective is very helpful, for it gives all emotion both a good and a dark side, and this approach is illustrated throughout the Old Testament. Love could be righteous or unrighteous, as could fear, anger, peace, shame, etc. This contrasts with Greek thought, which like us today, saw emotion as divided so that some feelings were good (e.g. love, joy, laughter etc.), and some bad (e.g. anger, hate, jealousy etc). Clinically, we follow the Hebrew model in CCD, echoed and supported in the life of Christ (Law 1915), and the writings of Paul (Eph. 4:26).

[It is important to me] that Christ Church recognizes emotions are valid and that every emotion has a place. And that there is a righteous side as well as an unrighteous side to every emotion so you can get redemption (W4-5).

Within my own practice there are a number of similarities with the underlying theories of Gestalt, arguing that 'a person is inseparable from his environment' (Passons 1975:49), so this therapeutic approach, (not to be confused with Gestalt Psychology) requires we possess what we really feel *now*. 'Observe the feelings you are experiencing now....do you become

---

untrustworthy, and not of help in the Christian walk. Interestingly, William James saw the importance of emotion in human experience (1884). Also Macmurray has made the connection of the importance of emotion in both one's personal life and the life of the community (1976).

[101] When teaching about emotion I describe our feelings as a stunning bouquet of unique flowers, around 120 blooms, that I catalogue into families. The word 'emotion' describes the full bouquet, while each individual bloom in this bouquet is a 'feeling', and must be appreciated for its own uniqueness. Emotion is a vast and controversial subject, and we can hardly do it justice in this short account. For a neural biological introduction, see Lewis and Havilland (1993) or Oatley and Jenkins (1996). Looking at the brain as the seat of emotion, see le Dioux (1998) and for a positive Christian view of emotion, see Baars (1979).

[102] The emotion-spirit link that I am suggesting is not my idea. Many have thought this before me. See, for instance, Hillman (1960:231ff.). Some of the other phenomena that transcend both realities are words, the Trinity, especially the Holy Spirit, our will, and whenever they wish, spiritual beings both good and bad.

[103] The Church is trapped here by anthropomorphic language, and I also am in danger of speaking anthropopathically, attributing human emotion to God. However, from God's perspective and based on Scripture it is we who mirror His nature as emotional beings, rather than us attributing human emotional characteristics to God. We do not impose emotion on God, merely interpret His emotional action in our world. Our disdain of emotion here in the West, at least in part, follows Greek Stoic thinking which saw emotion as unhelpful in the pursuit of pure intellectual thought.

aware of any physical sensations related to the feelings?....Attend to these...' (Passons 1975:53). The founder of Gestalt, Frederick Perls stated: 'emotion is understood to be not a threat to rational control of your life but a guide which furnishes the only basis on which human existence can be ordered rationally, then the way is open to the cultivation of its wise promptings' (1951/1977:100).[104]

In our practice of catharsis, however, we encourage the person to go much further, letting the emotion 'flood' them,[105] and in this engaging teach the person to let go the pain in such a way that they will never need to engage it again.

[I am encouraged to] be utterly and bitterly and deeply honest and frank about my feelings and explore them (M13-1).

We teach people to engage emotion with the support of others, never alone, so the process makes one vulnerable to others in the group thereby strengthening the bond of deepening relationship. This in turn strengthens the individual's willingness to trust others in the group (Bishop 1985:14).[106] For both men and women, these deepening relationships will be essential to the successful journey. But the process of learning positive catharsis is something you cannot hurry, for as with many other aspects of the journey toward permanent positive change, letting things happen is more important than the desire to make things happen (Martin 1962:164). Empowerment in the community is both something given and something taken.

So what I am proposing, and practise, is not just the use of catharsis as a healing tool, but something much broader, where catharsis is one key aspect. CAT seems to go further than most therapeutic counselling schools, including psychoanalytic or CBT. (See Marzillier and Butler 1995.) But even CAT does not see emotion as the strategic tool I do. My approach allows people to emotionally engage pain and its scripts, while at the same time cognitively denying what they feel. By finding and letting go of toxic emotion the person has permission to become someone new. We teach them to let their emotion flood them, and encourage them to declare 'I don't want this anymore!', by giving it to the Lord. This emotional

---

[104] Our own experience in CCD is that emotion becomes an ally as we clear out all the toxic past it is entangled in. This 'frees-up' our emotion to be more spontaneous, and able to be coached more spontaneously by the Holy Spirit. For us to become more fully human, emotion must become an ally in our wholeness journey rather than an area of deep vulnerability. One of the most balanced recent approaches, enlarging on this principle, was Bassett and Hill (1998), who proposed the possibility of 'living Christ while experiencing emotion'.

[105] This is a term I find helpful, borrowed from Goleman (1995:138), but adapted by me to describe the peaking release of emotion. Tears and deep convulsing will often accompany this process. (See Kottler 1996.)

[106] Haigh saw two distinct levels of emotionality, *primary emotional development*, when things go seriously wrong with a child's environment, and *secondary emotional development*, when we try to recreate the psychic space where things originally went wrong or got stuck, so they can be re-experienced and re-written (1999:256).

engaging is sometimes accompanied by a colourful range of expletives that we do not discourage. These profound moments are a declaration of emotional *engagement* or owning what they no longer want to carry. They are touching the dark toxic pain and trauma, formerly hidden to them, in order to rid themselves of it for ever. They are letting this baggage go, once and for all.

This ventilationist therapeutic approach also has an important community aspect, allowing people to go deep with one another, especially men.[107]

> *[I would describe] the capacity of the congregation, especially the men of the church, to support outsiders, to support men, men who come in great damage, great pain, rejection, great isolation (M9-1).*

Using this affective model demonstrates to the person how small choices and decisions from their past, e.g. 'I will never let him do that to me again!' have had a torrid impact on their lifestyle over many years. It is the emotional breaking of scripts and their schemas, bringing a cleansing to the person, especially to their choked up emotion. It is a practical way of possessing wholeness in body spirit unity. We frequently see distinct physical change and better health as indivduals go through this process.

Spiritual body language

For those who experience unexpected physical sickness at the beginning or during their journey of wholeness, we would usually expect this to be temporary, going as they deal with the issue related to it. Typical of these types of disorder are back ache, stiff necks and shoulder pain, headaches, skin rashes and the feeling of having a great 'lump' in ones stomach that needs to come up. Improvement is usually related to successful homework, where complete recovery follows this diagnostic process, with the help of their mentor.

> *[An example of 'spiritual body language']* Back pain (spasm) left as I returned *and took back to and from men what had been given and received by me from them (08F-6.6).*

The body spirit unity model is particularly helpful when talking about and experiencing physical disorder in the body. What impacts our emotional spiritual lives will often show itself in our bodies physically. Likewise, what happens to us physically will impact emotional spiritual aspects of our nature. Like Benner, I see much physical illness as 'a voice of the soul' (1998:102), a cry for help from the suffering *ruah* (Goldbrunner 1955:12).

---

[107] Alternate Monday evenings CCD has a men's meeting where between 15-25 men come together to make declarations publicly, and to engage emotion. We talk about these sessions as 'blood on the rug' times. Men do this like a rugby team, openly declaring matters previously kept secret by them, breaking the hidden power of baggage by speaking it out. Engaging such deep emotion draws together the man holistically, sometimes quite dramatically.

Physical pain attacks us all at our weakest point - our physical bodies and our minds (Goldbrunner 1966:56). Much of the time these 'diseases of the soul' (Weatherhead 1951:318), out of our interior world, are unrighteous jealousy, hate, malice, anger, revenge, resentment, worry, guilt, shame, etc. All these words we are seeking to recover in CCD and *Rapha*.[108] As our emotion surfaces, these 'voices of illness' as Dr John Jelfs[109] calls them, physically manifest themselves in our bodies as organic sickness and disease. I see this as a psycho-physiological response to the baggage of our core nature and spirit.[110] Such sicknesses, and their location in our body, can be helpful clues on the journey for diagnosing the condition of the human spirit or 'heart'.

Such thinking is beginning to find wider acceptance both in the Church (Wolff 1973:143-148, Siegel 1991, Wright 1999) and in medicine (Jobst, et al. 1999). It is one of the avenues we gently pursue when medical tests have exposed no neural or biological reason for a physical condition, or where the person has been unable to find relief in other ways.[111] But the release of emotion is more fundamental than just for physical healing, since it also brings relief in our spirit, thereby helping the body heal itself. Everyone doing this journey will need to learn that *feeling is healing*, and as pain goes we can be sure the issue is dealt with.

Some of the distinctives of my process

Where has the therapist gone?

Like Seymour Halleck I acknowledge that neutrality in the therapist is largely myth (1971/1994:19). But our using a didactic model, and no therapist as such, makes matters more complicated because teaching by its very nature is directive. After a long hard struggle I have made peace with this and like Culley concede it is impossible not to be directive in some

---

[108] 'Flesh and bone are only as healthy as the spirit they encase' (Brown 1995:16, quoting Wengrov 1982:152 commenting on Pr. 14:30).

[109] Dr John Jelfs is a medical doctor in general practice, with a special interest in spirituality and its psychophysiology. He mentioned this in a personal conversation, and I am grateful to him for permission to use the concept.

[110] It is not either/or, but rather a combination of both medical and emotional/spiritual. Spiritual body language is one of the spin-offs of working with people who have complex disorders. But I stopped many years ago recording incidents of people coming to me with stubborn physical disorders, which dissipated when they had completed the 'spiritual surgery' homework. To achieve complete success in seeing the disorder go sometimes takes several rounds, or layers. In this sense my model is both endogenous, having internal drives, and exogenous, having external 'causes'.

[111] We work closely with local GPs and health care professionals. Everyone joining the community is encouraged to register with a local practice. We do not view ourselves as an alternative to the medical model, but as a partner, bringing additional expertise and resources that will compliment other more traditional approaches.

measure in teaching, mentoring and in counselling (1991:48). Being non-directive, I have always thought, was the holy grail in professional counselling. This knowledge was reinforced in numerous pastoral settings, as I am aware of our power to mislead and harm. But I began to see that for any change to occur, the person must be intellectually convinced and/or emotionally driven, by learning alternative ways of living. Learning new ideas, and truth about oneself, becomes emancipatory, but only follows instruction, either from the community or God. People who want to change, especially the emotionally ill, are expecting instruction in how they might change to be well.

The safeguards we put in place focus around some simple principles. For instance, we encourage all members to hear and trust their inner voice (or God), and to expect this be the initiator of major areas of healing in their lives. It is not what *we* think, but what *they* know. We take for granted that God will set the agenda with them, not us.[112] We help facilitate what they are hearing and accepting about themselves. We also train mentors not to discuss major issues in people's lives until the person is already beginning to address them. In this sense the Lord, through the whole community, becomes the *Rapha* therapist. The wisdom behind this is significant, as a group of people, not one therapist, carries each newcomer. The individual also benefits from a diversity of experience and counsel. Diagnostic counselling sessions merely help clarify and supplement what is already happening.

As in all therapeutic practices, when allowing an individual to raise issues, one inevitably faces the question 'did it really happen?' Our view in CCD, following Epictetus and May among others, is that it is not the facts of the events that necessarily damage us, but our perception of them (May, et al. 1958:26).[113] The ongoing toxic damage in a person's life is more often the result of their *perception of what they believe happened*, rather than the facts of the actual event.[114] If they believe a matter, or show the damage of

---

[112] Some, like Lambourne, would see counselling, even in a pastoral context, as *ethical persuasion* (1983:136). Although I am sometimes guilty of 'bold love' (Allender and Longman 1994), our safeguards and group social process remove the need for such persuasion.

[113] I am sometimes asked what we do with psychotic people, especially those with delusional disorder (First 1995, DSMF22.0, for instance). In sessions I would refuse to talk to their alternative personas, requiring they exhibit their true selves, be present to us. Within the community members accept the validity of, say, a person's fear ('there's an alien after me'), choosing initially not judge it, but instead take them back to the time they began thinking or feeling this way.

[114] What I am suggesting here is that whether the event took place or not is not so relevant as the person's perception of whether it did. If they carry the damage, then they need to take responsibility for letting go of the damage, even if the facts they 'remember' are not objectively accurate, or even contradict what they feel (as they often will). This is a big issue in psychological therapies today. For instance, a recent major conference focused on this at the Royal Society of Medicine, 4/9/03, *Remembering trauma: Current theory, research and practice, with part of the day devoted to real and fabricated accounts of the past.*

it in their lives, then we should honour them by also accepting it. For instance, rape may or may not have taken place, but if they carry the damage then we meet them in this. An example was a woman who came to us feeling she had been raped around 10-11 years of age, but she had good parents and no memory of any such event, just the profound feelings of being violated. In talking it through with her mentor she began to recall an uncle who lived in the house for a year or so when she was at that age, who spied on her every time she undressed or had a bath. She remembered it happening. He was stripping her with his eyes. This was emotional rape, and this was what she was feeling.

So we do not trust memory that much, as the person will have emotionally and cognitively re-written their history many times. But if the person can be seen to carry the damage as though it did happen,[115] then that damage has to be removed by them, with the help of others.[116] Taking the person's viewpoint on any issue, and not questioning the validity of the 'facts', is one of the most liberating aspects of our model, as it means the person is not judged, but is able to begin believing they are trusted and understood. What we are actually doing is seeing matters from their perspective, not judging them through ours.

Supervision[117] of one another also plays a key role in our work. Personally I am accountable to both my colleague Susan Williams, as a peer supervisor on a daily basis, and fortnightly to the Leadership Team of CCD. Our supervision regime seeks to take account of current standard rules and conventions governing psychological therapies, designed to both protect the client and make life manageable in the community (cf. Bond 1993/2000:63ff.). Also, CCD is a member of the Association of Therapeutic Communities and part of the joint Community of Communities project with the Royal College of Psychiatrists (UK). Within this

---

[115] When questioned as to whether a rape might be a fantasy or fact Rollo May commented, 'we have....a continent of new knowledge about inner dynamics when we take the approach that the relation to a fact or situation is what is significant for the patient or person ....[not] whether or not something objectively occurred' (May, et al. 1958:26).

[116] The so-called 'reconciliation' movement concerns me, suggesting as it does that a matter is not fully dealt with until there is repentance on behalf of the perpetrator, and reconciliation with all parties. In CCD and *Rapha* we seek the wholeness of the individual, and for this we argue it is unnecessary for the person to ever meet their abusers. Our experience is that it often leads to further trauma and abuse. Also, the abuser may already be dead. We use Gestalt, which allows the person to confront their abuser without ever meeting them, and this together with the laying down of revenge (see 'Some examples: Fear, forgiveness and grief, page 157), means they can walk away with a new wholeness, without actual contact with their abusers.

[117] Traditional supervision in a counselling situation is provided by someone who is not in a line management position with them. So the *Ethical framework for good practice in counselling and practice* states, 'there is a general obligation for all counsellors, psychotherapists and trainers to receive supervision, consultative support independently of any managerial relationships' (British Association for Counselling and Psychotherapy 2002).

relationship we have an annual internal and visiting peer review from a team from another therapeutic community. This programme is designed to set best practice within the community, and it is hoped in time will lead to a set of standards for the over 300 therapeutic communities in UK. In addition, I am also a Lead Reviewer for this programme, in visiting other therapeutic communities, while CCD has recently been a peer reviewer for a community in Liverpool.

So we have designed a complex internal and external co-relational accountability and supervision system. This shows itself in numerous practices in the community, in that all mentoring is gender exclusive, and that during counselling sessions a scribe or mentor is also always present. The vulnerability of the one to one exclusive relationship is not pursued. Likewise, all support groups are either exclusively male or female, none are mixed. Such disciplines safeguard everyone. The community and its practices are believed by us to be the best supervisor,[118] most of the time acting as an early warning system when things are going wrong.[119]

We are also cautious about traditional pastoral 'follow-up', instead relying on the mentors and friends to keep the Leadership Team informed where necessary. In previous churches I have noted that from the church member's perspective much pastoral care can feel manipulative.

I have just heard people talk about it, [that is, being a Christian], and you are supposed to be it and you have all these charges against you because you are not it and you have all these charges against them because they are not it either (M13-1).

With such a diverse lay team of experienced helpers functioning as a therapeutic community,[120] the issue of confidentiality also becomes complex. We have adapted the guidelines proposed by Bond (1993/2000:150ff.), and have used this in both our mentor training and our Confidentiality Policy (appendix 6). With a community IQ comprising of such diverse backgrounds, the issue of counselling dependency is not relevant. As people's trust grows, so does their ability not to look to any one individual for support. The focus, ultimately, is their relationship with Christ, though one of the key abilities needed by mentors, what Culley calls *reflective* skills (1991:41ff.), articulates the internal frame of reference of the person back to the person. The community is good at being this mirror for people.

You are allowed to grow into the truth almost before it is exposed and spoken about. So there is a personal responsibility rather than a confrontation that makes you feel a failure or inadequate (W5-8a).

---

[118] Having said this, I am aware of the dangers of groupthink. See Janis (1994).

[119] Modern responses to the possibility of abuse are numerous. See, for instance, POPAN, The prevention of professional abuse network, helping those who have suffered the devastating effects of professional abuse {www.popan.org.uk}.

[120] Chapter 6 introduces the principles of therapeutic community.

The combination of hearing God's voice, mentoring, diagnostic sessions and the narrative culture of a therapeutic faith community provides a radically different approach from traditional psychological therapies, or from 'doing church'. But I also believe it offers a clinical framework for ongoing creative change within a Trinity model of community. In such a culture people can develop all of their natural skills and spiritual gifting.

The place of intuit

Intuit, intuition or insight is something I am fully committed to. With the increasing emphasis on the science of psychological therapies, it is disturbing to note the apparent diminishing role of 'insight' in the therapeutic process. In contrast, soul care should always practice an *insight focused* therapy (Davison and Neale 1998:505), a Holy Spirit-quickened perception of hidden repressed drives, coupled with the skill of identifying and interpreting these. In CCD we see the whole Trinity being present whenever we seek God. But in many circles this intuit, Holy Spirit quickened or not, is now considered 'unscientific'. Consequently, there has been a great deal of debate regarding the clinical or actuarial method, between the intuitive, (e.g. having no formula) (Meehl 1957), or the scientific.

In response to this trend, some are now calling for a return to greater use of insight (Kleinmuntz 1990), arguing that like the soul carer, the successful therapist must also have skills of an experiential, subjective and intuitive nature (Phares and Trull 1997:268). My one reservation, well known in CCD, is that in encouraging insight pastorally, we are always in danger of promoting a 'messianic' type of image of the carer/mentor (Krasner 1963). In our case this is filtered by 'homework', mentoring and the transparency of the grace culture of faith community. By encouraging people to practise on one another, social rules begin to develop between them which moderate extreme behaviour.[121] But the debate on intuit begs the prior question of how we might get ill in the first place.

How do we get sick?

Over the years I have developed a model that outlines the origins of some of our more common human damage. This helps people by removing the mystery of why they are 'sick'. But my model does not include organic illness, for instance toothache, heart surgery and other aging disorders, but

---

[121] A typical example was when a new member, but a Christian of many years, tried to begin telling people what was wrong with them 'in the Lord's Name'. He was quickly advised by an un-churched member, 'we don't do that here!' Likewise, a visitor recently tried to share what he thought the Lord wanted to say to a person, and was told to write it down, and give it to the person's mentor.

does cover lifestyle disease like addictions,[122] smoking, alcohol, street drugs, medication and obesity etc. However, we do not focus on the physical dimensions of illness, instead on the emotional/spiritual drives behind such disorders. Most of the illness we confront is long-term and intransigent, often complex, bringing people to a place of despair because they cannot find a way out of the downward spiral.

Typical symptoms of these drives are sleep deprivation, inability to give and receive love, persistent failure and recurring self-harm, and a range of cyclic emotional and mental illnesses that entrap and isolate the person from both relationships and themselves.[123] So the people we are most able to help in CCD are those born 'healthy' and who grow up 'normally', but then inexplicably slip into mental illness. Such people, like all of us to varying degrees, are the victims of ideas and relationships that have contributed to our becoming sick. Each of us must now use new ideas, from God's perspective, alongside new relationships of trust within community, to reverse these disorders.

Most people ask us how they got sick in the first place, so over the last 30 or so years I have developed a model illustrating where many of these problems come from. We see three possible sources. The first, and often the most controversial, is inherited disorders. We all benefit from both a material and spiritual heritage of our parents, but we also inherit baggage, its weaknesses and consequential sin. It can be as innocent as looks, attitudes or values, sometimes later manifesting as physical or mental disorder, or organic disability.[124] We teach people to possess the emotional and spiritual good they have inherited, for instance their intellectual skill set, or natural gifting, while encouraging them to separate from what is dark, for instance repeated marriage failure, a phobic state or a need to control everything. This process needs God's perspective, supplemented by the wisdom of the IQ, EQ and SQ of the community. It is a willingness to admit that not everything from one's parents was good. Instead of just accepting fate as many do, 'I've always been like this', we teach people they can separate themselves from the darkness in their heredity.

---

[122] The model we use for tackling substance addictions is a three level one with a biochemical, social and emotional layer to the addiction. Much of the time it is the emotional attachment to the addiction that is the 'root' or drive, that has to be owned and removed by the person. We see little point in temporarily breaking the biochemical aspects of the addiction until the emotional drive or attachment is dealt with, since the person will often merely return to the habit. Once the drive(s) have been undone, it is easier to let go of the addiction. See 'An example: Lifestyle disease and iatrogenic illness (page 236).

[123] The background medical concept I am using here is the distinction between *organic psychosis*, those psychiatric disorders that have an organic/neural dimension that can be treated with medication, and *functional psychosis,* those disorders with no organic explanation. See Grof and Grof (1989b:1ff.) for an enlarging of these distinctions.

[124] See Friedman (1985), Fabiano and Fabiano (2003) or Gothard (1998) for further discussion of these areas of damage.

The second area is what others, outside of our family, have done to us. This can take the form of physical, emotional, spiritual, sexual or verbal abuse, among others. All of us, from conception, can be victims of such abuse. Most people see this as the greatest source of damage in their lives, and take every opportunity to blame others for the state they are in. When people first contact us they normally have this mindset, clearly unwilling to change, while they blame others. Blaming others is a coping mechanism which they will maintain until they can confidently see a way out of the sicknesses they have. Accepting responsibility without having a way out is unwise. But over time, living in the community, or on the journey personally, as well as accepting responsibility, they will also come to learn, as we all do, the third and biggest area of damage.

During the first workshop they are introduced to the simple concept that it is not what others have done, but what they have done with what others have done. For most of us, with the passing of time, this will be the area of greatest damage. As mentioned earlier, in CCD we describe this as 'sin against ourselves'. People are disturbed not by things, but the view they take of them (Davison and Neale 1998:537). This concept, first popularised by Epictetus, the Stoic Greek master, was taken up by the followers of Freud, particularly Mahler's *object relations theory* (Carver and Scheier 1996:295), and person-centred counselling (Mearns and Thorne 1988/1999:31). For many of us, our own cognition of past events (Phares and Trull 1997:464, Gleitman 1995:663) is the real block in our path to wholeness.[125] But knowing the damage we have done to ourselves is not enough, as we need to act on that knowledge so that it changes both our perception and our lives.

Introducing scripts and schemas

A person's attitude to themselves will be written in their scripts and schemas,[126] mostly hidden to them. So the process of taking responsibility means confronting some of these unhelpful scripts and schemas that they and others have written. Scripts and schemas are our organisation of knowledge (scripts) and propensity for action (schemas). To break toxic

---

[125] This is not the only one, for instance spiritual crises have the potential of doing us much harm or being turned to good, depending on our view and the therapists. For a key text, including a plea to therapists to see religious experience as an opportunity for growth, not giving it a diagnosis of pathology, see Grof and Grof (1989b).

[126] Scripts and schemas, concepts borrowed by me from psychology, help us all live in a routine way. For instance, our ability to make a cup of tea, or drive a car, and not having to re-learn these processes every time we want to go somewhere or have a hot drink. But many scripts and schemas are not of the helpful type, instead being toxic to us, especially those that stop us from entering long-term relationships, or take risks or learn new things. My observation is that God is keen to help dismantle these bad scripts, as they get in His way as well as ours. For a comment on scripts from a psychological perspective, see Berne (1976).

scripts we must do daily exercises, together with gaining new knowledge and engaging cathartic experience.[127] With the removing of these scripts one has also to confront and dismantle the historic cognitive dissonance.[128] This is the process of the person owning and then dismissing contrary and negative views of themselves and their lifestyle. Their disorders form the basis of the person they have believed they were, but as the person begins tentatively to possess God's perspective, through life in the community, they build the foundation for new values, habits and scripts. They gain these new perspectives through several avenues: sharing stories and experiences, the diagnostic sessions, what they hear from their inner voice, or the Lord telling them etc. The options for learning change are numerous. Others in the community will add words of knowledge, pictures, encouragement, hope and love.

Some examples: Fear, forgiveness and grief

Fear is part of the brain stem,[129] and offers a useful example of how psychiatry and my model respond differently. A Biblical view of, say, fear requires we be free from its unrighteous or toxic impact, accepting, for instance, only a righteous fear of God.[130] Part of this process will be the need to re-write scripts, for instance, faith demands we abandon ourselves to trusting this personal, but largely unknown God. Resisting this trust can expose us to fear without faith, which Christians suggest will undoubtedly imperil one's health (McMillen 1963:31ff.). Here, for the Christian, lies the 'slender channel where sin leads to disease' (Goldbrunner 1955:28). Toxic fear can become psycho-physiological, whereas God becomes the author, not of unhealthy fear, but of rest (Heb 4:1ff.), a freedom from toxic fear and its consequences. To be in Christ, therefore, is to live a healthier life, free of toxic fear, by responding in trust to God in a manner exemplified in Christ's own life.

---

[127] I am suggesting that where an event has been so traumatic, or the person so stuck in a role dictated by scripts, they need to rewrite the scripts and schemas. See McLeod (1997). For a comment on the spiritual dimensions of trauma, and its clinical release, see McBride (1998).

[128] In using this term I am retaining the classic sense, first suggested by Festinger (1956), though much has been written since to refine the concept.

[129] The fear system in the body has neural components extending from the temporal lobe (the memory storage area for facts and events) through the hypothalamas (hormone control via the pituitary), down through the lower brainstem (via the periventricular gray) and into the autonomic output components of the lowest part of the brain-stem and upper spinal chord (which controls the basic physiological responses). 'A growing consensus is emerging that this neural system mediates a fundamental form of unconditional fear' (Panksepp and Panksepp 2000:113).

[130] It would be naïve to suggest all emotion only has this 'black and white', good and bad side, since my own experience over many years has shown me that many of the good and bad characteristics of emotion are both held and experienced more in common. For instance, with fear it can be awe-ful or awful, both often appearing and feeling the same. Some would say that it was Otto (1917/1959) who first put emotion back on the Church's map.

Psychological therapies on the other hand see fear, with all its baggage, as peripheral to our well-being. But when fear reaches a 'phobic state', it will probably be 'organically treated' with medication, to ease the stress it is creating. However this often merely gives permission to sublimate, control or ignore the fear, its physiology and drives. Rarely do people seem to ask why they fear, maybe because it seems easier, quicker and cheaper to treat the symptoms with medication? The problem is that such an approach does not lead to wholeness, instead often resulting in the fear expressing itself in other ways.[131]

> *The reason I didn't want to ring people is, one, through my own shame, through not thinking I was worth being made time for, or something like that, but also because I was so frightened of rejection (W4-1).*

Likewise, forgiveness is a subject we handle in a distinctive way in CCD and *Rapha* from either a psychological, therapeutic or traditional Christian approach.[132] Pressing a person to forgive without mentoring them to engage a cathartic release can lead to repression of the emotional damage, often causing pain and an ongoing simmering revenge.

With people seeking our help we require much more than to have them merely forgive, focusing instead on the laying down of the right of revenge. For instance, someone was raped 20 years before, and might have undergone much 'ministry' and 'counselling'. Although her abuser has died, we ask her what she would do if she had a gun in her handbag and saw him in the supermarket aisle. 'I'd kill him', she shouts. Such an honest admission is a recognition that though she believes herself to have forgiven, she has not been able to lay down feelings of the need for revenge. We then explain that she has the right of revenge through the due process of law, and God shares her anger about the abuse. But to live in wholeness she must now give this right of revenge to the Lord, allowing Him to deal with the abuser according to His justice. She will think about this and when ready, often symbolically, surrender the power of revenge to the Lord. This will most often be accompanied by toxic convulsions, deep tears and profound pain. But the person is then free to get on with their lives. They no longer have the duty to carry the revenge. This whole process will be supported by a group of mentors, friends and fellow-travellers within the community.

> *You can look at the betrayal, and feel anger and pain and face it as a reality rather than pretending everything is fine and it was all your fault (W5-4).*

Connected to this will be the grieving and loss for the many years the person may have carried this revenge unwittingly. We have begun writing a

---

[131] I liken this process to garden mint or bindweed growing wild. You chop it back, trying to dig it up at the roots, but is guaranteed to reappear somewhere else if you don't remove it all.

[132] Many books exist on the subject of forgiveness in the Church, e.g. Smedes (1976), Taylor (1956), Cook (1979), MacDonald (1984), Mayer (1988), MacDonald (1989), Schlink (1992), Miller (1994) etc. among others.

'theology of loss', of how people in Scripture, and through the modern *Rapha* journey have to deal with loss in their lives. Part of this process will often be the need to 'forgive' God for how they perceive *He* has treated them. 'Where was He when I was raped?' We encourage the person to reconnect with the feelings at the time of the abuse, meeting Christ in them.[133] By giving Him their pain, they see the whole experience redeemed for them. This is a strategic step for many,[134] allowing them to begin a new relationship with God. With issues like revenge, or dealing with major abuse, we will often see these moments as 'tipping points' in the person's life, a specific moment or event that positively tips the scales for them, allowing them to quickly begin to reap the benefits from often months of working through major issues. Borrowed from sociology, this concept of tipping points is becoming a field of research in its own right (Gladwell 2000).

The area of homework they have been dealing with and the baggage they have let go of, it has been so significant it is like the balance has been tipped (W13-9).

Gender and marriage

Our position on gender is a controversial one. From early contact with people we explain that male and female are different, not androgynous. Also, that part of a person's wholeness journey will be their welcoming of their gender, for this is part of their *imago Dei*. But we seek to avoid gender typecasting, instead teaching that within their gender they are unique.[135] We point to neurological research that illustrates the distinctives between the male and female brain (Moir and Jessel 1989, Kandel, et al. 2000:1134-1148).[136] Many experience this as liberating, being given permission to embrace their own personal strengths and weaknesses in the context of their

---

[133] This practice is not dissimilar to Theophostic counselling. See {www.theophostic.com}.

[134] On the matter of estrangement from God among Christians, see Wurtz and Bufford (1997).

[135] To demonstrate this I have developed a simple tool that I call the Gender Continuum, being a straight horizontal line representing both male and female. Then I bisect this line vertically at the centre, with one side becoming male, the other female. Everyone is somewhere on the horizontal line. All men will be on the male side of the line, although some may be closer to 'female' in their skills and preferences. Likewise all women will be on the female side of the line, although some may be closer to 'male' in their skills and preferences. I propose to them that Christ represents the whole line, as an example for both male and female. We have also developed a questionnaire that helps people to locate themselves on the line. This Gender Continuum is a particularly beneficial concept for those believing they are trapped in unhelpful gender stereotyping.

[136] This is a most contentious issue, and although Moir and Jessel is now dated, Kandel, a Nobel prize-winner in medicine outlines in detail in his book *Neural Science* (with Schwartz and Jessel) the hormone-dependent sexual differentiations of mammalian (including human) brain structures, and refers to the fact that the 'default setting' for brain architectures is female (2000:1134-1148).

gender.[137] We have found a number of distinct differences between the way men and women wish to tackle baggage and its homework. For instance, most men will think about it only briefly, make up their minds, then do it quickly, while women will often decide sooner but move more cautiously.

Also, in our community and the work of *Rapha* we go against much of the tradition in both Church and psychological therapies, especially in the USA, by treating couples as singles therapeutically, regardless of how long they have been married.

> *What Peter did immediately was insist that we stood on our own two feet instead of leaning on each other. For me that was a whole new beginning. I had always lent on someone or had someone lean on me, that is what life was about as far as I knew (M13-1).*

So we do not need to work conjointly, as in some 'family' and 'marriage' psychological therapies (Davison and Neale 1998:566).[138] We remind couples that it is not so much what we do in our marriage as what we *bring into* our marriage from our earlier history, that is most often the real cause of conflict (Tournier 1966:25). This principle is highlighted in Ellis' *rational emotive therapy* (1962 passim), emphasising we are all in part the sum of our heredity and past relationships, needing to look *insightfully* beyond both what we see and who we have become. On this basis couples continue to live out their baggage in marriage, often abusing the other person the way they are already abusing themselves.[139] The longer one is married the more this abusive cycle can grow. The approach of CCD releases both parties from the often heavy guilt of the failure of their marriages, and helps prepare each of them to take personal responsibility for their own wholeness, not continue blaming their partners.

In summary

Wheeler Robinson proposed that fellowship is the essence of practical theology (1930:140ff.), being the most important thing in life in both soul care and psychology (Carver and Scheier 1996:324). This I describe in CCD as *koinonia* community. But to this concept I would want to add the important role of honour and love for oneself and others, all needing to be learned in relationships.[140] Over the years we have learned that the

---

[137] Once a person becomes familiar with this idea, they find numerous good reasons for this practice, including the ease of being vulnerable, the safety of only having men or women present, and the contrast of how men and women behave when the other sex is not present.

[138] For background to family therapy, see Goldenberg and Goldenberg (1991).

[139] The difference for many of us is that when we are single if we want friends we cannot abuse them or we will end up alone, whereas in marriage we are given a 'licence' to blame the other person for all the unresolved issues we brought into the marriage. This is especially the case in a Christian marriage where our partner is contracted never to leave us.

[140] This is demonstrated in numerous ways. For instance, we have a 24-hour telephone line, linking those in need with one of our team or myself, similar to that offered by Higgins (1997).

experience *between* sessions, the *koinonia* relationships, can significantly positively impact outcomes, often more so than the session itself (Frank 1982). We have therefore come to rely heavily on the social process. The dynamics of this relationality we call *therapeutic faith community*, for people always seem to suffer from what they have lost of themselves in relation to the world of objects, events and relationships (Cassell 1982:642). My process goes some way to helping recover *koinonia* and its healing relationships within therapeutic faith community. With faith at the centre, this symbolises Christ at the centre as Redeemer.

What we are practising is a pastoral therapeutic discipleship model that brings together all the dimensions so far noted. It places holistic personhood at the centre, gives personal meaning to people's pasts as they are helped in letting go and re-writing their history, and is a practical discipleship model that specifically moves toward relationship with, and likeness to Christ. Salvation and the process of Christ-likeness become a wholeness journey.

It is also in line with the *Rapha* concept and practice of Exodus 15, promoting personal positive change. It sits comfortably alongside stage development theory as an alternative model. Also it is spiritually orientated, and can be used by anyone wishing to undertake it, Christian or otherwise. The fruit of this journey is becoming free from one's past, having a greater capacity to love one's self and others, thereby helping facilitate divine and human community. The one element still missing in this process however, is the role of community, for here in CCD this earths the whole process of becoming more fully human through therapeutic discipleship.

Chapter 5

Community; its loss in a faith context; our need to recover it; what it could look like today

Introduction:
My personal journey toward community

Participants in Susan Williams' research placed a surprising value on community. They felt they had been looking for authentic relationships for many years, often without realising it, and that their *Rapha* discipleship journey into wholeness would have failed had it not been pursued with the support of the wider community. This is consistent with Martsolf and Mickley, who recognise 'connecting' as a key component in the quest for spirituality.[1] Here in CCD adopting a social Trinity perspective places relationship at the heart of Godhead and personhood. However in beginning to see local congregations in community terms, I have been a grudgingly reluctant convert. Reproducing traditional institutional Church has been much easier over the last 35 years than creating a new model of church *as* community.[2]

Like many others, it seems, I had assumed that by merely meeting as a local congregation, for say Sunday worship, this was being a community, and it need go no further. We are community by merely doing church. So I carried a deep prejudice against other ideas of community, seeing these only for the weak and vulnerable, not a priority for mainstream Church. It is now hard for me to confess this, but to my shame I did not believe that any deeper form of 'community' was essential for growing churches, because they are already full of 'strong Christians' living 'successfully'. My flawed assumption was that being church automatically created community.[3] The Lord and CCD had a lot to teach me about community.

---

[1] Likewise, Pinnock cited the existence of community as one of the five reasons why a person should consider Christianity (1980:93ff.).

[2] Christ Church is the fourth congregation I have helped plant, the first in the Middle East, the second in Ash Green in Kent, the third on the Downham estate in south-east London, and then Christ Church, Deal. Though I believe all the previous congregations still exist, with these I merely reproduced what its members and I were most familiar with. Here in CCD we seem to be doing something more unusual.

[3] I am aware that the whole Church, worldwide, in any form, is *koinonia* (Heb. 12:22-23), a natural bond of fellowship in the Holy Spirit (Eph. 4:3). But what I have been taught by CCD is

But I also had a gender issue to work through. My perception was that women required attachment (e.g. community) (Gilligan 1982/1993 passim), but for men wholeness and maturity meant independence. I needed to change my view, beginning to admit through my experience of CCD, that men need community as much as women.

> *Where else can you have deep relationships with other men, where you are being honest and intimate, that doesn't happen. You don't meet many places, even in church, which is supposed to be the place where [you can]. I don't remember really having any deep relationships with any men in church until I came down here (M10-7).*

It has been a long, humiliating road, having to admit I was wrong on both counts, but at last I am able to agree with Oden, that Ecclesiology should reflect the Spirit's work, in bringing communities into being, in response to grace (1994/1998:280).[4] Also, like Clark, I now look at groups of believers, and their environment,[5] as the essence of Church life, and the most effective agents of change (1972:23) for both men and women. I had chosen independence (individualism) rather than community (Crabb 1999:180). My own personal journey illustrates, as it has for so many, how far the Western Church has drifted from the simple model of church as community: a womb for authentic change, relationality and wholeness, toward Christ-likeness.

To help unpack these broad issues this chapter is in three sections. In the first part I will note how we have lost community here in the Western world over the last several hundred years, as a quality of life today. To illustrate, I will note some of the forces that have contributed to the dismantling of community, and then offer hope through one 20th century philosopher who gives me some of the intellectual framework for both a relational and change theology.

But the core of the chapter is a return to a theme of Hebrew ideas, this time focusing on what Yahweh may have intended for community in adopting Israel. I will note some of the characteristics of how this worked out in early Israel's life, while also suggesting that what Yahweh actually wanted was to be a 'kinship ruler' among His people, head of a *Theocentric* community. I will suggest this offers a foundation for the creation of an alternative community model for local congregations in the 21st century.

---

that *koinonia* in itself does not make community of the type many of us wish for. This chapter unpacks this idea.

[4] Like Oden, in my emphasising the sociality of Christianity I am not denying the fact that each person must decide for himself or herself whether God's Word is trustworthy, and whether salvation is for them (1994/1998:282). I in no way wish to deflect from my personal responsibility in emphasising community.

[5] For this book the term *environment* defines a stable social situation or a stable pattern of interactions between human beings (Clark 1972:25).

In the third and final part of the chapter I will take these Hebrew ideas of kinship community and *Theocentricity*, tracing them through Christ and Paul, arguing that both these men sought to remain faithful to Yahweh's model of kinship community, noting especially which changes and features were key for them. In the final chapter, before concluding, I will draw all these ideas together, proposing community as a place of *therapeutic* personal change, not based on individualism but instead on the social process of *therapeutic* faith community.

The loss of community

The toll of Enlightenment ideas

In no area of contemporary culture do we seem to have the communities we are all seeking. Maybe this is because every generation needs to re-invent community for themselves[6] and we cannot, for example, return to the Victorian village of the 1800s.[7] So I will not be talking about the 'recovery' of community, except in a Biblical sense, for I am not sure how past models would fare in the 21st century. Instead, I will be suggesting we need to take a range of fundamental concepts regarding community, many of which the Church has either forgotten or never known, and then re-invent out of them a new type of community for ourselves in the 21st century.

The Newtonian world of individual atoms in motion, seeded by Aristotle and taken up by Hobbes the political social philosopher, Locke the philosopher of the Pilgrim Fathers and Descartes the mechanist, established reductionist thinking as the bedrock of our modern commonwealth. All of these men contributed to a social model of atomistic contractarianism, presenting personhood as private, individual and supremely as a thinker (Kirkpatrick 1986:19ff.). This thinking birthed Deism and scepticism, giving people, along with other things, permission not to believe in Christianity. What remained of nominal Christian community has since been absorbed by 'secularization' and the Church's own mistakes. For instance, as the drive toward selfism began, the Church, as one of its 'victims', never challenged such values. As Banks observed, Catholicism followed the cultic path of structure and control, seeking to hold on to some

---

[6] As Hanson commented, 'The Biblical notion of community, and the vision of an order of righteous compassion and peace that the community was to embody, experienced rebirth and renewal in the concrete situation faced by each new generation of believers' (1986:488).

[7] Most accept today that community as we believe it was in the past is gone forever. Some, like Winter (1989) suggested we are not seeing a total loss of community, just a time of change, with the emerging of a new deepening communal sensibility and interdependence. See chapter 6 for my expanding of some of these social themes.

ideas of community, while Protestantism followed the path of synagogue, in worshipping a book (1980/1988:112).[8]

The Protestant Church's new position was illustrated in the winter semester of 1899-1900 when Adolf von Harnack delivered his sixteen lectures at the University of Berlin, entitled *The Essence of Christianity* (1900). 'The kingdom of God comes by coming to individuals, making entrance into their souls,[9] and being grasped by them. The kingdom of God is indeed God's rule – but it is the rule of a holy God in individuals' hearts' (cited in Lohfink 1985:1-3). Such thinking was and continues to be firmly rooted in Western Protestant thought. Ideas and the practice of community, under the heat of the Enlightenment, have all but evaporated. Individualism rules.

Until recently this was also true outside the Church. But from the 1960's (Minar and Greer 1969) there has been a growing awareness of the loss of community. Etzioni (1992, 1993/1995), for instance, with his Hebrew roots and his training under Buber argued that we are beginning to ride a wave returning community to us. But he suggested it needed to be more a social, political and personal agenda if it was to work. Bellah (1985) likewise, called for a renewed understanding of the crucial role of community in constructing personal identity. Rapport summarised the beginnings of this growing awareness, 'recent decades have seen an upsurge in "community consciousness", "community development and rebuilding", and "values and works" (1996/2000:116ff.).

Noting some of the social forces against community

In my use of the term community I am not thinking of *communes,*[10] conjuring up images of hippies, ashrams and flower power. The modern sense of the word 'community' was probably first introduced by the German, Ferdinand Tönnies. He described *Gemeinschaft* as a way of life, typical of the German peasant in the countryside (1887/1955). In English, the term came to prominence in the 19th century through a cluster of authors as awareness grew, of the appalling impact on the poor of the hideous, soulless industrial revolution. The working classes had given up

---

[8]   Some Christians would be surprised at the suggestion that a book, even the Bible or its Bibliolatry, should be a substitute for the worship of Christ.

[9]   There was also a post-Reformation tendency to 'spiritualize' and internalize faith, which became easier as everyone gained personal access to a Bible. Protestantism allowed people to be more free, but also more alone (Walton 1946:108). Lindbeck described this as a 'Marcionite tendency' (1990:493), to spiritualize and privatize Christianity, and this has taken its toll on the community quest for a corporate faith. Robinson supported this: 'Christians should be the last people to be found clinging to the wrecks of an atomistic individualism, which has no foundation in the Bible' (1952:9).

[10]   This is itself a large, separate field of research. See Roberts (1971), Lockley (1976), etc.

rural communities, and there was a subsequent desperate need to recover lost relationship.[11]

Shenker suggested that alienated people are those who accept the need for a stable identity provided by society, but because of personal circumstances, either reject or are unable to internalize these criteria (1986:25). Ultimately the breakdown in community, as with psychotic breakdown, usually produces alienation, an isolation that in turn leads to internalized fragmentation that isolates one further. Healthy people are much more able to live in relationship than those that have all kinds of disorder in their lives. Such people need to be helped. For increasing numbers, the forces of individualization work with the pathological forces of broken personhood, to produce toxic loneliness, and a fragmentation of their culture.[12]

What saves most of us is the 'communal urge', a sort of biological imperative intrinsic to human nature. We want to be in relationship. This does not mean there are not times when we need to be alone. But if we remain healthy, most of the time for most of us relationships will prevail. Every one of us needs companionship. There are, no doubt, many reasons for this desire, but within community, being together is constitutive of selfhood, giving all of us the potential of 'fleshing out' the portrait of the personal self (Schrag 1997:78).[13]

> Every one of those relationships [in Christ Church] is benefiting me in some way, even if I think it isn't. Because it is all an aspect of my own personality which is being exposed in that relationship that wouldn't be exposed otherwise. Therefore it is another part of myself, another part of God which I am meeting because of the range of people that we have got here (M7-1).

But this is not always adequate motivation for those that have disorder in their lives, or are either emotionally unwell or relationally unskilled. I frequently observe that the damage done to us, and the subsequent damage we do with this damage (sin against ourselves), will mostly move us toward intrinsic fragmentation, and extrinsic isolation. Logically, one would assume it would drive us, instead, toward a need to learn community, as a way back from disorder in our lives. But this is not the case, as the conventional view is that most of us have lost community through social forces outside of our control. The Church, like the individual, is merely a victim. Although numerous movements within the church have sought to

---

[11] See Williams (1976:65-66). For an illustration of this current barrenness regarding the importance of relationships, note the absence of an entry or section on *relationship* in Atkinson and Field (1995), or its Catholic equivalent, Downey (1993).

[12] In modern times some of the social constructs are positivism, reductionism, relativism and determinism. For an introductory comment, see Mayes (1989), especially his helpful comments on social constructs (120ff.).

[13] Schrag (1997) is particularly helpful in identifying a number of the main thinkers in the modern debate regarding community. See especially chapter 3: *The self in community.*

respond to this need, e.g. the Bruderhof, Jesus Army etc., few models have so far endured.[14] Likewise, outside the Church, numerous sociologists have noted the loss of community, but few propose ways forward toward its restoration.

Kirkpatrick identified three systems from the Middle Ages which have contributed toward constructing modern thought regarding community. The first is the atomistic contractarian model (e.g. Hobbes, Locke and free market individualism) (Kirkpatrick 1986:13-61) that I have identified above, that in some ways brought devastation to the working classes, while failing to address the loss of community. But this is followed, secondly, by the organic functional model (e.g. Hegel, Burke, Marx, socialism, followed by Whitehead, Pols and others) (62-98) that responded to earlier models by seeking to make the social whole take precedence over the individual parts, the organic metaphor of 'society'. Such imagery is now almost universal among social theorists. Hegel epitomised such thinking by suggesting reality is fulfilled only in and through the whole, not in and through the parts alone (67). The Absolute, or Spirit, is the Whole of Reality. The community, for instance, is the embodiment of *Geist.* This in turn sowed the seeds of Marxist totalitarianism, for when one pushes too far the notion of society as an organism, the organic whole can take on a personality of its own, to which all its subsidiary parts must be subservient (83). The consequence of such thinking is a functionalism that discards all that is not useful, in Marx's case seeing society as diseased and its pathology needing revolutionary purging (1963). Such thinking did nothing to build community, until Whitehead, along with his comprehensive metaphysics (1929/1947), developed an organic model of community through his concept of 'occasion', seeking as he did to redress the fragmentation of prevailing dualism.

Kirkpatrick noted that the organic functional model creates one central problem, among others: how to reconcile our Western liberal insistence on the freedom of the individual with our desire to enter into interpersonal relations with others (Kirkpatrick 1986:137). The answer he proposed was the mutual personal model (e.g. Buber to Macmurray). Kirkpatrick introduces us to Buber, whom he suggested, guided by Feurbach (1841/1956), has done more than anyone else to establish the essential

---

[14] Many books, for instance, have been written on the theme of building Church community through cells (Clinebell 1972, O'Halloran 1984, Wuthnow 1994, Bilezikian 1997, Martin and McIntosh 1997, etc.). I particularly like Gorman's *Community as Christian*, who noted that since the Enlightenment we have seen a subversive undermining of community to such an extent that she saw little true community in either society or the Church today. For her, true community was that which looks out for others, and is not, like many small groups are today, consumed by self-centredness, a cultural cult of narcism (1993:13). Rasmussen (1993) is also helpful here, focusing on the moral ethical aspects of the loss of community, with guidance on how the Church could respond.

nature of human relationship (141). Only in relations, Buber argued, is the self fulfilled, for 'the primary word *I-Thou* can only be spoken with the whole being' (1958/1996:54). For Buber, unity with God, and community among creatures belonged together (1966:158), for such a community will arise through persons 'first, taking their stand in living mutual relation with a living Centre, and, second, their being in living mutual relation with one another. The second has its source in the first, but is not given when the first alone is given, …. The community is built up out of living mutual relations, but the builder is the living effective Centre' (1958/1996:94). Kirkpatrick observed that because of his ambivalent use of organic language and symbols, not unlike Hegel, Buber left the way open for a philosophy of persons that preserves the uniqueness of persons. John Macmurray took up this challenge, seeing personhood and more specifically relationship as priority over Cartesian individualism. His mutual personal model, drawing also on Hebraic traditions, creates the possibility of unique body spirit unity within community.

Enter John Macmurray

John Macmurray is one of the few major philosophers of our time to place the category of 'persons in community' at the centre of his metaphysical system. In doing so he moved against the massed consequences of Enlightenment ideas. Almost single-handedly[15] his writings go some distance to providing a metaphysical foundation for community. His philosophical system starts from and returns to the ontological primacy of person in relation, in many ways compatible with Cappadocian thought. He suggested that Cartesian man, and his dualism, made it impossible to argue for personal knowledge of another, because it is not what we *think,* but instead, what we *do* in relation to other agents (1957/1991 passim). He moved from the intrinsic to the extrinsic.

Knowing I am in relation to another person must be the 'starting point of all knowledge' (Macmurray 1961:76). To be a person is to be in communication with the Other,[16] meaning knowledge of the Other should

---

[15] Some would argue that Levinas went some distance to standing with Macmurray, arguing as he did for a re-think of a new ethics of inter-personal relationship. See the summary of his thinking in Robbins (2001). But it is generally agreed that his work does not move outside the context of a fellow Jew, Buber, who also stayed within a one-to-one relationship (1958/1996, 1965). Neither went beyond this, as Macmurray did, to talk in community terms.

[16] Macmurray saw the individual organism as unique, by stating that the unity of the organism is not a unity of functions (1933:111). Instead, 'we may define the schema of Organism as the conception of a unity which is unique harmony of complementary functions, expressing itself in a structural harmony of different organs' (1929:171). In this sense the differences of the elements determine their harmonious relations in an organic complex (170-171). This is how we will define 'Other'. Although Macmurray was ahead of his time, as he developed his thinking he also sadly found himself increasingly unable to share in the life of the Church as he knew it.

be the presupposition of all knowledge (1961:77). By making the self the primary agent, no dualism between thought and practice arises. Action (and therefore *becoming*) rather than being, is the basis of self, thereby allowing self to be understood as a unified whole (1957/1991:86). Macmurray therefore called this the personal model (Kirkpatrick 1986:146), and person is constituted by their relation to the Other. That is, we have our being in relationship, and this relationship is necessarily personal (i.e. communal) (Macmurray 1961:17). Our own human nature lies always beyond us as a goal to be aimed at, and this goal of freedom can ultimately only be realized in and through fellowship or community, the complete realization of the self through a complete self-transcendence (1950:16).

Macmurray's additional step was to locate his principle of relations in God's love and its flowing into Church life. For full realization of person in relations also requires the power of God. Macmurray, like myself, saw the importance of recovering a Hebrew model of *Theocentric* community (Kirkpatrick 1986:198, Macmurray 1973 passim). He claimed that Jesus must be understood in Hebrew terms, not in the categories of Greek Platonic or Aristotelian philosophy. At the heart of Hebraic monotheism in the Hebrew Bible, he argued, is the conviction that the union of mankind into one community is the intention of God (1 Sam. 25:29, 1 Cor. 3:16, Eph. 2:13-14; 4:13) and so the necessary end of the historic process (1961:60-61). Macmurray understood Christianity to be a religion that superseded Judaism's task of preparing the universal community, but that this is not possible unless man wills it, for the structure of all human relationships is the expression of human intention (1938a:100). Only life in intentional community can fully reflect human nature (1938b:9). This is echoed by Levinas; 'The human accomplishing its destiny of being human...merits the name *spirit*. It is with the other man that this spirit rises up in being' (cited in Robbins 2001:112-113).

Some of Macmurray's thinking is now considered quaint.[17] But Kirkpatrick argued that Macmurray is still relevant today, for most of us now live in a rootless culture, requiring numerous correctives in our thinking. For instance, we must recognize spiritual reality in both us and in our world. We must also acknowledge our sin in making self the centre of this world, rather than community and the Other.[18]

[Relationships didn't work] because of largely my own selfish motive for relationship and what I am trying to get out of it rather than what I am trying to put in (M14-11).

---

[17] See Kirkpatrick's observations of some of the weaknesses in Macmurray's thought (1986:137).

[18] This needs widening to include both the original damage of sin, our own 'sins' and our living of these damaging values. Bishop noted that Church culture recognizes both a personal and collective 'spiritual sickness' (1985:19).

Kirkpatrick called for a new reality of *Theocentric* Christianity, drawing on Macmurray, who gave us two further ingredients to our concept of community: first, a philosophical framework prioritising relationship over individualism, the concept of *Theocentric* community and its spiritual reality, and secondly proposing to the wider Church that such a shift is necessary.[19] What is being suggested is far more radical than first appears. On the basis of these men's work, any definition of spiritual personhood must include a relational community aspect. Prevailing thought, both inside and outside the Church, is that we are not yet doing this instinctively. For instance, Benner, a therapist and Christian, typically defined spirituality as the 'human response to God's gracious call to a relationship with Him' (1992:173). There is no mention of community, especially not as a *felt* experience.[20] In fact, the idea is absent much of the time in Christian writing. Buber and Macmurray are two of only a few thinkers proposing a community priority. Some would argue an exception would be the community Church movements, and outside the Church, communitarianism. But as exceptions they illustrate that individualism and its selfism still largely prevails.

Introducing *Theocentric* kinship community

Returning to the Early Hebrew period, Israel had struggled to survive the Exodus, the wilderness experiences and now the rugged Northern Palestinian hill country. This led to the forging of an egalitarian culture with a corporate identity, family solidarity and the growth of maturity as community. Most social scientists who study the Ancient Near East would say that what I am describing is typical of all Ancient Near East cultures of that day, that is, the type of corporate identity, village solidarity, etc. But what this section will suggest is something unique about Israel that sets it apart, with its focus on Yahwistic kinship and *Theocentricity*.

Macmurray's philosophy of relations draws from Hebraic ideas, and I likewise have found it helpful in CCD to explore some of these, especially Yahweh's early relationship with Israel. Within CCD we have an emphasis on 'Christ in our midst', His dwelling within our community, which as an idea is first seen in the Hebrew[21] Old Testament.[22] Johnson noted that the

---

[19] Some, like Grenz, are already suggesting we are moving into a 'post-individual' age (1996:167).

[20] For a comment on this sad state of affairs see Pingleton (1992).

[21] The problems of using Biblical, especially Old Testament material today are enormous in trying to understand, for instance early Israelite family life. (See Meyers 1997:4ff.) For a helpful, uncritical background, see Pedersen's two books (1926, 1946). We have watched a shift in fields of research like Biblical archaeology from being a servant of Biblical studies, to it now sometimes being a critical master. See Dever (2003:56-61). Rogerson suggests the Church is still some

historic[23] period of the Early Settlement was dominated by the concept of kinship (Johnson 1942:11), where Yahweh sought to create a people with several distinct features that may possibly be of relevance to us today.[24] I will highlight two, *Theocentricity* and *kinship community*.

The formation of community was Yahweh's central act (Ernest Wright 1954:19). From the time of the Exodus He emphasised '*Theocentric* community' with Himself as kinsman in their midst (Ex. 34:4-7; 40:34 etc.), what could be described as 'a society without rulers'.[25] Israel's population instead had a special 'kinship' with Yahweh, a community with no king but Yahweh.[26]

Yahweh can mean 'I will be God for you' (Fretheim 1996b:1296),[27] but this could only be authentically achieved by Him through fellowship with His people, whereby He Himself gives them the means to fulfil His requirements (e.g. Ezk. 11:19ff., Je. 31:33-34.) (Wheeler Robinson 1913:86). Such an attempt at 'rule by fellowship' within Israel seems

---

distance from a proper interpretive framework for examining Scripture the way we are seeking to here (2001:362).

[22] Part of the modern change in Old Testament studies has been the emergence of disciplines like social anthropology. These modern tools, for instance, have helped us reconstruct our understanding of the Early Hebrew family, and its social context. Through these we are able to build a better picture of life, for say, the women. (See Meyers 1988.) For an introduction to some of these general concepts, see Mayes (1989:18ff.). For a typical example of this new sociological approach, see Gottwald (1985). However, we should always be mindful of Rodd's caution, that in using sociological instruments in a hermeneutical way one is in danger of succumbing to their historic duplicity in cognitive dissonance (1997:22ff.). Sociology, used as a historic discipline can be promiscuous, whereas using it as a research tool on contemporary cultures is much less problematic.

[23] In using the term 'history' I am not taking sides in the debate on whether these early writings were 'history' or propaganda. See Coote and Whitelam (1987 passim). Today, some scholars question the reliability of early Biblical 'history', seeing modern scientific method (e.g. sociology, archaeology etc.) as more reliable than Scripture. In its extreme form this critique becomes deconstructionist (see McNutt 1999:11ff.). For a modern statement on this debate, see Shanks (2002:36). McNutt, like numerous modern scholars, preferred to begin the 'history' of Israel at the time of the highland occupation or settlement period, claiming we cannot externally verify the Exile (1999:40ff.). For a recent defence of Biblical narrative and the integrity of the Hebrew text, see Dever (2001).

[24] Little work focusing on early Yahwistic community seems to have been done. For instance, in over 100 works referred to by Carol Meyers in her *The family in ancient Israel* (1997), not one article takes up the theme of village or community. Like Grenz, I am suggesting we still have much to learn from Early Hebrew history (2000:158, 162, etc.).

[25] A phrase I have borrowed from Lang (1985b), quoting Sir Edward Evans-Pritchard, speaking about the Nuer of Africa. For a more extended comment on this comparison, see Fiensy (1997).

[26] For a different view, that much Hebrew thought came from mingling with the people groups around them, see Kiefer (1988:34).

[27] The word 'God' appears over 6,800 times in the Old Testament. For this book, I have been assuming God is who God is, and God is the only God, so that He might rightly be regarded as 'He who governs'.

unique among these ancient peoples. Most other ethnic groups around Israel had gods that typically ruled by fear and conniving. Bright argued that Israel's notion of God was entirely unique, bringing Yahweh with them from the desert (1960:132).[28] Although this position has been challenged,[29] what is clear is Yahweh sought from the Exodus onwards to promote a unique type of community,[30] with Himself being present, in fellowship, through the *mishpachah*,[31] the extended family, to all His people.

Gottwald characterizes Israel as a 'socially revolutionary movement primarily of peasants' (1993:142). The focus of the disclosure of Yahweh was among the settlement households, where He was active (Wheeler Robinson 1913:128). Many of these *mishpachah* lived in unique 'four-roomed (pillared) houses',[32] (appendix 7) (Buminovitz and Faust 2002:32-41) that helped accommodate this relationship.[33] Therefore, what united the tribes as a unified people was a strong sense of solidarity, cohered by the will of Yahweh toward them (Eichrodt 1961/1975:39).[34] With this concept

---

[28] Both Mendenhall (1962) and Gottwald (1975/1979) emphasise the equality of social life in these Israelite communities. Before and during this Early Hebrew period Canaanite society was collapsing, preparing the ground for Israelite monarchy.

[29] See for instance, Mendenhall (1962:66-87), and Gottwald (1975/1979). For a literary critical view of Israel as 'an artificial creation of the scholarly world of the modern age', see Lemche (1988:163). For a critical view of who lived in this region of Palestine before Israel, also see Lemche (1991).

[30] See for instance Kohler (1953/1973) who saw some 40 local regions being occupied during the settlement period. On the question of who wrote the Joshua conquest narrative, see Rowlett (1997).

[31] By noting the *mishpachah*, a clan or extended family, I am not suggesting these sought to replace the shrine centres of Shechem, then Bethel and Shiloh, which appear to have had an important cultic role, particularly for both the annual feasts (Bright 1960:147), and as a base for some of the cultic leadership (1 Ki. 12:23, etc.). Neither am I suggesting that by using such words we fully understand terms like *mishpachah* (see Gottwald 1975/1979:245ff.).

[32] This phrase best describes the clusters of houses accommodating the unusual extended families in this region in the Iron Age 1 period. Ahlstrom has noted this type of house was not unique to early Israel settlers (1993:339ff.), Bietak finding them as far away as Syria and Egypt (2003:41ff.). Buminovitz and Faust argue they are exclusive to Israel, even when found outside this region (2002:34-35). This view was expressed earlier by Shiloh (1970). For an exquisite example of this house see Ottoson (1993). For a summary of views, from an archaeological perspective, see Finkelstein (1988:254ff.).

[33] Architecturally, the design followed the demands of Jewish purity Law. Each room could be entered from a central space, without passing through other rooms, therefore purity could be strictly maintained, even where a ritually impure person resided in the dwelling. For instance, it gave men the ability to avoid menstruating women (Buminovitz and Faust 2002:39). Commitment to Yahweh and community apparently even influenced the design of the home one lived in.

[34] I am not claiming knowledge of Yahweh's perspective, only that in viewing the surface evidence and interpreting it in the light of subsequent recorded events, this seems to be the case. I am following here the 'logic of hermeneutics' (Sanders 1962), in its notion as an act of 'reasonable faith'. But I am not suggesting *how* Yahweh revealed Himself to the settlers, whether it evolved or was supernaturally revealed. For one view of this process of revelation of Yahweh to His people, see Wheeler Robinson (1913:102ff.).

of *Theocentricity* the eternal will of Yahweh was given visible form among them, expressed as a redeeming divine grace, a Triadic notion of community, that sought to incorporate social righteousness (e.g. the Law), compassion (e.g. in relationship) and worship (e.g. community and Temple).[35]

Righteousness, a promoter of community

Yahweh's desire to be King of Israel, to live in fellowship within His community,[36] was reinforced by His giving of the Law Code at Sinai (Ex. 19-Nu. 10:10), after receiving the *Rapha* principle. It is through the *Book of the Covenant* (Ex. 20:1–23:19), argued Hanson (1986:44ff.), that Yahweh set forth a pattern of behaviour in keeping with His nature, seeking just harmony between and within the families.[37] This was a type of mutuality.

> [It is very helpful] to come into a situation where it is righteous, equality in relationships, women who understand how men work, men who have learnt how women work, and to have that mutual respect of each other, that is the word, isn't it, mutuality (M9-7).

By this relationship Yahweh helped shape households, structured the economics, blessed reproduction, was nurtured as Creator and Redeemer, the teacher, warrior, lawgiver, judge, head of the household, mother, *go'el* (redeemer, kinsman), redeemer of Israel's slaves, seeking to be Israel's husband (Perdue 1997:225ff.) .

Yahweh emphasised the righteous and just expression of the Law (Eichrodt 1961/1975:249). If righteousness is injured, the orderliness of life is disturbed. The righteousness of the Law should be the guarantor of peace, and therefore successful community, so the righteous person is the one who carries out justly all the demands of community life (Kohler 1953/1973:174), which itself embodies and reflects the nature of Yahweh.[38]

---

[35] Taken from Hanson, but adapted by me (1986:30ff.).

[36] One is tempted to reflect on what this says about Yahweh Himself. For instance, is there an analogous sense in which Yahweh cannot be thought of as being alone or isolated? Modern Trinitarian studies, as we have noted, would certainly argue this is the case.

[37] A word of caution is needed in that this 'household' is not the 'family' as we know it today. Two factors make it unique, the one being its extended nature of several generations living together, and the other its essential cohesion. (See the following section.) Unlike today, people needed one another in order to survive.

[38] As a result, later Judaism's piety underwent a transformation of the greatest consequence, turning the religion of Yahweh into a religion of observance (Eichrodt 1961/1975:177), not relationship. The monarch, as the divinized representative head, was no longer capable of providing a single unified framework for all the diversity of life as it was being lived at its roots within a strong sense of community (Eichrodt 1961/1975:354). For instance, Yahweh claimed to be omnipresent. The king was not. Having said this, one must also note that some of the stronger focuses of *Theocentric* community never really left centre stage, reappearing in post-exilic desires (Ez. 3:8ff., Ne. 8–9, etc.). A number of the Hebrew ideas noted in this book did survive one way or another into post-Exilic times.

It is interesting that each community interpreted the Law as they felt best for themselves.[39] But as the prophets later noted, the idea of mutuality, solidarity and corporate responsibility (Is. 1:17) was not always realized (Je. 7:5-7; 22:1-5 etc.). It would seem that even by the time of the monarchy this focus had begun breaking down.[40]

Compassion, the individual and Theocentric community

The Hebrew model of community formulated under Yahweh placed relationship at the heart of wholeness. Individualism as we conceive it today would be inconceivable to people in these communities. Relationships were with Yahweh, the community and one's self, all contributors to the welfare of the *mishpachah*, or village community. Because Yahweh was at the heart of this process, all relationships became anointed with the holiness of Yahweh, as stated in Decalogue No 1, 'Hear, O Israel: The Lord our God is one Lord; and you shall love the Lord your God with all your heart, and with all your soul, and with all your strength' (Dt. 6:4-5).

But what does one mean by 'holy'? Often we take it to mean 'separate', but this is not how we see it in CCD. The traditional view of holiness was also a problem because it was at odds with principles of wholeness we find in Hebrew thought. It might be better, as we do in our community, to think of holiness as being whole or 'real' (e.g. authentic), whereby others are also part of the process of making a human what they can fully become.[41] In this sense holiness is not a separating, but a making whole. For instance, Yahweh wanted to be kin, with everyone focused around Him, a *Theocentricity*. Holiness in this sense is our becoming more whole. In CCD

---

[39] This is illustrated in that the Law Code points to a weakening of clan loyalties in favour of state control (see for instance Steinberg 1991, quoted in Perdue 1997:243), which would have weakened local community. This was clearly noted by the prophets, who saw it threatening relationship with Yahweh (cf. Is. 5:8-10, Mi. 2:1-3,8-9; 7:5-7), as well as competing with household allegiances. It represented two different ways of understanding first of all Yahweh, then Israel, history, creation, ethics, and the relationship of Israel to the nations (Perdue 1997:254). This weakened Yahweh's direct links with His people through community and is probably one of the reasons why Yahweh initially resisted so strongly the shift to monarchy (1 Sam. 8:6ff.; 12:12ff.,17b; 15:11, etc.).

[40] Yahweh elected the dynasty of Saul and David (1 Sam. 16:14ff., Ps. 89) and monarchy brought many unique features of both a positive and negative nature. On the positive side these included endorsing the nomadic value system that all men were brothers, not merely slaves, the way other contemporary monarchs often saw their subjects. (See for instance Robinson 1929:41, 44., quoted in Wheeler Robinson 1981:43). However, collective views were not so important, in fact liability for one another is categorically rejected (Eichrodt 1967/1972:241), illustrated in that blood revenge was constrained by the right of sanctuary (Ex. 21:12-14, Nu. 35:13-29, Jos. 20, etc.). All in all, we see the beginnings of an unmistakable heightening of the value of the individual. For other changes brought about by the monarchy, see Eichrodt (1967/1972:242ff.).

[41] This idea emerged following discussions with Dr Kenneth Wilson.

we seek to live with this 'Holy' God in our midst, for we believe that without Him at the core of human community no one can be truly whole, 'real', holy or an authentic person. Likewise, without this 'holiness' no-one can become more fully human, or be able to know authentic internal wholeness. God's authenticity, His type of holiness, calls all of us to personal and corporate authenticity.

Therefore, somewhat paradoxically, a holy person, household or nation is for us in CCD, a person who is most natural, in a profound sense. Holiness is a willingness to change, thereby increasingly moving us toward harmony with ourselves, others and God. The building of us into harmonic union with ourselves, others and God. Sin is therefore most *un*-natural, being selfishly destructive of the relationships that help make all of us both holy and more truly human. To reach a place of personal harmony, of wholeness within authentic community, requires a journey by individuals who together are willing to change in accordance with God's *Rapha Theocentric* wishes. To achieve this in Early Israel was the responsibility, within community, of everyone, both Jew and stranger as kinsman. Based on the Covenants, everyone was required to be holy, so that both life and community could be constructed in a real, authentic holy way. Holiness as wholeness was both learned, then lived relationally.

Theocentric kinship community

What I am noting here is that in Hebrew thought, begun in the Early Settlement period, the concept of the social unit is dominated by the idea of kinship (Johnson 1942:11). Israel often understood itself as a community of clans and households (Je. 2:4-8; 31:1 etc.), where Yahweh was the Father, Israel the son, wife, foundling, slave and resident alien within each *mishpachah*. This strong sense of Yahwistic *Theocentric* community dominated Israel's and early Judah's social and religious life,[42] shaping corporate identity, and creating sustainable local communities.[43] 'You will be my people, and I will be your God' (Lv. 26:12). Yahweh was Himself the common cause, the cohesive centre. But this was tempered with a strong tribal or clan sense of independence, which naturally resisted any serious limitation of tribal freedom. One has the sense that the internal core of these *mishpachah* sustained each individual against all external forces. The internal culture, with its allegiance to Yahweh, was intended to be stronger that its pagan hostile surroundings. Such a social system would exert decisive influences on the individuals, as givers rather than takers, so that life shared relationally was the priority, at both a local and tribal level.

---

[42] See Perdue (1997:255, footnote 14) for some of the sources arguing this point.

[43] I would not want to idealise Israel and its relationship with Yahweh. From what we know of Yahweh's ambitions, they were far from fulfilled. Hebrew history was one of continual recidivism, an ebb and flow of buying-in and then quitting.

Yahweh wanted a people for Himself, and went to great lengths to be their king. By the practice of worship, and seeking His will through interpreting the Law and its Traditions, local communities engaged with Him at all levels. He would be their Protector, Guide and Friend, the centre and focus of daily life. In fact, He was conceived as having anthropomorphic qualities, possessing an indefinable extension to His personality, that enabled Him to exercise a mysterious influence on His people, the power to release blessings or curses (Johnson 1942:20).

When covenant was broken with Yahweh, so was the motivation and power to *live* community (Kraus 1979:122). Restoration of covenant was first needed through corporate obedience, releasing a certain power to sustain *Theocentric* community. He provided a Yahweh-centred drive to actively live *Theocentric* community. It suggests a release, a synergy through righteousness, compassion and worship, not otherwise accessible to any of us alone. The tough character building of the Exodus and wilderness, then the Settlement period toward the Monarchy, all helped promote a distinct *kinship Theocentricity.*[44]

Some of these distinctives included a collective liability for the trespasses of the individual (Eichrodt 1967/1972:233). The 'sins of the fathers' being visited on the children is seen as an expression of God's righteousness (Ex. 20:5-6, Nu. 14:18-19, Dt. 5:9-10 etc.), a gift to change our heredity, not as the Church often sees it today as an offence or curse He has laid on us all. Ancient Israel saw its obligation to keep itself holy, and this was a community responsibility, since the sin of one affected everyone else (Johnson 1942 passim) (e.g. Achan, Jos. 7).[45] Likewise, people *belonged* to a family rather than *had* a family (Elliott and Dickey 1994, quoted in Meyers 1997:22). But this common cause and identity within the early Israelite *mishpachah* facilitated a certain type of relationship with Yahweh, one that allowed the individual to see their life in community as worship.

Old Testament faith knew nothing in any situation or at any time of a religious individualism granting a private relationship with Yahweh,[46] unconnected with the community either in its roots, its realization or its

---

[44] Johnson is interesting in his 'oscillation' concept in Hebrew thought between the one and the many, in areas like kinship, king and people, nation and individual, and finally Yahweh Himself and the 'angel' or 'messenger' (Johnson 1942:32).

[45] Such ideas are returning today, drawing together quantum thinking and Hebrew ideas. Gleick described his 'butterfly effect', the notion that a butterfly stirring the air today in Peking can transform storm systems next month in New York (1987:76). For a helpful introduction to some of these concepts, as they relate to theology and the Church, see O'Murchu (1997). I enlarge on some aspects of this theme in chapter 6.

[46] Wheeler Robinson began the debate regarding the place of individuality and the reality of 'corporate' Israel. See his original paper (1981) and the response challenging this by Rogerson (1985). See also Porter (1965:3661-380).

goals.[47] It is the formation of a divine centred society that gave meaning to divine demands, summoning the individual to live in permanent response to Him and others. The household, or households, were in their entirety regarded as a psychical whole (Johnson 1942:8). It was toward a perfected people of Yahweh that an individual's hope was directed (Eichrodt 1967/1972:265). I am not suggesting a return to such values, but instead to note the centrality of Yahweh's *Rapha* role, and to find for ourselves more balance regarding the ideas of the individual in community. The Hebrew community, creatively[48] assumed motherhood[49] of the religious life of the individual (Eichrodt 1967/1972:266).[50] It was only later prophetic thought that saw community and individuality together in fruitful interaction (267).

In Summary

Through the Hebrew Scripture, from the Settlement Period onwards, we see that all unity, by revelation, is created and maintained by the power of God, so that when one breaks covenant law one also breaks the grounds of one's own unity (Lambourne 1963:31),[51] a social pathology of disease is a normative assumption in the Old Testament, and the final aetiological factor is Adam's, 'man's' sin (58).[52] We see a view of the Christian 'soul' as the communally constituted self of the people, who by the indwelling Spirit finds full identity (Grenz 2001:20). It seems that Israel substantially lost this *Theocentric* way of life as a God-centred community, initially by moving toward the Monarchy, then the ritual of the Temple, and despite valiant efforts, finally during the Babylonian Exile (e.g. Am. 5:15). The concept of life as communal worship was breaking down.

Although a remnant returned and sought to develop a community around the Temple (Mal. 3:16-18), this new community focused more on the Torah, and eventually became formative in the Synagogue.[53] Yahweh increasingly became more transcendent, rather than *Theocentrically* living

---

[47] For a different emphasis, see Sheriffs (1996).

[48] God's creativity, then and now, I see as eternally redemptive. We change through His bidding, possessing progressively more wholeness now, allowing our life and faith to be more seamless. We need to live this ongoing redemption communally as a sacrament of life as worship.

[49] This term embraces my concept of community being 'a womb', a centre of formative (gestative) change. My belief is that such authentic *Theocentric* community carries the potential today of positively impacting all those who steps into its orbit.

[50] A modern parallel can be seen in the base church communities of South America, who share many of CCD's values, with a focus on the poor, being lay led etc. See Torres and Eagleson (1980), Barreiro (1984) or Boff (1986, 1988).

[51] This summary, and particularly this concept, underlies life in CCD. It is, I believe, a part of the implicit theology that makes the community a success, journeying together toward our own unique authenticity with one another, into Christ.

[52] For the impact of sin on Christian community today, see Hinnenbusch (1974:140ff.).

[53] The Synagogue became the depository for the written Law and Prophets. For an interesting introduction to this process, focused around the Septuagint (LXX), see Muller (1996).

among His people. In spite of the best efforts of Ezra, Nehemiah and others, *Theocentric* community as I have described it, stalled. Relationship with Yahweh increasingly focused around the Law, not Him. But what little remained came under an even greater threat, Hellenization,[54] with the coming of Christ and the birth of the Church.[55]

Christ, Paul and community

Christ and community

The idea that Christ was born into a backwater of Palestine has now given way to new ideas, based mainly on social archaeology. Christ was probably multi-lingual and from His Nazareth home could walk daily the five kilometres to Sepphoris, 'the ornament of all Galilee',[56] a new city being built by Herod at the time Jesus was a builder (Chancey and Myers 2000). Christ was part of a literate culture (Millard 2003) on the doorstep of one of the most cosmopolitan cities in the Middle East. But it seems He never really liked city life, avoiding the more urban areas, instead returning again and again to Bethany, a quiet village east of Jerusalem. He may have been drawn to Jerusalem by destiny, but focused much of His ministry around the shores of Galilee (Stambaugh and Balch 1986b:103) where He gathered His disciples, did many of His miracles, and where the 500 followers said good-bye to Him at His ascension (1 Cor. 15:5-8). This process of the re-framing of His personal life is currently underway academically.

But what has always been known is that He valued Yahwistic tradition and desired to birth a new type of family which He called Kingdom, emphasising new covenant relationships focused around Him. He also saw many obstacles set against this Kingdom's success (Mk. 4:26ff.; 10:14,

---

[54] The impact of Hellenism cannot be over-emphasised (Hengel 1989). Hellenization was a complex issue and differing groups within Judaism responded differently; some with accommodation, others with hostile derision. The Temple desecration by Antiochus IV Epiphanes in 167 BCE and subsequent Maccabean revolt saw Judaism finally break up. The Pharisees' Messianic hopes kept them aloof from Rome; the Sadducees embraced Rome, while the Essene Qumran community set themselves apart. It was a period of profound social and spiritual crisis. (See Skarsaune 2002:23ff.). But each contributed to Rabbinical Judaism, and hence to Christianity, though the last threads of traditional *Theocentric* community had already been virtually lost. After the fall of Jerusalem, 70CE, within Pharisaism, for instance, the people of Israel became the community, instead of the Temple (Neusner 1979:22, quoted in Stambaugh and Balch 1986a:100), preparing the way for radical shake up (Oesterley 1941).

[55] The birth of the Church saw Pharisaism still moving toward modern Judaism. The Pharisees took the Hebrew Bible, making it a religion of words rather than relationship with Yahweh. But the fall of Jerusalem in 70CE led to the establishing of the Academy of Jabneh as the centre of Jewish research. This helped birth Judaism and its community of the Synagogue as we know it today. For views on its impact on the Early Church, see Hull (1974) or Skarsaune (2002).

[56] For a list of some of the key titles focusing on Sepphoris, see Skarsaune (2002:70, n8).

24ff.; 12:32ff., etc.).[57] He therefore needed to equip His followers with a unique new outlook, echoing a *Rapha* or Yahwistic perspective, that would give them the spiritual and intellectual capital to hold steady in the battles that lay ahead. Just as in Exodus 15, Jesus' disciples were told to 'listen to Him' (Lk. 9:35). Their wholeness, like that of the Hebrew community, was to be found in relationship with Him and one another. For example, His special presence was manifest when two or three of them were together (Mt. 18:20). Christ lived the recovery of *Theocentric* community, though not focused around Yahweh, but Himself.

Christ's coming, with His teaching of a personal Satan (Mt. 4:1-11), the demonstrating of spiritual reality (Lk. 10:9, Jn. 14), permission to call God *daddy* (Mt. 6:9) and a challenge to all to treat this world with a 'light touch' (Lk. 12:31), all birthed a new wave of reality regarding Kingdom community.[58] Christ taught of a spiritual Kingdom[59] that existed in everyone who wanted it (Lk. 17:21), while in another sense would not exist until His rule was finally established on earth (Jn. 18:36, Rev. 12:10 etc.). In Christ, community[60] returned to a focus on Yahweh, and kinship relationship, but relationship centred not on the *mishpachah* or the Temple, but on Christ Himself as Son of the Father, Yahweh.[61] Jesus brought a return of immanence to the receding transcendent relationship with Yahweh. He set its personal expression in Himself, calling together a living community focused around Him, no longer in a Temple of stones.[62]

Jesus was also concerned about physical health. God's new, eschatological society would be known by the vanishing of disease and

---

[57] *Shalom* in the Old Testament becomes the Kingdom of God in the New. In Hebrew thought, well illustrated in Christ Himself, to be in sickness of body or weakness of circumstances is to experience the disintegrating power of death, while to enjoy health and adequate provision is to be allowed to walk with Him in fullness of life (Johnson 1964:108-109). However this is not guaranteed. See for instance the way God treated Jeremiah (Middlemiss 1996:165ff.).

[58] For a now dated, but helpful overview of 'man in community' from Early Hebrew times to Paul, see Shedd (1958).

[59] The Church announces the Kingdom, but is not the Kingdom. See Harrington (1980:27).

[60] Much is now being written on the ministry of Christ and the Early Church from a sociological perspective. On the theme of community in first a Judaic, then a Christian context, as well as a good recent introduction noting some of the social tools for analyzing Christian origins, see Kee (1995:13ff.). For a social study of how people lived in these times, following the theme that the early Christian family was the Greek Roman family, with some changes, see Osiek and Balch (1997). For a social history of the first century, see Stegemann and Stegemann (1999). For an interesting sociological comment on the growth of the Early Church, see Stark (1996). For a now dated, but interesting social focus on the Early Church's formative liturgies, see Swanston (1967).

[61] In moving from Hebrew Judaic ideas to Christ I would not want to imply a marked separation. See for instance Kee (1995).

[62] Commented Bilezikian, 'Jesus expressly and severely forbade his followers to structure their communities according to patterns borrowed from the secular world (Mt. 20:25-28). The only model they were allowed to follow was the interrelationship of oneness within the Trinity (Jn. 17:11,20-22)' (1997:49).

health miraculously appearing in Israel. The testings of the past were over, because everyone could now see the Lord revealed as Israel's physician (Lohfink 1994:95) (Is. 33:24), in the tradition of *Rapha,* 'I am Yahweh, your physician' (Ex. 15:26). Christ even suggested we would do greater miracles than Him when He had gone (Jn. 14:12).

Christ's emphasis on an individual's relationship with Him and His Father was revolutionary, setting new standards of intimacy with God, personal health, capacity for relational intimacy, faith between Christ and the individual, and through this to one another (e.g. Jn. 12-14). This became the foundation for *Kingdom community,* which was both taught and caught. With the Atonement there is forgiveness and the guarantee of the *Rapha* journey with Christ, with forgiveness there is reconciliation, adoption and connection, and with connection there is the community of faith (Crabb 1997:46). The eternal Son becomes, through *Theocentric* community and its Everlasting Covenant, the Incarnate Christ (Volf 1998a:85) (Eph. 2:4-7, Col. 2:9-10, Heb. 2:11-18).[63]

Christ and His disciples clearly saw themselves continuing in the tradition of Hebrew ideas, of both community and its spiritual heritage.[64] Christ restored something largely lost. He practised the concept of community Assembly (Heb. 12:22-24), where community is the leader, and each person contributes their own unique gifting toward it. The essence of Christ's teaching was the Kingdom of God, the core of Christianity here and now, while also being a spiritual kingdom which all of us with a struggle (Mt. 6:33) can enter, be part of and contribute to. Some, like Barth, saw Christ bringing in the Kingdom, though in his later life it is noted he recognized Christ *was* the Kingdom. Others, more specifically, have argued that Christ stands at the beginning of a new fellowship of humans, forming its foundation and being its fountainhead (Grenz 2000:352). But whatever the view on Kingdom, the core *Theocentric* emphasis of Hebrew community was being restored, now not calling Yahweh, but Christ as kin (Jn. 14:8-10; 20:28, 1 Cor. 8:6, Eph. 4:4-6).

The essence of this shift is defined in Christ's teaching us His prayer to His Father, and inviting us to make it ours (Mt. 6:9-13) (Hanson 1986:411). This Kingdom was spiritual, while Incarnate among us, worked out in grace, through believers (Kasemann 1982:65)(Phil. 2:13). But this Kingdom is also prophetic, stretching into future history, helping write it, the ultimate destiny for all of us, demonstrating the living reality of divine community within human relationality.

---

[63] Commented Volf, 'Christ….who is present in the local church through His Spirit and in this way makes it into the church in a proleptic experience of the eschatological gathering of the entire people of God, connects every local church with all other churches of God, indeed with the entire communion of those who through the same Spirit are 'in Christ'' (1998a:145).

[64] See, for instance, Miller (1979) and Hanson (1986:382ff.).

Christ birthing a *Theocentric* community

While Christ was teaching the nature of a spiritual kingdom, He also created a community of men and women that would be *ekklesia*,[65] here and now. For about three years He travelled, taught, loved and rebuked these disciples, forming a core community based on radical Kingdom principles that created a *koinonia,* ultimately capable of shaping human history. He demanded personal integrity, the willingness to speak truth at all times, and the importance of one's personal reputation before others. Such qualities were the outcome of solidarity with God in Christ, who focused this unity around His people together in intimate *communion* (Clark 1984:19ff.).[66] Christ was building a divine human interdependency, where everyone had an active unique contribution. Today *koinonia* embraces the Hebrew concept of *Theocentric* community, God with us, with Christ's own brand of spiritual community, Kingdom. In Christ, kinship *Theocentricity* fulfilled Yahwistic promise.

Christ's ministry seems to have created two inter-related communities of followers; those who during His life mostly stayed in their villages (Mk. 5:19-20), and a second core group of twelve disciples, that could become seventy (Lk. 10:1), or even five hundred (1 Cor. 15:6). Christ also instituted a renewed 'family' in Covenant with His Father (Mt. 10:37, Mk. 3:33-35, Lk. 14:26 etc.).[67]

Although He drew His followers from a broad social spectrum, on the whole they were from the poorer classes. He successfully moulded these into a community that stayed together, in obedience to Him, focused on Him.[68] Christ's strategy was to consolidate all aspects of their worlds into one (Frazee 2001:35), in bringing a unity reminiscent of a way of life in the early settlements. But to do this He needed every one of them to change, maturing the way He saw wholeness, through His words spoken to them about them.[69] This community developed a single-mindedness, leading to the birth of the Church and the subsequent proliferation of numerous communities. Christ's core community became the basis of all successive communities in the Church, showing many of the qualities of the Hebrew *mishpachah.*

From an Old Testament perspective Christ's death and resurrection brought about a renewing of the Triadic foundation of worship, righteousness and compassion by hearing the Word (Mt. 28:20, Lk. 8:21).

---

[65] For some of the formative influences on the Church's beginnings, see Swanston (1967).

[66] For a comment on the importance of the Eucharist in the context of contemporary spirituality, see Ballard (2003:364ff.).

[67] This is an important theme. See Lohfink (1985:31-73).

[68] Not always, e.g. Mt. 26:56, Jn. 6:60-66.

[69] We see fascinating insights into this process with, for instance, Peter the Apostle, who from the New Testament record clearly had a rugged journey toward greater maturity.

His teaching focused on all three (Mt. 14:14). But from Pentecost onwards the Kingdom and its *koinonia* was driven by another divine person, the Holy Spirit (Mk. 13:11). This added dimension quickened the reality of community, by promising all of us God's supernatural life in a consistent way (Jn. 14:26ff.). But Pentecost (Acts 2:1ff.) meant that any relationship in Christ now had the quickening immanent presence of God (Ps. 51:11-12; 143:10), giving it a supernatural dimension. Divine Trinity in human community became *Theocentric* once again, the dwelling place of God. Christ left the beginnings of a community model (Mt. 18:20), but it was the task of His Disciples, one of them in particular, Paul, to teach *Theocentric* community to the Greek Roman world.

Introducing Paul[70]

Paul[71] brought to the Church the most distinct models of community.[72] His thinking was highly developed, and represented a coalescing of Hebrew thought, Christ's own teaching and the wisdom of common sense in responding to practical problems. In essence, his thinking was shaped by local situations. *Theocentric* communities (Banks 1980/1988:150) were built, focusing on *charisma* (the exercising of spiritual gifts) within flat organizations by a living *koinonia* honouring both men and women.[73] Paul believed reconciliation (2 Cor. 5:7ff.) was only possible between one person and another when they were first reconciled to God (Rom. 15:7). Christ, like Yahweh before Him, promoted the building blocks of healthful one-to-one relationships, thus creating communities. Paul in turn emphasised the need to build up the Body of Christ by deepening relationship with Christ (Col. 1:15ff.), but all the time being mindful of the vulnerability of the weaker brother and sister (Rom. 15:1-3) (Bonhoeffer 1953:188-189).

As a guiding principle, Paul, the grounded realist, sought to adapt to the social culture around him, his thinking being the fruit of interaction between his Hebrew/Judaic, Hellenistic and Roman surroundings.[74] He had

---

[70] In choosing Paul I am mindful that in New Testament times there was not a monolith of what Church should be, since the first Christians left behind a range of models of Church. See Brown (1984).

[71] Although I am focusing on Paul and his communities, much has been written on other communities. See for instance Gager (1975) and Overman (1990).

[72] Drawing out the theology of Paul relating to community is in itself a formidable task. But then noting, even with a light touch, the cultural and local social applications of his model that are no longer directly relevant to us today, makes the whole task even more ambitious. For that reason I will only be focusing on specific features of Paul's models.

[73] The issue of gender is substantial, and currently in vogue. See Hooker (1963-64), Loewe (1966), Caird (1971), Pomeroy (1976), Banks (1980/1988:122ff.) and Podles (1999) etc.

[74] The modern study of the social world of the Early Church probably began with Meeks (1983), but was followed by a plethora of writings. Two of the most significant are Ascough

a unique background to achieve this. But he only accommodated or borrowed from the Greek Roman culture where it did not impinge on the freedom of the Gospel, or the person and work of Christ Himself. 'Being baptized into Jesus Christ signalled for Pauline converts an extraordinary thoroughgoing re-socialization in which the sect was intended to become virtually the primary group for its members, supplanting all other loyalties' (Meeks 1983:78, 104ff.).[75] *Theocentric* ideas were maturing, and the dynamic of being taught a new way of life promoted learning relations and its narrative culture.

First century turmoil[76]

The Graeco-Roman world of Paul's time was itself undergoing huge change, with increasing polarity between the rich and poor, the political elite and the masses.[77] There was also disenchantment with the *polis*, or state. Increasingly people were finding their desires fulfilled in voluntary associations, based on *koinonia*, a voluntary sharing or partnership, offering many people the community denied them elsewhere (Banks 1980/1988:15ff.). Into this social vacuum stepped two main claimants; a range of philosophies like the Stoics and Cynics (Sandbach 1975), and various 'mystery' or secretive religions or cults. Paul's communities must be seen as part of this wider movement of people seeking association with other individuals in society. Christians would be a cult, in the club or association sense of the word.[78] For instance, Zizioulas noted that although Greek thought had no ontology of personhood, Roman ideas supported the importance of personal relationships with others, because they focused on organizational and social concerns. This was expressed in the ability to form partnerships and associations, enter contracts, set up *collegia* to organize human life in the state, and to recognize the freedom that can be exercised by the group (Zizioulas 1985/2002:34). This was a good climate for the Hebrew Assembly, with its community leadership, to be re-born. It is self-evident that the wider climate at the time of Christ was conducive to new ideas, and Christianity proved the most radical and enduring. The

---

(1998), covering the social history of the Early Church, and its sociological analysis by Osiek (1992) and Stegemann and Stegemann (1999).

[75] In saying this, Meeks did not imply a cultish separation, '....they remained in the city, and their members continued to go about their ordinary lives in the streets and neighbourhoods, the shops and agora. Paul and the other leaders did not merely permit this continued interaction as something inevitable; in several instances they positively encouraged it (e.g. 1 Cor. 5:9-13)' (1983:105).

[76] For a number of the thoughts in the next three sections, I am indebted to Banks (1980/1988), who has done much of the work for me.

[77] For a scholarly focus on Jews and Judaism, as a background to understanding the early New Testament times, see Borgen and Giversen (1997), Scott (1995/2000) and Skarsaune (2002).

[78] For one modern view of when a local church becomes a cult, see Wookey (1996).

Early Church began to reclaim Hebrew community concepts in acknowledging the centrality of Christ.

Christ, the axis of *Theocentric* community

The conceptual bedrock of Paul's community, following the Hebrew model, was relationship with God through Christ as part of Trinity. The obstacles to this happening, according to Paul, were summarized in our compulsion to sin (Rom. 6:17,20; 7:14,25), our being hampered in finding God (as Jews Rom. 2:23, or anyone else Rom. 10:1-3) and our being in bondage to realities outside ourselves (2 Cor. 4:4, Eph. 2:2). Christ came to give us freedom from these (e.g. the *Rapha* principle), but this freedom can only be possessed in relationship with Him and *one another*. Paul saw salvation not only in personal terms (Rom. 11:17ff.), but also focused on encounter with Christ within community. It required maturing personal integrity and reputation with others (1 Cor. 11:27-32), having the Eucharist at its heart (1 Cor. 11:2ff.). This makes Paul's expression of Christ a corporate relational personality *now* (Banks 1980/1988:25). As we possess this new liberty in God in relationality it can lead to new freedom towards others, which must at all times be birthed in love (1 Cor. 9:19, 1 Thes. 2:8). This theme of love, and its binding interdependence, is central to Christ, Paul and Johannine thought.[79] As in the Hebrew *mishpachah,* everyone had an active and unique contribution to make to this community.

CHRIST THE HEAD OF COMMUNITY

In Pauline community we see the earlier Yahwistic example of a deliverer-God inviting personal transformation from both the individual (Col. 3:12-15a) and the community (Eph. 4:31-32), eliciting praise, righteousness and compassion (Phil. 2:1-7). Paul's deliberate policy was to bring people into intimacy with God in Christ, which in turn would lead to deeper personal relationships with one another (Rom. 15:7). Accepting Christ should compel us to accept all those already in Christ. For the Gospel (Phil. 4:2-3) and the Spirit (2 Cor. 13:14, Eph. 4:3, Phil. 2:1) are both shared. Therefore, to embrace the Gospel is to enter community.[80] This event and all of its processes Paul describes as *ekklesia*, an assembly or gathering of people.[81]

---

[79] You will have noted at several key places in this book the theme of love is noted. It has always been a prominent theme in the Church. In fact whole Christian movements have been birthed on it, for instance, the Lundensians (see Nygren 1932/1982, or Ferre 1939).

[80] Theologically one's instinct, like that of Paul (e.g. Rom. 15:7), is probably to put relationship with God first. In practice in my own experience I often see the opposite in CCD and *Rapha*, with people first learning to trust one other, then extending this to a circle of others. Then in time deciding they will begin to trust God in this same way. This reverses traditional 'evangelism', but, I suggest, may be more acceptable to the contemporary un-churched.

[81] For a more extensive discussion of the Catholic, Orthodox and Free Church view of *ekklesia,* see Volf (1998a:137ff.)

But unlike any other meeting of people in the Hellenic sense, the Church is described as belonging to the one who has brought it into existence, Christ Himself. This makes Christian *ekklesia* divine and supernatural (Rom. 16:16, 1 Cor. 1:1, 2 Cor. 1:1 etc.). Its owner, Christ himself, remains it Head.[82] On this basis Christ's mission[83] and its commission continued corporately after His ascension as a household, family and community church (Oden 1994/1998:280).

Birthing a community movement

This community or local church is a voluntary association, existing by divine authority, expressed in household units.[84] From these 'house churches' we see the visible manifestation of a universal eternal spiritual commonwealth in social relations now. Paul's model, some argue, is conceptually richer and more socially relevant than others advanced in his own day (Banks 1980/1988:50), and this may be true. Banks further noted that Paul nowhere addresses his major letters to specific men or women as 'leaders of the church', though sometimes mentioning them in the text (Col. 4:15,17 etc.). For Paul, all who belong to the community share in the responsibility for the general conduct of its proceedings (Banks 1980/1988:139). Paul gave to everyone the responsibility to hear and discern God's view (Rom. 15:14, 1 Cor. 14:31, Eph. 4:15, Col. 3:16), unlike the Theocratic system of the Old Testament, where the Elder and prophet normally had this responsibility, then in time the priest. In Paul's communities, as in Hebrew communities, leadership seems to have been a corporate affair.[85] Paul grounded equality in the divine act of Christ being available to all, but for Paul equality was subservient to unity. Sociologically, the persistence of such Hebrew ideas over Hellenistic ideas is now being accepted.[86]

---

[82] On the issue of Church as *ekklesia*, Pauline thought implies it is not all the Christians in a particular area, but rather the whole Church of which any part is representative. This body exists on earth, meeting intermittently, while permanently in session as a heavenly community (Col. 1:2; 3:3-4 etc.) (Banks 1980/1988:41ff.). See also Oden (1994/1998:283) for a similar view.

[83] For a comment on the 'mission' of Christ, see Kostenberger (1998).

[84] Suggested by Stuhlmacher (1981), quoted in Lohfink (1985:98). See also Ellison (1963) and Gehring (2004).

[85] A qualification. I am not arguing priests are wrong, only that leadership was clearly shared. In this I am echoing Bucer's concerns (1538, cited in McNeill 1951/1977). Bucer, the third man of the Reformation, saw it as a step back for Protestantism to adopt the Catholic one-priest-one-congregation tradition. Instead, he argued that no one man has all the gifts, therefore churches should have teams of leaders, chosen from across the social spectrum.

[86] The orthodox view has been that Hebrew influences were lost quickly in the Early Church, but this is being challenged by Skarsaune, who argues 'for the persistence of the Jewish heritage' (2002:279ff.), that early faith communities were far more mixed than we sometimes think. He proposes that Christology, the formation of liturgy, worship, calendar, Passover and Eucharist all had profound Hebrew influences. Also, the traditional view is that Gentile expansion of the Church,

We know surprisingly little on the subject of how the Early Church was structured, so it seems dangerous to speculate. But we do know that practically and theologically it was built, like the Old Testament *mishpachah*, around the concept of the Greek Roman family. Community was family (Gehring 2004).[87] Paul used the terminology of family creatively as body, household, family, steward, slave, brethren, neighbour, my brother, and my child, for it is around the metaphor of the family, with Christ as the Head, that He builds the spiritual community. It is interesting that the obviousness of Paul's use of these familial terms is largely overlooked today, that these local communities saw one another primarily as members of a common larger family (Gal. 6:10).[88] The radical nature of this family concept is not fully comprehended until one notes that nowhere in the Old Testament is Israel called *God's family*, though it is sometimes referred to as a *household* (Je. 38:26, Am. 5:25). But Paul was not the first to use this analogy.

Paul actually stands behind Christ in using a language of both family and love to describe the community of believers (Mk. 3:34-35; 12:30-31). Paul saw Christ as truly and wholly present in any group of believers (1 Cor. 12:13), which is theologically essential, for it endorses the *Theocentric* possibility of full relationship with Christ for anyone. Although Paul used the terms *elder* and *deacon*,[89] he nowhere used the common Greek word *hierus* or priest.[90] Christ returned to the ideal of Yahweh being the head, with everything under Him.[91] Paul understood better than most what Christ intended, and in taking up this concept required all believers acknowledge Christ, and He alone, as the Living Head. Paul is building on the Hebrew Theocratic community concept, the ground of which was prepared for him by Christ Himself.

---

away from Jerusalem and Jewish cultural centres, meant the Church absorbed more and more Hellenic ideas. Again, Skarsaune points out that Paul went to the Synagogues in each city, suggesting Jews and Gentiles would both make up any local faith community.

[87] The word 'family' today can be inclusive and divisive. So it is best to interpret it in this context in symbiotic and osmotic terms, in partnership with other ideas and concepts, while noting it has the power to gradually, unconsciously, assimilate other ideas in a modern context.

[88] As mentioned above, we must be careful here, since our society uses the same word 'family', but not in the sense that Paul used it. For Paul it meant an extended adoptive and impartial social grouping called church (*ekklesia*), living by fellowship (*koinonia*).

[89] I wish to thank Prof Mary Kate Morse for the reminder that Greek does not distinguish between male and female deacons.

[90] One of the foundations of Protestant Christianity is Luther's strong stand on the priesthood of all believers, even though today most Protestant denominations are clericalized. As in early Methodism, I personally would expect a whole congregation should rise to their individual full potential in Christ, not just its leader(s). See Henderson (1997:149).

[91] Christ was the ultimate Priest because He made the last great sacrifice of Himself once and for all. Therefore no one else could be a priest, and the ceremonial sacrifices are now redundant (Rom. 5:6ff., Heb. 7:11-28; 9:25-28).

The Church is not just the 'body of Christ' but 'one body in Christ' (Rom. 12:5a). Christ is the source of its unity and the means by which it exists. For everything in creation owes its life to Christ (Col. 1:15ff.). He alone is the image of the invisible God and the Church as Kingdom community is to grow up in every way into Him (Eph. 1:12,15-17). According to Paul, all who are genuine members of this community have the Spirit of Christ (e.g. 1 Cor. 12:13, 2 Cor. 3:18, Eph. 2:18, Gal. 5:22ff. etc). This means that all are spiritual in a Christ-centred sense, all having capacity not only for relationship with God, but also for hearing Him for themselves (Jn. 14:26). Both intimacy with Christ, and holiness through Him, is for everyone. In this sense Christ is building on the *Theocentric* principle, by making Himself fully available to everyone at a personal level. This is the authority of our claim to be able to become more fully human.[92]

Maturity plus community
as wholeness in Christ

The experience of CCD suggests a *Rapha* discipleship journey requires community as a means of achieving personal wholeness. To be more fully human one must live as a 'person in relation', within relational community with others. However, as we have learned, such community requires deep commitment, takes maturity to live authentically, and only happens over time. But this, I am suggesting, is the landscape of Christ's and Paul's discipleship models.

Spiritual growth, maturity and community in Paul's writings

This community context toward Christ-like wholeness brings a number of implications with it. Throughout Scripture the model of becoming more fully human is neither exclusively personal nor entirely private. For Paul, growth and maturity is spoken of in terms of ever-increasing integration into Christ, a living love in and through one another (Eph. 4:15). 'Since for Paul Christ's resurrection and the abiding presence of Christ's Spirit within the community of faith formed the centre of God's new initiative, he defined the Church as the body of Christ, called by grace to carry on the mission of reconciliation it had already experienced' (Hanson 1986:485).[93] It is important to note that most of the time, when Paul spoke of maturity,

---

[92] Beyond Paul we see the importance of the family, and the strategy to extend these Christian ideas of family into community. For the first three hundred years it is thought communities remained relatively small and tightly knit. Large crowds drew too much attention to themselves. So these small groups clearly had a high degree of autonomy, and moral and social cohesion. Many were persecuted. To survive, they needed stronger social processes over the individual, generating their own internal integrity that held *Theocentric* value systems in place.

[93] For a seminal work on this subject covering both Biblical and modern mission, see Bosch (1991).

he addressed the issue corporately (1 Cor. 1:10; 14:20, 2 Cor. 1:13-14, Eph. 4:11-16; 5:25-27, Col. 1:21-22; 4:12 etc.). Maturity was defined as an ever-closer approximation to the 'likeness' of Christ, an increasing reflection in our lives of His values and attitudes, and our mutual participation in His activities (Col. 1:15-19).[94] In this sense it is Christ speaking to us both personally and corporately that helps promotes authentic community. Wholeness is holistic, embracing every one of us faith lived out in corporate relationship.

For Paul, this process of 'maturity' was through the imparting of the knowledge of Christ (Eph. 4:20, Col. 1:7, etc.). It was taught by both Paul's words and his life (Acts 19:11ff.). This knowledge was specific and exclusive to promoting relationship with Christ. Paul was not prepared to tolerate any other talk except that which promoted personal and corporate deepening of relationship with Christ. He specifically stated that growth took place only as the members of the community are 'increased with', 'enriched by', 'renewed through' and 'filled with' such Christ-centred knowledge (Phil. 1:9, Col. 1:9-10; 3:10).

This growth for Paul was a rational and ordered process, described in numerous Greek terms, some of which are: *nous* – mind, *noema* – thought, *gnosis* – knowledge, *sophia* – wisdom, *sunesis* – understanding, *aletheia* – truth, *phronein* – to think, *logizein* – to consider, *anakrinein* – to discern, *peithein* – to persuade, *dokimazein* – to test etc. Each person internalizes this truth by their commitment to it (Rom. 10:9-10). Paul is describing a learning journey. Since God Himself is Truth, this commitment produces over time a growing deepening knowing of Christ. Knowledge from the Holy Spirit is the vehicle through which such faith and knowledge in the person of Christ grows.[95] Without this possibility of *knowing* and changing, the Church is left with an eternal (transcendent) God, but not an Incarnate Christ. As Banks noted, Paul nowhere limited this knowledge of maturity to an elite (1980/1988:149). In fact, as already noted, one major distinctive of this new divine Assembly of all members was the strong culture of personal change demanded of every new disciple, as they sought acceptance into the Kingdom family.

Since such spiritual growth is a gradual thing, the fruit of a person's life in Christ, within community, it becomes incumbent on all of us to minister into the lives of others. 'Leadership' is earned through integrity, the fruit of one's own journey, not merely by appointment to an office.[96] Scripture

---

[94] In spite of such apparent clear teaching in Scripture, most modern Christian writing on the subject of maturity in Christ virtually always reduces this process to a personal, even private level.

[95] I am aware that speaking this way I could be accused of slipping into the Charismatic camp, as described by Middlemiss, 'The main stream of religion is condemned as being an affair of simply outward form and ordinances, whereas authentic Christianity is now being restored as an affair of the heart' (1996:7).

[96] Though appointment is not contradictory to it (1 Tim. 3:1-7, Tit. 1:5-11).

suggests that for Paul, leadership seems to have been a 'lay' movement. Therefore, one's acceptance into the community in terms of leadership must correspond to the degree with which one already genuinely lives Christ in the lives of others.

At least one other key element was required in Paul's community, the presence of love in relationship. This love surpasses knowledge (1 Cor. 13:8, Eph. 3:19), whereas knowledge without love merely feeds pride (1 Cor. 8:1; 13:2). Love, for Paul, within community created the most conducive environment for a fuller understanding of Christ (1 Cor. 12:31ff., Col. 2:2). Pastoral responsibility to act in love at all times is assumed to be the obligation of every community member.

Also, for Paul, people did not go to church to 'worship' (Banks 1980/1988:91). Instead Paul saw one's whole life as worship (Rom. 12:1-2). To use a modern term, the meeting of the community together would best be described as 'mission', not worship. The mission seems to have been to express *'Theocentric'* community in Christ. Paul saw the purpose of meeting corporately as the spiritual strengthening of one another (1 Cor. 14:12,19,26).[97] This is done through sharing gifts in mutual ministry or *charisma* with one another (Eph. 5:19, Col. 3:16-17), exercising gifts for the benefit of all present. Christ Himself is the first gift (Eph. 2:8), and all the other gifts exercised through the gift of the Holy Spirit should reflect and point to Him. Though the gifts differ in their *effect*, the entire thrust of 'giving of gifts to one another' must ultimately deepen one's individual relationship with Christ, and subsequently further transform the group.

The fullest expression of this love within the community was around the Eucharist or Breaking of Bread - the bread during the meal, the wine at the end - and in between the experience eating the food of warm relationships (1 Cor. 11:23-5). Communion is a community meal, focused around a proper family event, usually with guests. For Paul, this event was something to be shared with Christ and one's friends in Christ. So strong was Paul's belief in the power of the community/communion aspect of this meal, that he warned them that if they were not sensitive to the physical needs of others in the community, in taking the meal they may insult Christ and harm themselves (1 Cor. 11:27-29). Paul is invoking a *diachronic* principle (Banks 1980/1988:150), encouraging a participatory society involving all in mutual allegiance within community in Christ.

---

[97] In CCD we also seem to do a number of things in a counter-intuitive way. For instance, we always take the last Sunday of the month off as a break, with no Sunday meetings at all. This gives people time to do tasks that cannot be done on any other day (e.g. travelling to meet family etc.) without missing church. But this also allows us to make the other three Sunday's special, a treat. For most of the community the Sunday off is a nuclear and corporate family day for spending more time together.

Early Church Incarnational community

In both Christ and Paul we see the maturing of the ideas we noted from the Hebrew period; *Theocentricity* and its learning relationships, the concept of Assembly and its community leadership, the importance of personal integrity and reputation, promoting community interdependence. Here everyone has an active unique contribution to make, and everyone shows a willingness to change and mature in order to express more fully 'God in our midst'.

For Paul community is the gospel in corporate, visible, enticing form. It was as fluid as the *mishpachah,* but as stable as the Assembly. Banks suggested that Paul may well have been the first individual to formulate and implement an idea of religious community that was not subservient to the family or the state (1980/1988:189). Paul's communities were clearly not based on one specific analogical model. Each community matured, having unique characteristics. They were experimental, non-standardized and genuinely 'incarnational' (Ascough 1998:98-99).[98]

The picture emerging from Paul is of a Church meeting in homes, probably no larger than around 30 in any one household, and culturally adapted to the climate prevailing at the time. They were focused around Christ and described by Paul as 'family'.[99] Life was structured to bring everyone to a mature personal knowing of Christ, at all times in the context of relationship with one another. Each person, through the *charism,* heard Christ for themselves and this released the *charismata.* Each community was conceived in love, focused around 'Communion' and energized spiritually through the Holy Spirit by the exercising of spiritual gifting and fruit. Leadership emerged on the basis of an individual's anointing, though everyone must be honoured, particularly the least esteemed in the community. This practice of Christ-centred *Theocentric* communities would extend into a world that was created to participate in the life of the social Trinity (Grenz 2000:112).

Our journey so far

We are beginning to visualize a divine community and a redeemed people, living within a renewed community, enjoying the presence of their God (Grenz 2000:113). Such community is the life of Christ on earth, having a *Theocentric heart,* where God speaks to each personally, while actively and manifestly dwelling among them corporately. Yahweh's speech, through His covenants, and His personally speaking to individuals about

---

[98] A long debate has continued over what Paul actually used as a model for his churches. I am suggesting it is the concept of *Theocentricity,* but Judge (1960b) argued that he used a rhetorical model. Common sense prevails in the view expressed by Ascough (1998). But the truth is we do not actually know, though it clearly took different forms in different places.

[99] See, for instance, Nardin (1996).

themselves, established Israel as a community (Plaskow 1999), This Christ also adopted, repeated and endorsed. Language, and its teaching and power to change us is the marrow of community, the coherence for human beings to live together in wholeness. Just as Yahweh spoke His Covenants that formed community, the Church still integrates the learning of the message of the Kingdom with communal formation through the social nature of language (Christians 1998:2).

The relationship of God to us is the one on which all other relationships must be built.[100] Triadic Covenant with Yahweh established a foundation of of righteousness,[101] compassion and worship within the community. The suggestion is that divine presence rests in community in a uniquely powerful way (Plaskow 1999:407). God, through such community has the capability of creating a single unified world (Kirkpatrick 1986:198-201).[102] In CCD such community is an essential contributor to our becoming more fully human. Therefore:

> The Western Church needs to learn to dialogue with, not condemn a world 'come of age' without God. The Church must seek to authenticate capacity in God and change in people, thereby building faith communities around those who acknowledge such personal need.

---

[100] This is echoing Bonhoeffer (1949/1970). For the view that community should be focused around the sacraments, e.g. meeting Christ, see Maertens (1970) and Pannenberg (1984). For the idea that healing is sacrament, see Israel (1984).

[101] The issue of righteousness and sin is a huge subject. But I see righteousness, as Hanson did, as corporate. 'In considering the Biblical notion of righteousness, we thus must conclude that an asocial private piety is simply unbiblical' (1986:510).

[102] Please note that although these references are in Kirkpatrick, some of the ideas are John Macmurray's. See Macmurray and Grant (1938) and Macmurray (1973) for an expansion of some of these community ideas.

Chapter 6

Seeking a model for the Church of therapeutic faith community

What happened to faith *community*?

Apprenticeships are not popular today. They take too long. Likewise, so do communities of the type which we all dream of belonging to. For living in community, as Susan Williams' research indicates, takes tenacious maturity, and like an apprenticeship, is only learned over an extended period of time.

> That is why [Christ Church] is so unique, people are buying into the principle of giving. We can only do that as we let go of the baggage and realize we have been selfish, and arrogant and full of pride, all our motives are wrong (M14-11).

Congregations becoming communities do not happen 'naturally' or spontaneously; they have to be intentional.

However, as already noted, creating faith communities is not helped by Western models of Trinity, personhood and discipleship. To become communities of the type any of us want, I am suggesting that at their heart must be a lived personal transformational theology, focused around both God and our changing self in inter-relationship. I believe that such personal change is what the contemporary un-churched are seeking: community with an immanent tangible spirituality, promoting therapeutic personal change, toward corporate maturity.

In this chapter I wish to introduce a new way of looking at faith community, by proposing that change,[1] even in Scripture, Christ's ministry and the Early Church's lifestyle, had a personal maturing therapeutic dimension. I also wish to press further, by suggesting this therapeutic change aspect was *implicit* in Hebrew and Early Church communities, illustrated by the journey toward maturity of many Biblical personalities (e.g. Abraham, Moses, David, Jeremiah, Peter, Paul etc.). But today this discipleship wholeness journey needs to be more *explicit*, because our

---

[1] Some argue that change is already a popular theme in the contemporary Church. For instance,we have noted above the huge number of Christian self-help books currently on the market. What I am suggesting is that what is missing is the internal personal change, and its corporate expression. Such a feature in faith community is rare, though not entirely extinct. One encouraging example is the survey done for the Religious Education Association in the USA, which makes the observation that faith community is the most effective place for personal change (Religious Education Association 1987:Foreword).

contemporary culture is now also living in similar ways. As Lucado stated, 'God loves you just the way you are, but He refuses to leave you that way. He wants you to be just like Jesus' (1998:subtitle). This chapter presents a contemporary rendition of Yahwistic, Christ-centred and Pauline models of therapeutic faith community.[2]

Christ-centred community in Trinity

When I first committed to Christ in the early 1960's I was told I should not look to others as they would all fail me at one time or another: only Jesus never fails. Such thinking, suggesting the Church will fail us, may in some ways be true, but is also a denial of what I now see as foundational to the Gospel, the incarnation of Christ *through* His Church, as community.[3] Our lives within faith community must demonstrate to others both who Christ is, and that they as individuals are loved. To belong to Jesus is to belong to one another, being part of a continually changing faith community. My observation is that in the Western Church, orthodoxy has been separated from orthopraxy. I have had to concede that if the Gospel does not drive the believer toward community, it is not the authentic Gospel.[4] For what is truly alive, grows (Snyder 1977:119). An authentic community is not a collection of individuals (e.g. members of a congregation), but a fellowship of likeminded persons, making the I-Thou relationship the heart of community (Buber 1958/1996 passim).

My call for discipleship as a means to creating community is not unique. Wallis (1980) suggested the greatest need within the Church was authentic *koinonia.* Dulles described the Church as needing *communities of disciples* that live a journey of personal and corporate change, with the goal of being together, with and like Christ (1974/1987:7ff.).

When I describe Christ Church in detail I actually talk about myself. I tell them what has happened to me and then, I tell them about my journey, and then I tell

---

[2]   CCD is not my 'finished' example or prototype therapeutic faith community, as it does not yet have all the aspects I am describing, e.g. its power to replicate itself and to continue developing independently etc.

[3]   This idea is more radical than it may at first sound. Take, for instance, the Lausanne Committee for World Evangelism's report, *Evangelism and social responsibility: An Evangelical comment* (1982), which looks at the Gospel in relation to issues of the Church's social responsibility. Here, at least, you would expect to find substantial references to the social role of faith community in drawing people to Christ, but nowhere in the entire document does it refer to community in any form as either a base or a strategy for evangelism.

[4]   Grenz went further. He argued that modernism, being a child of Enlightenment epistemology, glorifies reason and deifies science. But our postmodern age, tossing aside as it has the correspondence theory of truth, removes Christian objectivity (1996:163). This denial of rational scientific method benefits us, as postmodernism argues, as none of us are outside historical process. But Grenz proposed that the postmodern Gospel, even as a Gospel of individuality, must still remain within community/relationships (167). Grenz's approach contrasts with postmodern theory, suggesting all of us must create our own reality (Becvar 1997:dustcover).

people about the fact that others are doing the same as me but they have come from somewhere different and we are all in this community, entity, where we are all on a journey in a similar vein to mine (W9-2).

Koinonia of mutual need, expressed in love, is for me now the bedrock of living, breathing, loving communities[5] of faith.[6] It starts with a personal admission of one's need to change in order to possess wholeness in Christ, in fellowship with other like-minded people.[7] *Kerygma, diakonia, charisma* or even *propheteia* are not the priority. What is the priority is common purpose – all doing the same journey, toward the same end, together. Biblical community is the need, expressing the life of Christ on earth as one (Frazee 2001:22). This spiritual community first celebrates God (Crabb 1999:135) as a *Theocentric* community.[8] In putting these principles into practice, the Church would truly become counter-culture, rather than sub-culture.

---

[5] For a brief history of the Christian community movement in UK, touching some of these themes, see Clark (1984:92ff.). For a dated though helpful review of the problem of Church within a community, see Lovell (1972). For a comment on the phenomenal growth of communities within the Church, see Card (1988:25ff., 105ff.). For new thinking regarding the Church reconstructing the concept of communities, see Greenwood (1987).

[6] Many others have been calling for the same thing within the Church. For instance, Clark (1972) proposed a new holistic view of how Church should be based on a series of principles, including personal renewal, and its promulgation. He warned, however, that building such new communities would cause traditional congregations to resist such change. Westerhoff (1976) suggested that education oriented communities of faith were exhausted in the USA, and a new type of community needed to emerge to replace and reinvigorate the teaching of faith. Greenwood more recently argued the Church needed to move towards a more laity-driven structure, with less clerical control, and the building of local ministry teams. He even stated the Holy Spirit desired such change (1996:4-5). A similar thing had been said by Leslie Paul 40 years before (1964:171, quoted in Gill 2003:204). But none of these suggest the need for personal transformative change as the basis of authentic community. In fact Greenwood (1996) suggested that reorganizing the structures, allowing a laity orientation and building ministry teams will itself bring about this renewal of community.

[7] Others agree with me. Kraus argued that 'awareness of one's new individual identity before God inevitably and necessarily involves one in community' (1979:90). Bishop took it further by observing that *koinonia* potentially gives the Church a significant advantage in the healing community field (1985:20).

[8] There is a long history of returning to such community themes. Eberhard Arnold, the founder of the Bruderhof movement described it: 'We acknowledge Christ, the historical Jesus and with Him His entire message...we stand as brothers and sisters with all those who have joined together to live in community through the long course of history. They appeared among the Christians of the first century; in the prophetic movement of the Montanists in the second; in the monasticism of the following centuries; in the revolutionary movement of justice and love led by Julian of Brescia; in the Waldensian movement; in the itinerant communities of Francis of Assisi; among the Bohemian and Moravian brethren, and the Brothers of the Common Life; among the Beguines and Beghards; in the Anabaptist movement of the sixteenth century; among the early Quakers; among the Labadists of the seventeenth and eighteenth centuries, among the early Moravians and among many other denominations and movements down to our present day' (1967/1995:8-9). (For further comments by Arnold on community, see 1994:96ff., and 1984/1999.)

Scirghi (2002) helpfully summarizes this view, following Himes and Himes (1993:55-73) and Boff (2000), that the three persons of the Godhead are a model for human community, through both *kenosis* and inclusion. Following Eastern Orthodoxy, Scirghi sees *perichoresis* as an interpenetration of all persons who are a perfect harmony through their relation with one another. His argument, countering modalism and tritheism, depicts a Trinity of three persons in a perpetual state of self-giving (e.g. a type of kenosis), a kenotic perichoretic experience of Trinity in corporate humanity. He sees that the self-giving of the Incarnation of the Son of God interpenetrated the Trinity community, pouring out into human history. This allows us to model a community theology that resembles Trinitarian reality, where there is no being without belonging, and no being without giving oneself, as the Trinity fully did and still does. We belong to Christ eternally by our belonging to one another now. This is the authentic ground of all human becoming. To become is to be in ever deepening relationships. Like the Trinity itself with its intra-Trinitarian relationships, the more we commit to one another the more we personally fully wholely exist. This, I believe, is what it means to become more fully human. Like Boff, I believe the Church must shift from a Church-as-society, to a Church-as-communion (Boff 2000:65).[9] On such a foundation I am now able to go one step further.

Imago Dei

Like others have before me (Volf 1998a passim), I have gradually moved toward a view of *imago Dei* as needing to be a corporate reality, not a singular human-spirit-after-the-Holy-Spirit-in-me theology. We are a community-building species (Gardner 1996) just like our Creator. Miller (1979) built a solid theology of community around the concept of God's image, whereby the proclamation of the Word of God has to be accompanied by the image of God lived out. He systematically presented a cluster of ways whereby this image could be displayed in community, suggesting we are all created to bear this image before the world (95), and the Church *in its corporate identity* bears and displays this image of God (67). However, I am disappointed that he failed to take one further step, arguing as I am that the most basic way to learn how to live in such a community requires our willingness to positively change in order to learn, and learn in order to change. The Church today needs to mirror this kenotic Trinity.

Here Scirghi helps me, by suggesting that since the human being is made in the image and likeness of God, the human person has the *capacity* of

---

[9] Boff is a helpful introduction to the concept of the communion of the Trinity, with a useful summary of this doctrine to date (2000:111-115), that includes a brief but informative glossary (117-125).

becoming a self-gift to others (2002:341). This suggests human nature exists most healthily in relationship, within a climate of personal positive change. Where there is no ongoing change, there will be little authenticity.

In most places you could hide in the baggage where you can be somebody who, you can live in a fantasy, get away with it 'coz your relationships are so shallow, whereas here there is a requirement on you that you be real (M10-1).

None of us live this way ordinarily by choice. It is something we must all learn, in order to mirror social Trinity more fully. As Volf observed, the two fold activity of the Spirit is unifying, while differentiating (1998a:282). We must all honour our uniqueness, while learning the voluntary interdependence of authentic community (Covey 1989:183).[10]

Recovering imago Dei in community

CCD has taught me many things, but particularly that *imago Dei* in community is not easily acquired. For us, it has needed both a personal therapeutic discipleship journey supported by a culture of change in community. However, such a path is fraught for any church with numerous obstacles, including our prejudicial attitudes, our cognitive dissonance, scripts and schemas etc., that all construct and guide our values, expectations and actions. For instance, there is a belief among many churchgoers that congregational life should be warm and friendly,[11] rather than a more authentic place of discipline and painful ongoing self-reflection,[12] as the *Rapha* journey sometimes requires. Droege, along similar lines, also observed that the Church has a tradition of faith as 'unchanging', which makes recognition and acceptance of faith as 'developmental' difficult for people to accept (1992:40). Also, there is in some parts of the Church a type of piety in resisting change, while a 'triumphalist' trust in God can mean we give God responsibility for reversing falling numbers. Another similar attitude is that the Church does

---

[10] Once they have completed the first part of their journey some members need to make the decision that being part of the community is something they now really want long-term. This is a healthy process. (See, for instance, Pingleton 1992:111, who has observed the same process.) When they return, as most do, they are choosing to stay together within the community, even though they have reached a point in their wholeness where they could, if they wished, stand alone (Pingleton 1992:107). Instead, they voluntarily choose to come back and settle, to give back, even though in one sense they do not need the community any longer. This commitment creates a 'giving' culture of additional voluntary interdependence of community members.

[11] Bringing together the two ideas of the apprenticeship and the friendly congregation is not my idea. I have borrowed it from Hauerwas. 'We have underwritten a voluntaristic conception of the Christian faith....one can become a Christian without training.....any alternative cannot help appearing as an authoritarian imposition' (1993:153). Hauerwas then went on to suggest we all need to learn how to learn, because transformation is required (157).

[12] Bauman goes further by noting that today the successful do not need community (Bauman 2001:28), but then notes that without others we are not in charge of our own destiny. He further notes it is in this area of self-reflection that community is most missed (149).

not need a new message for the 21st century, just a redoubling of evangelistic efforts the way we have done it in the past.[13] My own past experience is similar to the Whiteheads, 'Having given ourselves generously to the effort of community formation, we come away with a sense of frustration and failure' (1992:1). These are just a few of the numerous obstacles to authentic faith community.

Within the Church change is more often associated with management restructuring, about *external* organisational change and conformity.[14] But such management change clearly does not achieve authentic community. Instead, I am suggesting authentic community needs to be driven by individual *internal* change. I believe without this internal personal change the building blocks are missing for authentic faith community. The experience of CCD is that such a community grows naturally when a group of people commit to personal change, led by Christ, choosing to do this therapeutic journey together. On this basis, my concern is that if the Church cannot find ways to allow people to pursue a personal journey of discipleship change, it will not be able to create authentic *Theocentric* community. The individual must first be *becoming* the new person in Christ, who then commits through shared experience to creating authentic communities of interdependence. The creating of such communities could, I believe, help reverse the attrition the Church is currently experiencing.[15] Renewed community only happens with renewed people, though recent history in the Church suggests that human nature will *always* prefer minimal change (Schaller 1994:152).[16] Faith community, built on a

---

[13] These are not the only reasons for the Western Church's sad state. There are many others. For instance, the love of leisure over commitment, the offence of modern Church to contemporary people, the fear many Christians have of changing ecclesial routines, the sanctity of un-changeableness, etc. See Wansey (1978/1987) for a comment on some of these areas of resistance, in his case focused on the Church of England, or Harris (1982), who focused more on the small American congregation. See Tomlinson (1995) for a modern call for change. Michael Green (1990) wrote a substantial tome for the decade of evangelism (1990s), anticipating some of the initiatives we have found helpful in CCD.

[14] '…..he regards himself as "religious" and as a believer in God, but usually his religion is outward and conventional, and when he has conformed to the injunctions of his church and shared in its rites he feels that he has done all that is required of him' (Assagioli 1989:32).

[15] Cobb, following the same theme, outlined the Church battling with three major problems: alienation from the Bible, boredom with worship, and a failure to encourage people into spiritual reality (1977:18ff). 'A full Christian goal is a new wholeness centering on spirit' (23).

[16] Having said this, it is interesting to note that in the United States, especially over the last 20 years, we have seen a range of specialist churches seeking to confront some of this resistance. For instance *The Saddleback Church,* pastored by Rick Warren in California, emphasises the need for a common purpose. *Willow Creek* in Chicago, emphasises community and a seeker-sensitive worship. *The Vineyard Fellowship* birthed by the late John Wimber in Anaheim, California has its emphasis on worship and healing. *The Crystal Cathedral,* led by Robert Schuler in New York, challenges us all to move from sin to salvation, from depravity to our being created in Christ's image. Also Michael Slaughter, *Ginghamsburg United Methodist Church,* is famous for worship as

therapeutic discipleship model, with a suitable Trinitarian theological framework can be an alternative to contemporary non-religious spirituality, and also a way forward for those Christians wanting more of Christ and the experience of authentic church. People today need good reasons to follow Christ and stay together, and doing a journey of personal positive change, with the Lord's help, in community, has to be one of the best?

Contemporary faith community

In response to the contemporary quest for authentic spirituality and its community, the modern Western Protestant Church, especially in North America, has adopted family models as the building blocks of Church 'community' (Sherrill 1937, Hamilton 1960, Morris 1990, Foley 1995, Freudenburg 1998, Erwin 2000). Families have become the 'ideal' for both pursuing personal faith and building community.[17] Unfortunately families are often also the context for much of the historic damage that an individual will need to expropriate on their *Rapha* journey.[18] So using a family model can actively resist therapeutic discipleship. It can become an exclusive rather than inclusive model, because mature singles, one parent families, and the emotionally ill all remain outside this model. The modern breakdown of traditional family life,[19] representing a substantial part of the population, places them on the fringes of Church life today. Broken, single, divorced and damaged people, as well as one-parent families and serial monogamists (Vanzetti and Duck 1996, quoted in Duck 1986/1998:96)[20] are not traditionally perceived as the ideal raw material of a familial *ekklesia*.[21] But with my model, as we have already shown in CCD, such people become the ideal building blocks for authentic therapeutic faith community, by turning their disorder and sicknesses into an asset for wholeness.

When Nisbet wrote his seminal work in 1953 on the quest for faith community, he noted that three characteristics were needed. First, the need

---

a sensory experience, and Keith Anderson, *Woodvale Church*, Minnesota, uses a business CEO model, adapting different services to different audiences, etc.

[17] Clapp questioned the New Testament provenance of the nuclear family, calling it instead a 19th century western capitalist construct (1993 passim).

[18] 'The family is the most physically violent group or institution that a typical person is likely to encounter' (Straus 1985, quoted in Duck 1986/1998:96).

[19] Duck, quoting Lawson in personal correspondence (16th April 1999), suggested that in the USA only 10% of 'families' now follow the 'Waltons' ideal (1986/1998:95).

[20] The observation that throughout their lives many people will move from one relationship to another, maybe staying with a person for three to four years at a time, living with them in a monogamous way, but then tiring and moving on.

[21] This family model is not so prevalent within Catholicism, as Lohfink noted. Since Catholicism has always insisted on the principle of community, and as recently as the end of the Middle Ages, contrary to Protestantism, still emphasized concrete, identifiable and salvific community (1985:5).

for people to work together on problems;[22] secondly, the autonomous and collective fulfilment of internal objectives; and thirdly, the experience of living under codes of authority set in large measure by the persons themselves. Each of these qualities can be observed being worked out in Hebrew communities. But Nisbet then went on to argue that the failure of community 'today' (e.g. 1953) was because there were no common problems, functions or a given authority within churches.[23] He further noted that community thrives on 'self-help' and a little disorder, and that the drive for people coming together was because they cannot meet their personal needs alone.[24] In essence, Nisbet suggested it is our life in Christ, experienced as a journey together, that heals us of our hate, selfishness, and desire for power etc. Nisbet wrote in formative personal terms of a type of community that brings about change, but is driven by social process or discourse of both personal change and common purpose. His vision for *Theocentric* community was therapeutic.

These observations contrast with Schaller, who more recently noted four distinctives of new paradigm churches: 'that they respond in a meaningful way to seekers (e.g. seeker sensitive); have a strong teaching ministry; a commitment to discipleship; and send people out on mission' (1994:151).[25] None of these, I believe, strike at the core of both promoting relationship and building authentic community.[26] In fact, they focus around programme, effort and initiatives, and a 'personal' discipleship, rather than a corporate focus. This is an interesting contrast of foci, illustrating Nisbet's emphasis on the social process of community life, in contrast to the modern structural management initiatives of much contemporary Christianity.

---

[22] This is key, as most of us are reluctant to spend time with others, especially when it may probe our own nature and motives. We are often unwilling to leave the control of our comfort zones. Shenker made a similar comment when he noted that we will often voluntarily choose to act in ways consistent with others, to avoid the fear of engaging the conflicting chaos within us (1986:26). Later in this chapter I will be suggesting that such behaviour reduces the possibility of authentic community.

[23] By 'given authority' Nisbet was speaking in terms of members of a community giving authority to the leaders e.g. bottom-up, as in CCD, rather than in conventional organizations, and many traditional churches, where it is top-down through hierarchies.

[24] Taken from the Preface to the 1970 edition of Nisbet:xvi.

[25] The type of discipleship advocated here is not that of personal growth and maturity, but rather more focused around action in mission. The problem I have observed so often is that until a person is 'cleaned up' emotionally, they are far less able to stand in the face of adversity. The battle merely damages them more, and they become the walking, disenchanted wounded.

[26] In suggesting, as I am about to, that a new type of community is needed, I am not advocating 'one type fits all', but that were we able to grasp certain fundamentals consistent with the needs of many contemporary people, the Church would begin to have a new, and for many an attractive alternative to other attractive options already being offered outside the Church.

Stringer, bringing these together, notes[27] two types of church, those with either a 'transformative', or with a 'coping' theology. He sees 'transformative' describing those churches with a thoroughly transcendent view, which can appear irrelevant to modern people with modern concerns, while those with coping theologies deal with the real, authentic problems of people's lives. On this basis, broadly speaking, Nisbet would be describing a coping model, while Schaller cites a transformative model. Put another way, virtually all the types of church I have outlined so far, except Nisbet, fall into what is often called 'maintenance' ministry, or a transformative type. Like Nisbet hinted at, I believe, as an alternative, the Church needs a 'coping' approach to help create faith community, a type of experiential changing congregational life where each member feels they are formatively contributing, what CCD call themselves: a therapeutic faith community.

Introducing therapeutic communities

As the Second World War ended, British hospitals began filling with more and more emotionally and mentally ill men, traumatized in numerous ways by their war experiences. Dr Tom Main, a psychiatrist at Northfield Military Hospital was overwhelmed by this need, and quickly recognized that the medicalized treatment environment itself could be detrimental, while one-to-one counselling would be inadequate for meeting the wide-ranging needs of these men. So he began to introduce the concept of the *whole* hospital being a therapeutic community (TC) (Main 1946).[28] It developed into a philosophy that can now be applied to both in-patient and out-patient settings, as well as both specialized and general psychiatric populations (Wright and Woo 2000).[29]

---

[27] This is from an unpublished paper presented at a seminar for the Worship in Birmingham series at the University of Birmingham, presented by Dr Martin Stringer on the 1st October, 2001. I thank him for permission to use this idea.

[28] The first hospital based on these principles was the Cassel, founded originally by Sir Ernest Cassel in 1919. It was developed by Dr Tom Main, and sought to be a community of healing. (See, for instance, Chiesa, et al. 1996.) These ideas from the early fifties were in turn taken up by Maxwell Jones and others (Jones 1953, 1962, 1965, Jones and Rapoport 1955, etc.).

[29] For an initial introduction to TCs, see Rosenthal (1991) or Knowles (1995). The concept of therapeutic communities has slipped in and out of favour over the last few decades. In the 1980's, for instance, it lost ground as mental hospitals closed, budgets were cut, individualized treatment chimed with political ideology, and evidence of successful outcomes was demanded. But TCs are now returning, especially due to the government's recent emphasis on 'care in the community' (Leff 1997). A good place to start is still Rossi and Filstead (1973), which though dated, names many of the early key players (Jones, Rapoport, and Etzioni etc.). The standard introductory text on TCs today, here in UK, is Kennard (1998a). The *Kennard and Lees Audit checklist* is a good example of the modern trend in TCs toward consolidation of thinking, while diversifying into numerous fields of health care (Association of Therapeutic Communities 2001). For an introduction to some of the areas where TCs are thriving, see Worrall (2002). For recent changes in TCs, see Kennard (1998b).

The principles were simple: that every human encounter could have therapeutic benefit, and everyone in the hospital was equal, both patients and staff having a comparable significant part to play in the running of the wards and the therapeutic process.[30] The key elements included self-responsibility, joint decision-making, not judging who was well and who was sick, open communication, as well as a belief that all community members, staff and patients alike were active agents on the healing journey. This practice became known as a therapeutic community.[31]

Haigh (1999) has refined these practices into what he calls the 'quintessence of a therapeutic environment'. These five characteristics resonate with both Martsolf and Mickley's expression of spirituality, and also with Hebrew community principles:

1. Attachment: the culture of belonging
2. Containment: a culture of safety
3. Communication: a culture of openness
4. Involvement: a culture of participation and citizenship
5. Agency: a culture of empowerment

The key qualities listed above are now widely accepted as the prevailing features in many therapeutic communities.[32] They have then been re-written and enlarged for a modern definition of a TC: 'A therapeutic community is a planned environment which exploits the therapeutic values of social and group processes. It promotes equitable and democratic group living in a varied, permissive but safe environment. Interpersonal and emotional issues are openly discussed and members can form intimate relationships. Mutual feedback helps members confront their problems and develop an awareness of interpersonal actions' (Haigh, et al. 2002).

The history of TCs and the Church

Healing faith communities have become increasingly common over the last two decades. In some ways this is inevitable, as our culture is becoming more and more psychologically informed (Furedi 2002 passim). But healing communities have also been a feature of the Church's tradition. In recent years we have seen a number birthed (e.g. Harper 1973, Tidings 1977, Vanier 1979 etc.). Clinebell, in his *Growth Counselling* suggested that the role of the Church should be as a therapeutic community (1979:46),

---

[30] Although not quite the same with children, TCs also work well with them. See Little and Kelly (1995).

[31] The idea of therapeutic community is not new. It has been practiced for centuries. For instance, in Geel in Holland it is thought that boarders suffering mental illness have been cared for by this local community since 1250 (Roosens 1979:27). Likewise, the Modum Bads Nervesanatorium in Vikersundm Norway (Ravensborg 1982) and the York retreat (Rosenblatt 1984) all reflect TC elements.

[32] Not all TCs use these five, but recent research features them, worded slightly differently and sometimes enlarged. They form a concordance. See for instance Melnick and De Leon (1999).

as did Becken (1984). Along similar lines, Bufford and Bratten-Johnstone (1982), in reviewing the rapid growth of the community mental health movement, observed that the Church needed to begin harnessing the therapeutic potential of the Church community to become healing communities. Booth (1987:10ff.) and Crabb and Allender (1996:168ff.) have suggested likewise. More recently Woodhouse (1999) noted that when a congregation pastors God's people properly, it becomes a healing community. Tidball summed this up, 'The church should be the best therapeutic community in the world. Unlike any TC built around a psychological counsellor for his clients, it is not an artificial community. It emphasises acceptance (Rom. 15:7), forgiveness (Eph. 4:32), compassion (Phil. 2:1, Col. 3:12) and grace, an unconditional and divine love (Jn. 13:34-35, Rom. 12:9-10, 1 Cor. 13, Gal. 5:13)' (1995:47).

But here we are in danger of becoming confused between healing 'ministry' and healing as a way of life. Specialised 'healing ministry' has been and still is significant as part of the Church's mission, but this is not what I am describing. Instead, I am suggesting certain congregations need to become healing communities. Supporting this, Bishop noted that the Church as a sharing community is particularly compatible with the social psychiatric concept of healing community (1985 passim). What I am suggesting is that many of my ideas are not new, but may be timely. Let me illustrate.

In 1962 Dr Denis V. Martin wrote *Adventures in psychiatry: Social change in a mental hospital.*[33] The book is a useful document of early TCs in the Claybury hospital, but of more interest to us is one of the final chapters which outlines the possibility that local congregations need to become therapeutic communities (1962:179-196). Martin chastised churches for their failure to seek healing for those with mental and emotional illness (179ff.), suggesting instead that much of the culture of the Church exacerbated problems for those with inner conflict. He argued that the Church is ideally situated to suffer the full impact of the evil and suffering of disease,[34] learning caring and acceptance (183) as redemption by love (185). But instead, rather sadly, he saw much Christian 'love' as little more than 'a superior brand of human kindness, based upon the suppression of bad feeling' (186).

---

[33] I have also found references in my research to a pamphlet written by Martin published in 1958 titled *The church as a therapeutic community,* but have so far failed to track down a copy.

[34] In the community of Christ Church Deal, taking up this theme, we speak of the local congregation's ability to 'absorb evil', in that much behaviour, especially from newcomers, requires high levels of grace, forgiveness and teaching from the rest of the community. Some of the abuse from newcomers can be testing, especially its selfish persistence.

Because of this and other reasons, Martin feared traditional Church was far too respectable for such a redemptive process as a TC (185).[35] For him a faith TC would take people as they were, while seeking their change through mutual love and the capacity to absorb their suffering alongside them (189). He believed people would come to such a faith community because they were admitting need (191). But he also conceded that faith TCs would, by their nature, be in conflict[36] with traditional Church.[37]

> *My experience is that the people who have turned away from [Christ Church] are usually experienced Christians, who have done well out of the church structure as it stands, they have status (M14-6).*

'It may well be that the time is ripe for experimental ventures of faith within the Church to demonstrate that the open acceptance of conflict and bad feeling in a spirit of sacrificial love is a more constructive approach than control by suppression' (191-192). That was 1962. Little has happened since.[38]

What is interesting to me is that some 40 years after Martin's call CCD has adopted many of these TC principles in a most natural way, without either reading his book or studying anything about TCs. CCD had been birthed several years, and was living as a TC when I stumbled across the idea in my research. What is ironic is that members of CCD feel that what they are living as a therapeutic faith community is 'normal' Church.[39] It has worked just like Martin suggested.

> *[Christ Church] is a church, but it is really a therapeutic community. It is something people come to, to find the truth, the truth of why they are in the position that they are in and to find some truth that can set them free from this pain and damage (M9-2).*

---

[35] Appendix 8 of this book outlines my summary of the comparison Martin makes between a normal local church and a traditional mental hospital. It is disturbing reading. I then follow this in the appendix with a summary of some of the features of a TC.

[36] This has also been our experience, as it has sometimes proven difficult to teach Christians what we are seeking to do. CCD is a complex model of TC and church, with many similarities and also many distinctives. Other faith communities can easily misunderstand these characteristics, and sadly, when this prejudice is in place, it is very difficult to turn it around.

[37] Since this time others have echoed the same concerns. For a faith community to help sick people it is helpful to have it lay-led, without the hierarchical structures of traditional Church. See, for instance, Lydic (1981). The nature of a TC is to have everyone with equal responsibility, a flat organisation. There is within society a certain dislike and even a fear of the emotionally ill, which naturally leads to a desire to separate from them, to become inclusive.

[38] Not every church ignores those with emotional disorders, but at a congregational level support is extremely limited. For an upbeat view of the potential, with recommendations of how to develop this, see McNair and Swartz (1997).

[39] In this we are not alone. Almond (1974) noted the need for some of these features, but in a global, multi-faith context. He particularly took up the traditional Christian ideas of *communitas* (community) and *healing charisma.*

I believe there is much the 21st century Western Church can learn from the therapeutic community movement, especially in helping recover the practice of authentic *Theocentric* community.

A healing therapeutic Theocentric community

Like Crabb, I believe connected community is the defining centre of God (1997:40), often taking on a therapeutic or healing aspect.[40] The Church's call has always been to the poor, destitute and vulnerable (Lk. 4:18; 14:13 etc.), and many down the centuries have expected the Church to maintain its tradition of responding innovatively to the prevailing human needs of the day.[41] In many ways the State has stolen the provision of medical and social services from the Church. The exception would be in the area of mental illness, where even the State has few answers, therefore providing a possible growth area for the Church.[42]

All of us suffer from the spiritual disease sin, so all of us are sick to one degree or another. I would therefore suggest the most natural faith community for anyone to be part of should be a *healing* one, where the individual can change and find wholeness, while also meeting Christ (e.g. the *Rapha Theocentric* aspects). In the remaining part of this chapter I want to bring together the five basic aspects of a therapeutic community noted by Haigh, then add a sixth, the spiritual and theological aspects of a *Theocentric* TC. In each I will unpack some observations about the practice of TC's, then note from Susan Williams' research and the experience of CCD, both distinctives and parallels found in the therapeutic faith community of CCD. The comparisons and relationships of Hebrew and New Testament communities will become clear. I believe that these 6

---

[40] Healing has always been an aspect of faith community. From the Early Church onwards, care of the sick and vulnerable is noted (Acts 5:12, etc.). But one of the earliest references to care of the sick is from the time of Caesar Julian, when he chastened the pagan priests to begin emulating Christians in charity and care (Foakes-Jackson 1891/1965:581). Also, Eustathius of Sebaste is connected with establishing hospitals, but they had probably been in existence within the Church long before the middle of the fourth century. This tradition of health care, and later the prevention of disease, looks back to the Hebrew Scriptures where the priests were the physicians.

[41] The rise of the medical model as part of the new sciences in the 1800s prepared the path for modern medical services, progressively seeing a movement from charity to state-controlled medicine. Not everyone has welcomed this as a beneficial shift. For instance, Lambourne, (1963) following Main (1946), was also a psychiatrist, but retrained as a theologian in the 1960's. On a somewhat prophetic note he saw serious flaws in the treatment of mental illness by the state. He also challenged the Church in his writings to begin opening their doors to the ill, creating *therapeutic communities* (1963). This type of thinking has been taken up by various writers more recently (e.g. Baum 1975, Peck 1987, Snyder 1996a, 1996/1998 etc.).

[42] Crossan (1998) noted that the process by which the powerless are healed entails three critical factors: supportive companionship, religious faith, and covert resistance (to a prevailing power structure and its values)(cited in Angrosino 2003:950).

features could help build a new model of Church, a type of church for the 21st century.

(1)   ATTACHMENT: A CULTURE OF BELONGING

Haigh suggested that if the bond is not secure for the infant, neither is the adult that grows from it (1999:247).[43] In joining a TC, the first contact is important. Members need to convince the newcomer their TC is a place worth belonging to (248), a safe place for them. Belonging is one of the most basic human needs, which when met, is one of the best predictors of well-being.[44]

Belonging is part of this social process. Sickness isolates us, whereas community and the culture of TCs help us to belong.[45] The interaction and the learning to belong is a social process, *social interaction*, and is a widely used concept in sociology (e.g. Giddens 1989:89ff., Brown 2000:35ff.). It includes non-verbal interaction, social rules, all forms of communicating, face, body and speech processes, micro and macro social behaviour, and the context and location of such interaction. It is an increasingly complex field with new and widening research being published all the time.[46]

In a TC this social process is taken several steps further than in more traditional social groups. In the TC environment even normal social relations are seen as therapeutic. In fact, everything one does and says is seen as potentially therapeutic (Martin 1962:46). Everyone has an ongoing therapeutic contribution (146). Life is learned as therapeutic. Normal relations for most of us do not fit this therapeutic frame, though we may have some sense of belonging. CCD offers this, with a specific emphasis on spiritual personhood and its exploration.[47]

Within *Theocentric* community: In Hebrew community belonging was essential. One could not easily survive alone. Interdependence was a key feature, with everyone having a unique contribution to make. In CCD the importance of belonging cannot be over-emphasised.

Members were clear that:

> *[most people] could probably never remember any time in their life where they were in some kind of community (M9-3).*
> *Our society is just made up of isolation (M9-11).*

They described a:

---

[43]   In this Haigh is borrowing from Bowlby's *Attachment Theory* (1980).

[44]   Being spiritually committed to a spouse and a community is still the best predictor of health and personal well-being (Myers 2000:64).

[45]   This is particularly true with certain disorders like addictions, that tend to cut us off from social networks (Kooyman 1993). Also, for a broader view of TCs and addictions, see de Leon and Ziegenfuss (1986).

[46]   Even a sociology of TCs is beginning to be written. See Manning (1989:183ff.).

[47]   Little has been written on the spiritual aspects of a traditional TC. One of the exceptions is Bloom (1997:238-247).

nomadic relational experience that is so un-fulfilling, that is so empty (M10-7).

Community

was the most important thing to each one of us. That is the thing that most people want and don't ever find (M14-3).

The friendships created by belonging are particularly significant, to both men and women.

One of the benefits of Christ Church is that after church there isn't enough time to hug all your friends, there just isn't enough time to go round (M12-1).
I think I have got more friends now than I have ever had. And I mean friends, not just people I say hi to. And I love it (W14-1).

However the therapeutic focus of CCD is also high on members' priorities.

[CCD] stands with and supports people that are showing the wear and tear of life. And it can empathise from experience (M2-3).
We are a church of emotionally troubled people 99% of whom are troubled to a greater or lesser extent. And the other one is lying! (M2-3).

This kind of damage is 'normal' in the congregation and creates a greater belonging.

There is safety in knowing there is other people doing the same thing (W3-11).
It has put me in touch with a whole community of people who want to do the same thing that I want to do (M7-1).

The 'social rules' provide a secure foundation, whilst also facilitating ongoing change:

The [social] rules are constantly changing as we change, and so is the language. We are the ones who are writing the 'social rules' so I don't think we consciously register the impact. Although we call them 'rules', they actually give us a freedom, e.g. to be real, or cry, which wouldn't otherwise be acceptable. (04F-8.30)

Here is the *'common goal' (W9-11)* which facilitates belonging.

You actually constantly have a focus, which is your journey (W9-1).

Those who are not ready to do such a journey will not feel they belong.

If you want to change [CCD] is like a blessing. If you don't want to change it is like a curse (W1-2).
It is a deep place, not to be trifled with. And being desperate is a qualification for knowing about us (M12-2).
The church is full of people that it is a last chance for (M11-4).

(2)   CONTAINMENT: A CULTURE OF SAFETY

Haigh defined this as a place where we can express our deepest and most primitive feelings without criticism, judgement or rejection. Safety requires limits, rules, and a permissiveness within structure. But somewhat perversely, within a TC this is only experienced when the person is being contained (Haigh 1999:249, Campling and Lodge 1988/1999). The TC can create this 'play space' with a richness, intensity and variety few other psychological therapies can: supporting, enforcing rules and holding the boundaries (250). However, such a culture of safety can only be experienced where there is unconditional acceptance, and no judging of the individual. A person is defined not by their sickness, but by their growing wholeness. This turns medical labelling on its head.

The primary focus of a TC is to facilitate therapeutic change. Santos and Hinshelwood (1998) observed three therapeutic stages that can normally be seen in a member engaging their pain and trauma. The first is described as projection, whereby the distress is externalized and absorbed by the community. The second is the community's reaction, being the distress members experience by needing to absorb this baggage (e.g. absorbing the evil). Thirdly is re-introjection, being the person's experience of observing the ability of others to carry what they have given in a toxic way, to the community. This cyclic process allows the individual to benefit from the trust they gain by the success of the cycle (1998 passim). These cycles will happen many times, promoting trust and behavioural modification,[48] and are the beginning of the process of healthy autonomous identity.

For the individual joining a TC this journey usually takes three stages as well. On entering the TC they begin *role paralleling*, requiring the person behave as the wider community already does. This in turn, and in time, leads to *identification*, a personal incorporation of the qualities of the more experienced members into the new member's life. This in time leads to the final stage, which is *integration*, whereby the member begins actually embracing the norms and values of the community (Bishop 1985:15). At all stages this perceived intra-psychic change is rewarded by affirmation of the wider community. This 'safety' will be tested by the new member in various ways, for instance they will seek to teach more mature members how they should treat and therapeutically support them (Martin 1962:150). This is both accepted and challenged.

But within TCs, learned by experience, is the belief that most clients know and understand their problems themselves already, and merely need the opportunity and space to articulate them. Personal growth occurs as these two forces play out in relationships. As one works through these issues one can begin to help lead others (149).[49] Watzlawick et al. suggested this occurs in two stages, *first order change*, the result of new knowledge or circumstances that externally change us, and *second order change*, where one internalizes and adapts this change (1974:10). All these processes help contribute to a safe place for the individual.

<u>Within *Theocentric* community</u>: Safety was probably the highest priority in Hebrew community, ultimately centred around trust in Yahweh. This is

---

[48] One is always aware of the danger of manipulation or coercion in facilitating social change. For some of these concerns, see Hinshelwood (1990).

[49] Not every TC is a success. See, for instance, Hobson, who outlined three stages of 'disease' that a TC can go through (Hobson 1979:231ff.).

not only against the outside world, but also to avoid damage from within. The Assembly's just application of the Law released a return to peace. No Hebrew community would have survived distinctively without the stability of Yahweh and the Law. CCD, likewise, has needed the same. It mirrors the TC in its culture of not judging a person, and the banning of ill-timed and inappropriate lectures telling others what they should do.

> *Being not judged or limited has been a most amazing experience (M13-1).*
>
> *I think for myself I am owning, just coming to the point where I am realising it, it is the fact that I am free to be me, I am not judged, not looked down upon, not condemned by anyone, that there is a freedom (M3-1).*
>
> *Complete acceptance of everybody, no matter how sick, damaged, how bad their life has been, how bad their life is (M9-2).*

It is self-evident that there needs to be a deep capacity within the TC to absorb bad behaviour, and tolerate for a season the expression of historic damage in the person's life, while newcomers adjust and learn how to let go.

> *It is OK to be me and if I'm a bastard that's OK (M13-1).*

This is essential in allowing the individual to discover the depth of the damage...

> *men talking honestly with each other about things that have gone wrong, about not being afraid, and having a safe place with which to say goodbye to it and supporting each other in a real open and honest atmosphere with each other (M15-5).*

This is quite different to CCD's members' historic experience of Church.

> *Before I always thought the last place they are going to be accepted is the church where I go so where do I take them? (M14-2).*

Instead of enjoying freedom to express themselves, members were more accustomed to being told

> *pick yourself up, pull yourself up, don't worry about it, just shrug it off (M6-1).*

To change one's way of life is a big risk, requiring a suitably supportive environment.[50]

> *For me safety was a massive importance. Without that safety I couldn't disassemble all that defence mechanisms (W4-3).*

A focus on growing wholeness creates a dynamic where

> *we are constantly being encouraged to go beyond what we think we can do (W9-1).*

Here the community plays an integral part.

---

[50] It is self-evident that people will talk as though they are in a good space until they find answers to deep problems they know they are carrying. When they see people living these answers they will quickly change by beginning to address the issues, and fall apart. This is why we often talk about it getting worse before it can get better.

The things she thought she couldn't do, I always thought she could and vice versa.
So I used to think, if she thinks I can do it, then maybe I can (W9-1).

But within CCD there are also a number of distinctives. To begin with, it is an open community, not a confined environment like many TCs. Everyone lives in their own homes and pursues daily life within community life.[51] In CCD we take the principle of not separating the sick and the healthy one step further, by acknowledging that we are all sick and in need of a journey of wholeness. The sense of safety, of acceptance, grows within a person as they begin to believe in the community's culture.

I thought when I came here I'd move into equal relationships, feel safe with
everybody, but that wasn't the case. But what has happened is that relationships
like that have been built on forgiveness and it is just open and deep and real
(M12-1).

(3)   COMMUNICATION: A CULTURE OF OPENNESS

The concept of openness takes many forms in a TC: qualities of communalism, opportunity for enquiry and questioning, permission for commentary, conveying a subjective sense of freedom, movement and the possibility of change. A culture of openness questions motives, relentlessly challenges defences, and explores relationships. Part of the success of the TC is its breakdown of the 'them and us' culture implicit in most medical institutions (Haigh 1999:251). Instead, a TC demands transparency and accountability from everyone (252), staff and clients alike. You must live your journey, otherwise you have no right to talk about it.

Sickness is never discrete. It will always create a climate of illness around it, what I often describe as a 'poisoned pond'.[52] The person will often need help to break these cycles in their life, or may even need to leave their environment for a period of time. This process is sometimes called *system intervention* (Jones 1973:326). As a person begins to experience the change and openness of the community, a 'process of transaction' begins (Bishop 1985:12), requiring change in the individual, and a moving toward the wholeness others are already experiencing. This immersion can be called a 'saturation of attention', whereby each individual moves away from isolation and obsession, with all their accompanying baggage, to focus on the community's processes and values, a shift from intrinsic to extrinsic perception. Like a startled clam, in time they begin to open to others.

Through the church I have learned to start letting down my barriers and to start
trusting people (M9-11).

---

[51]   Some purists might argue that an 'open' TC cannot be a TC. This I challenge by pointing out that some of the most successful TCs in the past are more open, e.g. Geel (Roosens 1979) and Caldicot (Little and Kelly 1995).

[52]   The analogy is of a goldfish in a bowl, living increasingly in its own urine and waste, slowly poisoning itself.

This is a long and hard journey, often fraught with clumsy calls for help, and numerous false starts. But for the cycle to be complete, the values and capacity of other more seasoned members must eventually be internalized by the individual. Jones (1979) called this new journey and new climate 'social learning' or 'social change'.

Within *Theocentric* community: It is impossible to conceive of not having openness in a Hebrew *mishpachah,* where several generations living together in extended four-pillar houses in communal clusters. Everyone would know everyone else's every move. In a culture of openness it is difficult to fake personal progress if you are not really living authentically. Likewise in CCD, we have learned that enforced change or progress is always in danger of promoting or reproducing the symptomatology it is intended to remove.

> *By not being judged it allowed me to come to my own decision about my own behaviour. But if somebody had said 'thou shalt not go out and get drunk', I would have gone, 'excuse me, are you talking to me' and gone and done it (W10-7).*

If openness or 'transparency', as we call it, is promoted too aggressively, it closes people down, causing reactance.

Transparency is a concept familiar to the Church (Howard 1979) and welcomed in a therapeutic community.

> *it is probably what we are searching for in relationship, to have an equal understanding, that love, wanting, openness of relationships, transparency,.. (M9-7).*

This requires all members

> *get more used to opening yourself up and bearing everything (M5-2).*
> *[It is] a real value, real benefit that we talk so openly about where we have come from (M15-5).*

In previous churches '*[you] are expected to conform' (M10-4).* Personal perspectives were not permitted.

> *There was such a lack of reality in church amongst relationships that I had, you couldn't have another perspective, other than the Bible, you couldn't ask questions (M10-4).*

Instead, in a healthy faith community;

> *... I was given a choice. 'This is the help we are offering, you can take it or leave it, you don't have to agree, this is not the way, it is a way'. I didn't agree but it didn't mean to say I had to leave. I chose to stay in good faith, in good spirit and free to disagree. Incredible. Because elsewhere you have to agree or you are in trouble (M12-1).*

In CCD we intentionally seek to open up the one-to-one counselling relationship, by bringing numerous others into supporting roles. Hence our 'Confidentiality Policy' acknowledges that much pathology is the person's inability to 'talk out' what they fear, or what it is that entraps them (appendix 6.). Implicit in this practice is the concept that when one openly 'confesses' a matter, its power is usually broken, whereas if one allows it to remain hidden by keeping it 'confidential', it retains oppressive power over us. We suggest in CCD this verbal owning of damage is best achieved in the presence of two or more witnesses.[53]

> *Some of the guys have been able to stand with you and push you to communicate , push you in a non-aggressive way, non-threatening way, push you in way that is supportive, push you in a way that is righteous and enable you to break down the barriers that have been suffocating you, suffocating you all your life, for me anyway (M9-1).*

Other features intended to gently 'open' the person include mentoring, a narrative story telling culture, a regime of shared homework, discipleship groups and workshops, all fulfilling the same function as the daily morning meeting in the TC, or the Assembly in Hebrew community. Unless we can get the person to talk openly, we have little hope of helping them. Also, in Hebrew community, the TC and CCD we have few people living alone.[54]

(4)   INVOLVEMENT: A CULTURE OF PARTICIPATION AND CITIZENSHIP

A TC is intended to be a 'living-learning' culture (M. Jones 1968:105ff.), where social cohesion as a group or team is the dominant aim, countering individualism and self-ism. This involvement is intended to push interdependence as far as one can (Haigh 1999:253), stressing all the time both duty and responsibility.[55] It is a process of drawing baggage to the surface, often by peer pressure, rules, procedures and intervention. The meetings create a world-view or value system that teaches civility and respect for the others, requiring trust, mutuality, integrity and confidentiality (254). Put another way, the heart of the TC is relationship, what Buber called the 'we' or 'thou' (1958/1996). It is a willingness to let others close, since intimacy is both the key to trust (Kron 1990) and the agent of deep change. The ultimate goal is open mutual sharing, a letting go in pastoral terminology of the self-hate, harm and abuse, much of it sin against one's self.

   Within *Theocentric* community: Citizenship in Hebrew community depended on a number of factors, including personal integrity, a reputation for being just, and a willingness to change, mature and learn from others. Without this, one would never be fully accepted. To a Hebrew, full citizenship would be the goal of every adult. This is the ultimate honour. In this area CCD is more like a Hebrew community than a TC.[56] Membership

---

[53]   The concept of confession or penance within community has a tradition in Scripture and the Church. See Dallen (1986) for an introduction.

[54]   Susan Williams' research showed only 9 members out of 117 living alone.

[55]   For a definition of mature relationship, and of interdependence, 'preferring to be together, while being able to stand alone', see Pingleton (1992:107).

[56]   A key aspect of a successful local congregation is the degree of local civic community involvement it has. Brierley comments, 'people do not wish to stay in churches which are not doing

in a TC, by its very nature, would be fulfilled when the person is able to leave because either they have successfully completed their term of treatment, or they are now well. In CCD the highest achievement is when a person remains, or returns after an absence enjoying their new-found wholeness, and begin to give back to the community. For this they will be honoured, say, in leadership.

Interdependence in CCD, as in most therapeutic communities, is a sensitive balance between personal freedom and consideration for others. Transparency requires an individual be honest, and act authentically.

> *And if I'm nice it is because I want to be, not because someone else wants me to be. I'm stopping being what I think other people want me to be (M13-1).*

And yet safety requires each person takes account of the impact of their behaviour on others.

> *[There are] all these social rules, like honouring, a whole list of them. The one that I find most challenging is the idea that my behaviour impacts everyone else. So if I have a bad day that bad day impacts everyone else because I am grumpy (W10-12).*

This growing awareness requires increasing levels of maturity from all members.

> *it is seeing the truth about your own life and how much pain you carry yourself, and dealing with that pain in such a way that you can interact deeply with other people without their pain or manifestations of their pain kicking yours off and you reacting inappropriately back to them (M7-13).*

Membership in the community for both men and women,[57] like almost everything else, is the result of people taking the initiative themselves.[58] With much to do, the level of commitment is at the person's discretion. From the moment people arrive they are reminded they are not going to be entertained. Newcomers are takers, whereas full citizenship in the community means one is an acknowledged giver, with the increasing capacity to give more and more, without burnout. We are therefore careful to avoid the temptation to see people for what they can do for the community (or its leadership), e.g. pianist, teacher, accountant etc. Instead, we begin each person's journey by asking in what way the community can

---

something for the local community' (2003) (personal email correspondence dated 22/11/03). CCD is actively involved with several substantial local civic initiatives for building community leisure, youth and health facilities.

[57] We are developing a number of gender distinctives, based on the concept that male and female are different, doing the same journey, but differently. On the whole we have found that mixing genders inhibits change, its homework and progress.

[58] For the first six months we require no-one take any active responsibility in the community, allowing them instead just to settle. Likewise, we have no written membership criteria, merely asking people when we are printing a new 'members list', (every two to three months), whether they would like to be included. This is available to everyone on the list, with addresses, telephone numbers, email, etc.

serve them. This will help give them hope, and empower them. They are honoured for who they are, not what they can do.

CCD already has a mature culture and numerous unwritten social rules one is expected to live by. Like a TC it has both a deep centre, and capacity to respond, but newcomers must still prove they have the commitment, thereby earning the right to belong. Most newcomers are given up to six months to begin to change, and acknowledge they need help. They need to begin to get honest with the community. If, during this period, they show no signs of progress and effort at change, they will find themselves at the edges, where less and less people will give them time.

> *I certainly endorse the empathy and care etc., but I would put a reservation that the commitment [of CCD] is conditional. In other churches in it's not conditional, it is unconditional. 'We will help you whatever, we will help you' and the responsibility becomes the church's. But here the commitment is in equal measure. When someone comes to the church, [they have to commit too]. And that is subject to the state of their emotions. If they can't commit anything and they are like a squashed worm then they need picking up, but when they are able to stand, [they are expected to] face the responsibility and we will match that with commitment, and once people are fully committed - We will meet them with their commitment (M12-5)*

The Leadership Team has to let this process happen: if they do not, they risk creating a culture of dependency, where the community becomes responsible for alleviating sickness. We have noticed a tension between the person's need to prove themselves, and the member's need to love and accept them as they are, especially with newcomers. But in due course it is the newcomer's duty to earn the love of the community, not for the community to show unconditional love forever. Many congregations struggle with numerous demanding people. This can leave the pastor or the most committed members feeling exhausted and abused,[59] whereas a belonging culture has conditions attached to it for the benefit of everyone. I am not saying our community team leadership model is the only good one. A single pastor in a small community can get along fine where there are few if any sick demanding people. But where we want to be known for our care and/or healing of people we will need a team to distribute the load.

> *We have a beloved community on the ground that we don't openly allow others' [baggage] to flow into us. We challenge it head on and openly invite that people to explore where the baggage was coming from (M9-11).*

(5)   AGENCY: A CULTURE OF EMPOWERMENT

The TC fundamentally challenges more traditional authorities in people's lives, both in the individual and in the group. The deepest therapeutic

---

[59] In a traditional church the 80/20 principle probably applies. 20% of the congregation create 80% of the problems, whereas in a faith TC this does not apply, since everyone is responsible for absorbing whatever is given. It is shared across the community.

impact will be seen in how the person treats themselves. Therefore the group process must serve this personal process, for without relational contact there is no change or growth (Erikson and Erikson 1997:8). On this basis, all forms of labelling and reification are seen as external and authoritarian. Everyone must have equal agency, suggesting that the responsibility for everything that happens is in one way or another carried by everyone. We are all responsible for requiring each other be present. Agency means everyone is empowered to do whatever they need to do, in order to change (Haigh 1999:254). What they suffered from in the past is not important, because the power to shed it is presumed. My observation, supporting Haigh, is that true authority is something *between* people, given to people by one another, not just *in* people (255), not merely what they take. Living is a process of breakdown and repair in relationships: discord, followed by increases in understanding (Josselson 2000:94). It is a strenuous process, but we become empowered together as we search the basis of our own personal agency, and the negative authorities over and in us.

The community, rather than the therapist or professional, becomes the diagnostic counsellor, empowering the process. This is mainly through shared experience, *'getting it out of my system'*, that the shared social process precipitates. As already noted in CCD, the community is the analyst (Hinshelwood 1979, Rapoport 1959). In effect, the combination of the person's increasing knowing of themselves, drawn out of themselves with the help of others as part of the community social process, allows the person to begin to redefine their perception and behaviour of what was previously 'sick' in their lives.[60] The community appeals to the healthy part of each person, calling them away from their toxic pasts, while acknowledging its trauma and pain. The new member begins to believe they can change, like everybody else already is, by taking responsibility for their lives, thereby becoming who they are meant to be and not who they have previously been.

Within *Theocentric* community: In the Biblical Hebrew period empowerment of the individual was clearly important, though within the context of extended family and community. Each person had a unique part to play with their IQ, EQ and SQ, all of which would need to mature in order for them to become a full citizens. The social complexity of these small communities required everyone pull their weight. But the first step is one of becoming authentic.

> *You can be real, you can be and you can be real. You can be honest, you can be true (W12-1).*
>
> *Dare to let yourself out of the cage (M15-2).*

---

[60] Jones, though dated, is still one of the most useful books on this process of how people change by learning (M. Jones 1968:68ff.).

I can only be mature when I am being the real one (W6-9).

Finding the courage to be one's self includes the recognition of limitless potential and opportunities,[61] and the responsibility to make right choices.

> *You can be anything you want to be in Christ Church (M4-1).*
> *You can be yourself and are encouraged to be yourself and like what you like (W9-7).*

This was not always people's experience of previous churches.

> *When I was a Christian before that I would stress out that it has got to be a certain way and right (W10-3).*

Instead, in a therapeutic environment uniqueness is recognised.

> *Whatever you do it is your journey, no-one else's. How it works for you, do it. Don't try and do it how everyone else does. What works for you (M8-10).*

Likewise, in a TC and CCD one learns hope and begins valuing other people, and relationship with them. But relationships become fundamentally different without the baggage.

> *that [there] is a sense of being a man, not being under another person's authority but being a man in equal relationships, in equality (M9-7).*
> *It is empowering, not coming under people (W11-10).*

Also, in CCD, as noted already, we take the diagnostic idea one step further, by seeing Christ as diagnostician, working through community members. This gives the individual both the empowerment of the community as well as personal empowerment. This releases to them new-found hope, knowledge and support in their *Rapha* journey.

> *[The community] holds up a mirror to myself, everywhere I turn, everywhere I look there is an aspect of myself if I choose to see it (M7-2).*

(6) 'WITH CHRIST IN OUR MIDST'

This sixth feature is one I wish to add to Haigh's list, articulating *Theocentric* therapeutic faith community. We have noted that in Hebrew community Yahweh is central, especially in His Covenants, Feasts and individual households, where oral tradition passed on accounts of His faithfulness. Although absent in TCs,[62] in CCD God is seen by us not only as the audience, but also as an essential presence within community. He talks to people (e.g. Ex. 15:26), 'meddling' in all of our lives. By borrowing Yahweh's words and putting them into practice as an act of worship we become more fully participants within Trinity. Our response, our life of

---

[61] It is my observation that almost any one is more intelligent and capable than their standing in life might suggest.

[62] Oden suggested Bonhoeffer would disagree. In summarising Bonhoeffer's theology in this area, he stated, 'Christ and the world cannot be separated. Wherever therapy is, theology is present. Helping that nurtures selfhood is Christian, regardless of whether or not the name of Jesus is mentioned' (Oden 1983:199).

worship, further empowers us.[63] The *Theocentric* aspect, in the words of Josselson, offers the community a language of transcendent growth (2000:90).

But I am also suggesting that Church, to be authentic community, must also have an acknowledged pathological dimension to its culture, with people being honest enough to admit they are sick, needing help and needing to change. As Lambourne noted some 40 years ago, I see that it is in its healing, its preaching and its suffering (e.g. by absorbing the darkness in people as they enter community and let their pasts go) that a community enters into Christ (1963:49).[64] The healing of one becomes the gift of healing to the whole community. By this process we both demonstrate the love of Christ through one another, and also enter into Christ together in a way we cannot achieve privately

Within *Theocentric* community: The bringing in of a faith dimension helps off-set some of the dependency problems,[65] by teaching newcomers to focus on the 'inner voice', rather than the voice of the therapist, or even that of others in the community. A faith in God also adds a further safety level in meeting deeper spiritual personal need.[66] It also offers a cohesion, giving people a common bond beyond their illnesses.

It has enabled me to start to become a human being with other human beings, no facades, or less facades. And that is everything (M12-1).

In such a culture as CCD the therapeutic discipleship journey is not an optional extra. It is the main reason members have joined, and continue in the congregation.

I don't think again I have ever been in a church where I have felt there has been the pastoral support system in place to actually help me to grow as a Christian (W13-1).

They discover discipleship and personal wholeness are both inextricably linked.

Surely also the closer you get to God the more you become you (W4-10).

---

[63] Along with Zizioulas I would agree that the Eucharist should remain central in *Theocentric* community (1985/2002:209ff.).

[64] Lambourne argued, following Hebrew ideas, that to remove sickness without removing its sin is impious (1963:58). See Clark (1984:48ff.) for alternatives to my pathological model of community.

[65] I have been accused of creating dependency on myself with people I am seeking to help. Shenker went some distance toward answering this: 'only when people are equally dependent on the community and know that this is the case, will they be prepared to commit themselves unconditionally to it' (1986:192). I have always encouraged a healthy dependence on Christ. In CCD today we would argue that such dependency, even on the Lord, is merely the first stage toward voluntary interdependency.

[66] A National Opinion Research Center survey conducted in the USA revealed higher levels of 'very happy' people among those who feel 'extremely close to God' (41%), rather than 'somewhat close' (29%) or not close or unbelieving (23%). (Quoted in Myers 2000:64).

They are looking for a type of discipleship that encompasses personal reality.

It has to do with yourself, getting rid of your own stuff and not just like, not only reading the Bible and listening and praying for the world and everything (W12-10).

[CCD is based] not on the foundation of religion, concepts, traditions. But being built on the foundation of God who is love (W4-3).

But in addition to providing greater depth to personal discipleship, the therapeutic process also makes it attractive to outsiders.

I said I was part of a therapeutic community, if you say that people don't put all the barriers up that you are part of a church (W4-2).

The social life and meetings communicate the experience of God's love.

If [an outsider comes] along to a service, they have got it, they feel it, they walk in. You only have to be away for a week, two weeks and you come back into it and you feel it, the warmth of the congregation, the atmosphere, and the spirit and worship and it is just so tremendous. But we get so used to it, we lose sight of that, but when people walk into it. It is quite spectacular for them, isn't it (M13-6).

Members are excited that CCD is attractive to the un-churched.

That is such an important thing about Christ Church that people can come in and it doesn't matter.   In a normal church if someone comes in with different viewpoints, e.g. I don't believe in God - , (M10-2) (imitating a gun) bang, bang, (M3-2) - whereas in Christ Church people can go for a year and say well 'I don't believe in Christ yet and I don't believe in it all' but they are not rejected from the church because they don't believe. They are given that permission to have space (M10-2).

This is a holistic approach to congregational life, integrating a personal healing journey, with discipleship as daily reality. Stringer's 'coping theology' is a key attraction.

this is bloody good really. It is challenging, hard to take in, there is a lot to know, and that is a pretty important thing for me. It is not just explaining the Bible but going far deeper than that, far wider. Slowly getting a bigger understanding of the whole thing (M5-1).

The *'intensive care'* (W13-5) of a *Theocentric* therapeutic community offers the individual an opportunity for both healing oneself, learning successful relationships and meeting God.[67]

A loyalty network thing going on that allows a community to work really. The practical as well, practically the loyalty being practical as well as spiritual. Being there for their journey but it is also being there for the whole self, the whole of their lives, not just one aspect of it. The whole of their lives matters to the other people in the community (W9-11).

---

[67] This avoids the indictment that 'The community-based approaches are not much use to people with underlying social skill deficits since, "Go out and meet more people" really just amounts to "Go out and be rejected by more people" unless the underlying problem is solved first' (Duck 1986/1998:62).

So community becomes possible because therapeutic discipleship toward Christ-likeness is the 'driver' behind the common goal.

But if we are trying to be more Christ like and if the reason we are there is because of God, then it is going to be safer than anywhere else (W4-3).

Many who join CCD are driven by their personal need, rather than looking for *Theocentric* community. But as their needs are met, and they meet Christ in others, they begin to want to know Him for themselves.

In summary: A community built on the 'solidarity of the shaken'

This chapter is suggesting that through the TC concept and its practices, anyone can enter the therapeutic change process, whoever they are, regardless of damage and however little they think they have to offer, or need to change. Such a community is built on those who admit they are sick and need to change (Shanks 2001).[68] Christ in Trinity is already the full expression of all that we are becoming. Dr Tom Main birthed a movement which I believe needs to be welcomed into Church life, by the creating of specific therapeutic faith communities. The implications of local congregations beginning to offer such wholeness journeys, helping those who are willing to admit they need to change, are un-measurable. Many contemporary people in our psychologically informed culture are being told they are less than they should be, but are being given few ways to change this. Therapeutic faith communities would be well placed to do this, offering the shaken a solid place to become, because deep change can only emerge through deep intimacy of relationality within support groups or community.

---

[68] Shanks has concluded, based on Patocka's concept of the 'solidarity of the shaken', that the Church and its theologians need to define a set of key solidarity-articulating concepts, unfold them, and then help shape a suitable programme of ritual practice (2001:195).

Chapter 7

Reviewing the implications
of the CCD/*Rapha* model
for the wider Church

This book is drawing attention to a significant rift between the Western Institutional Church and contemporary Western culture. It suggests that the structures that have made the Western Church distinctive in the past are today in some respects becoming its liability, especially where it is seeking to be relevant to the contemporary un-churched. Rahner observed theology was tired (cited in McCoy 1980:108), McCoy that it was sick, verging on exhaustion (1980:227) and Rauschenbusch, that the world was full of stale religion (McCoy 1980:226, quoting Walter Rauschenbusch 1917:128). Many contemporary people, voting with their feet, would seem to agree. To the contemporary un-churched, traditional values and ideas within the Church are unimportant, irrelevant, or even offensive, e.g. the unyielding dogmatism of tradition, resistance to change and the rugged private individualism of modern faith in a post-individual culture (Grenz 1996:167). So I have begun suggesting in this book some of the initiatives we may need to see within the Church:

1) Change In God:
Within Trinitarian relations in local faith community, change is His endless capacity, guided by His unchanging Covenant commitment, to support our continual becoming through both the *Rapha* principle, and His facilitating this in our life in Christ.

2) **Change In People:**
The harnessing through Christ of the human capacity for personal positive transformative change, toward Christ-likeness, by owning our dark side and letting go our toxic pasts. This is a gradual salugenic discipleship journey, within the womb of faith community, possessing together the fullness of who we might become. This is our personal journey, possessing our full creative potential as part of *imago Dei*, no longer wishing to remain, individually, the person we now are

3) Change In The Church:
The Western Church needs to learn to dialogue with, not condemn a world 'come of age' without God. The Church must seek to authenticate capacity in God and change in people, thereby building faith communities around those who acknowledge such personal need.

This book[1] is suggesting that distinctive alternatives do exist within a Trinitarian theology to build new types of faith community. This gives us the platform to develop a discipleship journey into wholeness as Christ-likeness. But what this book is also suggesting is that the CCD model can also become a template for our becoming more fully human. This successful process has its price.

However, what I have also been saying is that this approach to church is not for the faint hearted. For we are all always vulnerable to the baggage in peoples lives as we seek to stand with them and help them, despite claims of the help and protection of the Lord. When the journey is difficult or unacceptable to a person they leave, sometimes even vindictively turning against the community. In not doing the journey they then sometimes need to justify their actions, so accuse the community, and those in it, of being manipulators or abusers, or even a cult. Sometimes these attacks are quite slanderous. The issues people do not wish to resolve they can turn into coping mechanisms, seeking to justify their unwillingness to face up to the pain, trauma and even revenge that they may be carrying.

In the field of mental illness, as with certain other sub-groups like new or 'mature' Christians, vindictiveness and even slander are sadly not uncommon. The community has to absorb such abuse, without retaliation, and move on pained and bloodied. But in an unexpected way the Lord has so many times redeemed very bad situations, drawing the community and individuals further forward, more redeemed, more mature and much more wiser. One is reminded of the simple truth that if a matter is important to the Lord, it will also be important to the Enemy.

So in this final chapter I would like to consider some of the implications of what we are learning in CCD, mistakes and all, by drawing out four of the key themes in this book; the challenge to the Church of the post-Christian spirituality movement, the usefulness of some Hebrew ideas, the need to rediscover relevant faith community, and the potential setting of all these within a therapeutic environment.

Theme one:
The challenge of the post-Christian spirituality movement

I adopted Martsolf and Mickley's meta-analytic summary as being a typical reflection of spirituality outside of religion. It offers a practical, clinical type of spirituality becoming more and more popular today, focused around five concepts; meaning, value, transcendence, connecting and becoming. Like myself, the authors assume a base spirituality in all humans. But I

---

[1] This book does not have a traditional concluding chapter, as the matters being examined are ongoing. So this chapter summarises the position we have so far reached in CCD in certain areas, while also introducing material that may be helpful in setting the landscape for the future.

have also noted how the Church has been by-passed by these spirituality movements, so that for many it now feels easier to talk 'spiritual' in a pub or night-club than in congregational life. This section notes six problems, among many others, that the Western Church probably needs to face before it is able to offer a spirituality more relevant to the contemporary un-churched.

Problem one: Immutability in God

Immutability, God's un-changeableness in character,[2] suggests an absolutist quality in the divine nature, His *unwillingness* to change (from a human perspective). I have suggested such dogma theologically obstructs Trinity in relational terms, instead portraying God as something like a brass Buddha. For contemporary people seeking out experience of 'connecting' with their spirituality, or that of others, such an immutable God cannot easily participate. *Theocentricity* is hindered. This is a serious problem, since what we cannot imagine we will rarely possess or experience. Such an immutable God may be worthy of worship, but not of relationship.

Gunton suggested that long before Kant, the Western Church had a theological tradition that encouraged thought in the essential un-knowability of God (1991a:31).[3] God's being in relation to the world was external, whereby God is not intrinsically touched by our world. This has led to the separation of God and the world, and a theology un-bending to the experience of intimacy with God.[4] One of the responses in the Western Church to this divine asiety, particularly since the Middle Ages, has been to develop ascetic theologies (Dillon 1995, Brown 1988 passim), practices intended to invoke God to appear and act.[5] Another response is to over-emphasise relationship with Christ, at the expense of the other two persons in the Trinity.

An immutable God does not bend to personal change. Rahner sought to break this impasse in what is now famously called 'Rahner's Rule', by stating "He who is not subject to change in himself can *himself* be subject

---

[2]   Hartshorne, among others, has addressed this issue, see *Omnipotence and Other Theological Mistakes* (1984), especially chapters one and two.

[3]   Others may challenge this by suggesting it is not His un-knowability, but the revelation of *mystery of God* (e.g., Eph. 1:17-18, 1 Tim. 3:16).

[4]   An increasing number of theologians are thinking this through. For instance Fretheim, '[it is God's openness to change] that reveals what it is about God that is unchangeable: God's steadfastness has to do with God's love; God's faithfulness has to do with God's promises; God's will is for the salvation of all. God will always act, even make changes, in order to be true to these unchangeable ways and to accomplish these unchangeable goals' (1991:287, quoted in Pinnock 1994). For some, proposing such a theology is dangerous. Is it better to speak of His essential graciousness, whereby He is seen able to absorb change in others without His need to change?

[5]   I am not saying these are wrong, but merely that the existence of them suggests the need for them.

to change *in something else"* (Rahner 1978a:220). Rahner was suggesting that God changes, becomes, in and through His relations with history, while remaining immutable (unchanging/consistent) in His (Covenant) relations with His people.[6] O'Donnell suggested the Church should see Yahweh's immutability not as a quality within His own nature, but instead in His Covenant relations with Israel *in concrete history* (my italics) (1983:48). This, as with Rahner, avoids the idea He cannot change in His relation with us, while offering an immanent dynamic spiritual relationality with Him. I am suggesting that perfection and immutability in God's nature have both become over-emphasised. Martsolf and Mickley do not claim to be theologians, but clearly reflect a belief that 'God' can be known now. The Church now needs a theology that recognises the responsiveness and knowability of God to those who seek relationship with Him.

Problem two: Remote transcendency

The transcendency of the Christian God in Western theology is a commonly-heard criticism. It adds to the sense of God's irrelevance. To the un-churched I fear the modern Western Church is sometimes seen having immature views of spiritual reality, where God is 'out there somewhere', 'in heaven' etc.[7] To my knowledge the Church currently has no credible theology that allows God to be transcendent, while also suggesting the Hebrew concept of a 'first heaven', allowing Him to be immanent to people (e.g. Ps. 139:7-12). The Church needs a theology of the immediacy of Christ-centred spirituality. Outside the Church numerous interesting concepts are being used that talk of spiritual reality, like the existence of a parallel universe alongside and/or within ours, popularized by movies like *Matrix* and the television series *Stargate SG1*. There are hundreds of publications outside the church focusing on, or emphasising personal spirituality, the spiritual world and its lived experience. At least one title seems to be in the bestseller list much of the time. Likewise, one can look to the arts, poetry, the novel and drama for accounts of what it is to be alive spiritually, to both oneself and others. The Church must find ways of expressing God's immanent transcendency, if the un-churched are to include Him in their journey.

But this absence of a theological framework of spiritual reality also harms the Church in another way. The term 'spirituality' leaves un-answered whether 'being spiritual' means transcending physical material reality now, or merely becoming more fully embodied here on earth. In a

---

[6] For another view of immutability, within the same school as Rahner, but from a philosophical perspective, see Norris Clarke (1994:183ff.).

[7] I have chosen not to cite particular authors, but a search for titles that mention 'heaven', or 'going to hell' illustrates the problem. Christian spiritual reality is based on theology, so has limited connection with contemporary culture and its continually evolving ideas.

contemporary sense, spirituality is not a word substitute for transcendency. Martsolf and Mickley accepted immanence as a fundamental feature of spirituality, assuming it can be experienced here and now. The Church needs a theology to describe this.

Problem three: Having few pneumatic models of human make-up

None of us in this life will ever know what it is to be *fully* human. But we must all learn what it is to be *more* fully human. Within the Church there are few mature models of human make-up that include a pneumatic dimension, able to be used by individuals to help them understand themselves, claim more of their personhood and assist in the possessing of their personal spirituality. Within Christian traditions, on the subject of human make-up, one finds anthropological confusion, demonstrated in the current proliferation of 'bipartite', 'tripartite' and 'dualistic' models, mostly claiming provenance from the New Testament.

Society constructs understanding from ideas, so where ideas are absent, so are the constructs. Then constructs, as they are understood, in turn lead to choices. Therefore, the absence of a model of human pneumatic personhood inhibits the Church's ability to describe its view to people interested in spirituality. Or how we get sick and what we need to do to get well. This contrasts with Martsolf and Mickley, who suggest the possibility of actively assisting clients possess their spirituality, on the assumption that to be more fully human they will need to engage and mature their personal spirituality.

Two recent books on spirituality illustrate this absence; the first Protestant (McGrath 1999), the other Catholic (Healey 1999). Both were entitled *'Christian Spirituality'*, both were published the same year, and both packed with a rich historic legacy of 'spiritual' theology. But neither book, despite their world-class authorship, mentioned 'wholeness', 'human spirit', what human spirituality was, or how one might develop a personal spirituality after learning about it historically. Neither do the books talk about being personally alive to the spiritual. In this book I am proposing a simple first step, by adopting a Hebrew body spirit unity model of human make-up.

> The Lord for me becomes an integral part of finding yourself, I can't separate the two (M13-2).

Problem four: The absence in the church of models of corporate spirituality

Martsolf and Mickley included connectedness and relationality in their understanding of spirituality. We all live in an age and culture where spirituality is 'lived' and expected to impact and change us. I have already noted that Biblical psycho-pneumatics and personal relations are barren and neglected fields of research today.

Some would argue that within the Christian tradition many, like Ignatius Loyola with his *Spiritual Exercises*[8] and Thomas Merton's extensive catalogue of spiritual writings, have developed both mature personal spiritualities, and shared their journey. This may be true, but these, like many others,[9] are on the whole guilty of promoting a private, self-centred spirituality. The Church does not yet have either a theology of personal, clinical or corporate spirituality, its relationality or its *communio*. I am not speaking of a theology of *ekklesia*, which I accept is well developed. Instead I am referring to a theology of human relations, able to be built on Cappadocian Trinitarian explorations. The contemporary un-churched seem to have accepted that authentic spirituality is not just private. A great deal of 21st century spirituality outside the church is finding expression in groups, seeking commitment to each other. Could it be they are discovering communal *imago Dei* in relationship together, albeit in a Christ-less way, while within the Church it continues to be assumed that one can be holy and mature alone?

Problem five: Where is transformative spirituality within the Church?

There are few constructs for a clinical transformational spirituality within the modern Western Church.[10] This contrasts with Martsolf and Mickley's tangible spirituality that is assumed to be part of both human make-up and its therapeutic change process. Within their nursing care context, growing in one's personal spirituality is part of personal healing toward maturity, with change assumed to be at its core. In this book I have suggested that before the Middle Ages the process of learning about one's personal spirituality traditionally included an expectation of personal sanctification as change. One's commitment and learning changed one. Even within the Church there is rising interest in spirituality courses in several Universities[11] and most Bible colleges in the UK, but where is clinical spirituality?

But there is also within the contemporary Church, as in the society it mirrors, a practice that separates academic study, and even Bible teaching, from personal change and maturity. This is evident in most professional and

---

[8]   English (1992) argued that Ignatian spirituality has communal aspect implicit in it.

[9]   See, for instance, Callen (2001:255ff.) who has sought to compile a list of these outstanding men and women who have mature personal spiritualities.

[10]   For instance, I have found little comparable in the Church to Quinn's book (1996), *Deep change,* suggesting corporate change can only follow personal change, or the idea of pursuing this in community as we are in CCD. Yet in a counter-culture way within the history of the Church there have always been movements, often on the fringes of the church, as we have noted earlier, that have continued to explore these ideas.

[11]   For instance, Heythrop and Kings College (London University), London Bible College (Brunel University), Sarum College (Lampeter), Queens Foundation (University of Birmingham), etc.

academic disciplines, but is particularly pronounced when considering spirituality within the Church. For instance, at Sarum College, Salisbury, UK, Philip F. Sheldrake, a former Jesuit, was until recently teaching 'Christian Spirituality', but did not, on his own admission, encourage students' expectations of experiencing a spiritual formation dimension from the course. His reason, perfectly acceptable, is that spiritual growth and health is too hard to grade. However, Sheldrake is aware that many of the students enter the courses expecting the learning process to include a spiritual formation dimension for them personally (2001:61).[12] Some, at least, are seeking to learn positive pneumatic change.

This expectation of being changed by what one learns, a sound Hebrew and New Testament idea, is also a post-Enlightenment reaction to modernity, consistent with contemporary people's search for spiritual reality (Heelas 1996:77). Without such a transforming corporate spirituality, the Church is in danger of remaining trapped in a static and intangible spirituality that 21st century people do not find particularly attractive.

Problem six: The Church giving away its birthright

In some ways what this book is saying is that authentic spirituality has been 'given away' by the Church. At a time when Christianity is competing for followers with numerous other world faiths (Sine 1991:173), the Western Church has either let go of or not developed some of its greatest assets, for instance, issues like pneumatic models of human make-up, their transforming spirituality, and its potential for creating authentic community. In the Western world both psychological therapy and contemporary spiritualities, in part because of their promise of change, are fast replacing Christianity.[13]

Woodhead and Heelas argue that while mainstream Christianity is dying, a Christian and non-religious spirituality defined by them as 'life' is replacing these traditions, both inside and outside the Church. 'Detraditionalisation embraces a number of interconnected processes. Essentially it involves a shift away from over-arching sacred canopies,

---

[12] Sheldrake's position is not unique. See McGinn (1993:1ff.), Kinerk (1981) or Schneiders (1998). There is an extensive historic literature on the subject of teaching spirituality within the Church, but much of it is academic, very little clinically pastoral. This contrasts with a great deal being written, mostly outside the Church, on what spiritual health is and how we can measure it. See, as an example, Chapman (1986, 1987a, 1987b).

[13] I am aware that the Western Church is in part the passive victim of wider mega-trends, like the failure of positivism and its hostile reaction to postmodernism. An already significant and still growing literature exists on the view that 'post-modernism since the 1960's, is really a thinly-disguised and hypocritical "anti-narrative" of the West, compounded with New Left political activism, multiculturalism, communitarianism, and universalism and doctrinaire feminism and environmentalism' (Gress, quoted in Dever 2001:291).

towards a spirituality taken to be integral to the self, its relationships, and the natural order. It is a shift from the given to the chosen, the external to the internal, the transcendent to the here-and-now' (2000:485). Dynamic though this spirituality may at first sound, and despite their optimism, I see little evidence within the Church that it is delivering what most contemporary people are seeking. The current sterility of Christian spiritualities speaks for itself in falling interest in Christianity.[14] There is much the Church can learn from other spiritualities like New Age and Buddhism,[15] as Church leaders have noted in the past.[16] We are giving away our birthright.

In a 'world come of age' without God, observed Bonhoeffer, 'man has learned to cope with all questions of importance without recourse to God as a working hypothesis....it becomes evident everything gets along without God' (1953:145-146). One aspect of this is that the Church can no longer easily be identified with people's search for a personal spirituality (Robinson 2001:11). For knowledge without the authority of experience is not what contemporary people want.

But it is the most amazing thing for me to see, that in Christ Church it actually works (W12-1).

The recovery of the Church's birthright in this area is not in its becoming like contemporary spiritualities, or mimicking them. Instead, the Western Church needs to begin constructing alternatives that are consciously spiritual, personally transforming, and having an unapologetic goal toward wholeness as Christ-likeness. This must take place within therapeutic faith community that loves generously, through the abundant capacity to absorb evil and the baggage of people's pasts. This, as we are experiencing at CCD, is proving irresistible to contemporary people.

Come [to Christ Church] and find out about yourself. If you want to (M7-2).

---

[14] Since some churches are growing in numbers, an argument exists that such churches must be healthy churches. Here I find Schwarz helpful, advocating as he does a replicating of a quality of maturity, rather than seeing a 'healthy' church primarily as a numerically growing one (Schwarz 1996, Schwarz and Schalk 1997).

[15] See for instance, Groothuis (1986), Tucker (1989b, 1989a), Streiker (1990), Osborn (1992), Perry (1992) etc., to name but a few.

[16] Merton's *New seeds of comtemplation;* '....sought to awaken the dormant inner depths of the spirit so long neglected by Western man, to nurture a deeply contemplative and mystical dimension in our spiritual lives' (1961/1972). Other titles by Merton focusing on comparative spirituality are *The way of Chuang Tzu* (1965) and *Zen and the birds of appetite,* (1968), etc. E. Stanley Jones (1884-1973) in *The Christ of the Indian road* (1927) focused on the truth that Christ did not come to destroy local culture, but complete it, while *Round table* (1928) focused on developing Christian ashrams within the USA, practicing a practical spirituality. In his *Spiritual Biography* (1968) Jones expressed a number of concerns regarding the inadequacy of Western Christianity, and the way it is 'exported'.

[What is amazing about Christ Church], I would say its ability to absorb whatever crap that we throw at it (M7-1). Put another way, it can accommodate all types of people (M2-1). [17]

Theme two: Hebrew ideas…

Hebrew ideas are used throughout this book, seeking in part the redressing of some of the imbalances created by Greek influences in our Western world. In CCD we have also found these ideas helpful as a relevant way to connect with the contemporary un-churched.

Adopting a Hebrew model of human make-up

In Hebrew thought personhood is viewed as an un-differentiated psycho-physiological oneness, whereby body and spirit co-mingle, interpenetrate within one another, in the same form, two aspects of the one nature, an amorphous wholeness. Both give form to each other, the body the domain of human spirit, the human spirit the domain of the body. Physical and spiritual co-exist within one another, a seamless reality, a perfect harmony.

Giving human nature a spiritual dimension in this way avoids the sterility of neurogenetic determinism (Rose 1998)[18] on the one hand, and the need for the complexity of non-reductive physicalism[19] on the other (See Brown, et al. 1998.). But it also allows the Church to move forward without the baggage of Cartesian dualism, avoids the shift of spirit to mind, and the minefield of needing to put back into contemporary human nature the 'spiritual' aspect it has lost. Our Western world has suffered profoundly by the abandoning of human spirit,[20] but this simple Hebrew model provides a 'base spirituality', representative of all humankind, that gives everyone a way of describing their spiritual nature, Christian and non-Christian alike. Interest in human spirit and its spirituality has seen some

---

[17] For growth to happen in any congregation, it must break the *Jones/Butler formula*, which suggests congregations die because they do not recruit from outside of existing churchgoers and their families. For a contemporary comment on this research, originally undertaken in the early sixties, see Gill (2003:156ff., 204). Becoming a TC would help any church to break this formula.

[18] This is sometimes called *biological determinism,* suggesting our genetic make-up, and its neurological networks guide our behaviour in such areas as sexual preferences, lifestyle and even gender.

[19] Nonreductive physicalism is used here in the sense that 'the soul is a functional capacity of a complex physical organism, rather than a separate spiritual essence that somehow inhabits the body' (Brown, et al. 1998:xiii). Human spirit is not seen as a distinct aspect of human make-up.

[20] However, merely adopting a model of human make-up that includes a spiritual dimension does not solve the Church's problems. I see such a move as merely a first step in a long journey. For instance, the Church also needs a fuller knowledge of the formation of self, a redefinition of spiritual personhood, a defining of the limits of human experience, and to learn how spirituality contributes to all aspects of human life.

revival in the last few years.[21] This seems mainly due to the significant interest in spirituality outside the Church, to the renewed interest in Trinitarian studies and the modern focus on the Holy Spirit.

At no time has the Church specifically denied the reality of spiritual personhood. After all, is not God spiritual? The failure is far more subtle, in that spiritual reality and human spiritual make-up have never been formalised into creeds, statements or doctrine.[22] Relations, for Western people, noted Kirkpatrick, remain within a Cartesian framework, and are a philosophical mystery (1986:160).

Traditionally the Church accuses Descartes of finally killing off spiritual personhood (Cooper 1989/2000:14ff.) and this is probably partly true. Greek modernist tendencies to rationalise everything are also partly to blame, but I see the greater guilt being Christianity itself. Only good ideas can counter bad ideas, so the Church needs a theology and Biblical anthropology of human personhood (Boyd 1994). Also, the Church is still some distance from a psycho-pneumatic theology of human make-up. It has been a combination of the Church's failure, together with the rise of atomistic contractarian thinking, seeded by Aristotle and articulated by Hobbes, that has created the intellectual tools which eventually dismantled and stole human spirituality from all of us.

Sin as an unwillingness to change

Living the *Rapha* journey and its promise requires continual personal positive change. Gotz (1997) suggested all material reality is static, while spiritual reality is in a permanent state of change. God dwells mainly in this spiritual reality, therefore for us to harmonise with Him we must also be willing to move personally into change through engaging spiritual reality. To *be* is to resist change. *Becoming* is a personal *spiritual* posture of permanent maturing change. On this basis, not seeking to change means we will not become more like Christ, and this condition in resisting change as God wishes, is sin. This concept fits well with Christ's own expectation of substantial change from all His followers (Mt. 18:3).

I am not proposing that a Church which resists change is necessarily in a place of sin, but that individuals within the church could be. The expectation of the Christian life should be toward permanent personal change, wholeness and Christ-likeness. We all need to change to be both

---

[21] In 2003 the *Journal of Psychology And Christianity* took the initiative to run a regular section in their Journal covering 'Christian Spirituality and Mental Health' (Vol. 22 (1) pp. 62-63).

[22] With few implicit statements or models of spiritual personhood in the culture of the Church I would argue it has already surrendered far too much to New Age, spirituality movements, and the occult. All have benefited from the Church's slumber. Many outside the Church now treat the mysteries of human spirituality and the spiritual worlds as though they invented the idea. For example, on the website of the Inner Bookshop, there are 2,451 books with 'spiritual' as the keyword (as searched on 6th April 2004 {http://www.innerbookshop.com/trade/booklist.asp}).

like Christ, and develop greater capacity for relationality. Members of CCD would accept that an unwillingness to seek this change takes one out of harmony with what God wants for them.[23]

Becoming Christian for some requires a moment of change, called conversion, followed by life in a spirit of ongoing change. Though many in CCD and *Rapha* see becoming Christian as a journey, most would have such a moment of meeting Jesus. Two Hebrew words describe this, *nacham,* to lament, grieve, be sorry, change one's mind, and *shub,* to turn back, to return (Woodbridge 1995:730). Christ took up this key theme at the beginning of His ministry (Mt. 4:17), and was still emphasising it toward the end of His life (Lk. 24:46-47). But the Hebrew idea of sin as resisting change also suggests a life of change. Reid sees sanctification as the process of becoming free from sin(s), and the process of eliminating personal evil dispositions and practices (Reid 1995:756), both key aspects of the *Rapha* journey. I am suggesting the Church as therapeutic community should be the agent of change.

Rapha: An empowering spirituality

In Exodus 15:26 Yahweh offers a model of change that contemporary people in CCD find conceptually attractive, with or without a faith. Listening to the voice of God (or their inner voice) gives them an intuitive way to begin exploring their personal spirituality. Both their own and others' spirituality begins to live to them.

> You can take your mask off and start to be honest about what you have really got (M15-2).

They learn to welcome God's perspective, for the *Rapha* promise, consolidated in the Atonement, is of a total provision for maintenance of the person's well-being throughout life, that includes a transforming pneumatology. We have already noted that the integration of spirituality into health and healing is now in hot debate (Miller 2000). Similarly, healing as a spiritual discipline is for some a key to new possibilities in relieving suffering (Becvar 1997, Brown 1998, Miller 1990, 1999). But few are looking to the church in this quest. [24]

By introducing people to the Hebrew *Rapha* perspective, the Church has a way forward, not in a dualistic binary sense, but instead simply by seeing spirituality as part of our nature. In CCD we encourage people to consciously begin grasping this within themselves, for hidden to them by them are the many drives that have contributed over the years to their

---

[23] The Western Church will need to find a balance between being the protector of tradition (implying a static role), and a leader of personal and group change.

[24] This was emphasised to me by Mark Sutherland at the conference, *Key Issues in pastoral care,* held at the University of Birmingham, 31st March 2001. 'Pastoral care must seek to revive the connection of deep spiritual reality we all actually live in'.

inability or unwillingness to change. God is able, by His Spirit, to bring to our consciousness what would otherwise be hidden to us by us (Ps. 25:4-9,14; 119.99). This is both Christ's and the *Rapha* promise, that the Holy Spirit will release the truth of the drives hidden within us (Jn. 16:13, 1 Tim. 2:4). This is empowering.

Borrowing a Hebrew view of emotion

One of the more significant things about the journey outlined in this book is its view of human emotion. In no other area are we more damaged than in our human emotion. The experience of the members of CCD is that we all need to move from a more Greek view of emotion, where in a dualistic way some feelings are good and others bad, and where emotion is not helpful in the pursuit of change, to a more holistic, rounded view, within Hebrew thought.[25] This view sees all emotion having both a good and bad side. Such a view of emotion is always personally liberating and allows us to embrace all our feelings. It does not condemn certain of them (e.g. anger, hate, jealousy etc.) within the bouquet of emotion, but instead allows us to cleanse toxic emotion, while encouraging the discovery of a righteous dimension to all feelings. Our contemporary age places much importance on the authority of experience. Therefore the 21st century is not a time to be showing contempt of emotion by not being willing to 'experience' God through emotion. It makes the Church appear even more out of touch. Even Christ Himself speaks in emotional terms about the person and work of the Holy Spirit (Jn. 14:25-27; 16:8-11).

By adopting a Hebrew view one is able, with the support of Scripture, to see emotion legitimately as an ally, part of the spiritual toolbox, helping permit people to *emotionally* experience God.

> *It touches you, you know it is Scriptural, you know you have heard it before, but it is the context it comes in and the living it out (W5-1a).*

Such an approach to emotion will need a complete reversal of current thinking in the minds of many Christians, from a Stoic Greek cerebral view that sees emotion as untrustworthy, to seeing emotion as an asset, and God's second chance to engage and let go of our toxic pasts with all its pain.

Theme three:
Rediscovering a relevant Church

Hebrew perspectives on personhood, communal spirituality and emotion offer a relevant framework to dialogue with contemporary people. But

---

[25] I would not want to be entirely either/or on this matter. For instance, Aquinas, working within this Greek philosophical framework (Hess 1981), had some helpful things to say about emotion (1965a, 1965b).

some existing theology and structures within the Western Church appear diseased.[26]

The failure of pastoral care[27]

In the absence of therapeutic discipleship, currently it is pastoral theology, pastoral care and practical theology that are the areas in the Church devoted to supporting personal change.[28] But these disciplines seem unable to offer a *distinctive* *alternative* to contemporary spiritualities and psychotherapeutic processes. In the 20th century religion and psychological therapies have been two of our prime meaning-givers here in the West, leaving God and the unconscious vying for supremacy in our thinking about ourselves. But as psychology continues to grow in popularity, Christian religion fades. Whole books have been devoted to this problem (Spezzano and Garguilo 1997), but without resolving the conflict between the two. Many see psychology as dangerous,[29] if not an enemy of Christianity. Others see Christianity needing a more comprehensive rapprochement,[30] a tool largely ignored by the Church.[31] Instead of the continuing 'them and us' debate, the practice of CCD is to see psychology's therapeutic toolbox as accessible, and offering additional helpful understanding of the human state already given by God. The Church must become willing to learn about

---

[26] The concept is not mine. McCoy headed a chapter in his 1980 book with the phrase, 'the disease of Western theology' (1980:108).

[27] The term *pastoral care* is a broad concept embracing a range of psychologically informed methods (Studzinski 1988:818ff.). On the question of whether pastoral care and pastoral counselling are the same thing, see O'Connor (2003). Part of this discussion is the ongoing debate of finding a definition for *pastoral care* and *pastoral counselling*. Prof. Brian Thorne at the conference, 'Key Issues in Pastoral Counselling' (University of Birmingham, 31st March 2001) suggested in his address that a contemporary definition for pastoral theology could focus on its prophetic role. (See Thorne 2001).

[28] The main task of pastoral care, I am assuming, is to see Christ formed in us. Firet would concur, 'Theology is not only the study of the knowledge of God; it is also the study of the process of getting to know God, of the events which happen between God and human beings, between persons, with a view to the process of getting to know, and knowing God' (Firet 1986). For the importance of pastoral theology in this task, see Hiltner (2000). For an overview of pastoral and practical theology, see Woodward and Pattison (2000). But these are new areas, even for the Church, and there is little consensus of what is meant by pastoral theology, especially in relation to modern psychological therapy. See Imbelli and Groome (1992), for a comment on this from a Catholic perspective. From a counselling psychotherapeutic perspective, see Crabb (1997:210). For a call to recover theology as a practical discipline, see Maddox (1990).

[29] For example, MacArthur and Mack (1994), Vitz (1977/1994), Bobgan (1987, 1989), Ganz (1993), to name but a few. We should also note here that parts of the Church have embraced a pastoral counselling stance while others, like those listed above, have on the whole rejected psychology as a tool.

[30] E.g. Narramore (1960), White (1960), Clinebell (1966/1984), Kirwan (1984), Collins (1988) Koteskey (1991), Miller-McLemore (1991), Bhugra (1996), Shafranske and Newton Malony (1996), Benner (1998:69) and Bilich et al. (2000), etc.

[31] Hurding (1995a) is a helpful introduction and overview.

human nature from these maturing fields, while also seeking to develop its own distinctives alongside them,[32] as CCD is seeking to do. This will require a new clinical relational pastoral theology.

In many disciplines today we see a dividing of the psychological from the spiritual.[33] Likewise within the Church, people are frequently expected to choose between spiritual (pastoral) and psychological (secular), when seeking help. Such dualism has been disastrous for both the Church and for psychology, since, from God's perspective, all disorder in peoples' lives, as spiritual beings, must have a spiritual dimension, and in certain cases the spiritual will be the primary drive for the sicknesses (Crabb 1999:180). This has led to a further division between what is spiritual and what is professional, creating further bifurcation in modern life.[34]

As noted earlier, a flawed Creation theology that fails to see Divine order in all material reality, compounded by dualism and other ideas, allows areas of material and spiritual reality to exist outside of Christ (Oden 1983:201). This makes Christ one choice among many, allowing people merely to ignore Him. Lambourne saw this whole process partly as a loss of theological nerve on the part of Christians (1963:91),[35] while others blame pastoral care (Oden 1980:4ff.).

The Church has also allowed personhood to be divided into parts,[36] physical, emotional, cognitive and spiritual, to name but a few. The failure

---

[32] In the practice of pastoral care I am comfortable with the simple metaphor of a shepherd. In this I am in good company. See for instance, Hiltner; 'that branch or field of theological knowledge and inquiry that brings the shepherding perspective to bear upon all the operations and functions of the Church and the minister, and then draws conclusions of a theological order from reflection on these observations' (2000:28). Likewise, Benner; 'across history, Christian soul shepherds have heard confessions, given encouragement and counsel, offered consolation, taken actions to protect the community from external and internal threats, preached sermons, written books and letters, visited people, developed and run hospitals, organized schools and offered education, and have undertaken political and social involvements' (1998:132).

[33] I am using the term 'spiritual' here, in the traditional sense of pastoral care. This should not be confused with my use of the term 'spirituality', that I am suggesting is conceptually absent from much pastoral care. A growing number are seeking a higher profile for spirituality. See, for instance, Benner (1992), Scott and Allen (1997), Cornett (1998), VanKatwyk (2002), etc.

[34] It is ironic, and somewhat sad, that increasing numbers of professionals, as we have noted, are redressing this imbalance by pursuing their own spirituality, outside of Christ and the Church. The best help for many are the writings of the spirituality, self-help movement, not Christ centred thinking.

[35] One is forced to note how serious the situation has become when journals like *Modern Believing* have to remind readers that pastoral care is the Church's essential task. See Walrond-Skinner (2002). This article, along with others, notes how seriously damaging the divide and its loss of focus really is. For a modern comment on how pastoral theology has been faring under postmodernism, see Graham (1996).

[36] There have been many attempts at reconciliation in both the bipartite and tripartite debate, and the desire in the Church for common ground with psychological therapy. For instance, Alcorn (1937) argued that if you seek out in the New Testament the words *soma*, *psyche* and *pneuma*, then you can see the id, ego and superego.

to put human spirituality at the core of personhood and treat both body and spirit as two aspects of our one nature, has blocked the path to developing an holistic clinical pneumatic theology. This in turn denies us the capacity to emotionally and spiritually 'stitch back together' fragmented people.[37] A kind of 'Humpty-Dumpty' syndrome has become inevitable, where the Church lives every day with the damage, but has not developed the tools to respond and begin to repair the person.

Although both psychology and Christianity may have fed off the same historic cultural heritage (Browning 1992:130), I believe the Church has made a strategic mistake allowing psychological therapies to appear to be more successful than the healing of Christ within community.[38] The failure of the Church to engage and develop these areas now means that at least in part it is forced to work with those psychology gives it.[39] The Church no longer believes it has the tools to help those with disorder in their lives, or those who are suffering mental and emotional illness, not even from a Christ-centred perspective. It has abdicated this role to the health care services and to spiritless psychological therapy. As North noted, therapists have taken on the role of *secular priest,* while themselves denying the power to transform and heal from the spiritual core of human nature (1968 passim).[40] Until the Church is bold in owning its language describing human sickness, people will have little permission in the Church to be real about their disorders.

What I am suggesting is that this amounts to a massive failure of pastoral care,[41] pastoral theology and practical applied theology within the Church. Having let go of many of its distinctives, the Church seems to have now become confused by the apparent similarities pastoral care has with psychology, seducing it in some ways away from its own rich traditions of

---

[37] McKenzie, as long ago as 1940, commented, 'twenty years....has convinced me that we shall not make progress in mental conflicts until we have taken full cognisance of the....spiritual spheres which are not covered by the Freudian topography of personality' (1940:15).

[38] By saying this I am not implying the Church has failed to develop psychologically informed therapeutic models. See, for instance, Benner who, in 1987, listed some 50 types of Christian counselling and group therapy (1987:93ff.). But it may be true that because the Church has been seduced into focusing on style and outcome in psychology, it has failed in articulating an apologetic of clinical content and meaning.

[39] Implicit in these models is the therapeutic one-to-one relationship, which much pastoral care now appears to have followed. In CCD we have abandoned this exclusivity for a model of mentors, troikas and community. McNeill illustrates in his 'cure of souls' that in the Old Testament this community kinship of 'wise men, Scribes and Rabbis' was part of religious wholeness tradition (1951/1977:1ff.).

[40] Orthberg (1995) noted the obvious, that the changes in life through the practice of faith within the Church, and what this brings about, is only superficially understood in psychology.

[41] Some argue pastoral care should not be entirely blamed, since authors have been saying for years that every counselling relationship should be healing for both parties (Dayringer 1998). But Dayringer illustrated the point by not using a pneumatic model of human make-up, or using the community social process aspects of psychological therapy.

therapeutically knowing Jesus. Making disciples, I am suggesting, should include a therapeutic dimension, and is a journey every one of us in the Church should do. But we are not doing this well, and it is now perceived to be a separate and lesser task than going to a therapist, who now helps us when we are sick.

What I am noting is that today discipleship is failing. In many circles pastoral care is now viewed as nothing more than the poor step-daughter to the real thing, clinical psychotherapy. But rather than seeking to redefine pastoral care, my own journey has been to develop an alternative therapeutic discipleship approach within the soul care tradition.[42] For, like McFadyen, I believe definitions of health need to be God-centred (1990:116). At CCD we are exploring this discipleship wholeness model, bringing new perspectives to what pastoral care and its theology can be. Let me illustrate some of the opportunities we are exploiting in CCD.

An example: Lifestyle disease and iatrogenic illness

Soul care, being seen as a therapeutic discipleship journey into wholeness, offers an holistic approach to human need, a radical 21st century message able to help meet some of the problems facing contemporary people.

A great amount of illness today is avoidable, so-called 'lifestyle disease' (Droege 1995:117), like alcohol abuse, smoking, street and pharmaceutical drugs, HIV and credit card addiction, etc. We are making ourselves ill, and even killing ourselves, by our own free choice. This is such a serious problem that medical professionals are asking why it is that so many of us are self-harming in this way. Such behaviour is now endemic. People do not need to smoke, or have casual sex, take street drugs and overspend, but they do. It almost seems there is something in human nature that drives them to it, half against their better judgement, but tinged with a certain arrogant defiance. A soul care model using Biblical language and concepts is able to recognise that human nature is cursed with a dark side, seducing us all into self deception and its self-harm (Eph. 2:3, 2 Pet. 1:4). In CCD we

---

[42] MacArthur and Mack (1994), coming from an American fundamentalist position, offer a useful indication of the distinctives of our approach in CCD. I admire Freud (8), have a respect for psychology, am non-exclusive clinically (9,11), borrow from psychology (50), and I integrate personhood, rather than divide it (10). Also, I do not condemn fetal therapy, as they do (12), nor do I accept that sickness is for the 'spiritually weak' (17). We also give people permission to use expletives where appropriate, which they condemn (17), and unlike myself they believe we need to know God before we know our true selves (29, 38). In addition, they see Christ-likeness as self-condemnation (33) and mortification (37ff.), whereas I see it as the liberating of life from within us. Also, they teach we do not need the voice of God, (puritanism sought the face of God, not His voice (41)), since we already have Scripture. They also have a distinct disdain for the integration of psychology and theology (49). To this I would add their belief that feeling good about one's self can be sinful (101), and that the Christian life is not about fullness now, but living under cruciform theology always.

are seeking out ways to teach people, how to break these self-harming drives, through theology, language and its empowering. As we are learning, therapeutic faith community is a suitable place to absorb and reverse this self-abuse.

But lifestyle disorders are also being matched by a new generation of mostly man-made disease within modern medicine, so-called iatrogenic sickness. This cluster of illnesses is caused by long-term or over-prescribing of medication, often described as poly-pharmacy (Pattison 1989:113, Young 1992:150ff.).[43] The modern chemical attack on sickness and mental illness, though remarkably successful in the past, is now spiralling out of control, generating its own range of illnesses. The health care services are dispensing far too many drugs in ever more complex cocktails. Iatrogenesis is potentially endemic.[44]

This cultural misbehaviour, a state-approved 'soft' drug-dependent sub-culture, is the result of indulgent catalytic or somatic intervention. It is an inevitable consequence of a medical model which has rejected many of the natural drives for healing in human nature, choosing instead pharmaceutical management of emotional and mental illness. Fighting such illness through medication has now subsequently created its own range of psycho-social diseases (Engel 1977:131). Today society is seeing a whole new generation of disorders endemic in all advanced cultures, condoning people's unwillingness to face the truth about how they feel, and what has really happened to them. Many are addicted to prescribed medication, with no message from modern medicine that there might be alternatives.

At no time in human history have we been more able to enjoy good health, but many of us are finding, through the driven-ness of our baggage, an inability to possess such health. Many who have talked with us have reached the end of the path with medication. We suggest that some of the drive into lifestyle disease and iatrogenesis is their unwillingness to admit they are choosing self-harm. Using the traditional language of soul care we are able to help them recognise their unrighteous harm of themselves, and its revenge against others. We suggest they must learn to love their body and cleanse their spirit. The contemporary Church has much to offer such people, trapped in these self-harming cycles.[45] Such practice would be

---

[43] In the USA alone it is estimated that each year 2 million become ill and 98,000 die from iatrogenic-related sickness. See {www.iatrogenic.org/index.html}. Psychiatry still sees human nature primarily as fragmented, and needing to be chemically re-tuned when not working correctly, so-called rational treatment therapy (Engel 1977:133). In talking with two UK pharmacists (28/9/03), they estimated that 80% of elderly are taking at least one medicine, while 10% (some suggest as high as 18%) of admissions are medicine related. They suggest that half are due to side-effects and toxicity of medicines, the rest treatment failure.

[44] Is the pharmaceutical industry helping facilitate this? See Moncrieff (2003).

[45] We frequently have folk in the community coming off medication, facing and overcoming addictions, in co-operation with local doctors, and with the support of pharmacologists within our

distinctive to the Church, for 'nothing is nobler than exposing man's misery' (Levinas cited in Robbins 2001:190).

> *I suddenly saw people changing, which is why I came [to Christ Church] and then other people have come for the same reason. Somebody has seen someone change and then they want it, and they come, and somebody else sees them change and then they come (W6-2).*

I am describing a working clinical model of discipleship, psychologically informed, that can respond to these lifestyle disorders and iatrogenic illness. The model we are developing meets a specific need at a specific time in a specific place in a specific way: people coming together to help one another on the same journey, with the Word of Christ directing them, releasing a dynamic social process that is biotic, birthing the wholeness experience within *Theocentric* faith community.

The growing rift between the Church and culture

Although theology and even philosophy have in the past proven worthy tools for exploring human personhood in its numerous dimensions, I observe the Church is now not always using these in a helpful way. Within contemporary culture there is a desire to re-invent oneself (Foucault in Rabinow 1984:41-42), but this desire no longer seems to include God or the Church.[46] Among contemporary un-churched peoples we see the creating of all manner of movements and ideas within our psychologized Western culture, where such a journey is becoming a way of life. Frankl, one of the gurus of modern spirituality, noted the idea that we are sick, having a dark side and therefore needing a sense of meaning to give coherence to our lives (1963). Society is demonstrably ready to embrace the concept that to be more fully human requires a therapeutic discipleship journey into wholeness.[47]

---

community. But on a day to day basis this is managed by lay people, whose principal qualification will be their own experience in breaking these cycles. Having said this, I am not against medication. It has an important part to play in managing extreme behaviour and mood swings, allowing people to live in community, whereas in the past they would have been sectioned or find themselves in managed accommodation.

[46] This can have a negative side: 'Whereas the crisis of subjectivity precipitated by modernity might be characterised as a crisis of (religious) *faith* following the erosion of traditional forms of belief and association, the postmodern condition entails a crisis of (secular) *meaning* based in sensory overload and the discontinuities and disjuncture engendered by new communication and information technologies' (Dunn 1998:88).

[47] This is not a new thought. Within the church, for instance, it is the opening remark of Calvin in writing his Institutes, setting the tone for all that is to follow: 'Institutes of the Christian Religion, Book First, Of The Knowledge of God the Creator: Chapter One, *The knowledge of God and of ourselves mutually connected* – The nature of that connection' etc., (my italics) (1960). Also Come had a similar emphasis, '...man's knowledge of God must not be developed in isolation from man's knowledge of himself. And man's knowledge of himself in Christ must not be isolated from

as I grow in finding myself, like you, I am finding God (M13-2).

Without such distinctive authenticity, the Church is in danger of forfeiting a relevant spirituality for the 21st century.

At the heart of these diseases seems to be a resistance within the Western Church to change, even a fear of change and new things. This expresses itself in numerous ways, like dogmatism over Scripture and doctrine, or dictating how people should live that requires a superficial conformity and compliance. But this is also often accompanied by putting rules before personal need or relationship, an absence of grace.[48] There is also a judging of others' views, on the assumption that they (the Church) are always right,[49] illustrated by traditional churches seeing new congregations and Church movements as cults because they have different values and practices. Yet another expression is passivity, an unwillingness to take personal responsibility for what is happening in the Church. Dogmatism, imperialism, pure reason, or pure empiricism, all modernist tendencies, are largely unacceptable to contemporary people.

From my own painful experiences as part of the Church for over forty years, I sometimes find myself talking about 'good and bad religion', or 'true and false religion', as Wright called it (1996:123). These phrases define, as we have been noting, either a type of Christianity that promotes positive change (e.g. true), or inhibits it (false) (126).[50]

The Church needs to move from being a 'maintenance organisation',[51] to seeking fresh authentically clinical thinking with the capacity to bring about personal and group change. Jamieson observed that the Church has much to learn from outside-the-Church-but-Christian cell groups in New Zealand, with values similar to Susan Williams' findings. They have a focus on community, have integrity of participation, dialogue in finding truth,

---

man's knowledge of himself apart from Christ' (1959:7). For a typical modern 'workbook' on this theme, see Keefauver (1997).

[48] One of the clearest examples is when a couple living together, but un-married, often with children, join a Christian congregation. Some congregations would require they separate until they get married, but instead, as a community, we support them fully, 'absorbing the sin' until they marry. We see such situations, when they arise, as a gift to the community. For it allows us time to help the couple work through the baggage they brought into their relationship, that they can now let go before 'marrying'.

[49] 'It is part of the sickness of the church that it so often acted through history as patron rather than as servant' (Fraser 1975:5).

[50] Wright is close in his conclusions to my own. For instance, that true religion reaches out to others, while false religion builds barriers against them (123); human expressions of truth are always capable of being improved (e.g. they are never absolute); and that the restrictivism of bad religion leads to judgementalism (124). This restrictivism I would describe as a pressure to comply. He also notes, as I have, that when we believe we are at our most 'Christian', we are also often at our most self-righteous. He likewise observes that truth sets people free and does them good (125), and people must always remain our priority, not the Church's creeds, Laws or tradition (125).

[51] For the misfit of traditional Church with modern culture, in this case the UK Anglicans, see Willmer (2001).

minimalist structures and transparent leadership (2003:217ff.). They are also people-centred, instead of message or belief-centred (223ff.). 'In the church I can't be me. In this group I can' (222).

> *I would say that [at Christ Church] you are encouraged to be who you are and you don't have to conform (W9-8).*

Theme four:
Community: A modern problem

The final theme I want to highlight in this book is to identify the need for a contemporary authentic therapeutic faith community, as a corporate expression of *imago Dei*.

Theocentric kinship community

'God in our midst' was Yahweh's desire (e.g. Ex. 33:13-14, Dt. 9:14b; 10.12ff., Jos. 21:43-45 etc.), to be 'kith and kin' with His people, without intermediaries. This was unlike the religions of the people surrounding Israel, with their proliferation of deities and their cultus. The early role of the Judges and Priests was to manifest God's rule, not be a substitute for Yahweh Himself (Jdg. 8:23-24). Yahweh wished to be an immanent deity, not transcendent. But this initiative did not last. Firstly the adopting of a king for Israel (1 Sam. 8:1ff.), then resistance to calls for holiness among Israel's own people, followed by Hellenistic Judaic thought[52] and Constantinian theology, all contributed, along with many other forces, to make God conceptually more remote.

The Western Church on the whole still has a transcendent God, burdened with static qualities (e.g. immutability, transcendence etc.) and few conceptual tools that allow us to believe He can be known and experienced. This lack of experience of God is one of the main reasons, I believe, why people today are bored with Church (Brierley 2000:87, 230). As Nietzsche once observed of the Church, its members do not *look* redeemed (Leech 1998:113, quoted in Brierley 2000:230).

> *[I told people] how I loved going to church and 3 years on was still loving going to church. That bowled them over, because they had stopped loving going to church (M13-4).*

I am suggesting that the Church is just beginning to find the theological tools, like Cappadocian theology and a Hebrew view of emotion, to assist making God more kin in the way the un-churched desire. I am also

---

[52] 'The term "Hellenistic Judaism" makes sense, then, only as a chronological indicator for the period from Alexander the Great to the Maccabees or perhaps to the Roman conquest of the 1st century BCE. As a descriptive term for a certain type of Judaism, however, it is meaningless, because all the Judaisms of the Hellenistic period were "Hellenistic"' (Cohen 1987:37, quoted in Skarsaune 2002:75 n20).

suggesting the Church needs to listen to contemporary thought and begin developing the kinship idea of 'God desiring to be in our midst', *Theocentric* kinship community.

The absence in Church of authentic community today

Mellor and Shilling (1997) pointed out that the Church has been in a constant state of change since the Middle Ages, and the formative and re-formative processes within Christianity have always centred around community, the 'binding' and 'unbinding' of social relations,[53] the essence of change. But this can imply that community has been a high priority and is thriving, which is far from the truth. Most churches today are not communities[54] in the sense that I am describing the concept.[55]

Some argue this waning of cultural Christianity may prove good for the Church and that out of its ashes could rise a type of congregation closer to the pre-Constantinian structure, maybe, even closer to that which birthed the Early Church (Lindbeck 1990:496). Others, like Greenwood, suggest that complex human organizations like the Church take time to make the profound changes required. We must be patient (1996:2). Wright defined true and false religion, arguing that false religion no longer welcomes uniqueness in the individual,[56] seeking instead conformity (1996:123ff.). Yet others suggest one of the reasons for the collapse of Church numbers and community is the 'believing without belonging' movement (Davie 1994), as well as the drift of what I describe as 'bedouin' Christians.[57] Such behaviour does not provide the basic building blocks of authentic community.[58] Wallis, along similar lines, observed that where we feel most rooted will also most determine our values, priorities, and the way we live

---

[53] Sociality within the life of the Church is becoming a common theme in recent literature. See for instance Baum (1975), Finger (1997), and Volf (1998a:181ff.).

[54] See for instance, Crabb (1999:xiv).

[55] See, for instance, Mellor and Shilling, who argued that the Church is now a victim of 'decivilisation' (1997:201).

[56] One of the key characteristics of CCD is its celebration of particularity, personal uniqueness of personhood. In this we go against the prevailing tide in renewed congregations, where Middlemiss observed: 'God wants all Christians to have a standard type of personality and an un-interrupted psychological smoothness...God always wants everyone to feel good' (1996:166).

[57] Having helped plant several congregations in the past, CCD was the first one that was not part of a larger urban community. This has meant that here in Deal the population is more stable. (Deal is on the way to nowhere.) We do not have a high proportion of visitors at our meetings that 'drink at the watering hole', whilst remaining un-willing to commit to either community or deep relationships. Davie (1994) looked at Christians with faith, while not necessarily committed to a local congregation, while Schaller (1994) notes the 'bedouin' Christian phenomenon is a migration across traditions and denominations. He noted, as one sees from his title, some 21 distinct features of this drift.

[58] For instance, in the churches I have helped plant, or been part of their Leadership Team, probably a third or more of the congregation appeared reluctant to commit, seeing Church purely in terms of a place to have their needs met.

(1980:12). This is indeed a problem for many of us, since our security is no longer based within the Church, even though we are Christian. In looking at these problems in this way we begin to see, with Lindbeck, that the weakening of communal commitment and loyalties is the fundamental disease of modernity, not just the Church (Lindbeck 1990:492). This suggests the Church is both victim and perpetrator.

Some are responding to this. Frazee sets out a model of community Church that in a Texan context is clearly working at restoring aspects of community (2001). He advocates working at *organizing* community back into people's lives. Although reference is made to the spiritual dimension of this community model, it is not the primary focus of his book. Others, like Larry Crabb, have been moving towards a commitment to community over the last few years.[59] 'I have come to believe that the root of all our personal and emotional difficulties is a lack of togetherness' (1997:32). A similar journey seems to have been taken by Scott Peck, from his early book (1978/1990), *A road less travelled*, focusing on one's personal journey, to his more recent call for authentic community, *The different drum: community making and peace* (1987:55-56). Another is Dallas Willard, who devoted a whole section of his *Divine Conspiracy* to the desperate state of the Church in lacking community (1998:215ff.). Willow Creek's Bilezikian (1997)[60] also described a new type of community they are seeking to create. Likewise Snyder, in his numerous books, called for the reform of the Church, the break-up of religious institutions, and the rise of laity as leadership. But unlike others, he assumed community has always existed, albeit in need of some restructuring.[61] What I observe is missing from all these models is a focus on spirituality, an emphasis on deep personal change, and its corporate therapeutic gains. All these have proven key in CCD.

---

[59] See, for instance, one of his early books *Inside out* (1988), a study noting what we are really like 'inside', and why we cannot get on with each other. In 1996 he published with Allender *Hope when you're hurting*, where a short section began to raise the issue of community (Part IV, Section 15). This was followed by his book *Connecting* (1997), a comment on our need to *spiritually* connect, and more recently his *Safest place on earth* (1999), a study of the need for deep trust within renewed community. His thinking was anticipated by Miller et al. (1988) in their interesting book on the battle to connect.

[60] In his *Community 101: Reclaiming the local church as community of oneness*, while emphasising the need for community, the author spent much time (p65-128) arguing a dual Pauline strategy for managing his sick and normative churches. He then used this to prepare the ground for rationalising the difficult passages in Paul regarding women.

[61] 'The church must increasingly take seriously its true nature as community and counterculture that reinforces and perpetuates its own values...it must be a community with the social strength to incarnate values that are antagonistic at key points to the world around it' (Snyder 1996a:115).

Like Volf, I believe spirituality is both part of our salvation history and social[62] in nature (1998a:188). But this *Theocentric* 'sociality of salvation' within the Church is quickened through human spirit, by the Holy Spirit, and is manifest corporately as *communio,* into *ekklesia.*[63] The indwelling of persons is an exclusive prerogative of God alone (Volf 1998a:211). I am suggesting that all humans are *imago Dei,* though many are so anonymously (Rahner 1969:390ff.).[64] But if *imago Dei* is to be restored in us together, we must first become familiar with our own spirituality.[65] This book, illustrated in CCD, suggests that kinship communities in Christ of the type many of us desire are not possible until a significant number of their members begin moving into therapeutic change, releasing people to become givers, rather than takers.[66] *Theocentric* community is the essential centre of this process. The life-in-Christ-in-me, speaking to me about me meets the life-in-Christ-in-another.[67] The active *perichoretic* principle (inter-penetration) within the kenotic Trinity[68] through my healing journey, draws me into divine harmonic community. I engage this dynamic spirituality, which progressively awakens in me a greater capacity for His voice and perspective, while giving me personally the courage to face both my own inauthentic story,[69] and to risk experiencing relationships. It is only within this total process that I believe we can be whole, and know what it is to be more fully human. Church as authentic therapeutic community is an ideal place to practice such a new way of living.[70]

---

[62] Some work is being done on the social dimensions of Church, salvation and spirituality. See Couture and Hunter (1995).

[63] The Church in its corporate identity bears this image of God (Miller 1979:67).

[64] We are here speaking of Rahner's concepts of the 'supernatural existential' (1961/1974:300-302, 310-315) and the anonymous Christian (1969/1974:390-391, 393-395).

[65] There can be no correspondence to the interiority of the divine persons at a physical human level. We are here speaking of spiritual reality for us as we reflect God. Neither can another human self be internal to my own self. See Volf (1998a:210-211).

[66] This is one of the reasons why CCD prefers a large Leadership Team, because by its nature you can end up with a whole congregation allowed to be takers and spectators, and one paid giver who burns out under increasing demands.

[67] Not everyone would agree with me centring this whole process on Christ. For instance, Ferry (2002) sees a drift from the 1800's, due to the presence of secular humanism, that has invoked from the Church the humanization of the Divine and the divinization of the human. He argues that a genuine spirituality must first be rooted in human beings, not the divine. CCD's experience, that most people find relationships of trust in community with others *before* they begin to trust Christ, lends support to his argument.

[68] For further comment on this *perichoretic* presence within the Trinity and its implications for the believer in Christ, see Volf (1998a:208ff.). For a recent comment on the key aspects of Trinity in relationship to therapeutic wholeness focused around the theme of sexual abuse, see McFadyen (1996). The church needs a theology of *perichoretic* human relations.

[69] For the link between Trinity and truth, conceiving of the Christian God as 'the truth', see Marshall (2000).

[70] Also, I see in CCD and communities like ours, a way for contemporary people coming to terms with and coping more easily with rapid change here in the West in the 21st century.

In Conclusion
'We speak God's wisdom in a mystery' (1 Cor. 2:7)

The rise of rationality and its atheism has resulted in a profound mistrust of the mystical, the intuitive and interiority (Moeller 1968, Watts 1988), so we urgently need a new theology of mystery (Rahner 1978b).

The use of the term *mystery* describes God giving Himself in relationship through Christ, speaking to us in a way that facilitates our personal positive change, harmonising us with others and Himself into the reconciliation of all things (Eph. 1:10-11, Col. 1:26-27, 1 Tim. 3:15-16). I am not speaking here of mystagogy, initiation into the Church through the rites of passage, or even using mystery in a Rahnerian sense (1966/1974, 1978b). Instead, maybe with new meaning, I am describing how Christ Himself by telling us about our sin and its baggage, helps take this from us by receiving our repentance. This transforms us. The Church could give mystery a new dimension in talking about a therapeutic discipleship journey within community towards Christ-likeness. This is a reconciliation both within our selves and toward all things in Christ (Eph. 1:22-23). How Christ does this and is this to us is a *mystery*.

This process within CCD has allowed people through listening, confession and forgiveness, to let go of lies, hate, shame, guilt and abuse, merely by Christ speaking to them, and by His taking their sin and its pain. Also, the language and reality of people's darkness is drawn to the surface within faith community, thus making Christ's redemption more visible. But as I have noted, such healing must be driven by a desire, unfulfilled in any other way, to be united with Christ *and* with others in deep personal love. The Church is able to speak of a response to such *mystery,* but can never truly define it. Our response must be a life of continual worship, our becoming like Him in this life. This is a journey into Christ, experienced with others as the Kingdom of God, and what it is to become more fully human.

This is the immediate self-bestowed presence of Christ Himself as the true vocation of all spiritual beings, whereby we both are, and are becoming, one with Christ. The incomprehensibility of the ground of humanity as the mystery of God who gives Himself in love (Rahner 1978b). Such an experience of this mystery must become our constant companion for *Rapha* healing to happen, beginning with a personal seeing of ourselves from God's perspective. This is His *Rapha* gift to us. For the desire of the Father in the mystery of His Son is that He touches nothing He does not transform, and this *becoming,* this transforming toward self-transparency is for us all (2 Cor. 3:18), Christ in Trinity in human community, becoming compelling to us all.

What I have been seeking over these many years is a contemporary re-inculturation of the actual experience of meeting and *knowing* Jesus (Regan

1994:116, 126-9). I have become increasingly convinced that it is possible to be both Christian orthodox as well as contemporary. The Church needs to seek such *mystery:* God's *Rapha* promises in a lived communal relationality. Like Jamieson I have had to concede that radical change in the Church is essential (2003:223), if the essence of Christianity - the person and work of Christ within Trinity community - is to be authentic to future generations. For the artwork of spirit-in-matter is to condition human nature to be receptive to divine life (Goldbrunner 1966:18-19). If the Church does not restore the authentic spirituality of the mystery of knowing Christ, it is in danger, in John Drane's words, of ending up a secular Church in a spiritual age (2002).

With Christ, I am proposing a journey whereby we possess more fully what has already fully possessed us. It is on such a journey, with others, that we are most able to change, to become more fully human. 'By implication, what Jesus is about is the retrieval of an *integral spirituality* that encompasses the whole of life in its personal, interpersonal, planetary and universal dimensions' (O'Murchu 2000:124). Some have said to me that such change within the Church would need a paradigm shift in the Thomas Kuhn (1962:19-20) tradition,[71] and this may be so. But I would prefer to describe it merely as a new wineskin for the same sweet wine of the aroma of Christ, passed on to a new generation.

---

[71] Kuhn introduced the concept to the humanities, but it was probably brought into theology by Kung and Tracy (1989).

Bibliography

Adams, B. and B. Bromley, *Psychology for health care: Key terms and concepts* (London: MacMillan, 1998)

Adams, J.E., *Competent to counsel* (Grand Rapids, MI: Baker Books, 1970)

---, *The Christian counselor's manual* (Grand Rapids, MI: Zondervan, 1973)

---, *The Christian counsellors casebook* (Grand Rapids, MI: Zondervan Publishing, 1974/1981)

---, *What about nouthetic counselling: A question and answer book.* (Grand Rapids, MI: Baker Book House, 1976)

Aden, L., 'Faith and the developmental cycle', *Journal of Pastoral Psychology* 24 (1976), 3. 215-230

Aden, L., et al. (eds.), *Christian perspectives on human development* (Grand Rapids, MI: Baker Book House, 1992)

Ahlstrom, G.W., *The history of Ancient Palestine from the Palaeolithic period to Alexander's conquest* (Sheffield: Sheffield Academic Press, 1993)

Alcorn, D.E., 'New Testament psychology', *British Journal of Medical Psychology* 16 (1937), 279-280

Allender, D.B. and T. Longman, *The cry of the soul: How our emotions reveal our deepest questions about God* (Colorado: NavPress, 1994)

Allport, G.W., *Personality: A psychological interpretation* (New York: Holt, Rinehart & Winston, 1937)

---, *The individual and his religion: A psychological interpretation* (New York: MacMillan Co, 1950)

---, *Becoming: Basic considerations for a psychology of personality* (New Haven: Yale University Press, 1955)

---, *Pattern and growth in personality* (New York: Holt, Rinehart & Winston, 1961)

Almond, R., *The healing community: Dynamics of therapeutic milieu* (New York: Jason Aronson, 1974)

Ammerman, N.T., *Bible believers: Fundamentalists in the modern world* (New Brunswick: Rutgers University Press, 1987)

Angrosino, M.V., 'L'Arche: The phenomonology of Christian counterculturalism', *Qualitative Inquiry* 9 (2003), 6. 934-954

Aquinas, T., *Summa theologiae* Vol. 21 of 60 *Fear and anger* Reid, J.P. (ed.), (London: Blackfriars, 1965a)

---, *Summa theologiae. The emotions.* (London 1965b)

Armirtham, S. and R.J. Pryor, *The invitation to the feast of life: Resources for spiritual formation in theological education* (Geneva: World Council of Churches, Programme on Theological Education, 1991)

Arnold, E., *Why we live in community: Two interpretive talks by Thomas Merton* (Robertsbridge: The Plough Publishing House, 1967/1995)

---, *God's revolution: Justice, community and the coming kingdom* (Farmington, PA: The Plough Publishing House, 1984/1999)

---, *Discipleship* (Robertsbridge: The Plough Publishing House, 1994)

Arnold, M.B. (ed.), *The nature of emotion: Selected readings* (Harmondsworth: Penguin, 1968)

Aronson, E. and J.M. Carlsmith, 'The effect of severity of threat on the devaluation of forbidden behaviour', *Journal of Abnormal and Social Psychology* 66 (1963), 584-588

Ascough, R.S., *What are they saying about the formation of Pauline churches?* (New York: Paulist Press, 1998)

Assagioli, R., 'Self-realization and Psychological Disturbances' in Grof, S. and C. Grof (eds.), *Spiritual Emergency: When personal transformation becomes a crisis* (New York: Penguin Putnam Inc, 1989) pp. 27-48

Association of Therapeutic Communities, *What is a therapeutic community? Kennard-Lees audit checklist 2,* (2001, Online). Available from http://www.therapeuticcommunities.org/klac.htm [Accessed 5th April 2004]

Atkinson, D., 'The Christian church and the ministry of healing', *Anvil* 10 (1993), 1. 25-42

Atkinson, D.J. and D.H. Field (eds.), *New dictionary of Christian ethics & pastoral theology* (Leicester: IVP, 1995)

Augustine, *Corpus Christianorum V.xxi* (L/LA: Turnout, 1968)

Augustine of Hippo, *Confessions* Boulding, M. (tr.) (New York: New City Press, 1997)

Baars, C.W., *Feeling and healing your emotions* (New Jersey: Logos International, 1979)

Bakken, K.L. and K.H. Hofeller, *The journey toward wholeness: A Christ-centred approach to health and healing* (New York: Crossroads, 1988)

Ballard, P., 'The Bible and Christian spirituality today', *Expository Times* 114 (2003), 11. 363-366

Bandura, A., 'Influence of model's reinforcement contingencies on the acquisition of imitative response', *Journal of Personality and Social Psychology* 1 (1965), 589-595

Banks, R., *Paul's idea of community: The early house churches in their historical setting* (Grand Rapids: William B. Erdmans Publishing Company, 1980/1988)

Barnard, A. and J. Spencer, ''Culture'' in Barnard, A. and J. Spencer (eds.), *Encyclopedia of social and cultural anthropology* (London: Routledge, 1996) pp. 136-143

Barnes, R., 'Psychology and spirituality: Meeting at the boundaries', *The Way Supplement* 69 (1990), 29-42

Baron, R.A. and C.R. Kempner, 'Behaviour and attraction toward the model as determinants of adult aggressive behaviour', *Journal of Personality and Social Psychology* 14 (1970), 335-344

Barr, J., 'The image of God in the book of Genesis : a study of terminology : [A lecture delivered in the John Rylands Library on the 14th of February 1968.]', *Bulletin of the John Rylands Library* 51 (1968), 1. 11-26

---, *The image of God in Genesis - Some linguistic and historical considerations* Ou-
testamentiese Werkgemeenskap van Suid-Afrika: Proceedings of the 10th meeting
1967, 1971) pp. 5-13

Barrerio, A., *Basic ecclesial communities: The evangelisation of the poor* (Maryknowle,
New York: Orbis Books, 1984)

Barresi, J., 'On becoming a person', *Journal of Philosophical Psychology* 12 (1999), 1.
79-98

Barrett, D., *The new believers: A survey of sects, cults and alternative religions*
(London: Cassell, 2001)

Barrow, S., 'From management to vision: Issues for British churches negotiating decline
and change', *International Review of Mission* 92 (2003), 364. 7-17

Barth, K., *Church dogmatics - Doctrine of the Word of God* Bromiley, G.W. and T.F.
Torrance (tr.) (Edinburgh: T&T Clark, 1956)

Bartunek, J.M. and M.R. Louis, *Insider-outsider team research* (London: Sage, 1996)

Basil of Caesarea, 'Letter 38 4 MPG 32 332a and 333d5-333el, ET' in Wiles, M. and M.
Santer (eds.), *Documents in Early Christian thought* (Cambridge: Cambridge
University Press, 1975)

Bassett, R.L. and P.C. Hill, 'The ACE model of emotion: Living Jesus Christ while
experiencing emotion', *Journal of Psychology and Theology* 26 (1998), 3. 232-
246

Bateman, A. and J. Holmes, *Introduction to psychoanalysis* (London: Routledge, 1995)

Bauer, L., et al, 'Exploring self-forgiveness', *Journal of Religion and Health* 31 (1992),
2. 149-160

Baum, G., *Religion and alienation: A theological reading of sociology* (New York:
Paulist Press, 1975)

Bauman, Z., *Community: Seeking safety in an insecure world* (Cambridge: Polity Press,
2001)

Baumohl, A., *Making adult disciples: Learning and teaching in the local church*
(London: Scripture Union, 1984)

Beasley-Murray, P., *Power for God's sake: Power and abuse in the local church*
(Carlisle: Paternoster, 1998)

Beaudoin, T., *Virtual faith: The irreverent spiritual quest of Generation X* (San
Fransisco: Jossey-Bass, 1998)

Beck, A.T., *Cognitive therapy and the emotional disorders* (New York: Meridian, 1975)

Becken, H.J., 'The Church as a healing community', *Mission Studies* 1 (1984), 6-13

Becker, P.E., *Congregations in conflict: Cultural models of local religious life*
(Cambridge: Cambridge University Press, 1999)

Becvar, D.S., *Soul healing: The spiritual orientation in counselling and therapy* (New
York: Purseus Books, 1997)

Begley, S., 'Your brain on religion: Mystic religion or brain circuits at work',
Newsweek, (2001, Online). Available from http://www.cognitiveliberty.org/neuro/
neuronewswk.htm [Accessed 26th Sep. 2003]

Bellah, R., *Beyond belief: Essays on religion in a post-traditional world* (New York:
Harper & Row, 1970)

Bellah, R.N., et al, *Habits of the heart: Individualism and commitment in American life* (New York: Harper & Row Publishers, 1985)

Benner, D. (ed.), *Psychotherapy in Christian perspective* (Grand Rapids, MI: Baker Book House, 1987)

---, *Care of souls: Revisioning Christian nurture and counsel* (Grand Rapids: Baker House, 1998)

Benner, D.G., 'Spirituality in personality and psychotherapy' in Aden, L., et al. (eds.), *Christian perspectives on human development* (Grand Rapids: Baker Book House, 1992) pp. 171-186

Benner, D.G. and J.H. Ellens, 'Conclusion' in Aden, L., et al. (eds.), *Christian perspectives on human development* (Grand Rapids: Baker Book House, 1992) pp. 251-254

Bensley, R.J., 'Definition of spiritual health: A review of the literature', *Journal of Health Education* 22 (1991), 5. 287-290

Benson, P.L., et al., 'The faith-maturity scale: Conceptualisation, measurement and empirical validation' in Lynn, M.L. and D.O. Moberg (eds.) *Research in the social scientific study of religion* Vol. 5 (Greenwich Conneticut: JAI Press Inc., 1993) pp. 1-26

Berger, J., *And our faces, my heart, brief as photos* (London: Writers and Readers, 1984)

Berger, P.L., *The sacred canopy: Elements of a sociological theory of religion* (New York: Anchor Books, 1969/1990)

Berkhof, L., *Systematic theology* (London: Banner of Truth Trust, 1939/1963)

Berkowitz, L., *Aggression: A social psychological analysis* (New York: Academic Press, 1962)

---, *Aggression: Its causes, consequences and controls* (New York: McGraw Hill, 1993)

Berman, J.S. and N.L. Norton, 'Does Professional Training Make a Therapist More Effective', *Psychological Bulletin* 98 (1985), 401-407

Berne, E., *Beyond games and scripts* (New York: Grove Press, 1976)

Bettelheim, B., 'Reflections: Freud and the Soul', *New Yorker* 58 (1982), 52-93

Beuchner, R., 'Journey toward Wholeness', *Theology Today* 49 (1993), 4. 454-464

Bhaskar, R., *A realist theory of science* (Leeds: Leeds Books, 1975)

Bhugra, D., *Psychiatry and religion : Context, consensus and controversies* (London: Routledge, 1996)

Bibring, E., 'The Development and problems of the theory of the instincts', *International Journal of Psychoanalysis* 22 (1941), 102-131

Biehl, B., *Mentoring: Confidence in finding a mentor and being one* (Nashville: Boardman and Holman Publishers, 1996)

Bietak, M., 'Israelites found in Egypt: Four-room house identified in Medinet Habu', *Biblical Archaeology Review* 29 (2003), 5. 41-49

Bilezikian, G., *Community 101: Reclaiming the local church as community of oneness* (Grand Rapids: Zondervan, 1997)

Bilich, M., et al., *Shared grace: Therapist and clergy working together.* (New York: Haworth Pastoral Press, 2000)

Bishop, L.C., 'Healing in the koinonia: Therapeutic dynamics of church community', *Journal of Psychology and Theology* 13 (1985), 1. 12-20

Bloom, S.L., *Creating sanctuary: Toward the evolution of sane societies* (New York: Routledge, 1997)

Bloor, M., et al., *One foot In Eden: A sociological study of the range of therapeutic community practice* (London: Routlege, 1988)

Bobgan, D. and M. Bobgan, *Psychoheresy: The psychological seduction of Christianity* (Santa Barbara: Eastgate Publishers, 1987)

---, *Prophets of psychoheresy* (Santa Barbara, CA: Eastgate Publishers, 1989)

Boff, L., *Ecclesiogenesis: The base communities reinvent the church* (London: Collins, 1986)

---, *Trinity and society* (Maryknoll: Orbis, 1988)

---, *Holy Trinity, perfect community* (New York: Orbis Books, 2000)

Boivin, M.J., 'The Hebraic model of the person: Toward a unified psychological science among Christian helping professionals', *Journal of Psychology and Theology* 19 (1991), 2. 157-165

Boman, T., *Hebrew thought compared to Greek* (London: SCM Press, 1954/1960)

Bond, T., *Standards and ethics of counselling in action* (London: Sage, 1993/2000)

Bonhoeffer, D., *Life together* (London: SCM Press, 1949/1970)

---, *Prisoner for God* (New York: Macmillan Co, 1953)

---, *Ethics* (London: Touchstone Books, 1955/1995)

---, *Creation and fall, Temptation: Two Biblical studies* (New York: Macmillan Company, 1959)

Booth, H., *Healing is wholeness: A resource book to encourage healing ministry initiatives in the local church* (London: The Churches Council for Health and Healing, 1987)

Borgen, P. and S. Giversen (eds.), *The New Testament and Hellenic Judaism* (Peabody, MA: Hendrickson, 1997)

Bornkamm, G., *Early Christian experience* (London: SCM Press, 1969)

Borresen, K.E., *The image of God* (Minneapolis: Fortress Press, 1995)

Bosch, D.J., *Transforming mission: Paradigm shifts in theology of mission* (New York: Orbis Books, 1991)

Botterweck, G.J., et al., *Theological dictionary of the Old Testament* Vol. 1-6 Willis, J.T. (tr.) (Grand Rapids: W.M.B. Erdmans Publ. Co. Inc., 1974)

Bowlby, J., *Attachment and loss series* (London: Hogarth Press, 1980)

Boyd, G.A., 'The self-sufficient sociality of God: A trinitarian revision of Hartshorne's metaphysics' in Bracken, J.A. and M.H. Suchocki (eds.), *Trinity in process: A relational theology of God* (New York: Continuum, 1997) pp. 73-94

Boyd, J.H., *Affirming the soul: Remarkable conversations between mental health professionals and an ordained minister* (Cheshire, Conneticut: Soul Research Institute, 1994)

---, *Reclaiming the soul: The search for meaning in a self-centred culture* (Cleveland, Ohio: The Pilgrim Press, 1996)

Bracken, J.A., 'Panentheism from a process perspective' in Bracken, J.A. and M.H. Suchocki (eds.), *Trinity in Process: A relational theology of God* (New York: Continuum, 1997) pp. 95-116

Bracken, J.A. and M.H. Suchocki, 'Concluding remarks' in Bracken, J.A. and M.H. Suchocki (eds.), *Trinity in process: A relational theology of God* (New York: Continuum, 1997a) pp. 215-224

--- (eds.), *Trinity in process: A relational theology of God* (New York: Continuum, 1997b)

Bresinger, T.L., "Be alive' (semantic field 2649)' in van Gemeren, W.A. (ed.) *New international dictionary of Old Testament theology and exegesis* Vol. 2 of 5 (Carlisle: Paternoster, 1996) pp. 108-113

Brierley, P., *Future church: A global analysis of the Christian community to the year 2010* (London: Monarch Books, 1998)

---, *The tide is running out: What the English church attendance survey reveals* (London: Christian Research, 2000)

---, *UK church religious trends, Number 4 2003-2004* (London: Christian Research, 2003)

Bright, B., *A handbook for Christian maturity: A compilation of 10 basic steps towards Christian maturity* (San Bernardino: Campus Crusade for Christ International, 1982)

Bright, J., *History of Israel* (London: SCM Press, 1960)

Briscoe, S., *Discipleship for ordinary people* (Wheaton: Harold Shaw, 1995)

British Association for Counselling and Psychotherapy, *Ethical framework for good practice in counselling and psychotherapy,* (2002, Online). Available from http://www.bacp.co.uk/ethical_framework/ [Accessed 5th April 2004]

Broadfoot, P., et al., *Developing an effective lifelong learning inventory - the ELLI project* (A Report to the Lifelong Learning Foundation produced by the Graduate School of Education, University of Bristol, 2002)

Brockway, R.W., 'Immortality of the soul: An evangelical heresy', *Religious Humanism* 13 (1979), 14-18

Brooks Hollifield, E., *A history of pastoral care in America* (Nashville: Abingdon Press, 1983)

Brown, C., 'Sophia (wisdom)' in Brown, C. (ed.) *The new international dictionary of New Testament theology.* Vol. 3 of 3 (Exeter: Paternoster Press, 1971) pp. 1026-1033

Brown, C.K., 'The integration of healing and spirituality into health care', *Journal of Interprofessional Care* 12 (1998), 4. 373-381

Brown, F., et al., *A Hebrew and English lexicon of the Old Testament with an appendix containing the Biblical Aramaic* (Oxford: Clarendon Press, 1907/1962)

Brown, L., *New shorter Oxford English dictionary* Vol. 2 (Oxford: Clarendon Press, 1993)

Brown, P., *The body and society: men, women and sexual renunciation in early Christianity* (New York: Cambridge University Press, 1988)

Brown, R., *Group process* (Oxford: Blackwell, 2000)

Brown, R.E., *The Semitic background of the term 'mystery' in the New Testament.*
(Philadelphia: Fortress Press, 1968)

---, *The churches the Apostles left behind* (New Jersey: Paulist Press, 1984)

Brown, R.H. and D. Goodman, 'Jurgen Habermas' theory of communicative action: An
incomplete project' in Ritzer, G. and B. Smart (eds.), *Handbook of social theory*
(London: Sage Publications, 2001) pp. 201-216

Brown, W.S., et al., *Whatever happened to the soul?* (Minneapolis: Augsberg Fortress,
1998)

Brown, W.T., *Israel's divine healer* (Carlisle: Paternoster Press, 1995)

Browning, D., 'Psychology in service of the church', *Journal of Psychology and
Theology* 20 (1992), 2. 127-136

Bruce, S., *God is dead: Secularization in the West* (Oxford: Blackwell Publishing, 2002)

Bruner, J., *Acts of meaning* (Cambridge, MA: Harvard University Press, 1990)

Brunner, E., *The Divine Imperative* (London: ET, 1947)

---, *Truth as encounter: A new edition, much enlarged, of the divine-human encounter*
(London: SCM Press, 1964)

Buber, M., *I and Thou* Kaufman, W. (tr.) (New York: Touchstone, 1958/1996)

---, *The knowledge of man* (New York: Harper Collins, 1965)

---, *The way of response: Martin Buber, selections from his writings* (New York:
Schocken Books, 1966)

Bucer, M., *De vera animarum curo veroque officio pastoris* (Strasbourg 1538)

Bufford, R.K. and T. Bratten-Johnstone, 'The Church and community mental health:
Unrealised potential', *Journal of Psychology and Theology* 10 (1982), 4. 355-362

Buminovitz, S. and A. Faust, 'Ideology in stone: Understanding the four room house',
Biblical Archaeology Review 28 (2002), 4. 32-41

Bunyan, J., *The pilgrim's progress* (London: Penguin, 1656/1987)

Burkhardt, M.A. and M.G. Nagai-Jacobson, 'Reawakening spirit in clinical practice',
Journal of Holistic Nursing 12 (1994), 1. 9-21

Burnard, P., 'Spiritual distress and the nursing response', *Journal of Advanced Nursing*
12 (1987), 377-382

Burrell, D.B., *Knowing the unknowable God: Ibn-Sina, Maimonides, Aquinas* (Notre
Dame: University of Notre Dame Press, 1986)

Butler, J., *The works of Joseph Butler* Vol. 2 *Fifteen sermons on human nature* (Oxford:
Clarendon Press, 1922/1986)

Byrne, R., 'Journey (Growth and development in spiritual life)' in Downey, M. (ed.),
The new dictionary of Catholic spirituality (Collegville, MN: Liturgical Press,
1993) pp. 565-577

Caird, G.B., *Paul and women's liberty.* The Manston Memorial Lecture (University of
Manchester, 1971)

Callen, B.L., *Authentic spirituality: Moving beyond mere religion* (Carlisle: Baker
Academic, 2001)

Calvin, J., *Institutes of the Christian religion.* (Philadelphia: Westminster Press, 1960)

Campling, P. and F.D. Lodge, 'Boundaries: Discussion of a difficult transition' in
    Campling, P. and R. Haigh (eds.), *Therapeutic Communities: Past, present and
    future* (London: Jessica Kingsley, 1988/1999) pp. 90-98

Card, T., *Priesthood and ministry in crisis* (London: SCM Press, 1988)

Carroll, J.T., 'Sickness and healing in the New Testament Gospels', *Interpretation* 49
    (1995), 2. 130-142

Carver, C.S. and M.F. Scheier, *Perspectives on psychology* (Boston: Allyn & Bacon,
    1996)

Cassell, E., 'The nature of suffering and the goals of medicine', *New England Journal of
    Medicine* 306 (1982), 11. 639-642

de Certeau, M., *The mystic fable* Vol. 1 *16th & 17th Centuries* Smith, M.B. (tr.)
    (Chicago: University of Chicago Press, 1992)

Chan, A.K.Y., et al., '*rp*', Healing' in van Gemeren, W.A. (ed.) *The new international
    dictionary of Old Testament theology and exegesis* Vol. 3 of 5 (Carlisle:
    Paternoster, 1996) pp. 1162-1173

Chancey, M. and E.M. Myers, 'How Jewish was Sepphoris in Jesus' time?' *Biblical
    Archaeology Review* 26 (2000), 4. 18-33

Chapman, L.S., 'Spiritual health: A component missing from health promotion',
    American Journal of Health Promotion Premier Issue (1986), 38-41

---, 'Developing a useful perspective on spiritual health: Well-being, spiritual potential
    and the search for meaning', *American Journal of Health Promotion* 1 (1987a), 3.
    31-39

---, 'Developing a useful perspective on spiritual health: Love, joy, peace and
    fulfillment', *American Journal of Health Promotion* 2 (1987b), 2. 12-17

Charmaz, K., 'Grounded theory: Objectivist and constructivist methods' in Denzin,
    N.K. and Y.S. Lincoln (eds.), *Handbook of qualitative research* (Thousand Oaks:
    Sage Publications, 2000) pp. 509-536

Chiesa, M., et al., 'Changes in health service utilization and by patients with severe
    personality disorders before and after inpatient psychosocial treatment', *British
    Journal of Psychotherapy* 12 (1996), 4. 501-512

Childs, B.S., *Exodus: A commentary* (London: SCM Press, 1974)

Chriss, J.J. (ed.), *Counseling and the therapeutic state* (New York: Aldine de Gruyter,
    1999)

Christians, C.G., 'The Sacredness of Life', *Media Development,* (1998, Online).
    Available from http://www.wacc.org.uk/publications/md/md1998-
    2/christians.html [Accessed 26th Mar 2003]

Chu, J., 'O Father, where art thou?' *Time Magazine* 161 (June 16th 2003), 24. 22-30

Church, L.F., *More about the early Methodist people* (London: Epworth press, 1949)

Clapp, R., *Families at the crossroads: Beyond traditional and modern options*
    (Leicester: IVP Press, 1993)

Clark, D., *Basic communities: Toward an alternative society* (London: SPCK., 1977)

---, *The liberation of the church: The role of basic Christian groups in a new re-
    formation* (Birmingham: National Centre for Christian Communities and
    Networks, 1984)

Clark, D.K., 'Interpreting the Biblical words for the self', *Journal of Psychology and Theology* 18 (1990), 4. 309-317

Clark, S.B., *Building Christian communities: Strategy for renewing the church* (Notre Dame: Ave Maria Press, 1972)

Clark, S.R.L., *Aristotle's man* (Oxford: Clarendon Press, 1975)

Clark, T.E. and M. Thompson, 'Psychology and spirituality: Meeting at the boundaries', *The Way Supplement* 69 (1990), 29-42

Claxton, G., *Live and learn: An introduction to the psychology of growth and change in everyday life* (London: Harper and Row Publishers, 1984)

Clayton, P., 'Pluralism, idealism, romanticism: Untapped resources for a Trinity in process' in Bracken, J.A. and M.H. Suchocki (eds.), *Trinity in process: A relational theology of God* (New York: Continuum, 1997) pp. 117-145

Clinebell, H., *Basic types of pastoral care and counselling : Resources for the ministry of healing and growth* (London: SCM Press, 1966/1984)

---, *Growth counselling: Hope centred methods of actualising human wholeness* (Abingdon, Nashville 1979)

---, *Counselling for spiritually empowered wholeness: A hope centred approach* (New York: Haworth Pastoral Press, 1979/1995)

---, 'Six dimensions of wholeness centred on spirit' in Newton Maloney, H., et al. (eds.), *Spirit centred wholeness: Beyond the psychology of self.* (New York: The Edwin Mellen Press, 1988)

---, *Ecotherapy : healing ourselves, healing the earth : a guide to ecologically grounded personality theory, spirituality, therapy and education* (Minneapolis: Fortress, 1996)

Clinebell, H.J., *The people dynamic: Changing self and society through growth groups* (New York: Harper and Row Publishers, 1972)

Clines, D.G.A., 'The image of God in man', *Tyndale Bulletin* 19 (1968), 53-103

Coakley, S., 'Rethinking Gregory of Nyssa: Introduction - Gender, trinitarian analogies and the pedagogy of 'The Song'.' *Modern Theology* 18 (2002), 4. 431-444

Cobb, J. and D. Griffin, *Process theology: An introductory exposition* (Philadelphia: Westminster Press, 1976)

Cobb, J.B., *Christ in a pluralistic age* (Philadelphia: Westminster Press, 1975)

---, *Theology and pastoral care* (Philadelphia: Fortress Press, 1977)

---, *Reclaiming the church: Where the mainline church went wrong and what to do about it* (Louisville: Westminster John Knox Press, 1997)

Cohen, A.P., *The symbolic construction of community* (London: Routlege, 1985/1992)

Cohen, S.J.D., *From the Maccabees to the Mishnah* (Philadelphia: Westminster Press, 1987)

Cole, G.A., 'Responsibility' in Atkinson, D.J. and D.H. Field (eds.), *New dictionary of Christian ethics & pastoral theology* (Leicester: IVP, 1995) pp. 734-736

Collins, G., *Can you trust counselling?* (Leicester: IVP, 1988)

Collins, G.R., *Fractured personalities: The psychology of mental illness* (Carol Stream: Creation House, 1972/1975)

---, 'Lay counselling: Some lingering questions for professionals', *Journal of Psychology and Christianity* 6 (1987), 2. 7-9

---, *Christian counselling : A comprehensive guide* (Dallas: Word, 1988)

Collins, K.J., *The Scripture way of salvation: The heart of John Wesley's theology* (Nashville: Abingdon Press, 1997)

Collins, P.M., *Trinitarian theology: West and East, Karl Barth, the Cappadocian Fathers and John Zizioulas* (Oxford: Oxford University Press, 2001)

Collinson, S.I., *An enquiry into the congruence of discipling as an educational strategy with the objective of Christian faith communities* PhD thesis (Murdoch University, 1999)

Come, A.B., *Human spirit and Holy Spirit* (Philadelphia: Westminster Press, 1959)

Conger, J.J., *Adolescence and youth: Psychological development in a changing world* (New York: Harper and Row, 1973)

Conn, J.W., *Spirituality and personal maturity* (New York: Integration Books, 1989)

Conn, W.E., 'Self-transcendence: Integrating ends and means in value counselling', *The Journal of Counselling and Values* 38 (1994), 176-186

Conran, T., 'Solemn witness: A pilgrimage to Ground Zero at the World Trade Center', *Journal of Systemic Therapies* 21 (2002), 3. 39-47

Cook, J. and S.C. Baldwin, *Love, acceptance and forgiveness: Equipping the church to be truly Christian in a non-Christian world* (Ventura, CA: Regal Books, 1979)

Cooper, J.W., *Body soul and life Everlasting: Biblical anthropology and the monism-dualism debate* (Grand Rapids: Michigan Erdmans, 1989/2000)

Coote, R.B. and K.W. Whitelam, *The emergence of Early Israel in historical perspective* (Sheffield: The Almond Press, 1987)

Cornett, C., *The soul of psychotherapy: Recapturing the spiritual dimension in the therapeutic encounter* (New York: The Free Press, 1998)

Cornwell, J., *Consciousness and human identity* (Oxford: Oxford University Press, 1998)

Couture, P.D. and R.J. Hunter (eds.), *Pastoral care and social conflict: Essays in honor of Charles V. Gerkin* (Nashville: Abingdon Press, 1995)

Covey, S.R., *Spiritual roots of human relations* (Salem: Deseret Book Company, 1970)

---, *The seven habits of highly effective people: Powerful lessons in personal change* (New York: Simon and Schuster, 1989)

---, 'Principles hold key to leadership success', *Professional Manager* 41 (September 2001),

Cowen, E.L., 'Help is where you find it: Four informal helping groups', *American Psychologist* 3 (1982), 7. 385-395

Cowper, W., *A narrative of the life of William Cowper*: Bielby & Knotts, 1817)

Cox, H., *The secular city* (London: SCM Press, 1965)

Crabb, L., *Basic principles of Biblical counselling* (Grand Rapids: Zondervan Publishing House, 1975)

---, *Inside out: Real change is possible - if you are willing to start from the inside out.* (Colorado Springs: NavPress, 1988)

---, *Connecting: Healing for ourselves and our relationships, a radical new vision* (Nashville: Word Publishing, 1997)

---, *The safest place on earth: Where people connect and are for ever changed* (Nashville: Word Publishing., 1999)

Crabb, L. and D.B. Allender, *Hope when you're hurting* (Eastbourne: Kingsway, 1996)

Cray, G., *Postmodern culture and youth discipleship: Commitment or looking cool* (Cambridge: Grove Books, 1998)

Creel, R.E., *Divine impassibility: An essay in philosophical theology* (Cambridge: Cambridge University Press, 1986)

Crick, F., *The astonishing hypotheses: The scientific search for the soul.* (London: Touchstone Books, 1995)

Croft, S., *Transforming communities: Re-imagining the church for the 21st century* (London: Darton Longman & Todd, 2002)

Crossan, J.D., *The birth of Christianity: Discovering what happened in the years immediately after the execution of Jesus* (San Francisco: Harper, 1998)

Culley, S., *Integrative counselling skills in action* (London: Sage, 1991)

Cupach, W.R. and B.H. Spitzberg, *The dark side of interpersonal communication* (New Jersey: Erlbaum, 1994)

D'Costa, G., *The meetings of religions and Trinity* (Edinburgh: T&T Clark, 2000)

Dallen, J., *The reconciling community: The rite of penance* (New York: Pueblo, 1986)

Davidson, A.B., *The theology of the Old Testament* (Edinburgh: T. & T. Clark, 1961)

Davie, G., *Religion in Britain since 1945: Believing without belonging* (Oxford: Blackwell, 1994)

Davis, C., *Body as spirit* (London: Hodder and Stoughton., 1976)

Davis, R. and G. Rupp (eds.), *A history of the Methodist church in Great Britain* (London: Epworth Press, 1965)

Davison, G.C. and J.M. Neale, *Abnormal psychology* (New York: Hayworth Press, 1998)

Dayringer, R., *The heart of pastoral counselling - Healing through relationship* (New York: Haworth Pastoral Press, 1998)

Deere, J., *Surprised by the voice of God* (Eastbourne: Kingsway Publications, 1996)

Dennett, D.C., *Consciousness explained* (New York: Little, Brown & Co., 1991)

Dever, W.G., *What did the Biblical writers know and when did they know it* (Grand Rapids, Michigan: William B. Erdmans Publishing Company, 2001)

---, 'Whatchamacallitt: Why its so hard to name our field', *Biblical Archaeology Review* 29 (2003), 4. 56-61

Diamond, J., *Life Energy: Using the meridians to unlock the hidden power of your emotions* (St Paul, MN: Paragon House, 1985/1990)

Dillon, J.M., 'Rejecting the body, refining the body: Some remarks on the development of Platonist asceticism' in Wimbush, V.L. and R. Valantasis (eds.), *Asceticism* (New York: Oxford University Press, 1995) pp. 80-87

le Dioux, J., *The emotional brain: The mysterious underpinnings of emotional life* (London: Weidenfeld & Nicholson, 1998)

Dodds, L.A., 'The role of the Holy Spirit in personality growth and change', *Journal of Psychology and Christianity* 18 (1999), 2. 129-139

Downey, M. (ed.), *The new dictionary of Catholic spirituality* (Collegville, MN: Liturgical Press, 1993)

Drakeford, D., *Integrity therapy* (Waco, Nashville: Broadman Press, 1967)

Drane, J., *The MacDonaldization of the church: Spirituality, creativity and the future of the church* (London: Darton Longman & Todd, 2000)

---, *Rebuilding the house of faith: Being spiritual, human and Christian in today's world,* (2002, Online). Available from http://www.ctbi.org.uk/assembly/Drane.doc. [Accessed 29th Feb. 2004]

Droege, T.A., 'Adult faith development and ministry' in Aden, L., et al. (eds.), *Christian perspectives on human development* (Grand Rapids, MI: Baker Book House, 1992) pp. 35-52

---, 'Congregations as communities of health and healing', *Interpretation* 49 (1995), 2. 117-129

Dubois, J.M. (ed.), *Moral issues in psychology: Personalist contributions to selected problems* (Lanham, NY: University Press of American, 1997)

Duck, S.W., *Human relationships* (London: Sage, 1986/1998)

Duffy, S.J., 'Evil' in Downey, M. (ed.), *The new dictionary of Catholic spirituality* (Collegville, MN: Liturgical Press, 1993) pp. 361-364

Dulles, A., *Models of the church: A critical assessment of the church in all its aspects* (Dublin: Gill & MacMillan, 1974/1987)

Dunn, J.D.G., *Unity and diversity in the New Testament: An enquiry into the character of earliest Christianity* (London: SCM Press, 1977)

Dunn, R.G., *Identity crises: A social critique of postmodernity* (Minneapolis: University of Minnesota Press, 1998)

Durlak, J.A., 'Evaluating comparative studies of paraprofessionals and professional helpers: A reply to Nietzel and Fisher', *Psychological Bulletin* 89 (1981), 566-569

Edwards, D.L., *The church that could be* (London: SPCK, 2002)

Egan, G., *The skilled helper: A model for a helping and interpersonal relating systematic* (Monterey, CA: Brooks Cole, 1975)

Ehrlich, J.D., *Plato's gift to Christianity: The Gentile preparation for and the making of the Christian faith* (San Diego: Academic Christian Press, 2001)

Eichrodt, W., *Theology of the Old Testament* Vol. 1 (London: SCM Press, 1961/1975)

---, *Theology of the Old Testament* Vol. 2 (London: SCM Press, 1967/1972)

Eims, L., *The lost art of disciple making* (Grand Rapids: Zondervan, 1978)

Ellens, J.H., 'The unfolding Christian self' in Aden, L., et al. (eds.), *Christian perspectives on human development* (Grand Rapids:: Baker Book House, 1992) pp. 127-144

Elliott, M. and C. Dickey, 'Body politics', *Newsweek* (September 12 1994), 24-25

Ellis, A., *Reason and emotion in psychotherapy* (New York: Lyle Stuart, 1962)

Ellis, C. and M.G. Flaherty, 'An agenda for the interpretation of lived experience' in Ellis, C. and M.G. Flaherty (eds.), *Investigating subjectivity: Research on lived experience* (Newbury Park: Sage Publications, 1992) pp. 1-13

Ellison, H.L., *The household church* (Exeter: Paternoster Press, 1963)

Engel, G.L., 'The need for a new medical model : A challenge for biomedicine', *Journal of Science* 196 (1977), 4286. 129-136

English, H.B. and A.C. English, 'Catharsis' in English, H.B. and A.C. English (eds.), *A comprehensive dictionary of psychological and psychoanalytical terms: A guide to useage* (London: Longmans, 1958) p. 54

English, J., *Spiritual intimacy and community: An Ignatian view of the small faith community* (London: Darton, Longman & Todd, 1992)

Enquist, D.E., et al., 'Occupational therapists' beliefs and practices with regard to spirituality and therapy', *American Journal of Occupational Therapy* 51 (1997), 3. 173-180

Erickson, K.C. and D.D. Stull, *Doing team ethnography: Warnings and advice* (London: Sage, 1998)

Erikson, E.H., *Childhood and society* (New York: WW Norton & Co., 1950/1963)

---, *Identity and the life cycle* (New York: Norton, 1959/1980)

---, *Identity: Youth and crisis* (New York: Norton, 1968)

Erikson, E.H. and J.M. Erikson, *The life cycle completed* (New York: Norton, 1997)

Erland, W., 'Shalom and wholeness', *Brethren Life and Thought* 29 (1984), 145-151.

Ernest Wright, G., *The Biblical doctrine of man in society* (London: SCM Press, 1954)

Erwin, P.J., *The family-powered church* (Loveland, CO: Group Publishing Inc., 2000)

Etzioni, A., *The spirit of community: The reinvention of American society* (New York: Touchstone, 1992)

---, *The spirit of community: Rights, responsibilities and the communitarian agenda* (London: Fontana Press, 1993/1995)

Evans, C.S., *Preserving the person: A look at the human sciences* (Downers Grove: IVP, 1979)

Faber, H., *Toward a contemporary spirituality* (London: SCM, 1988)

Faber, R., 'Trinity, analogy and coherence' in Bracken, J.A. and M.H. Suchocki (eds.), *Trinity in Process: A relational theology of God* (New York: Continuum, 1997) pp. 147-171

Fabiano, F. and C. Fabiano, *Healing the past, releasing your future: How to discover the roots of adult problems, experience healing and break through to your God-given destiny* (Tonbridge: Sovereign World, 2003)

Fackre, G., 'Book Review: Pinnock C.H.: Most moved mover: A theology of God's openness. Vanhoozer, K.J. (Ed). Nothing greater, nothing better: Theological essays on the love of God.' *Theology Today* 59 (2002), 2. 319-323

Fairchild, L., '"... As thyself"', *Journal of Religion and Health* 17 (1978), 3. 210-214

Farrow, D.B., 'Irenaeus of Lyon' in Hart, T.A. (ed.), *Dictionary of historical theology* (Carlisle: Paternoster, 2000) pp. 273-275

Ferre, N.F.S., *Swedish contributions to modern theology: With special reference to Lundensian thought* (London: Harper & Bros., 1939)

Ferry, L., *Man made God: the meaning of life* (Chicago: Chicago University Press, 2002)

Festinger, L. and J.M. Carlsmith, 'Cognitive consequences of forced complicance',
　　Journal of Abnormal and Social Psychology 58 (1959), 203-210

Festinger, L., et al., *When prophesy fails* (New York: Harper Torchbooks, 1956)

Feuerbach, L., *The essence of Christianity* (New York: Harper & Row, 1841/1956)

Fiddes, P.S., *Participating in God: A pastoral doctrine of the Trinity* (Louisville:
　　Westminster John Knox Press, 2000)

Field, A., *From darkness to light: How one became a Christian in the Early Church*
　　(Ben Lomond, CA: Conciliar Press, 1978/1997)

Fiensy, D., 'Using the Neur culture of Africa in understanding the Old Testament: An
　　evaluation' in Chalcraft, D.J. (ed.), *Social scientific Old Testament criticism*
　　(Sheffield: Sheffield Academic Press, 1997) pp. 43-52

Finger, T.N., *The self, earth and society:Alienation and Trinitarian transformation*
　　(Downes Grove: IVP, 1997)

Fink, P.E., 'Celebration' in Downey, M. (ed.), *The new dictionary of Catholic
　　spirituality* (Minnesota: Liturgical Press,, 1993) pp. 130-133

Finkelstein, I., *The archaeology of the Israelite settlement* (Jerusalem: Israel Exploration
　　Society, 1988)

Finn, T.M., *Early Christian baptism and the catechumenate: West and East Syria*
　　(Minneapolis: Liturgical Press, 1992)

Firet, J., *Dynamics in pastoring* (Grand Rapids: Michigan, 1986)

First, M.B., *Diagnostic and statistical manual of mental disorders* (Washington D.C:
　　American Psychiatric Association, 1995)

Fitzpatrick, G., *How to recognize God's voice* (Fairy Meadows, NSW, Australia:
　　Spiritual Growth Books, 1984/1987)

Flannery, A., *Vatican Council II: The conciliar and postconciliar documents* Vol. 1
　　(Dublin: Cominican Publications, 1988)

Flory, B.M., 'Holistic ministry - Challenge to growth and wholeness within the local
　　congregation', *Brethren Life and Thought* 28 (1983), 101-106

Foakes-Jackson, F.J., *History of the Christian Church: From the earliest times to 461*
　　(London: George Allen & Unwin, 1891/1965)

Foley, G., *Family-centred church: A new parish model* (Kansas City, MO: Sheed &
　　Ward, 1995)

Ford, D.F., *Self and salvation: Being transformed* (Cambridge: Cambridge University
　　Press, 1999)

Ford, L., 'Contingent Trinitarianism' in Bracken, J.A. and M.H. Suchocki (eds.), *Trinity
　　in process: A relational theology of God* (New York: Continuum, 1997) pp. 41-68

Ford, L.S., 'An alternative to creatio ex-nihilo', *Religious Studies* 19 (1983), 2. 205-213

Fortman, E.J., *The Triune God: An historical study of the doctrine of the Trinity*
　　(London: Hutchinson & Co. Publishers Ltd, 1972)

Foskett, J., *Meaning in madness* (London: SPCK., 1990)

Foskett, J. and D. Lyall, *Helping the helpers: Supervision and pastoral care* (London:
　　SPCK., 1988)

Foster, R., *Celebration of discipline* (London: Hodder & Stoughton, 1978)

Fouch, R.E., *What Is The Experience Of Spirituality Within Psychotherapy? A heuristic study of seven psychotherapists' experience of spirituality within psychotherapy* An Unpublished Dissertation (The Union Institution, USA, 1997)

Fowler, J.W., 'Religious institutions 1: Toward a developmental perspective on faith', *Journal of Religious Education* 69 (1974), 2. 207-219

---, *Stages of faith: The psychology of human development and the quest for meaning* (San Francisco: Harper, 1981)

---, 'Theology and psychology in the study of faith development' in Kepnes, S. and D. Tracy (eds.), *Concilium: Religion in the eighties* (Edinburgh: T&T Clark, 1982)

---, *Faithful change: The personal and public challenges of postmodern life* (Nashville: Abingdon Press, 1996a)

---, 'Pluralism and oneness in religious experience: William James, faith development theory and clinical practice' in Shafranske, E.P. (ed.), *Religion and the clinical practice of psychology* (Washington DC: American Psychological Association, 1996b) pp. 165-186

Frank, J.D., 'Therapeutic components shared by all psychotherapies' in Harvey, J.H. and M.M. Parks (eds.) *Psychotherapy research and behaviour change* Vol. 1 (Washington DC: American Psychological Association, 1982)

Frankl, V., *Man's search for meaning* Lasch, I. (tr.) (New York: Washington Square, 1963)

---, *The doctor and the soul: From psychotherapy to logotherapy* (New York: Vintage Books, 1965/1973)

Fraser, I.M., *The fire runs: God's people participating in change* (London: SCM, 1975)

Frazee, R., *The connecting church: Beyond small groups to authentic community* (Grand Rapids: Zondervan Publishing., 2001)

Freeman, A., 'Styles of discipleship: personal growth models in the New Testament', *Studies in Formative Spirituality* 5 (1984), 2. 171-188

Fretheim, T.E., *Exodus* (Louisville, KY: John Knox Press, 1991)

---, 'Knowledge' in van Gemeren, W.A. (ed.) *The new international dictionary of Old Testament theology and exegesis* Vol. 2 of 5 (Carlisle: Paternoster, 1996a) pp. 409-414

---, 'Yahweh' in van Gemeren, W.A. (ed.), *The new international dictionary of Old Testament theology and exegesis* (Carlisle: Paternoster, 1996b) pp. 1295-1300

Freud, A., 'The bearing of the psychoanalytic theory of instinctual drives on certain aspects of human behavior' in Loewenstein, R.M. (ed.), *Drives, affects, behaviour* (Oxford: International Universities Press, 1953) pp. 259-277

Freud, S., *Studies in hysteria: The standard edition of the complete works of Sigmund Freud* Vol. 2 (London: Hogarth Press, 1893-1895)

---, *Introductory lectures on psychoanalysis* Vol. 15, 16 (London: Hogarth, 1905/1965)

Freudenburg, B.F., *The family-friendly church* (Loveland, CO: Vital Ministry, 1998)

Friedman, E.H., *Generation to generation: Family process in church and synagogue* (New York: The Guilford Press, 1985)

Fullan, M., *Change forces: The sequel* (Philadelphia, PA: Falmer Press, 1999)

Fuller, R.C., *Religion and the life cycle* (Philadelphia: Fortress Press, 1988)

Furedi, F., 'The silent ascendancy of therapeutic culture in Britain', *Society* 39 (2002), 3.
    16-24

Gager, J.G., *Kingdom and community: The social world of early Christianity* (New
    Jersey: Prentice-Hall Inc., 1975)

Ganje-Fling, M.A. and P.R. McCarthy, 'A comparative analysis of spiritual direction
    and psychotherapy', *Journal of Psychology and Theology* 19 (1991), 1. 103-117

Ganoczy, A., 'Entelechy' in Arnold, F.X. (ed.) *Handbuch der pastoraltheologie* Vol. 1
    of 5 (Freiburg: Herder, 1964) pp. 208-209

Ganss, G.E. (ed.), *Ignatius of Loyola : The spiritual exercises and selected works* (New
    York: Paulist Press, 1991)

Ganz, R., *Psychobabble: The failure of modern psychology - and the Biblical alternative*
    (Wheaton, IL: Crossway Books, 1993)

Gardner, J., 'Building community', *Community Education Journal* 23 (1996), 3. 6-9

Garfield, S.L. and A.E. Bergin, *Handbook of psychotherapy and behavior change* (New
    York ; Chichester: Wiley, 1994)

Garzon, F., Burkett, L., 'Healing of memories: Models, research, future directions',
    Journal of Psychology and Christianity 21 (2002), 1. 42-49

Gay, V.P., 'The ego's complicity in religion', *Journal of the American Academy of
    Religion* 47 (1979), 4. 539-555

Gebser, J., 'Foreword' in Saher, P.J. (ed.), *Eastern wisdom and western thought: A
    comparative study in modern philosophy of religion* (New York: Barnes & Noble,
    1970) pp. 3-12

Geen, R.G., 'Some effects of observing violence upon the behaviour of the observer' in
    Maher, B.A. (ed.) *Progress in experimental personality research* Vol. 8 (New
    York: Academic Press, 1978)

Geertz, C., 'Religion as a cultural system' in Banton, M. (ed.), *Anthropological
    approaches to the study of religion* (London: Tavistock Publications, 1966/1977)
    pp. 1-47

Gelpi, D.L., *The turn to experience in contemporary theology* (New York: Paulist Press,
    1994)

van Gemeren, W.A. (ed.), *The new international dictionary of Old Testament theology
    and exegesis* NIDOTTE (Carlisle: Paternoster, 1996)

Gerkin, C.V., *The living human document: Re-visioning pastoral counselling in a
    hermeneutical mode* (Nashville: Abingdon Press, 1984)

Gibson, T.L., 'Wholeness and transcendence in the practice of pastoral psychotherapy
    from a Judaeo Christian perspective' in Young-Eisendrath, P. and M.E. Miller
    (eds.), *The psychology of mature spirituality* (Philadelphia: Routledge, 2000) pp.
    175-186

Giddens, A., *Sociology* (Oxford: Polity Press, 1989)

---, *Modernity and self-identity: Self and society in the late modern age* (Stanford:
    Stanford University Press, 1991)

Gilbert, P. and V. Nicholls, *Inspiring hope: Recognising the importance of spirituality in
    a whole person approach* (Leeds: NIMHE Central Team, 2003)

Giles, K., *The Trinity and subordinationism: The doctrine of God and the contemporary gender debate* (Downers Grove, IL: IVP, 2002)

Gill, R., *The myth of the empty church* (London: SPCK., 1993)

---, *The empty church revisited* (Aldershot: Ashgate Press, 2003)

Gilligan, C., *In a different voice* (Massachusetts: Harvard University Press, 1982/1993)

Gladwell, M., *The tipping point: How little things can make a big difference* (London: Little Brown & Company, 2000)

Glaser, B.G., *Emergence vs forcing: Basics of grounded theory analysis* (Mill Valley, CA: The Sociology Press, 1992)

Gleick, J., *Chaos: Making a new science* (London: Sphere books, 1987)

Gleitman, H., *Psychology* (New York: W.W. Norton & Co., 1995)

Goddard, N.C., 'Spirituality as integrative energy: A philosophical analysis as requisite precursor to holistic practice', *Journal of Advanced Nursing* 22 (1995), 808-815

Goldbrunner, J., *Holiness is wholeness* (London: Burns and Oates, 1955)

---, *Realization* (Dublin: Herder and Herder, 1966)

Goldenberg, H. and I. Goldenberg, *Family therapy : An overview* (Pacific Grove, California: Brooks Cole, 1991)

Goldsmith, M., *God on the move: Growth and change in the church worldwide* (Carlisle: OM Publishing, 1991)

Goleman, D., *Emotional intelligence* (New York: Bantam Books, 1995)

---, *The new leaders: Transforming the art of leadership into the science of results* (London: Little Brown, 2002)

Gorman, J.A., *Community that is Christian: A handbook on small groups* (Wheaton, IL: Victor Books, 1993)

Gothard, B., *Iniquities of the forefathers*: Unpublished paper, received in personal correspondence, April 9th 1998, 1998)

Gottwald, N.K., *The tribes of Yahweh: A sociology of the religion of liberated Israel - 1250-1050BCE* (London: SCM Press, 1975/1979)

---, *The Hebrew Bible: A socio-literary introduction* (Philadelphia: Fortress Press, 1985)

---, 'Sociological method in the study of ancient Israel' in Gottwald, N.K., et al. (ed.), *The Bible and liberation: Political and social hermeneutics* (MaryKnoll, NY: Orbis Books, 1993)

Gotz, I.L., 'On spirituality and teaching', *Philosophy of Education,* (1997, Online). Available from http://www.ed.uiuc.edu/EPS/PES-Yearbook/97_docs/gotz.html [Accessed 13th Jan. 2003]

Graham, E.L., *Transforming practice - Pastoral theology in an age of uncertainty* (London 1996)

Gray, T. and C. Sinkinson, *Reconstructing theology: A critical assessment of the theology of Clark Pinnock* (Carlisle: Paternoster, 2002)

Green, M., *Evangelism through the local church* (London: Hodder & Stoughton, 1990)

Greenberg, D. and E. Witztum, 'Problems in the treatment of religious patients', *The American Journal of Psychology* 45 (1991), 4. 554-565

Greenberg, L.S. and J.D. Safran, *Emotion in psychotherapy* (New York: Guildford, 1987)

---, 'Emotion in psychotherapy', *American Psychologist* 44 (1989), 19-29

Greene, T.A., 'Persona and shadow: A Jungian view of human duality' in Moore, R.L. (ed.), *Carl Jung and Christian Spirituality* (New York: Paulist Press, 1988) pp. 167-180

Greenwood, R., *Reclaiming the church* (London: Fontana, 1987)

---, *Practising community: The task of the local church* (London: SPCK, 1996)

Gregory of Nyssa, 'Contra Eunomium' in Migne, J.-P. (ed.), *Patrologia Graeca* (Paris1857-1866) p. 45

Grenz, S.J., *A primer on postmodernism* (Grand Rapids: William B. Eerdmans, 1996)

---, *Created for community: Connecting Christian belief with Christian living* (Grand Rapids: Baker Books, 1996/2000)

---, *Theology for the community of God* (Grand Rapids: Erdmans, 2000)

---, *The social God and the relational self: A Trinitarian theology of the imago Dei* (London: Westminster John Knox Press, 2001)

Gress, D.R., *From Plato to Nato: The idea of the West and its opponents* (New York: Free Press, 1988)

Griffin, D.R., 'A naturalistic Trinity' in Bracken, J.A. and M.H. Suchocki (eds.), *Trinity in process: A relational theology of God* (New York: Continuum, 1997) pp. 23-40

Groeschel, B., *Spiritual passages: The psychology of spiritual development* (New York: Crossroad Publishing, 1992)

Grof, S. and C. Grof, 'Epilogue: Spiritual emergence and global crisis' in Grof, S. and C. Grof (eds.), *Spiritual emergency: When personal transformation becomes a crisis* (New York: Penguin Putnam Inc, 1989a) pp. 233-235

--- (eds.), *Spiritual emergency: When personal transformation becomes a crisis* (New York: Penguin Putnam Inc, 1989b)

Grogan, G.W., 'Image of God' in Atkinson, D.J. and D.H. Field (eds.), *New dictionary of Christian ethics & pastoral theology* (Leicester: IVP, 1995) pp. 476-477

Groothuis, D., *Confronting the New Age* (Illinois: IVP, 1986)

Guest, M., et al., *Congregational studies: Taking stock* Colloquium on Congregational Studies (University of Lancaster, 2001)

Gugenbuhl-Craig, A., *Power in the helping professions* (Dallas: Spring, 1985)

Guigo II, *The ladder of monks: A letter on the contemplative life & twelve meditations* Colledge, E. and J. Walsh (tr.) (London: Mowbrays, 1978)

Guiness, O., *Dining with the Devil: The megachurch movement flirts with modernity* (Grand Rapids: Baker Book House, 1993)

Gundry, R.H., *Soma in Biblical theology: With emphasis on Pauline anthropology* (Cambridge: Cambridge University Press, 1976)

Gunn, G., *Office Feng Shui* (Abingdon: Hodder & Stoughton, 1999)

Gunton, C.E., *Becoming and being: The doctrine of God in Charles Hartshorne and Karl Barth* (Oxford: Oxford University Press, 1978)

---, *Enlightenment and alienation: An essay towards a Trinitarian theology* (Grand Rapids, MI: Willam B. Eerdmans Publishing, 1985)

---, *The promise of Trinitarian Theology* (Edinburgh: T&T Clark, 1991a)

---, 'Trinity, ontology and anthropology: Toward a renewal of the doctrine of the *imago Dei*' in Schwobel, C. and C. Gunton (eds.), *Persons, Divine and Human* (Edinburgh: T&T Clark, 1991b) pp. 47-61

---, *The one, the three and the many: God, creation and the culture of modernity.* (Cambridge: Cambridge University Press, 1993)

---, *Act and being: Towards a theology of divine attributes* (London: SCM Press, 2002a)

---, 'Book Review: Jungel, E. God's being is in becoming: The Trinitarian being of God in the theology of Karl Barth', *Theology Today* 59 (2002b), 2. 310-311

Guttmacher, S., 'Whole in body, mind and spirit: Holistic health and the limits of medicine', *Hastings Center Report* 9 (1979), 15-21

Guy, J.D. and G.P. Liaboe, 'Isolation in Christian psychotherapeutic practice', *Journal of Psychology and Theology* 13 (1985), 3. 167-171

Haaga, D.A.F. and G.C. Davison, 'Cognitive change methods' in Kander, F.H. and A.P. Goldstein (eds.), *Helping people change: A textbook of methods* (Elmsford, New York: Pergamon, 1991) p. 218ff.

Habermas, J., *Knowledge and human interests* (Boston, MA: Beacon Press, 1986)

Hadidian, A., *Successful discipling* (Chicago: Moody, 1979)

Hadot, P., et al., *Philosophy as a way of life : Spiritual exercises from Socrates to Foucault* (Oxford ; New York: Blackwell, 1995)

Haggard, P., 'Healing and health care of the whole person', *Journal of Religion and Health* 22 (1983), 234-240

Haigh, R., 'The quintessence of a therapeutic environment' in Campling, P. and R. Haigh (eds.), *Therapeutic communities: Past, present and future* (London: Jessica Kingsley, 1999) pp. 246-256

Haigh, R., et al., 'The derived definition from the foreword to the final revised version of the therapeutic community standards, which form the basis for the Quality Network Mutual Exercise', *Association of Therapeutic Communities Joint Newsletter* 4 (March 2002), 13

Halleck, S., *The politics of therapy* (New York: Science House, 1971/1994)

Halling, S., 'Embracing human fallibility: On forgiving oneself and forgiving others', *Journal of Religion and Health* 33 (1994), 2. 107-113

Halmos, P., *The faith of the counsellors* (London: Constable & Co. Ltd, 1965)

Hamilton, H.A., *The family church in principle and practice* (Wallington: Religious Education Press, 1960)

Hamilton, M.C., 'Masculine bias in the attribution of personhood: People = male, male = people', *Psychology of Women Quarterly* 15 (1991), 3. 393-402

Hand, Q.L., 'Pastoral counselling as theological practice', *Journal of Pastoral Care* 32 (1978), 100-110

Hanegraaff, W.J., *New Age religion and Western culture: Esotericism in the mirror of secular thought* (New York: State University of New York Press, 1998)

Hanks, G. and W. Shell, *Discipleship* (Grand Rapids: Zondervan, 1993)

Hannaford, R., *The church for the 21st century: Agenda for the Church of England* (Leominster, Hereford: Gracewing Publications, 1998)

Hanson, P., *The people called: Growth of community in the Bible* (San Francisco: Harper and Rowe, 1986)

Haring, B., *Sin in the secular age* (Slough: St Paul Publications, 1974)

---, *Christian maturity: Holiness in today's world* (Slough: St Paul Publications, 1983)

von Harnack, A., *The essence of Christianity (Das Wesen des Christentums)* (Leipzig 1900)

Harper, M., *A new way of living* (Plainfield: Logos International, 1973)

Harrington, D., *God's people in Christ: New Testament perspectives on the Church and Judaism* (Philadelphia: Fortress Press, 1980)

Harris, J.C., *Stress, power and ministry* (Bethesda, MD: Alban Institute, 1982)

Hartshorne, C., *The divine relativity: A social conception of God* (New Haven: Yale University Press, 1948)

---, *Omnipotence and other theological mistakes* (Albany, NY: The State University Press, 1984)

Hattie, J.A., et al., 'Comparative effectiveness of professional and paraprofessional helpers', *Psychological Bulletin* 95 (1984), 534-541

Hauerwas, S., 'Discipleship as a craft, church as a disciplined community' in Walker, S. (ed.), *Changing community* (St Paul: Gray Wolf Press, 1993) pp. 151-162

Haughton, R., *The transformation of man: A study of conversion and community* (Springfield: Templegate, 1967)

Hay, D. and K. Hunt, *Understanding the spirituality of people who don't go to church* (Nottingham: Nottingham University Press, 2000)

Healey, C.J., *Christian spirituality: An introduction to the heritage* (New York: Alba House, 1999)

Heelas, P., *The New Age movement: The celebration of the self and the sacralisation of modernity* (Oxford: Blackwell Publishing Ltd, 1996)

Hegel, G.W.F., *Phenomenology of mind* (Oxford: Oxford University Press, 1807/1977)

Heller, M.S. and S. Polsky, *Studies in violence and television* (New York: American Broadcasting Companies, 1975)

Helminiak, D.A., *The same Jesus: A contemporary Christology* (Chicago: Loyola University Press, 1986)

---, *The human core of spirituality: Mind as psyche and spirit* (New York: State University of New York Press., 1996)

Hempel, J., *Theologische literaturzeitung* Lambert, W.A. and H.J. Grim (tr.) (Philadelphia: Muhlenberg Press, 1957)

Henderson, D.M., *John Wesley's Class Meeting; A model for making disciples* (Nappanee: Evangel Publishing House, 1997)

Hengel, M., *The Hellinisation of Judea in the first century after Christ* (London: SCM Press, 1989)

Hess, C.R., 'Aquinas organic synthesis of Plato and Aristotle', *Angelicum* 58 (1981), 339-350

van der Heyden, P.A., 'Religious addiction: The subtle destruction of the soul', *Journal of Pastoral Psychology* 47 (1999), 4. 293-302

Higgins, B., 'Does anyone feel they need support tonight? 24 hour care on a day unit.'
    Therapeutic Communities 18 (1997), 1. 55-61

Hill, E., *Being human - a Biblical perspective* (London: Geoffrey Chapman, 1984)

Hillman, J., *Emotion* (London: Routledge & Kegan Paul, 1960)

Hiltner, S., *Pastoral counselling* (Nashville, TN: Abingdon Press, 1949)

---, 'The meaning and importance of pastoral theology' in Pattison, S. and J. Woodward
    (eds.), *The Blackwell reader in pastoral and practical theology* (Oxford:
    Blackwell Publishers Ltd., 2000) pp. 27-48

Himes, M. and K. Himes, *Fullness of faith: The public significance of theology* (New
    York: Paulist Press, 1993)

Hindman, D.M., 'From splintered lives to whole persons: Facilitating spiritual
    development in college students', *Journal of Religious Education* 97 (2002), 2.
    165-182

Hinnebusch, P., *Friendship in the Lord* (Notre Dame: Ave Maria Press, 1974)

Hinshelwood, R.D., 'The Community as analyst: Current issues - theory' in
    Hinshelwood, R.D. and N. Manning (eds.), *Therapeutic communities: Reflections
    and progress* (London: Routlege & Kegan Paul, 1979) pp. 103-112

---, 'Therapy or coercion: A clinical note on personal change in a therapeutic
    community', *International Journal for Therapeutic and Supportive Organisations*
    11 (1990), 1. 53-59

Hobart Mowrer, O., *The crisis in psychiatry* (New Jersey: D. Van Nostrand Co. Inc.,
    1961)

Hobson, R.F., 'The Messianic community: Clinical case studies' in Hinshelwood, R.D.,
    & Manning, N. (ed.), *Therapeutic communities: Reflections and progress*
    (London: Routlege & Kegan Paul, 1979) pp. 231-243

Holmes, P.R., 'Some of the problems studying spirituality: Facing its challenges,
    landscaping its domain' in Flanagan, K. and P.C. Jupp (eds.), *The Sociology of
    Spirituality*: To be published, 2006)

Holmes, P.R. and S.B. Williams, *Developing a new model for care in the community:
    The results of a pilot study conducted to assess the benefits and drawbacks for
    people with mental health problems of a new rehabilitation programme focused on
    a therapeutic community* (Deal, Kent: Community Therapy and Rehabilitation
    Ltd, 2002)

--- (eds.), *Changed lives: Extraordinary stories of ordinary people* (Milton Keynes:
    Authentic, 2005)

Honderich, T. (ed.), *The Oxford companion to philosophy* (Oxford: Oxford University
    Press, 1995)

Hooker, M.D., 'Authority on her head: 1Cor 11.10', *New Testament Studies* 10 (1963-
    64), 410-416

Hopewell, J.F., *Congregation: Stories and structures* (Philadelphia: Fortress Press,
    1987)

Hoskins, M. and J. Leseho, 'Changing metaphors of the self: Implications for
    counselling', *Journal of Counselling and Development* 74 (1996), Jan/Feb. 243-
    252

Houlden, L., 'Why were the disciples ever called disciples?' *Theology* 105 (2002), 828

Houston, B.M., et al., 'Distinctive components and perceived sources of gain in Christian counselling', *Journal of Psychology and Christianity* 19 (1999), 3. 238-253

Howard, J.G., *The trauma of transparency: A Biblical approach to interpersonal communication* (Portland: Multnomah Press, 1979)

Howe, L.T., 'Faith in the quest for wholeness', *Religion in Life* 49 (1980), Fall. 289-306

Huffman, D.S. and E.L. Johnson (eds.), *God under fire: Modern scholarship reinvents God* (Carlisle: Zondervan, 2002)

Huggett, J., *Living free: Becoming the person God intends you to be* (Leicester: IVP, 1984)

---, *Listening to God* (London: Hodder & Stoughton, 1986)

Hull, J., *Hellenistic magic and the Synoptic tradition* (London: SCM Press, 1974)

Hull, J.M., *What prevents Christian adults from learning?* (Philadelphia: Trinity Press International, 1991)

---, 'Spiritual development: Interpretations and applications', *British Journal of Religious Education* 24 (2002), 3. 171-182

Hunt, D. and T.A. McMahon, *The seduction of Christianity: Spiritual discernment in the last days* (Oregon: Harvest House Publishers, 1985)

Hunter, G.G., *Church for the unchurched* (Nashville: Abingdon Press, 1996)

---, *The Celtic way of evangelism: How Christianity can reach the West.... again* (Nashville: Abingdon Press, 2000)

Hurding, R., *The Bible and counselling* (London: Hodder & Stoughton, 1992)

---, 'Pastoral care, counselling and psychotherapy' in Atkinson, D.J. and D.H. Field (eds.), *New dictionary of Christian ethics & pastoral theology* (Leicester: IVP, 1995a) pp. 78-87

---, 'Pathways to wholeness: Christian journeying in a postmodern age', *The Journal of Psychology and Christianity* 14 (1995b), 4. 293-305

---, *Pathways to wholeness: Pastoral care in a postmodern age* (London: Hodder & Stoughton, 1998)

Illingworth, R.J., *Personality, human and divine* The Bampton Lectures for 1894 (London, 1894)

Imbelli, R. and T.H. Groome, 'Signposts toward a pastoral theology', *Theological Studies* 53 (1992), 127-137

Isaacs, M.E., *The concept of Spirit* (London: Heythrop College, 1976)

Israel, M., *Healing as sacrament* (London: Darton, Longman and Todd, 1984)

Izzard, S., 'Holding contradictions together: An object relational view of healthy spirituality', *Contact* 1 (2003), 140. 2-8

Jacobs, M., *Toward the fulness of Christ: Pastoral care and Christian maturity* (London: Darton, Longman and Todd, 1988)

James, W., 'What is an emotion?' *Mind* 9 (1884), 188-205

---, *The varieties of religious experience* (New York: Longman Green and Co, 1902/1928)

Jamieson, A., 'Churchless faith: Trajectories of faith beyond the church from evangelical, pentecostal and charismatic churches to postchurch groups', *International Review of Mission* 92 (2003), 365. 217-226

Janis, I.J., 'Groupthink and Poor Quality Decision Making' in Clark, H., et al. (eds.), *Organisation and Identities: Text and readings in organisational behaviour* 1994) pp. 279-294

Janov, A., *Primal scream: Primal therapy, the cure for neurosis* (New York: Delta, 1970)

---, *Primal revolution* (London: Abacus, 1972/1975)

Jenson, R.W., *God after God: The God of the past and the God of the future, seen in the works of Karl Barth* (New York: Bobbs-Merrill Publishing, 1969)

---, *The Trinity identity* (Philadelphia: Fortress Press, 1982)

Jewett, R., *Paul's anthropological terms: A study of their use in conflict settings* (Leiden: EJ Brill, 1971)

Jobst, K.A., et al., 'Editorial: Diseases of meaning, manifestations of health and metaphor', *The Journal of Alternative and Complementary Medicine* 5 (1999), 6. 495-501

John of Climacus, *The ladder of divine ascent* (London: SPCK, 1982)

Johnson, A.R., *The one and the many in the Israelite conception of God* (Cardiff: University of Wales Press, 1942)

---, *The vitality of the individual in the thought of Ancient Israel.* (Cardiff: University of Wales Press., 1964)

Johnson, D. and J. Van Vonderen, *The subtle power of spiritual abuse; Recognising and escaping spiritual manipulation and false spiritual authority within the church* (Minneapolis: Bethany House, 1991)

Johnson, E.L. and S.J. Sandage, 'A postmodern reconstruction of psychotherapy: Orienteering, religion, and the healing of the soul.' *Psychotherapy* 36 (1999), 1. 1-15

Jonas, H., *The imperative of responsibility: In search of an ethics for the technological age* (Chicago: University of Chicago Press, 1984)

Jones, E.S., *The Christ of the Indian road* (London: Hodder & Stoughton, 1927)

---, *Christ at the round table* (London: Hodder & Stoughton, 1928)

---, *A song of ascents: A spiritual autobiography* (Nashville: Abingdon Press, 1968)

Jones, M., *The therapeutic community* (New York: Basic Books, 1953)

---, *Social psychiatry* (Springfield, IL: Charles Thomas, 1962)

---, *Beyond the therapeutic community* (New Haven: Yale University Press, 1965)

---, *Social psychiatry in practice: The idea of the therapeutic community* (Harmondsworth: Penguin, 1968)

---, 'Therapeutic community concepts and the future' in Rossi, J.J. and W.J. Philstead (eds.), *The therapeutic community: A sourcebook of readings* (New York: Behavioral Publications, 1973) pp. 325-336

---, 'The therapeutic community: Social learning and social change' in Hinshelwood, R.D. and N. Manning (eds.), *Therapeutic communities: Reflections and progress* (London: Routlege & Kegan Paul, 1979) pp. 1-10

Jones, M. and R.N. Rapoport, 'Administrative and social psychiatry', *Lancet* 2 (1955), 386-388

Jones, S.L., 'A constructive relationship for religion with the science and profession of psychology: Perhaps the boldest model yet' in Shafranske, E.P. (ed.), *Religion and the clinical practice of psychology* (Washington, DC: American Psychological Association, 1996) pp. 113-148

Josselson, R., 'Relationship as a path of integrity, wisdom and meaning' in Young-Eisendrath, P. and M.E. Miller (eds.), *The psychology of mature spirituality* (Philadelphia: Routledge, 2000) pp. 87-102

Judge, E.A., 'The early Christians as a scholastic community', *Journal of Religious History* 1 (1960a), 4-15, 125-137

---, *The social pattern of groups in the first century: Some prolegomena to the study of New Testament ideas of social obligation* (London: Tyndale, 1960b)

Jung, C.J., *Modern man in search of a soul* Dell, W.S.B., C.F., (tr.) (London: Kegan Paul, Trench, Trubner & Co., 1933/1973)

Jungel, E., *The doctrine of the Trinity: God's being is in His becoming* (Edinburgh: Scottish Academic Press, 1976)

---, *God as the mystery of the world: On the foundation of the theology of the Crucified One in the dispute between theism and atheism* (Edinburgh: T&T Clark, 1983)

---, *Theological essays* (Edinburgh: T&T Clark, 1989)

---, *God's being is in becoming: The Trinitarian being of God and the theology of Karl Barth - a paraphrase* (Edinburgh: T&T Clark, 2001)

Kalweit, H., 'When insanity is a blessing: The message of Shamanism' in Grof, S. and C. Grof (eds.), *Spiritual emergency: When personal transformation becomes a crisis* (New York: Penguin Putnam Inc, 1989) pp. 77-97

Kandel, E.G., et al., *Principles of neural science* (New York: McGraw Hill, 2000)

Kao, C.C.L., *Maturity and the quest for spiritual meaning* (New York: University Press of America, 1988)

Kapelke, C., 'Community is king: Companies are reaching out with online communities', *Continental* (April 2001), 38-40

Kasemann, E., *Essays in New Testament themes* (Philadelphia: Fortress Press, 1982)

Keating, T., *The spiritual journey: A guide book with tapes* (Colorado Springs, CO: Contemporary Publications, 1987)

Kee, H.C., *Who are the people of God? Early Christian models of community.* (Yale: Yale University Press, 1995)

Keefauver, L., *Experiencing the Holy Spirit: Transformed by His Presence - A twelve week interactive workbook* (Nashville: Thomas Nelson, 1997)

Keil, C.F., *Commentary on II Chronicles* (Edinburgh: ET Publishers, 1872)

Kelly, G.A., *A theory of personality: The psychology of personal constructs* (New York: W.W. Norton & Co., 1955/1963)

Kelsey, M.T., *Companions on the innerway: The art of spiritual guidance* (New York: Crossroad, 1989)

Kennard, D., *Introduction to therapeutic communities* (London: Jessica Kingsley, 1998a)

---, 'Therapeutic communities are back - and there is something a little different about them', *International Journal for Therapeutic and Supportive Organisations* 19 (1998b), 4. 323-329

Kenny, A., *The self* (Milwaukee: Marquette University Press, 1988)

Kenny, J.P., *The supernatural* (New York: Alber House, 1972)

Kernberg, O.F., 'Self, ego, affects and drives', *Journal of the American Psychoanalytic Association* 30 (1982), 893-915

Kerr, F., *After Aquinas: Versions of Thomism* (Oxford: Blackwell, 2002)

Kidder, R.M., *Shared values for a troubled world* (San Francisco: Jossey-Bass Publishers, 1994)

Kiefer, C.W., *The mantle of maturity: A history of ideas about character development* (New York: State University of New York Press, 1988)

Kimmel, M.S., *The gendered society* (New York: Oxford University Press, 2004)

Kinerk, E., 'Toward a method for the study of spirituality', *Review for Religious* 40 (1981), 1. 3-39

Kirkpatrick, F.G., *Community - a Trinity of models* (Washington: Georgetown University Press, 1986)

Kirwan, W.T., *Biblical concepts for Christian Counselling: A case for integrating psychology and theology* (Grand Rapids: Baker Book House, 1984)

Kleinmuntz, B., 'Why we still use our heads instead of the formulas: Toward an integrative approach', *Psychological Bulletin* 107 (1990), 296-310

Knowles, J., 'Therapeutic communities in today's world', *Journal of Therapeutic Communities* 16 (1995), 2. 97-102

Koch, S., *Psychology: A study of science* Vol. 6 (New York: McGraw-Hill, 1959/1963)

---, 'The nature and limits of psychological knowledge: Lessons of a century of qua science', *American Psychologist* 36 (1981), 257-267

Koenig, H.G., et al., 'Religion, spirituality and medicine: A rebuttal to skeptics', *International Journal of Psychiatry in Religion* 29 (1999), 2. 123-131

Kohlberg, L., 'Stage and sequence: The cognitive developmental approach to socialisation' in Goslin, D.A. (ed.), *Handbook of socialisation, theory and research* (Chicago: Rand McNally, 1969) pp. 347-480

Kohler, L., *Hebrew man* (London: SCM Press, 1953/1973)

Kohut, H., *The restoration of the self* (Madison, Conneticut: International Universities Press Inc, 1977/1988)

Kooyman, M., *The therapeutic community for addicts: Intimacy, parent involvement and treatment success* (Amsterdam: Swets & Zeitlinger, 1993)

Kornfeld, M.Z., *Cultivating wholeness: A guide to care and counselling in faith communities* (New York: Continuum Publishing Co, 1998)

Kostenberger, A.J., *The missions of Jesus and the disciples according to the fourth gospel: With implications for the fourth gospels purpose and the mission of the contemporary church.* (Grand Rapids: Erdmans Publishing, 1998)

Koteskey, R.R., *Psychology from a Christian perspective* (New York: University Press of America, 1991)

Kottler, J.A., *The language of tears* (San Fransisco: Jossey-Bass Publishers, 1996)

Krasner, L., *The therapist as a social reinforcer: Man or machine?* A meeting of the American Psychological Association, Philadelphia, 1963)

Kraus, C.N., *The authentic witness: Credibility and authority* (Grand Rapids, Michigan: Erdmans Publishing Co., 1979)

Kraybill, R., 'Toward encountering divine presence in the classroom', *Journal of the Henry Martyn Institute* 20 (2001), 1. 50-61

Kretzmann, N., *The metaphysics of theism* (Oxford: Clarendon Press, 1997)

Kron, T., 'The "we" in Martin Buber's dialogical philosophy and its implications for group therapy and the therapeutic community', *International Journal for Therapeutic and Supportive Organisations* 11 (1990), 1. 13-20

Kubler-Ross, E., *On death and dying* (London: Tavistock, 1970)

Kugelmann, R., 'Becoming responsible for emotion: Contradictions in pain management' in Dubois, J.M. (ed.), *Moral issues in psychology: Personalist contributions to selected problems* (Lanham, NY: University Press of American, 1997) pp. 81-97

Kuhn, T.S., *The structure of scientific revolutions* Vol. 2 (Chicago: University of Chicago Press, 1962)

Kung, H. and D. Tracy, *Paradigm change in theology: A symposium for the future* (Edinburgh: T&T Clark, 1989)

Kvalbein, H., 'Go therefore and make disciples... The concept of discipleship in the New Testament', *Themelios* 13 (1988), 2. 48-53

Lakeland, P., *Postmodernity: Christian identity in a fragmented age* (Minneapolis: Fortress Press, 1997)

Lambourne, R., *Explorations in health and salvation* (Birmingham: Birmingham Institute for the Study of Worship and Religious Architecture, 1983)

Lambourne, R.A., *Community, church and healing* (London: Darton, Longman & Todd, 1963)

Lampel-de Groot, J., 'The theory of instinctual drives' in Lampel-de Groot, J. (ed.), *Man and mind: Collected papers of Jeanne Lampel-de Groot* (New York: International Universities Press, 1985) pp. 175-182

Lang, B., *Anthropological approaches to the New Testament* (London: SPCK, 1985a)

---, *Anthropological approaches to the Old Testament* (London: SPCK., 1985b)

Lapierre, L.L., 'A model for describing spirituality', *Journal of Religion and Health* 33 (1994), 2. 153-161

Lapointe, F.H., 'Who originated the term psychology?' *The Journal of the History of the Behavioral Sciences* 8 (1972), 328-335

Lather, P., 'Postmodernism, post-structuralism and post (critical) ethnography: of ruins, aporias and angels' in Atkinson, P., et al. (eds.), *The handbook of ethnography* (London: Sage, 2001) pp. 477-492

Lausanne Committtee for World Evangelization & The World Evangelical Fellowship, *Evangelism and social responsibility: An evangelical commitment* (Exeter: Paternoster Press, 1982)

Law, R., *The emotions of Jesus* (Edinburgh: T&T Clark, 1915)

Lazarus, A.A., *Behaviour therapy and beyond* (New York: McGraw-Hill, 1971)

---, *The practice of multi-modal therapy* (New York: McGraw Hill, 1981)

Lee, B.J., 'An "other" Trinity' in Bracken, J.A. and M.H. Suchocki (eds.), *Trinity in process: A relational theology of God* (New York: Continuum, 1997) pp. 191-214

Lee, J.Y., *God suffers for us: A systematic enquiry into a concept of divine passibility* (The Hague: Martinis Nijhoff, 1974)

---, *The theology of change: A Christian concept of God in an Eastern perspective* (Mary Knowle, NY: Orbis Books, 1979)

Leech, K., *Spirituality and pastoral care* (London: Sheldon Press, 1986)

---, *The sky is red* (London: Darton, Longman & Todd, 1998)

---, *Through our long exile: Contextual theology and the urban experience* (London: Darton Longman and Todd, 2001)

Lees, J., 'Research: The importance of asking questions' in Campling, P. and R. Haigh (eds.), *Therapeutic communities: Past, present and future* (London: Jessica Kingsley, 1999) pp. 207-222

van Leeuwen, M.S., *The person in psychology: A contemporary Christian appraisal* (Leicester: IVP, 1985)

Leff, J. (ed.), *Care in the community: Illusion or reality?* (New York: Wiley, 1997)

Lemche, N.P., *Ancient Israel: A new history of Israelite society* (Sheffield: Sheffield Academic Press, 1988)

---, *The Canaanites and their land: The tradition of the Canaanites* (Sheffield: Sheffield Academic Press, 1991)

de Leon, G. and J.T. Ziegenfuss (eds.), *Therapeutic communities for addictions: Readings in theory, research and practice* (Springfield IL: Charles C. Thomas, 1986)

Levinson, D.J., *The seasons of a man's life* (New York: Ballantine Books, 1978)

Lewis, M. and J.M. Haviland (eds.), *Handbook of emotions* (New York: Guilford Press, 1993)

Liebert, R.M. and R.A. Baron, 'Some immediate effects of televised violence on children's behaviour', *Developmental Psychology* 6 (1972), 469-475

Lincoln, Y.S. and N.K. Denzin, 'The seventh moment: Out of the past' in Denzin, N.K. and Y.S. Lincoln (eds.), *Handbook of qualitative research* (Thousand Oaks: Sage Publications, 2000) pp. 1047-1065

Lindbeck, G.A., 'Confession and community: An Israel-like view of the church', *The Christian Century* (1990), 492-496

Lindgren, K.N. and R.D. Coursey, 'Spirituality and serious mental illness: A two part study', *Psychosocial Rehabilitation Journal* 18 (1995), 3. 93-111

Ling, T., *The significance of Satan : New Testament demonology and its contemporary relevance* (London: SPCK., 1961)

Little, M. and S. Kelly, *A life without problems? The achievements of a therapeutic community* (Aldershot: Arena, 1995)

Lockley, A., *Christian communes* (London: SCM Press, 1976)

Loewe, R., *The social position of women in Judaism* (London: SPCK, 1966)

Lohfink, G., *Jesus and community* Galvin, J.P. (tr.) (London: SPCK., 1985)

Lohfink, N., *The theology of the Pentateuch: Themes of the Priestly Narrative and Deuteronomy* (Edinburgh: T&T Clark, 1994)

Lonergan, B.J.F., *Insight : A study of human understanding* (New York: Longmans Philosophical Library, 1957)

---, *Collection : Papers by Bernard Lonergan* (Montreal: Palm, 1967)

Loptson, P., *Readings on human nature* (Toronto: Broadview Press, 1998)

Loux, M.J. (ed.), *Metaphysics: Contemporary readings* (London: Routledge, 2001)

Lovell, G., *The church and community development - An introduction.* (Pinner: Grail Publishing, 1972)

Lucado, M., *Just like Jesus* (Nashville: Thomas Nelson Publishers, 1998)

Lukes, S., *Individualism* (Oxford: Blackwell, 1973)

Lull, T.F., *Martin Luther's basic theological writings* (Minneapolis: Fortress Press, 1989)

Lydic, R.F., 'Divestment of pastoral authority: A model for healing', *Journal of Pastoral Psychology* 30 (1981), 122-125

Lyon, D., *Jesus in Disneyland: Religion in postmodern times* (Cambridge: Polity Press, 2000)

MacArthur, J.F., *The Charismatics: A doctrinal perspective* (Grand Rapids, Michigan: Zondervan, 1978)

MacArthur, J.F. and W.A. Mack, *Introduction to Biblical counselling: A basic guide to the principles and practice of counselling* (Dallas: Word Publishers, 1994)

Macaulay, R. and J. Barrs, *Being human: The nature of spiritual experience* (Downers Grove: IVP, 1978)

MacDonald, G., *Forgiving: A real world faith* (Crowborough: Highland Books, 1989)

MacDonald, H.D., *Forgiveness and atonement* (Grand Rapids Michigan: Baker Book House, 1984)

MacDonald, M., *Insanity and the realities of history in Early Modern England* 1990)

MacMullen, R., *Christianizing the Roman Empire (AD 100-400)* (New Haven: Yale University Press, 1984)

Macmurray, J., 'The unity of modern problems', *Journal of Philosophical Studies* 4 (1929), 167-179

---, *Interpreting the universe* (London: Faber and Faber, 1933)

---, *The clue to history* (London: SCM Press, 1938a)

---, *The nature of religion* St Asaph Conference (London: SCM Auxiliary, 1938b)

---, *Conditions of freedom* (London: Faber & Faber, 1950)

---, *The self as agent* (New Jersey: Humanities Press, 1957/1991)

---, *Persons in relation* (London: Faber & Faber Ltd, 1961)

---, *The philosophy of Jesus* (London: Friends Home Service Committee, 1973)

---, *Reason and emotion* (London: Faber & Faber, 1976)

Macmurray, J. and I. Grant, *The provisional basis of the Christian left* (London: The Christian Left, 1938)

MacQuarrie, J., 'A theology of personal being' in Peacocke, A. and G. Gillette (eds.), *Persons and personality: A contemporary enquiry* (Oxford: Blackwell, 1987) pp. 172-179

Maddocks, M., *Journey to wholeness* (London: SPCK., 1986)

Maddox, R.L., 'The recovery of theology as a practical discipline', *Theological Studies* 51 (1990), 650-672

Maertens, T., *Assembly for Christ: From Biblical theology to pastoral theology in the twentieth century* (London: Darton Longman and Todds, 1970)

Main, T.F., 'The hospital as a therapeutic institution', *The Bulletin Of The Menninger Clinic* 10 (1946), 66-70

Malony, H.N. (ed.), *Wholeness and holiness: Readings in the psychology and theology of mental health* (Grand Rapids, Michigan: Baker Book House, 1983)

Mann, D., *Love and hate : psychoanalytic perspectives* (Hove, East Sussex [England] ; New York: Brunner-Routledge, 2002)

Mann, D.W., 'Theories of the self', *Harvard Review of Psychiatry* 4 (1996), 4. 175-183

Manning, N., *The therapeutic community movement: Charisma and routinisation* (London: Routlege, 1989)

Marsden, G.M., *The outrageous idea of Christian scholarship* (Oxford: Oxford University Press, 1997)

Marsh, C., 'In defence of a self: The theological search for a postmodern identity', *Scottish Journal of Theology* 55 (2002), 3. 253-282

Marshall, B.D., *Trinity and truth* (Cambridge: Cambridge University Press, 2000)

Martin, D.V., *Adventure in psychiatry: Social change in a mental hospital* (London: Bruno Cassirer Publications, 1962)

Martin, G. and G. McIntosh, *Creating community: Deeper fellowship through small group ministry* (Nashville: Broadman & Holman Publishing, 1997)

Martsolf, D.S. and J.R. Mickley, 'The concept of spirituality in nursing theories: Differing world-views and extent of focus', *Journal of Advanced Nursing* 27 (1998), 294-303

Marx, K., *Selected writings in sociology and social philosophy* (London: Penguin, 1963)

Marzillier, J. and G. Butler, "CAT in relation to cognitive therapy" in Ryle, A. (ed.), *Cognitive analytical therapy: Developments in theory and practice* (Chichester: J.Wiley & Sons, 1995) pp. 121-138

Maslow, A., *Religions, values and peak experiences* (New York: Viking Compass Books, 1964/1970)

---, *Motivation and personality* (New York: Harper, 1970)

Massie, J., 'Disciple' in Hastings, J. (ed.) *A dictionary of the Bible: Dealing with its language, literature and contents including Biblical theology* Vol. 1 of 5 (Edinburgh: T&T Clark, 1898) pp. 609-610

May, G.G., *Care of mind, care of spirit: Psychiatric dimensions of spiritual direction* (San Francisco: Harper & Row, 1982a)

---, *Will and spirit* (San Francisco: Harper and Rowe, 1982b)

May, R., 'The problem of will, decision and responsibility in psychological health', *The Christian Scholar* 66 (1963), 3. 235-244

May, R., et al. (eds.), *Existence - a new dimension in psychiatry and psychology* (New York: Touchstone/Simon & Schuster, 1958)

Mayer, J.E., *A song of forgiveness* (Eastbourne: Kingsway, 1988)

Mayes, A.D.H., *The Old Testament in sociological perspective* (London: Marshall Pickering, 1989)

McBride, J.L., *Spiritual crisis: Surviving trauma to the soul* (New York: Haworth Pastoral Press, 1998)

McCarthy, M., 'Spirituality in a postmodern era' in Pattison, S. and J. Woodward (eds.), *The Blackwell reader in pastoral and practical theology* (Oxford: Blackwell Publishers Ltd., 2000) pp. 192-206

McCool, G.A., 'The philosophy of the human person in Karl Rahner's theology', *Theological Studies* 22 (1961), 537-562

---, 'Rahner's anthropology', *America* (1970), 342-344

McCoy, C.S., *When Gods change: Hope for theology* (Nashville: Abingdon Press, 1980)

McFadyen, A., 'Healing the damaged' in Ford, D.F. and D.L. Stamps (eds.), *Essentials of Christian community: Essays for Danile W. Hardy* (Edinburgh: T&T Clark, 1996) pp. 91-101

---, *Bound to sin: Abuse, holocaust and the Christian doctrine of sin* (Cambridge: Cambridge University Press, 2000)

McFadyen, A.I., *The call to personhood : A Christian theory of the individual in social relationship* (Cambridge: Cambridge University Press, 1990)

McGarry, F.J., 'Balance, wholeness and healing in Christianity', *Journal of Religion and Health* 35 (1996), 2. 159-168

McGettrick, B.J., *Values and educating the whole person* (Dundee: Centre for Creative Communities and the Scottish Consultative Council on the Curriculum, 1995)

McGinn, B., 'The Letter and the spirit: Spirituality as an academic discipline', *Christian Spirituality Bulletin* 1 (1993), 12. 1-10

McGrath, A.E., *Christian theology - an introduction* (Oxford: Blackwell Publishers, 1994)

---, 'Sin and salvation' in Atkinson, D.J. and D.H. Field (eds.), *New dictionary of Christian ethics & pastoral theology* (Leicester: IVP, 1995) pp. 78-87

---, *Christian spirituality* (Oxford: Blackwell, 1999)

McKenna, S., *Introduction to Saint Augustine: The Trinity* (Washington DC: Catholic University of America Press, 1963)

McKenzie, J.G., *Psychology, psychotherapy and Evangelicalism* (London: George Allen and Unwin, 1940)

McKim, D.K., *The Westminster dictionary of theological terms* (Louisville: Westminster John Knox Press, 1996)

McLeod, J., *Narrative and psychotherapy* (London: Sage Publications, 1997)

---, *Qualitative research in counselling and psychotherapy* (London: Sage Publications, 2001)

McMillen, S.I., *None of these diseases* (London: Oliphants, 1963)

McNair, J. and S.L. Swartz, 'Local church support to individuals with developmental disabilities', *Education and Training in Mental Retardation and Developmental Disabilities* 32 (1997), 4. 304-312

McNeill, J.T., *A history of the cure of souls.* (New York: Harper and Row, 1951/1977)

McNutt, P.M., *Reconstructing the society of Ancient Israel* (Louisville, KY: Westminster John Knox Press, 1999)

Mearns, D. and T. Thorne, *Person-centred counselling in action* (London: Sage, 1988/1999)

Meehl, P.E., 'When shall we use our heads instead of the fomulas?' *Journal of Counselling Psychology* 4 (1957), 268-273

Meeks, W.A., *The first urban Christians: The social world of the Apostle Paul* (Newhaven: Yale University Press, 1983)

Mellor, P.A. and C. Shilling, *Re-forming the body: Religion, community and modernity* (London: Sage Publications, 1997)

Melnick, G. and G. de Leon, 'Clarifying the nature of therapeutic community treatment: A survey of essential elements questionnaire (SEEQ).' *Journal of Substance Abuse Treatment* 16 (1999), 4. 307-313

Mendenhall, G., 'The Hebrew conquest of Palestine', *Biblical Archaeologist* 25 (1962), 66-87

Menninger, K., *What ever happened to sin?* (New York: Bantum Books, 1988)

Mental Health Foundation, *Taken seriously: The Somerset spirituality project* (London: 2002)

Merton, T., *The ascent to truth* (London: Hollis & Carter, 1951)

---, *The new man* (New York: Farrar, Strauss & Giroux, 1961)

---, *New seeds of contemplation* (New York: New Directions Book, 1961/1972)

---, *Life and holiness* (New York: Doubleday/Image Books, 1963/1996)

---, *The way of Chuang Tzu* (New York: New Directions Books, 1965)

---, *Zen and the birds of appetite* (New York: New Directions Book, 1968)

Meye, R.P., 'Spirituality' in Hawthorne, G.D. and R.P. Martin (eds.), *Dictionary of Paul and his letters* (Leicester: InterVarsity Press, 1993) p. 765

Meyendorff, J., *Byzantine theology: historical trends and doctinal themes* (New York: Fordham University Press, 1974)

Meyers, C., *Discovering Eve: Ancient Israelite women in context* (New York: Oxford University Press, 1988)

---, 'The family in Early Israel' in Perdue, L.G. (ed.), *Families in Ancient Israel*: Westminster John Knox Press, 1997) pp. 1-47

Middlemiss, D., *Interpreting charismatic experience* (London: SCM Press, 1996)

Miles, M., 'Fragmentation and wholeness in Western culture', *Modern Church Peoples Union* 37 (1996), 4. 2-8

Millard, A., 'Literacy in the times of Jesus', *Biblical Archaeology Review* 29 (2003), 4. 37-45

Miller, H., *Christian community: Biblical or optional* (Ann Arbor, MI: Servant Books, 1979)

Miller, J.P., *Education and the soul: Toward a spiritual curriculum* (Albany: State University of New York Press, 2000)

Miller, S., et al., *Connecting with self and others* (Colorado: Interpersonal Communications Programs Inc, 1988)

Miller, W.E., *Forgiveness, the power and the puzzles* (Warsaw, Indiana: Clearbrook
     Publishers, 1994)
Miller, W.R., 'Spirituality: The silent dimension in addiction research. The 1990
     Leonard Ball Oration', *Drug and Alcohol Review* 9 (1990), 259-266
---, 'Researching the spiritual dimension of alcohol and other drug problems', *Addictions*
     93 (1998), 7. 979-990
--- (ed.), *Integrating spirituality into treatment: Resources for practitioners*
     (Washington DC: American Psychological Assocation, 1999)
Miller, W.R. and C.E. Thoresen, 'Spirituality and Health' in *Integrating Spirituality into
     Treatment: Resources for Practitioners* (Washington DC: American
     Psychological Assocation, 1999) pp. 3-18
Miller-McLemore, B.J., 'Thinking theologically about modern medicine', *Journal of
     Religion and Health* 30 (1991), 4. 287-298
Minar, D.W. and S. Greer, *The concept of community: Readings with interpretations*
     (Chicago: Aldine Publishing Company, 1969)
Mitchell, S.A., *Relational concepts in psychoanalysis: An integration* (Cambridge, MA:
     Harvard University Press, 1988)
Mitroff, I.I. and E.A. Dentron, *A spiritual audit of corporate America: A hard look at
     spirituality, religion and values in the workplace* (San Fransisco: Jossey-Bass,
     1999)
Moeller, C., 'Renewal of the doctrine of man' in Shook, L.K. (ed.) *Renewal of religious
     structures* Vol. 2 of 2 (Montreal: Palm Publishing, 1968)
Moir, A. and B. Jessel, *Brain Sex* (London: Michael Joseph, 1989)
Moltmann, J., *The crucified God: The cross of Christ as the foundation and criticism of
     Christian theology* (London: SCM Press, 1974)
---, *History and the Triune God: Contributions to Trinitarian theology* (London: SCM
     Press, 1991)
Moncrieff, J., *Is psychiatry for sale?: An examination of the influence of the
     pharmaceutical industry on academic and practical psychiatry* (London: Institute
     of Psychiatry, 2003)
Monlar, P.D., 'Barth, Karl (1886-1968)' in Hart, T.A. (ed.), *Dictionary of historical
     theology* (Carlisle: Paternoster, 2000) pp. 53-58
Moon, G.W., 'A personal journey to spiritually sensitive psychotherapy: An interview
     with David G. Benner', *Journal of Psychology and Christianity* 21 (2002), 1. 64-
     71
Morris, B., *Western conceptions of the individual* (Oxford: Berg, 1991)
Morris, R.C., *The family as the foundation for effective leadership in the church* Master
     of Divinity thesis (International School of Theology, Portland, Oregon, 1990)
Moseley, R.M., *Becoming a self before God: Critical transformations* (Nashville:
     Abingdon Press, 1991)
Moynagh, M., *Changing world, changing church: New forms of church, out of pew
     thinking, initiatives at work.* (London: Monarch Books, 2001)
Muller, M., *The first Bible of the church: A plea for the Septuagint.* (Sheffield: Sheffield
     Academic Press, 1996)

Murray, J., *Collected writings of John Murray* Vol. 2 (Edinburgh: Banner of Truth Trust, 1977)

Myers, D.G., 'The funds, friends and faith of happy people', *American Psychologist* 55 (2000), 1. 56-67

Myss, C., *Anatomy of the spirit: 7 stages of power and healing* (New York: Three Rivers Press, 1996)

Nardin, G., *The open family: The vision of the early church* (London: New City, 1996)

Narramore, C., *The psychology of counselling: Professional techniques for pastors, teachers, youth leaders and all who are engaged in the incomparable art of counselling* (Grand Rapids: Zondervan Publishing House, 1960)

Nash, R.H. (ed.), *On process theology* (Grand Rapids: Baker House, 1987)

Neusner, J., *From politics to piety: The emergence of Pharaisaic Judaism* (New York: KTAV, 1979)

Newlands, G.M., *Theology of the love of God* (London: Collins, 1980)

Nichols, B., 'The picture of health: Liturgical metaphors of wholeness and healing', *Studies in Christian Ethics* 15 (2003), 1. 40-53

Niebuhr, H.R., *The nature and destiny of man* Vol. 1 *Human nature* (London: Nisbet & Co. Ltd, 1943a)

---, *The nature and destiny of man* Vol. 2 *Human destiny* (London: Nisbet & Co. Ltd, 1943b)

---, *The responsible self* (New York: Harper & Row, 1978)

Nisbet, R.A., *The quest for community* (London: Oxford University Press, 1953/1969)

Nock, A.D., *Conversion: The old and the new in religion from Alexander the Great to Augustine of Hippo* (Oxford: Oxford University Press, 1933/1972)

Noffke, S., "Soul" in Downey, M. (ed.), *The new Catholic dictionary of spirituality* (Minnesota: Liturgical Press, 1993) pp. 908-910

Norris Clarke, W.S.J., *Person and being* (Milwaukee: Marquette University Press, 1993)

---, *Explorations in metaphysics* (Notre Dame: University of Notre Dame Press, 1994)

North, M., *The secular priests* (London: George Allen & Unwin Ltd, 1968)

Nouwen, H.J.M., *The three movements of the spiritual life* (London: Collins, 1975)

Nygren, A., *Agape & Eros* (London: SPCK., 1932/1982)

O'Connell, B., *Solution-focused therapy* (London: Sage, 1998)

O'Connor, T.J.e.a., 'Review of quantity and types of spirituality research in three health care databases (1962-1999): Implications for the health care ministry', *Journal of Pastoral Care & Counselling* 56 (2002), 3. 227-232

O'Connor, T.S.J., 'Pastoral counselling and pastoral care: Is there a difference?' *Journal of Pastoral Care and Counselling* 57 (2003), 1. 3-14

O'Donnell, J.J., *Trinity and temporality: The Christian doctrine of God in the light of process theology and the theology of hope* (Oxford: Oxford University Press, 1983)

O'Halloran, J., *Living cells: Developing small Christian community* (Dublin: Dominican Publications, 1984)

O'Murchu, D., *Quantum theology* (New York: Crossroads, 1997)

---, *Religion in Exile: A spiritual vision for the homeward bound* (Dublin: Gateway, 2000)

Oatley, K. and J.M. Jenkins, *Understanding emotions* (Oxford: Blackwell, 1996)

Oden, T.C., 'Recovering lost identity', *Journal of Pastoral Care* 1 (1980), 4-18.

---, 'Theology and therapy: A new look at Bonhoeffer' in Newton Maloney, H. (ed.), *Wholeness and holiness: readings in the psychology/theology of mental health* (Grand Rapids: Baker Book House, 1983) pp. 199-222

---, *Pastoral counsel* (New York: Crossroads, 1989)

---, 'The historic pastoral care tradition: A resource for Christian psychologists', *Journal of Psychology and Theology* 20 (1992), 2. 137-146

---, *Systematic theology* Vol. 3 of 4 *Life in the spirit* (Peabody, MA: Harper Collins Paperback, 1994/1998)

Oesterley, W.O.E., *The Jews and Judaism during the Greek Period: The background of Christianity* (London: SPCK., 1941)

Ogden, S.M., *The reality of God and other essays* (London: SCM Press, 1967)

Orchard, H. (ed.), *Spirituality in health care contexts* (London: Jessica Kingsley, 2001)

Ormerod, N., 'Wrestling with Rahner on the Trinity', *Irish Theological Quarterly* 69 (2003), 213-227

Orr, J., *God's image in man* (London: Hodder & Stoughton, 1906)

Orthberg, J., 'Rethinking the kingdom of God: the work of Dallas Willard and some applications to psychotherapeutic practice', *Journal of Psychology and Christianity* 14 (1995), 4. 306-317

Osborn, L., *Angels of light: The challenge of the New Age* (London: Darton Longman and Todd, 1992)

Osborne, C.G., *The art of learning to love yourself* (Grand Rapids: Zondervan, 1976)

Osiek, C., *What are they saying about the social settings of the New Testament?* (New York: Paulist Press, 1992)

Osiek, C. and D.L. Balch, *Families in the New Testament world* (Louisville, Kentucky: Westminster John Knox Press, 1997)

Otto, R., *The idea of the holy* (London: Pelican, 1917/1959)

Ottoson, M., 'The Iron Age of Northern Jordan' in Lemaire, A. (ed.), *History and traditions of Early Israel: Studies presented to Eduard Nielsen, May 8th 1993* (Leiden: E.J. Brill, 1993) pp. 90-103

Outhwaite, W., *Habermas: A critical introduction* (Cambridge: Polity Press, 1994/1996)

Overman, J.A., *Matthew's gospel and formative Judaism: The social world of the Matthean community* (Minneapolis: Fortress Press, 1990)

Owen, J., *Works* Vol. 16 Goold, W.H. (ed.), (Edinburgh: T&T Clark, 1862)

Owens, J., *An elementary Christian metaphysics* (Milwaukee: The Bruce Publishing Co., 1963)

Ozarowski, J.S., *Jewish pastoral theology and care at life's crisis points: Illness and grief (pastoral care)* Dissertation (Lancaster Theological Seminary, USA, 1992)

Panksepp, J. and J.B. Panksepp, 'The seven sins of evolutionary psychology', *Evolution and Cognition* 6 (2000), 2. 108-131

Pannenberg, W., *Christian spirituality and sacramental community* (London: Darton Longman & Todd, 1984)

Paranjpe, A.C., 'Style over substance: The loss of personhood in theories of personality' in Smythe, W.E. (ed.), *Toward a psychology of persons* (Mahwah, NJ: Lawrence Erlbaum Associates, 1998) pp. 49-71

Parkes, C.M., *Bereavement* (Harmondsworth: Penguin, 1972)

Pasnau, R., *Thomas Aquinas on human nature: A philosophical study of Summa theologiae 1a 75-89* (Cambridge: Cambridge University Press, 2002)

Passons, W.R., *Gestalt approaches in counselling* (New York: Holt, Rinehart and Winston, 1975)

Pattison, S., *Alive and kicking* (London: SCM Press, 1989)

Paul, L., *The deployment and payment of the clergy* (London: Church Information Office, 1964)

Peacocke, A. and G.R. Gillett (eds.), *Persons and personality: A contemporary enquiry* (Oxford: Blackwell, 1987)

Peck, M.S., *The road less travelled: A new psychology of love, traditional values and spiritual growth* (New York: Simon and Schuster, 1978/1990)

---, *The different drum: Community-making and peace* (New York: Simon & Schuster, 1987)

Pedersen, J., *Israel: Its life and culture* Vol. 1 (London: Oxford University Press, 1926)

---, *Israel: Its life and culture* Vol. 2 (London: Oxford University Press, 1946)

Peels, E., *Shadow sides: The revelation of God in the Old Testament* Lalleman, H. (tr.) (Carlisle: Paternoster Press, 2002)

Pelham, G., et al., 'A relational model of counselling' in British Association of Counselling Psychologists (ed.), *British Association of Counselling Psychologists Counselling Reader* 2001) pp. 113-118

Pennebaker, J.W., ' Emotion disclosure and health - an overview' in Pennebaker, J.W. (ed.), *Emotion disclosure and health* (Washington DC: American Psychological Association, 1995) pp. 3-10

Pennington, M.B., *A retreat With Thomas Merton* (New York: Amity House, 1988)

Perdue, L.G., 'The household, Old Testament theology and contemporary hermeneutics.' in Perdue, L.G. (ed.), *Families in Ancient Israel* (Louisville: Westminster John Knox Press, 1997) pp. 223-258

Perls, F.S., et al., *Gestalt therapy* (Harmondsworth: Penguin Books, 1951/1977)

Perry, C., *Listen to the Voice Within: A Jungian approach to pastoral care* (London: SPCK, 1991)

Perry, M., *God's within* (London: SPCK, 1992)

Pervin, L.A., *Personality: Theory, assessment and research* (New York: John Wiley & Son, 1984)

Peterson, E.H., *The message: The Bible in contemporary language* (Colorado Springs: Navpress, 2002)

van Peursen, C.A., *Body, soul, spirit: A survey of the body-mind problem* Hoskins, H.H. (tr.) (London: Oxford University Press, 1966)

Phares, E.J. and T.J. Trull, *Clinical psychology: Concepts, methods and profession*
(Pacific Grove: Brooks/Cole Publishing Co., 1997)

Philip, J., *Christian maturity* (London: IVP, 1964/73)

Phillips, K., *The making of a disciple* (Eastbourne: Kingsway, 1981)

Piaget, J., *The language and thought of the child* (New York: Harcourt Brace,
1926/1956)

---, 'Piaget's theory' in Mussen, P.H. (ed.), *Carmichael's manual of child psychology*
(New York: Wiley, 1970)

---, *The development of thought: Equilibration of cognitive structures* Rosin, A. (tr.)
(New York: Viking, 1977)

Pilgrim, D. and A. Rogers, *A sociology of mental health and illness* (Buckingham,
Philadephia: Open University Press, 1993)

Pingleton, J.P., 'A model of relational maturity' in Aden, L., et al. (eds.), *Christian
perspectives on human development* (Grand Rapids:: Baker Book House, 1992)
pp. 101-113

Pinnock, C., *The openness of God: A Biblical challenge to the traditional understanding
of God* (Downers Grove, IL: IVP, 1994)

---, *Most moved mover: A theology of God's openness* (Grand Rapids: Baker, 2001)

Pinnock, C.H., *Reason enough: The case for the Christian faith* (Exeter: Paternoster
Press, 1980)

Plaskow, J., 'Transforming the nature of community: Towards a feminist people of
Israel' in Bach, A. (ed.), *Women in the Hebrew Bible* (New York: Routledge,
1999) pp. 403-418

Pocock, N., *Amnon & Tamor: The conseqeunces of evil and the extent of personal
responsibility*: Self-published, 2001)

Podles, L., *The church impotent: The feminisation of Christianity* (Dallas: Spence
Publishing Company, 1999)

Pomeroy, S.B., *Goddesses, whores, wives, slaves: Women in classical antiquity* (New
York: Schocken Books, 1976)

Popkes, W., 'New Testament principles of wholeness: (and spiritual growth)',
Evangelical Quarterly 64 (1992), 319-332

Porter, J.R., 'The legal aspects of the concept of 'corporate personality' in the Old
Testament', *Vetus testamentum* 15 (1965), 361-380

Porterfield, A., 'Healing in the history of Christianity: A presidential address, January
2002, to the American Society of Church History', *Journal of the American
Society of Church History* 71 (2002), 2. 227-242

Pratney, W., *Handbook for followers of Jesus* (Minneapolis: Bethany House Publishers,
1975/1977)

Prestige, G.L., *God in patristic thought* (London: SPCK, 1936/1952)

Preuss, H.D., *Old Testament theology* Vol. 2 (Edinburgh: T&T Clark, 1996)

Puntel, L.B., 'Spirit' in Darlap, A., et al. (eds.) *Sacramentum Mundi: An encyclopaedia
of theology* Vol. 5 (London: Burns & Oates, 1970) p. 143

Purton, A.C., 'Unconditional positive regard and its spiritual implications' in Thorne, B. and E. Lambers (eds.), *Person centred therapy: A European perspective* (London: Sage, 1998) pp. 23-37

Puttick, E., *Personal development: The spiritualisation and secularisation of the human potential movement* (Edinburgh: Edinburgh University Press, 2000)

Quinn, R.E., *Deep change: Discovering the leader within* (San Fransisco, CA: Jossey-Bass, 1996)

Rabinow, P. (ed.), *The Foucault Reader* (New York: Pantheon, 1984)

Rahner, K., *Hominisation - The evolutionary origin of man as a theological problem* (Burns & Oates: London, 1958)

---, *Theological investigations* Vol. 1 *God Christ Mary and Grace* (London: Darton Longman & Todd, 1961/1974)

---, *Nature and grace* (London: Sheed & Ward, 1963)

---, 'The concept of mystery in Catholic theology' in Rahner, K. (ed.) *Theological Investigations* Vol. 4 (New York: Seabury Press, 1966/1974) p. 37ff.

---, *Spirit in the world* (London: Sheed & Ward, 1968)

---, 'Anonymous Christians' in Rahner, K. (ed.), *Concerning Vatican Council II* Karl, H. and B. Kruger (tr.) (London: Darton, Longman & Todd, 1969) pp. 390-398

---, *Theological Investigations* Vol. 6 *Concerning Vatican Council II* Karl, H. and B. Kruger (tr.) (London: Darton, Longman & Todd, 1969/1974)

---, *The Trinity* (London: Burn & Oates, 1970)

---, *Foundations of Christian faith: An introduction to the idea of Christianity* Dych, W.V. (tr.) (New York: Seabury, 1978a)

---, 'Mystery' in Darlap, A., et al. (eds.) *Sacramentum Mundi: An encyclopaedia of theology* Vol. 4 of 6 (London: Burns & Oates, 1978b) pp. 133-136

---, *Hearers of the Word* Donceel, J. (tr.) (New York: Continuum Publishing Company., 1994)

Raitt, J. (ed.), *Christian spirituality II: High Middle Ages and Reformation* World Spirituality Series (New York: Routledge & Kegan Paul, 1988)

Rapoport, R.N., *Community as doctor: New perspectives on a therapeutic community* (London: Tavistock Publishing, 1959)

Rapport, N., ''Community' in current use' in Barnard, A.S., J. (ed.), *Encyclopedia of social and cultural anthropology* (London: Routledge, 1996/2000) pp. 136-143

Rapport, N. and A. Dawson, 'Home and movement' in Rapport, N. and A. Dawson (eds.), *Migrants of identity: Perceptions of home in a world of movement* (Oxford: Berg, 1998) pp. 19-38

Rasmussen, L.L., *Moral fragments and moral community: A proposal for church in society* (Minneapolis: Fortress Press, 1993)

Raub, J.J., *Who told you that you were naked? Freedom from judgment, guilt and fear of punishment* (Slough: St Paul Publications, 1992)

Rauschenbusch, W., *A theology for a social gospel* (New York: Macmillan, 1917)

Ravensborg, I., 'The inpatient care of families at Vikersund' in Kaslow, F. (ed.), *The international book of family therapy* (New York: Brunnel/Mazel, 1982)

Rebillot, P., 'The hero's journey: Ritualizing the mystery' in Grof, S. and C. Grof (eds.), *Spiritual emergency: When personal transformation becomes a crisis* (New York: Penguin Putnam Inc, 1989) pp. 211-224

Regan, D., *Experience the mystery - Pastoral possibilities for Christian mystagogy.* (London: Geoffrey Chapman., 1994)

de Regnon, T., *Edudes de theologie positive sur la Sainte Trinite* (Paris 1893)

Reich, W., *Character analysis* (New York: Orgone Institute Press, 1949)

Reichenbach, B.R., 'By his stripes we are healed', *Journal of the Evangelical Theological Society* 41 (1998), 4. 551-560

Reid, M.A., 'Sanctification' in Atkinson, D.J. and D.H. Field (eds.), *New dictionary of Christian ethics & pastoral theology* (Leicester: IVP, 1995) pp. 756-757

Religious Education Association, *Faith development in the adult life cycle: The report of a research project prepared for the Religious Education Association of the USA and 22 partner organizations, sponsors of the project* (Minneapolis: Religious Education Association, 1987)

Reuther, R., *Liberation theology: Human hope confronts Christian history and American power* (New York: Paulist Press, 1972)

Richard of St Victor, *De trinitate* (Paris: Les Editions du Cerf, 1959)

Richards, P.S. and A.E. Bergin, *A Spiritual Strategy for Counselling and Psychotherapy* (Washington: American Psychological Association, 1997)

Rist, J., 'On Greek biology, Greek cosmology and some sources of theological pneuma' in Dockrill, D.W. and R.G. Tanner (eds.), *The concept of spirit: Prudentia supplementary* 1985) pp. 27-47

Rist, J.M., *Man soul and body: Essays in Ancient thought from Plato to Dionysius* (Aldershot: Variorum, 1996)

Robb, J.H., *Man as infinite spirit* (Milwaukee: Marquette University Publications, 1974)

Robbins, J. (ed.), *Is it righteous to be? Interviews with Emmanuel Levinas* (Stanford, CA: Stanford University Press, 2001)

Roberts, L., *The achievement of Karl Rahner* (New York: Herder & Herder, 1967)

Roberts, R.E., *The new communes: Coming together in America* (New Jersey: Prentice-Hall Inc., 1971)

Robinson, J.A.T., *The body: A study in Pauline theology* (London: SCM Press, 1952)

---, *On Being The Church in the World* (London: SCM Press, 1960)

Robinson, M., 'From a consultants desk: Spirituality and mission, a voice for the voiceless', *The Church Growth Digest* 22 (2001), 3. 11-12

Robinson, T.H., *Palestine in general history: The Schweich Lectures of 1926* (Oxford: Oxford University Press, 1929)

Rodd, C.S., 'On applying sociological theory to Biblical studies' in Chalcraft, D.J. (ed.), *Social scientific Old Testament criticism* (Sheffield: Sheffield Academic Press, 1997) pp. 22-33

Rogers, C.R., 'Significant aspects of client-centred therapy', *American Psychologist* 1 (1946), 420-421

---, *Client-centered therapy* (Boston: Houghton Mifflin Co., 1951)

---, *On becoming a person: A therapist's view of psychotherapy* (New York: Houghton Mifflin Co., 1961/1995)

Rogers, T.B., 'The look of depersonalization: Visual rhetoric in personality textbook covers' in Smythe, W.E. and e. al. (eds.), *Toward a psychology of persons* (Mahwah, NJ: Lawrence Erlbaum Associates, 1998) pp. 145-175

Rogerson, J., 'Epilogue' in Rogerson, J. (ed.), *The Oxford illustrated history of the Bible.* (Oxford: Oxford University Press, 2001) p. 362ff.

Rogerson, J.W., 'The Hebrew conception of corporate personality (A Re-examination)' in Lang, B. (ed.), *Anthropological approaches to the Old Testament* (London: SPCK, 1985) pp. 43-59

Roof, W.C., *Spiritual marketplace: Baby-boomers and the remaking of American religion* (Princeton, NJ: Princeton University Press, 1999)

Roosens, E., *Mental patients in town Life: Geel - Europe's first therapeutic community* (Beverly Hills: Sage Publications, 1979)

Rose, S., 'The rise of neurogenetic determinism' in Cornwell, J. and e. al. (eds.), *Consciousness and human Identity* (New York: Oxford University Press, 1998) pp. 86-100

Rosenblatt, A., 'Concepts of the asylum in the care of the mentally ill', *Hospital and Community Psychiatry* 35 (1984), 244-250

Rosenthal, M.S., 'Therapeutic communities' in Glass, I.B. (ed.), *The international handbook of addiction behaviour* (London: Tavistock Routledge, 1991)

Ross, A., *Evangelicals in exile: Wrestling with theology and the unconscious* (London: Darton, Longman and Todd, 1997)

Rossi, J.J. and W.J. Filstead (eds.), *The therapeutic community: A sourcebook of readings* (New York: Behavioural Publications, 1973)

Rowlett, L., 'Inclusion, exclusion and marginality in the book of Joshua' in Chalcraft, D.J. (ed.), *Social scientific Old Testament criticism* (Sheffield: Sheffield Academic Press, 1997) pp. 372-380

Russell, B., *A history of Western philosophy* (London: Unwin, 1946/1979)

Ryle, A. (ed.), *Cognitive analytical therapy: developments in theory and practice* (Chichester: J.Wiley & Sons, 1995a)

---, 'Difficult transferrence in the practice of CAT' in Ryle, A. (ed.), *Cognitive analytical therapy: developments in theory and practice* (Chichester: J.Wiley & Sons, 1995b) pp. 23-53

Sandbach, F.H., *The Stoics* (London: Chatto & Windus Ltd, 1975)

Sanders, J.N., 'The meaning and authority of the New Testament' in Vidler, A.R. (ed.), *Soundings* (Cambridge: Cambridge University Press, 1962)

Sanders, J.O., *The best that I can be* (London: OMF, 1965/1971)

---, *In pursuit of maturity* (Eastbourne: Kingsway Publications, 1985)

---, *Spiritual discipleship* (Chicago: Moody Press, 1990/1994)

---, *Problems of Christian discipleship* (London: Lutterworth Press, undated c.1945)

Sanford, J.A., *Dreams and healing: A succinct and lively interpretation of dreams* (New York: Paulist Press, 1978)

Sanford, M.J., *Principles of spiritual growth* (Lincoln, Nebraska: Back to the Bible, 1979)

Santos, A. and R.D. Hinshelwood, 'The use at the Cassel of the organisational dynamics to enhance the therapeutic work', *Therapeutic Communities* 19 (1998), 1. 29-39

Schadel, E. (ed.), *Biblitheca trinitariorum: The international bibliography of Trinitarian theology* (London: K.G. Saur, 1984)

Schaeffer, F.A., *True spirituality* (London: Hodder & Stoughton, 1972)

Schaeffer, F.A. and U. Middlemann, *Pollution and the death of man* (Wheaton, IL: Crossroad Books, 1970)

Schaller, L.E., *21 bridges to the 21st century* (Nashville: Abingdon Press, 1994)

Schermer, V.L., *Spirit and psyche: A new paradigm for psychology, psychoanalysis and psychotherapy* (London: Jessica Kingsley, 2003)

Schindler, F., et al., 'How the public perceive psychiatrists, psychologists, nonpsychiatric physicians and members of the clergy', *Professional Psychology Research and Practice* 18 (1987), 371-376.

Schippers, R., 'Telos' in Brown, C. (ed.) *The new international dictionary of New Testament theology.* Vol. 2 of 3 (Exeter: Paternoster Press, 1971) pp. 59-65

Schlink, M.B., *Repentance: The joy-filled life* (Darmstadt: Kanaan Publications, 1992)

Schmemann, A., *Church, world, mission* (Crestwood, NY: St Vladimir's Seminary Press, 1979)

Schneiders, S.M., 'Theology and spirituality: Strangers, rivals or partners', *Horizons* 13 (1986), 2. 253-274

---, 'Spirituality as an academic discipline: Reflections from experience', *Christian Spirituality Bulletin* 1 (1993), 2. 10-15

---, 'The study of Christian spirituality: Contours and dynamics...' *Christian Spirituality Bulletin* 6 (1998), 1. 1-12

Schrag, C.O., *The self after post-modernity* (Newhaven: Yale University Press, 1997)

Schultheis, G.M., *Brief therapy homework planner* (New York: John Wiley & Sons Inc, 1998)

Schwandt, T.A., 'Constructivist, interpretivist approaches to human enquiry' in Denzin, N.K. and Y.S. Lincoln (eds.), *The landscape of qualitative research* (London: Sage, 2003) pp. 221-259

Schwartz, R.C., 'Releasing the soul: Psychotherapy as a spiritual practice' in Walsh, F. (ed.), *Spiritual Resources in Family Therapy* (New York: Guilford Publications, 1999)

Schwarz, C.A., *Natural church development: A guide to 8 essential qualities of healthy churches* (Emmelsbull: C&P Verlags, Germany, 1996)

Schwarz, C.A. and C. Schalk, *Natural church development implementation manual* (Moggerhanger: British Church Growth Association., 1997)

Schwobel, C., 'Human being as relational being: Twelve theses for a Christian anthropology' in Schwobel, C. and C. Gunton (eds.), *Persons, divine and human* (Edinburgh: T&T Clark, 1991a) pp. 141-165

---, 'Introduction' in Schwobel, C. and C. Gunton (eds.), *Persons, divine and human* (Edinburgh: T&T Clark, 1991b) pp. 1-29

---, *God: Action and revelation* (Kampen 1992)

Schwobel, C. and C.E. Gunton, *Persons, divine and human: Kings College essays in theological anthropology* (Edinburgh: T&T Clark, 1991)

Scirghi, T.J., 'The Trinity: A model for belonging in contemporary society', *The Ecumenical Review* 54 (2002), 3. 333-342

Scott, J.J., *Jewish backgrounds of the New Testament* (Grand Rapids, Michigan: Baker Books, 1995/2000)

Scott, R.P. and E.B. Allen, *A spiritual stragegy for counselling and psychotherapy* (Washington DC: American Psychological Association, 1997)

Scripture Union, *Christian life and today's world: not conformed but transformed* (London: Scripture Union, 2002)

Seeber, J., 'Pathogenic/salugenic faith and integrative wellness', *Journal of Religious Gerontology* 13 (2001), 2. 69-81

Segundo, J.L., *The community called church* (New York: Orbis Books, 1968/1973)

Shafranske, E.P. (ed.), *Religion and the clinical practice of psychology* (Washington, DC: American Psychological Association, 1996)

Shafranske, E.P. and H. Newton Maloney, 'Religion and the clinical practice of psychology: A case for inclusion' in Shafranske, E.P. (ed.), *Religion and the clinical practice of psychology.* (Washington, DC: American Psychological Association, 1996) pp. 561-586

Shanks, A., 'The solidarity of the shaken' in von Harskamp, A. and A. Musschenga (eds.), *The many faces of individualism* (Leuven: Peeters, 2001) pp. 185-196

Shanks, H., 'Dancing in Denver', *Biblical Archaeology Review* 28 (2002), 2. 36ff.

de Shazer, S., 'Brief therapy with families', *American Journal of Family Therapy* 7 (1979), 2. 83-95

Shedd, R.P., *Man In community: A study of St Pauls application of Old Testament and Early Jewish conceptions of human solidarity* (London: Epworth Press, 1958)

Sheldrake, P., 'Teaching spirituality', *British Journal of Theological Education* 12 (2001), 1. 53-64

Shelton, R.L., *Divine expectations: Interpreting the atonement for 21st century mission* publication in process)

Shenker, B., *Intentional communities: Ideology and alienation in communal societies* (London: Routledge & Kegan Paul, 1986)

Sheriffs, D., *The friendship of the Lord* (Carlisle: Paternoster, 1996)

Sherrill, L.J., *Family and church* (New York: Abingdon Press, 1937)

Shiloh, Y., 'Four-room house', *Israeli Expeditions Journal* 20 (1970), 180

Shotter, J., 'Resurrecting people in academic psychology: A celebration of the ordinary' in Smythe, W.E. (ed.), *Toward a psychology of persons* (New Jersey: Lawrence Erlbaum Associates, 1998) pp. 245-271

Siegel, B., 'Healing of the spirit and curing of the body', *Studies in Formative Spirituality* 12 (1991), 143-147

Simmons, O.E., 'Grounded therapy' in Glaser, B.G. (ed.), *More grounded theory: A reader* (Mill Valley, CA: Sociology Press, 1994) pp. 4-37

Sine, T., *Wild hope: A wake up call to the challenges and opportunities of the 21st century* (Tonbridge Wells: Monarch, 1991)

Sinnott, E.W., *The biology of the spirit* (New York: Viking Pres, 1955)

Sisemore, T.A., 'St Augustine's confessions and the use of introspective counseling', *Journal of Psychology and Christianity* 20 (2001), 4. 324-331

Skarsaune, O., *In the shadow of the Temple: Jewish influences on early Christianity* (Downers Grove, IL: InterVarsity Press, 2002)

Smail, T.A., 'In the image of the Triune God', *International Journal of Systematic Theology* 5 (2003), 1. 22-32

Smart, N., *Religious experience of mankind* (New York: Fontana, 1971)

Smedes, *Sex in the real world* (Tring, Herts: Lion Publishing, 1976)

Smith, H., *Forgotten truth: The common vision of the religions* (San Fransisco: Harper, 1992)

Smith, M.L. and G.V. Glass, 'Meta-analysis of psychotherapy outcome studies', *American Psychologist* 32 (1977), 752-760

Smith, M.L., et al., *The benefits of psychotherapy* (Baltimore: John Hopkins Press, 1980)

Smythe, W.E., 'Folk psychology and the concept of person' in Smythe, W.E. (ed.), *Toward a Psychology of Persons* (New Jersey: Lawrence Erlbaum Associates, 1998a) pp. 23-40

--- (ed.), *Toward a psychology of persons* (New Jersey: Lawrence Erlbaum Associates, 1998b)

Snaith, N.H., *Distinctive ideas of the Old Testament* (London: Epworth Press, 1974)

Snyder, H.A., *The problem of wineskins: Church structure in a theological age* (Downers Grove: IVP, 1975)

---, *The community of the king* (Downers Grove: IVP, 1977)

---, *Liberating the church: The ecology of church and kingdom* (Pasedena: Wipf & Stock Publishers, 1996a)

---, *Radical renewal: The problem of wineskins today* (Houston: Touch Publications, 1996b)

---, *The radical Wesley and patterns for church renewal* (Eugene, Oregon: Wipf & Stock Publishers, 1996/1998)

Spence, A., 'Christ's humanity and ours: John Owen' in Schwobel, C. and C. Gunton (eds.), *Persons, divine and human* (Edinburgh: T&T Clark, 1991) pp. 74-97

Spencer, J., 'Ethnography after post-modernism' in Atkinson, P., et al. (eds.), *The handbook of ethnography* (London: Sage, 2001) pp. 443-452

Spezzano, C. and G.J. Garguilo (eds.), *Soul on the couch: Spirituality, religion and morality in contemporary psychoanalysis.* (Hillsdale, NJ: The Analytic Press, 1997)

Stafford Clark, D., 'The nature of the problem' in Mairet, P. (ed.), *Christian essays in psychiatry* (London: SCM Press, 1956) pp. 13-27

Stambaugh, J.E. and D.L. Balch, *The New Testament in its social environment* (Philadelphia: Westminster Press, 1986a)

---, *The social world of the first Christians* (London: SPCK, 1986b)

Stark, R., *The Rise of Christianity* (New Jersey: Princeton University Press, 1996)

Staub, E., *Positive social behaviour and morality* Vol. 1 *Social and personal influences* (New York: Academic Press, 1978)

---, *The psychology of good and evil* (Cambridge: Cambridge University Press, 2003)

Steele, L.L., *On the way: A practical theology of Christian formation* (Grand Rapids: Baker Book House, 1990)

Steere, D.A., *Spiritual presence in psychotherapy: A guide for care-givers* (New York: Brunner-Mazelle, 1997)

Stegemann, E.W. and W. Stegemann, *The Jesus movement: A social history of the first Christians* (Minneapolis: Fortree Press, 1999)

Steinberg, N., 'The Deuteronomic law code and the politics of state centralization' in Jobling, D.e.a. (ed.), *The Bible and the politics of exegesis* (Cleveland: Pilgrim Press, 1991) pp. 16-170, 336-338

Steinhoffsmith, R., 'Politics of pastoral care: An alternative politics of care' in Couture, P.D. and R.J. Hunter (eds.), *Pastoral care and social conflict: Essays in honor of Charles V. Gerkin* (Nashville: Abingdon Press, 1995) pp. 141-151

Stevens, R.P., *The abolition of the laity: Vocation, work and ministry in Biblical perspective* (Carlisle: Paternoster Press, 1999)

Stevenson, L., *Seven theories of human nature* (New York: Oxford University Press, 1974/1987)

---, *The study of human nature* (Oxford: Oxford University Press, 1981)

Stocker, M. and E. Hegeman, *Valuing emotions* (Cambridge: Cambridge University Press, 1996)

Stone, H.W. (ed.), *Brief pastoral counselling* (Minneapolis: Fortress Press, 1994)

--- (ed.), *Strategies for brief pastoral counselling* (Minneapolis: Augsberg Fortress Press, 2001)

Straus, M.A., *Family violence* HDFR (University of Conneticut, 1985)

Strauss, A.L. and J. Corbin, *Basics of Qualitative Research: Techniques and procedures for developing grounded theory* (Thousand Oaks: Sage Publications, 1998)

Strawson, P.F., *Individuals : An essay in descriptive Metaphysics* (London: Methuen, 1959)

Streiker, L., *New Age comes to mainstreet* (Nashville: Abingdon Press, 1990)

Strong, A.H., *Systematic theology: Three volumes in one.* (London: Pickering & Inglis., 1907/1962)

Studzinski, R., 'Psychology' in Komonchak, J., et al. (eds.), *New dictionary of theology* (Wilmington, Del.: Michael Glazier Inc., 1988) pp. 818-823

Stuhlmacher, P., *Der Brief an Philemon* (Zurich: Benzinger Neukirchen & Vluyn, 1981)

Sugden, C., *Radical discipleship* (London: Marshalls, 1981)

Swanston, H.F.G., *The community witness: An exploration of some of the influences at work in the New Testament community and its writings.* (London: Burns & Oates, 1967)

Swinton, J., *Spirituality and mental health care* (London: Jessica Kingsley, 2001)

Tan, S.-Y., 'Lay counselling: A Christian approach', *Journal of Psychology and Christianity* 13 (1994), 3. 246-269

Tanner, R.G., 'Early Greek origins of the idea of pneuma', *The concept of spirit.*
  Prudentia supplementary (1985), 49-53

Taylor, V., *Forgiveness and Reconciliation: A study in New Testament Theology*
  (London: Macmillan & Co. Ltd, 1956)

Teresa of Avila, *The interior castle or the mansions* (London: SCM Press, 1958)

Tertullian, *La pudicite (De pudicitia)* (Paris: Cerf, 1993)

Thiessen, G., *Psychological aspects of Pauline theology* (Edinburgh: T&T Clark, 1987)

Thomas, F.A., *Spiritual maturity: Preserving congregational health and balance*
  (MInneapolis: Fortress Press, 2002)

Thompson, J.H., *Spiritual considerations in the prevention, treatment and cure of*
  disease (Stockfield, Northumberland: Oriel Press, 1984)

Thoresen, C.E., 'Spirituality and health: Is there a relationship?' *Journal of Health*
  Psychology 4 (1999), 3. 291-300

Thorne, B., 'The prophetic nature of pastoral counselling', *British Journal of Guidance*
  and Counselling 29 (2001), 4. 435-446

Thwaites, J., *The church beyond the congregation: The strategic role of the church in*
  the postmodern era (Carlisle: Paternoster Press, 1999)

Tidball, D.J., 'Practical and pastoral theology' in Atkinson, D.J. and D.H. Field (eds.),
  New dictionary of Christian ethics & pastoral theology (Downers Grove: IVP,
  1995) pp. 42-48

Tidings, J., *Gathering a people* (Plainfield: Logos International, 1977)

Tillich, P., *The shaking of the foundations* (New York: C. Scribner's Sons, 1948)

---, *The courage to be* (Newhaven: Yale University Press, 1952)

---, *The new being* (New York 1955)

Tomlinson, D., *The post-evangelical* (London: SPCK., 1995)

Tonnies, F., *Community and association* Loomis, C.P. (tr.) (London: Routledge and
  Kegan Paul, 1887/1955)

Torrance, A.J., *Persons in communion: An essay on Trinitarian description and human*
  participation, with special reference to Volume 1 of Karl Barth's Church
  Dogmatics (Edinburgh: T&T Clark, 1996)

Torrance, T.F., *Theology in reconciliation* (London: Geoffrey Chapman, 1975)

---, *The Christian doctrine of God - One being three persons* (Edinburgh: T&T Clark,
  1996)

Torres, S. and J. Eagleson, *The challenge of basic Christian communities: Papers from*
  the International Ecumenical Congress of Theology, Feb 20-Mar 2, 1980, Sao
  Paulo, Brazil. (New York: Orbis Books, 1980)

Tournier, P., *The healing of persons* (Illinois: Good News Publishers, 1966)

Trautmann, R.L., 'Psychotherapy and spirituality', *Journal of Transactional Analysis* 33
  (2003), 1. 32-36

Trevarthen, C., 'Brain science and the human spirit' in Ashbrook, J.B.e.a. (ed.), *Brain*
  culture and the human spirit: Essays from an emergent evolutionary perspective
  (Lanham, MD: University Press of America, 1993) pp. 129-181

Trinkle, G., *Delivered to declare: Out of Satan's grip - one woman's powerful story of*
  deliverance (Sevenoaks: Hodder & Stoughton, 1986)

Tucker, R., *Another gospel: Cults, alternative religions and the New Age movement* (Grand Rapids: Zondervan, 1989a)

---, *Strange gospels: Comprehensive survey of cults, alternative religions and the New Age movement* (London: Marshall Pickering, 1989b)

Tuggy, D., 'The unfinished business of Trinitarian theorising', *Religious Studies* 39 (2003), 2. 165-183

Twelftree, G., *Jesus the exorcist: A contribution to the study of the historical Jesus* (Peabody, MA: Hendrickson, 1993)

Tyrrell, V.J., *Christotherapy: Healing through enlightenment* (New York: Paulist Press, 1975)

Underhill, E., *The spiritual life* (New York: Harper, 1936)

---, *The mystics of the church* (New York: Schocken Books, 1964)

Van Kaam, A., *On being yourself: Reflections on spirituality and originality* (Denville, NJ: Dimension Books, 1972)

---, *In search of spiritual identity* (Denville, NJ: Dimension Books, 1975)

---, *Fundamental formation* (New York: Crossroad, 1983)

Van Katwyk, P.L., 'Pastoral counselling as a spiritual practice: An exercise in the theology of spirituality', *Journal of Pastoral Care and Counselling* 56 (2002), 2. 109-119

Vanier, J., *Community and growth* (New York: Paulist Press, 1979)

Vanstone, W.H., *Love's endeavour, love's expense: A response of being to the love of God* (London: Darton, Longman & Todd, 1977/1993)

Vanzetti, N. and S.W. Duck (eds.), *A lifetime of relationships* (Pacific Grove, CA: Brooks/Cole, 1996)

Vattimo, G., *After Christianity* (New York: Columbia University, 2002)

Via, D.O., *Self-deception and wholeness in Paul and Matthew* (Minneapolis: Fortress Press, 1990)

di Vito, R.A., 'Old Testament anthropology and the construction of personal identity', *The Catholic Biblical Quarterly* 61 (1999), 217-238

Vitz, P.C., 'A Christian theory of personality' in Burke, T. (ed.), *Man and mind* (Hillsdale, MI: Hillsdale College Press, 1987) pp. 192-222

Vitz, P.C. and P. Mango, 'Hatred and forgiveness: Major moral dilemmas' in Dubois, J.M. (ed.), *Moral issues in psychology: Personalist contributions to selected problems* (Lanham, NY: University Press of American, 1997) pp. 67-77

Vitz, P.E., *Psychology as religion - The cult of self-worship* (Carlisle: Paternoster, 1977/1994)

Volf, M., *Exclusion and embrace: A theological exploration of identity, otherness and reconciliation* (Nashville: Abingdon Press, 1996)

---, *After our likeness: The church as the image of the Trinity* (Grand Rapids: Erdmans, 1998a)

---, 'The Trinity is our social programme: The doctrine of the Trinity and the shape of social engagement', *Modern Theology* 14 (1998b),

Wallis, J., 'Rebuilding the church', *Sojourners* 9 (1980), 1. 10-15

Walrond-Skinner, S., 'Pastoral care: The church's essential task', *Modern Believing* 43 (2002), 1. 3-11

Walton, R.C., *The gathered community* (London: Carey Press, 1946)

Wansey, C., *The clockwork church: Reform in the Church of England at worm's eye level* (Oxford: Becket Publications, 1978/1987)

Ware, K., 'The unity of the human person according to the Greek Fathers' in Peacocke, A. and G. Gillett (eds.), *Persons and personality: A contemporary enquiry* (Oxford: Blackwell, 1987) pp. 197-206

Watson, D., *Discipleship* (London: Hodder and Stoughton., 1981)

Watts, F., & Williams, M., *The psychology of religious knowing* (Cambridge: Cambridge University Press, 1988)

Watzlawick, P., et al., *Change: Problems of principle formation and problem resolution* (New York: W.W. Norton & Co., 1974)

Weatherhead, L.D., *Discipleship* (London: SCM Press, 1934)

---, *Psychology religion and healing* (London: Hodder and Stoughton, 1951)

Weber, R.J., *The created self: Reinventing body, persona, and spirit* (New York: W.W. Norton & Company, 2000)

Weisz, J.R., et al., 'Effectiveness of psychotherapy with children and adolescents: A meta-analysis for clinicians', *Journal of Consulting and Clinical Psychology* 55 (1987), 542-549

Wells, C.R., 'Hebrew wisdom as a quest for wholeness and holiness', *Journal of Psychology and Christianity* 15 (1996), 1. 58-69

Wells, D., *God in the wasteland* (Leicester: IVP, 1994)

Wengraf, T., *Qualitative research interviewing: Biographic narrative and semi-structured methods* (London: Sage Publications, 2001)

Wengrov, C., *Malbim on Mishley* (Jerusalem/New York: Feldheim, 1982)

Westerhoff, J.H., *Will our children have faith?* (Harper: San Fransisco, 1976)

Wheeler Robinson, H., *The religious ideas of the Old Testament* (London: Duckworth, 1913)

---, *The Christian experience of the Holy Spirit* (London: Nisbet & Co., 1930)

---, *Corporate personality in Ancient Israel* (Edinburgh: T&T Clark, 1981)

White, V., *Soul and psyche: An enquiry into the relationship of psychotherapy and religion* (London: Collins & Harvill Press, 1960)

Whitehead, A., *In the service of old age* (Harmondsworth: Penguin, 1970)

Whitehead, A.N., *Process and reality: An essay on cosmology* (New York: Free Press, 1929/1947)

Whitehead, E.E. and J.D. Whitehead, *Community of faith: Crafting Christian communities today* (Mystic, CT: 23rd Publications, 1992)

Whitlock, G.E., 'The structure of personality in Hebrew psychology: The implications of the Hebrew view of man for the psychology of religion.' *Interpretation* 14 (1960), 1. 3-13

Whitson, R.E., *The Shakers: Two centuries of spiritual reflection* (London: SPCK., 1983)

Wiersbe, W., *Be mature: How to break the mould of spiritual immaturity, and grow up in Christ* (Wheaton, IL: Victor Books, 1978)

Wilber, K., 'Spirituality and developmental lines: Are there stages?' *Journal of Transpersonal Psychology* 31 (1999), 1. 1-10

---, *A Theory of everything: An integral vision for business, politics, science and spirituality* (Boston: Shambhala, 2001)

Wiley, T., *Original sin: Origins, developments, contemporary meanings* (New York: Paulist Press, 2002)

Wilhoit, J.C., *Nurture that is Christian: Developmental perspectives on Christian education.* (Wheaton, IL: Victor Books, 1995)

Wilkes, K.V., 'DeltaNuOmegaThetaIotaSigmaEpsilonAlphaUpsilonTauOmicronNu (Know thyself)', *Journal of Consciousness Studies* 5 (1998), 2. 153-165

Wilkins, M.J., *Discipleship in the Ancient World and Matthew's gospel* (Grand Rapids: Baker House Books, 1988/1995)

---, *Following the master: A Biblical theology of discipleship* (Grand Rapids: Zondervan Publishing, 1992)

Wilkinson, J., *The Bible and healing: A medical and theological commentary* (Edinburgh: The Handsel Press Ltd, 1998)

Willard, D., *Divine conspiracy* (San Fransisco: Harper, 1998)

Williams, R., *Keywords* (Croom Helm: Fontana, 1976)

---, *Interiority and epiphany: A reading in New Testament ethics* (Oxford: Blackwell Publishers, 2000)

Williams, S.B., *Journeys of personal change in a therapeutic faith community: A congregational study of Christ Church Deal* M.Phil. Thesis (Department of Theology: University of Birmingham, UK, 2002)

Williams, S.B. and P.R. Holmes, *Passion For purity: Principles from a personal journey into wholeness* (Deal, Kent: Waterfront, 2000)

---, *Letting God heal: From emotional illness to wholeness* (Bletchley, UK: Authentic Media, 2004)

Willmer, H., 'The collapse of congregations', *Anvil* 18 (2001), 4. 249-260

Wilson, E.F. and W.B. Johnson, 'Core virtues for the practice of mentoring', *Journal of Psychology and Theology* 29 (2001), 2. 121-130

Wimber, J., *Dynamics of spiritual growth* (London: Hodder & Stoughton, 1990)

Winnicott, D.W., *The maturational processes and the facilitating environment: Studies in the theory of emotional development* (New York: International University Press Inc., 1965)

Winter, G., *Community and spiritual transformation: Religion and politics in the communal age* (New York: Crossroads Books, 1989)

Wise, C., *Pastoral counselling: Its theory and practice* (New York: Harper and Bros., 1951)

Wittgenstein, L., *Philosophical Investigations* Anscombe, G.E.M. (tr.) (Oxford: Blackwell, 1953)

Wolff, H.G. and H. Goodell, *Stress and disease* (Springfield IL: Charles C. Thomas, 1968)

Wolff, H.W., *Anthropology of the Old Testament* (London: SCM Press, 1973)

Wolfson, H.A., *The philosophy of the Church Fathers* (Cambridge: Harvard University Press, 1956)

Wolman, B., 'Catharsis' in Wolman, B. (ed.), *Dictionary of behavioral science* (New York: Van Nostrand Reinhold, 1973) p. 54

Wolpe, J., *Psychotherapy by reciprocal inhibition* (Stanford, CA: Stanford University Press, 1958)

Wolski Conn, J. and W.E. Conn, 'Christian spiritual growth and developmental psychology', *The Way Supplement* 69 (1990), 3-14

Wong, P.T.P. and P.S. Fry (eds.), *The human quest for meaning: A handbook of psychological research and clinical application* (New Jersey: Lawrence Erlbaum Associates Inc., 1998)

Wood, J.T., *Spinning the symbolic web: Human communication as symbolic interaction* (New Jersey: Ablex Publishing Corporation, 1992)

Woodbridge, P.D., 'Repentance' in Atkinson, D.J. and D.H. Field (eds.), *New dictionary of Christian ethics & pastoral theology* (Leicester: IVP, 1995) pp. 730-731

Woodhead, L. and P. Heelas, *Religion in modern times: An interpretive anthology* (Oxford: Blackwell Publishers, 2000)

Woodhouse, D., 'Building a healing community', *Renewal* 277 (1999), 16-19

Woodward, J. and S. Pattison, 'Introduction to pastoral and practical theology' in Pattison, S. and J. Woodward (eds.), *The Blackwell reader in pastoral and practical theology* (Oxford: Blackwell Publishers Ltd., 2000) pp. 1-19

Wookey, S., *When a church becomes a cult* (London: Hodder & Stoughton, 1996)

Worrall, A., *Service standards for therapeutic communities,* (2002, Online). Available from http://www.rcpsych.ac.uk/cru/CoC%20Standards%201st%20Ed%2002.pdf. [Accessed 5th April 2004]

Wright, D.C. and W.L. Woo, 'Treating post-traumatic stress disorder in a therapeutic community: The experience of a Canadian psychiatric hospital', *The International Journal for Therapeutic and Supportive Organizations* 21 (2000), 2. 105-118

Wright, H., *A more excellent way: 1 Corinthians 12.31. A teaching on the spiritual roots of disease.* (Thomaston, Georgia: Pleasant Valley Publications, 1999)

Wright, N., *The radical Evangelical: Seeking a place to stand* (London: SPCK, 1996)

Wright, N.G., *A theology of the dark side: Putting the power of evil in its place* (Carlisle: Paternoster Press, 2003)

Wurtz, K. and R.K. Bufford, *Predicting estrangement from God among Christians* Annual Meeting of the Christian Association for Psychological Studies (Vellevue, WA, 1997)

Wuthnow, R., *Sharing the journey: Support groups and America's new quest for community* (New York: The Free Press, 1994)

Yale, D., 'The heart connection', *Mediation Quarterly* 11 (1993), 1. 13-24

Young, F.M., *From Nicaea to Chalcedon: A guide to the literature and its background* (London: SCM Press, 1983)

Young, J., 'Health, healing, and modern medicine' in Montefiore, H. (ed.), *The gospel and contemporary culture* (London: Mowbray, 1992) pp. 149-158

Young-Eisendrath, P. and M.E. Miller (eds.), *The psychology of mature spirituality: Integrity, wisdom, transcendence* (London: Routledge, 2000)

Zizioulas, J.D., *Being as communion: Studies in personhood and the church* (New York: St Vladimir's Seminary Press, 1985/2002)

---, 'On being a person: Toward an ontology of personhood' in Schwobel, C. and C. Gunton (eds.), *Persons, Divine and Human* (Edinburgh: T&T Clark, 1991) pp. 33-45

Zohar, D. and I. Marshall, *SQ: Spiritual intelligence: The ultimate intelligence* (London: Bloomsbury Publishing Plc, 2000)

---, *Spiritual Capital: Wealth we can live by* (London: Bloomsbury, 2004)

Author Index

Subject Index

Scripture Index